in the Province of PENN...

— PHILADEL

7. Fr... ...harf

10. Sassafras Street   11. Chestnut Street

(from *London Magazine,* October, 1761)

REBELS AND GENTLEMEN

Philadelphia in the Age of Franklin

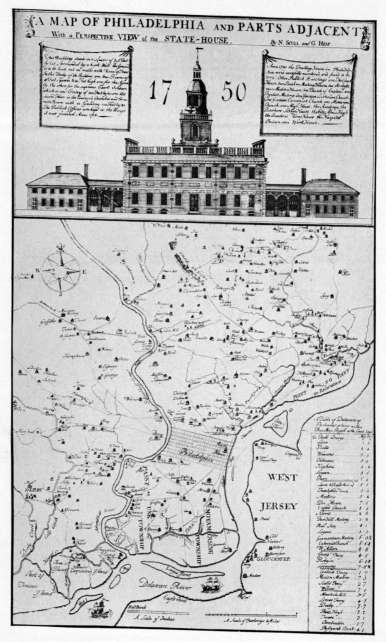

(*Courtesy Historical Society of Pennsylvania*)

REBELS

and

GENTLEMEN

Philadelphia
in the Age of Franklin

BY

Carl and Jessica Bridenbaugh

REYNAL & HITCHCOCK · NEW YORK

974.8
B

PRINTED IN THE UNITED STATES OF AMERICA
BY THE CORNWALL PRESS, CORNWALL, N. Y.

To
Charles and Mabel Bridenbaugh
Philadelphians

How much we are excelled by those in Europe.
                        —*Edward Shippen, 1749.*

*

*The Arts have always travelled westward, and
there is no doubt of their flourishing hereafter on
our side of the Atlantic, as the number of wealthy
inhabitants shall increase, who may be able and
willing suitably to reward them; since, from several
instances, it appears that our people are not
deficient in genius.*

                        —*Benjamin Franklin to Peale, 1771.*

*

*The Revolution was effected before the war commenced. The Revolution was in the minds and
hearts of the people. . . . This radical change in
the principles, opinions, sentiments, and affections of the people, was the real American Revolution.*

                        —*John Adams, 1818.*

PREFACE

THE rise in eighteenth-century Philadelphia of a mature, urbane and democratic culture constitutes one of the most curiously unchronicled phenomena of modern history. Yet it represents a major contribution of New World society while still in its Colonial period to the development of Western civilization, and a precious instance of the richness of our American heritage.

In the transfer of civilized institutions from Europe to America the seventeenth and eighteenth centuries form two great seminal periods. In the seventeenth century the Puritan strain, consequence of the Protestant Reformation, was brought by saints and elders to New England. Here after the extremes and vicissitudes of theocratic experiment, its individualistic and democratic elements remained to become permanent factors in American life. The eighteenth century brought to our shores a new strain, the Enlightenment, secular, humanistic, and also with democratic and individualistic implications. Becoming rapidly naturalized to its new environment, the Enlightenment met and blended with the earlier ecclesiastical culture of New England to flow in turn into the main channel of American thought.

For this later important element in our native inheritance Penn's city on the Delaware served as the port of entry, and its apostles there were not priests and elders, but laymen—scientists, philosophers, teachers, doctors, artists and craftsmen. Foremost among them was the printer-philosopher Benjamin Franklin. His entire career, from the boy whose whole capital numbered three loaves of bread to the New World democrat proudly wearing his squirrel

cap in European courts, so admirably expressed for both his American and his European contemporaries the mind and spirit of his
community as completely to overshadow the hundreds of his fellow
citizens whose accomplishments and aspirations made that community what it was.

The reason for the spectacular success of Philadelphia as the primary unit of reception and distribution for this second wave of European culture lay in its increasing importance as an urban center.
In the thirty-five years preceding Independence, trade and immigration made of Philadelphia the second city of the British Empire.
Here existed that full and free interplay of group and individual
activity, buttressed by fairly continuous economic prosperity, which
was necessary to the development of a vigorous cultural life. Here
also grew up a democratic society, product of the theory of its
founding and the conditions of New World existence. Education
was amazingly general; opportunity for talent and initiative, relatively free. Philadelphia presented therefore the outstanding, probably the first, example in the Western world of a culture resting on
a broadly popular base.

This culture was nourished not alone by the privileged, the
leisured, and the financially endowed. It depended to a remarkable
degree on the efforts of hundreds of able and energetic individuals,
men and women, sprung from all ranks of society and all motivated
by a love of learning, a curiosity in the world about them, a de-
vout belief in progress, and a burning personal desire to get ahead.
Some four hundred such citizens, perhaps 1 per cent of the city's
population in 1775, appear in the pages of this book, and but for a
desire to avoid needless repetition the authors might have called in
many more for witnesses. These men and women constituted the
component parts of the New World society of which Benjamin
Franklin became the perfect synthesis. Their less versatile accomplishments have been overlooked in the preoccupation, past and
present, with the life and character of Colonial America's greatest
citizen. While we have no wish, in the words of a colleague, to "res-
cue Philadelphia from Benjamin Franklin," we have tried to present

a picture, by means of brief biographical treatment of or allusions to
the many members who composed it, of this society which produced
the man who has been called the finest flower of the Enlightenment.

Two more factors, we believe, lift the story of pre-Revolutionary
Philadelphia above the realm occupied by mere local studies. One is
that it furnishes on an ample stage and with a large cast of characters an excellent example of the silent preparation of the mind of
America for independence of the old British Empire—what John
Adams called "the real American Revolution." From 1740 to 1775
Philadelphia presents a continuous struggle between two cultural
trends. On the one hand were the forces of colonialism, the society
of British-bred or would-be British gentlemen, usually aristocratic,
leisured or professional, who wanted the British colonies to accept
their social and cultural conventions direct from the mother country. Opposed to them were the many who, often unconsciously,
sensed in their new community the need for another set of cultural
standards and symbols fitted to the life they must express—in other
words, the forces of the New World.

Without the partial triumph of the latter group, in Philadelphia
and elsewhere, the Revolution might never have occurred nor the
appeal to arms have been made. Not until Americans had learned to
think like Americans, and not like transplanted Englishmen, were
they ready to sever the ties, political and sentimental, which bound
them to the Old World. In Philadelphia, rapidly growing, economically prosperous, secular, democratic and cosmopolitan, that process
—in microcosm—is best seen at work.

Finally, examination of eighteenth-century Philadelphia constitutes an introduction to knowledge of the Middle States. In the recent vogue for regional studies the Middle Atlantic States have been
largely neglected. Open to the north, west and south, they are not a
well-defined geographical area such as New England or the Old
South, or even the Ohio Valley. Nor has their culture ever been
characterized by one salient and overwhelming interest; it was dedicated neither to the maintenance of a single way of life nor to the
defense of a peculiar institution. Their society was eclectic and cos-

mopolitan; their agriculture and their industry, widely diversified. The section is thus probably more characteristic of American life as a whole, with its genius for variety, assimilation and compromise, than the more self-contained regions that have been so extensively studied. A possible method of approach to its complexities is through its capital city, its center of reception and distribution in the eighteenth century—Benjamin Franklin's Philadelphia.

C. B. and J. B.

June, 1942.

ACKNOWLEDGMENTS

THE authors are grateful for valuable suggestions and sympathetic encouragement to Mr. Carl Van Doren of New York and Mr. Julian P. Boyd of the Princeton University Library; for the generous loan of his family diaries to Dr. Cecil K. Drinker of Boston; for a critical reading of the chapter on the medical profession to Professor Richard H. Shryock of the University of Pennsylvania; and to Mr. I. Bernard Cohen, Fellow of the Carnegie Institution, for materials and a point of view which have been incorporated in the chapter on Philadelphia science.

For their kindness in replying to correspondence and their helpfulness in furnishing materials we thank Mr. Barney Chesnick of the Library Company of Philadelphia, Miss Florence D. Greim of the Pennsylvania Hospital, Dr. Robert J. Hunter of the Philadelphia General Hospital, Mr. William B. McDaniel, Jr., of the Philadelphia College of Physicians, Professor Joseph E. Johnson of Williams College, Dr. Clifford K. Shipton of the American Antiquarian Society, Mr. Brooke Hindle, now of the United States Navy, and Dr. Joseph T. Wheeler of the Minneapolis Public Library. We are grateful to Mr. William Reitzel of the Historical Society of Pennsylvania for permission to reprint a part of Chapter III which appeared as an article in the *Pennsylvania Magazine of History and Biography,* as well as for countless other favors; and to our friend Professor Raymond P. Stearns of the University of Illinois for his customary generosity in sharing his scholarly information.

A grant of money from the American Council of Learned Societies made possible research in Philadelphia in the summer of 1940.

The most pleasant obligation we have to discharge is our debt to our friends and colleagues at Brown University, who have provided the atmosphere of intellectual sympathy so indispensable to the happy writing of a book. Especially we wish to name with gratitude Mr. Lawrence C. Wroth of the John Carter Brown Library for his vast knowledge and historical insight and his unfailing kindly interest in views with which he was not necessarily in agreement; Mr. I. J. Kapstein for his sympathetic comprehension of the problems we encountered and for the suggestion which led to the title of this book; Mr. James B. Hedges for his genial and stimulating skepticism, which helped us to avoid certain pitfalls into which enthusiasm might otherwise have carried us; and Chester H. and Ethyn Williams Kirby for their reading and criticism of a large part of the manuscript in an early draft. A chance observation by Mr. S. Foster Damon greatly influenced the chapter on the arts. For valuable advice in their special fields that are not our own we are indebted to Professors Alonzo Quinn and J. Walter Wilson and to Mr. William Dineen. We have received helpful assistance from Miss Edith R. Blanchard of the John Hay Library and Miss Marion Adams and Miss Jeannette Black of the John Carter Brown Library, while for her labors in the final preparation of the manuscript we are deeply grateful to Miss Louise L. Waitt of the Department of History of Brown University.

Finally, when one of the authors entered the service of his country, the other was left solely responsible for all the tiresome and exacting jobs involved in the completion of a printed work. For inestimable assistance in such arduous tasks as reading proof she is therefore indebted to her parents, William Holway and Helen MacGregor Hill, of Wellesley, Massachusetts.

CONTENTS

ILLUSTRATIONS

Chapter I

THE PHILADELPHIA OF BENJAMIN FRANKLIN

O N October 11 in the year 1726, after a two years' residence in
London, Benjamin Franklin returned to Penn's city on the
Delaware. A young man of twenty, but made wise in the
ways of the world by the experiences of his English sojourn, he
seems to have selected his New World environment with an instinctive shrewdness, as if he found therein a promise of physical expansion and intellectual and spiritual growth that made a peculiar
appeal to the combination of the practical and the romantic in his
own complex character. Indeed, so well did man and city agree in
temperament that, as the years went by, Benjamin Franklin became
to many of his contemporaries the perfect expression of the spirit of
his chosen home, and posterity has followed them in ascribing to the
force of Franklin's versatile personality a tremendous influence in
the shaping of his surroundings.

Yet examination of Philadelphia in the fifty years prior to the War
for Independence reveals many lesser Franklins, friends, rivals, or
collaborators of the great philosopher, and the thought arises that the
society which produced such men may well be worth our deeper
knowledge. Perhaps the man owed as much to the environment as
did the environment to the man. Certainly, Franklin's Philadelphia
possessed a personality and a glory of its own, distinct from those
reflected to it by the character and accomplishments of its greatest
citizen.

On the autumn day when the young printer disembarked at Market Street wharf, the evidences of that personality lay still concealed beneath the beginnings of a sober commercial prosperity. The city had altered little during his brief absence. Less than a half-century old, its most prominent features were still the fine wharves along its river front, and its straight, right-angled streets, for the most part still unpaved, and lined with rows of small, plain brick houses, substantial but monotonous. The Court House in High Street constituted its only public edifice of any note, and throughout the town there was little indication of civic spirit or municipal pride.

Observers found few traces either of great wealth or of real poverty. The 11,000 inhabitants appeared thrifty and industrious, living in solid though unpretentious comfort. Making a living and acquiring an estate almost wholly absorbed their energies and interests. Trade and politics held sway in tavern discussions. The heavy, materialistic quality of the community appeared intensified by the solemn mien of its leading Quaker citizens, whose tolerance of all faiths seemed to some critics to stem from sheer indifference, so that their only true religion had come to be the equal neglect of all. There was little gaiety and less elegance; a dreary commercialism, clothed in the austere garb of Quaker principles, permeated the very air. "The generality of the people in Town," remarked one of their clergy, ". . . are well inclined, but want much more of the Gentleman to please them."

But Philadelphia in 1726 was a young place, and its inhabitants had perforce to devote themselves to mundane matters, to the physical business of building and growing, and to laying out economic patterns upon which their town might expand and thrive. It was indeed a community of future prospects rather than of present achievement. Largely under Quaker leadership, Philadelphians had established the firm foundations for the future commercial greatness of their city which, in population and volume of trade, was already threatening the supremacy of Boston. In social organization and civic and cultural accomplishment Penn's city still lagged far behind the metropolis of colonial America. But signs were present that the mind of Philadelphia was beginning to awake, to think about other things than flour and sugar and ships. Change and challenge were in the air. Philadelphia society was about to shake off its adolescence and enter into the full maturity of its manhood estate. Who can say— it is probably too much to say—that Benjamin Franklin consciously glimpsed the future of his chosen home? The fact remains that he grew up, and took his place in world society, along with Philadelphia and the Philadelphians.

The thirty-five years preceding the American Revolution constituted for Philadelphians a dynamic era of growth and progress that was charged with significance for the future of their country. The potential energy and intellectual vitality of this New World society, traces of which began to appear in the early thirties, revealed themselves clearly and unmistakably after 1740. Thereafter, despite two wars and the economic and social dislocations incident thereto, life in the Pennsylvania capital expanded continuously in all directions until the very outbreak of the War for Independence. Rapidly increasing population and geometrically mounting wealth accelerated the tempo of social and cultural as well as that of material advance.

This whole transformation of society took place in an environment which became each year progressively more urban. After 1740 Philadelphians dwelt no longer in a city in the wilderness, but in a pulsating metropolis, whose far-flung commerce drew it into the vortex of Western civilization, opening up new spheres of endeavor and achievement to its inhabitants, and attracting to it thousands of new citizens from the Old World. Such expansion demanded continual adjustments on the part of the citizenry of Philadelphia, some of whom achieved the necessary integration with their changing times, while others, failing to bow before the logic of events, retained a nostalgic attachment to their Old World origins. The simultaneous existence of these two streams of culture, and the repeated struggles between them, animate the whole social and intellectual development of these years.

The population of the city and its liberties increased from about 13,000 in 1740 to 22,000 in 1760, and finally to 40,000 by 1776. In the latter year Bristol, the second city of England, boasted a population of less than 36,000, while Edinburgh and Dublin were only slightly larger. Thus it is probable, as nearly as we can deduce from the imperfect statistics of the eighteenth century, that on the eve of the American Revolution Philadelphia ranked as the second largest city of the British Empire, surpassed only by the metropolis of London itself.

The great accretion of these years arose from two sources: the natural increase of population in a prosperous society, and continuous accessions from without. The small but steady flow of English newcomers was swelled in the 1720's by the arrival of the Scotch-Irish, and even more greatly augmented in the next decade by the flood tide of German immigration. Despite the passage of most of the newer elements through the city to take up farms in rural regions or back country, enough of both groups remained in Philadelphia to alter its population and affect its economic life. This was particularly true of skilled artisans, who needed a populous market for their wares, and of those who possessed sufficient capital or education to set themselves up in shops or professions.

In addition to these companies of "foreign Protestants" whom the propaganda of agents or ship captains had induced to migrate, many an energetic individual came on his own, seeking in the New World opportunity to better his station in life. Especially after 1745, a considerable number of men of substance arrived to engage in the expanding trade of the New World city, while at the same time ambitious men whose sole capital was training, capacity or native wit sought successfully to make their way to wealth and influence in Philadelphia. In this latter category the Scots, by their energy and ability, came to constitute an important element. Their number was never large, but its quality was fine, and they found in Philadelphia, where an intellectual awakening similar to that of their native country was taking place, an extraordinarily congenial environment for the exercise of their talents.

New World as well as Old yielded up its increase to the growing city, and from surrounding rural areas came able and energetic young men, eager to make use of the opportunities there afforded. New Jersey, the Delaware counties, and particularly the Eastern Shore of Maryland contributed heavily to the economic and cultural development of the Pennsylvania metropolis, which exerted upon these regions much the same sort of magnetic attraction that London held for all England.

Thus to the naturally increasing native population were added by immigration members at all economic and social levels. The newcomers contributed not only brawn but brains, not only numbers but wealth, to the service of their adopted home. Not a few of them provided that grace and "tone," that elegance and sophistication, absence of which observers had earlier deplored. With this infusion a cosmopolitan air came gradually to pervade the life of the city, to the partial dissipation of its localism, with the result that the intense and often narrow provincialism of New England towns became here virtually impossible.

The key to Philadelphia's prosperity, which excited comment and envious admiration from European travelers, lay in its ever increasing role as a commercial entrepôt. Almost from the time of its founding local merchants had engaged in a flourishing traffic with the West Indies in flour, breadstuffs, meat and lumber. At the same time continuous immigration and the constant need for European manufactured goods made for steady contact with Great Britain and Ireland, while Philadelphia ships sailed regularly to Madeira and Lisbon for cargoes of wine and salt.

The facts of this European traffic are too well known to require comment save in one particular. In 1760 the Shippens and the Allens sent two ships freighted with sugar to Leghorn, Italy, with instructions to bring back consignments of carpets and to investigate prospects for a regular Mediterranean trade. Thereafter a vessel or so a year was dispatched to Leghorn, and although the commercial value of this exchange never became important, its cultural effects were of the greatest significance, for thus it was that Philadelphians made contact with the art and thought of Italy and the ancient world.

The steady passage of Delaware-built ships over these lanes of commerce connecting Europe with the New World produced two results of almost revolutionary import: it yielded wealth to the merchants of Philadelphia and their dependents, and it brought to the Pennsylvania capital not only the material commodities of comfortable living, but also larger cargoes of people and ideas. Simultaneously, ships sailing for Europe carried Philadelphians in mounting numbers to the ports of England and the Continent, and made possible a fairly constant communication between Pennsylvania and the Old World by mail. In the rise of colonial Philadelphia its sea-borne commerce played as vital a cultural as an economic role; it enriched not only the pockets but the minds of its citizens.

The advantages of membership in the old British Empire fostered the development of both overseas and West India trade. Convulsions suffered by the Empire itself affected the general prosperity but little. When war threatened the disruption of normal commercial intercourse, many Philadelphians turned easily to privateering, profits from which were often enormous. In April and May, 1743, for example, two privateers brought in 60,000 pieces of eight to the port of Philadelphia, one of them returning again in October with a Spanish prize valued at £30,000 sterling. Pennsylvania merchants prospered under the Acts of Trade and Navigation during the years of "salutary neglect," and suffered few restraints in their pursuit of profit and advantage through illicit traffic with the French islands or in trade with the enemy.

Particularly during the Seven Years' War certain men in the city amassed considerable fortunes. Thomas Penn reported to Pitt in 1759 that the Delaware port was swarming "with shallops unloading these illegal cargoes, brought at their return, and cheating the King of his dutys, besides carrying provisions and ready money to the Enemy." That year and the next "a very great part of the principal Merchants" engaged in this treasonable trade, conducted under flags of truce, passes for which Governor Denny "scrupled not" to sell in blank form "at the low price of twenty pounds sterling or under." Legally or illegally, as one visitor noted, the merchants of

Philadelphia applied themselves strenuously to business, and in war or peace their wealth accumulated.

Perhaps equal in importance to the West India trade, and far surpassing that with Europe, was Philadelphia's coastwise commerce, which engaged a major proportion of its shipping. Especially profitable was the city's New England business, outweighing even its very substantial traffic in flour and breadstuffs with the Southern colonies. In the single year 1752, 103 vessels cleared the port of Philadelphia for New England, 39 of them for Rhode Island alone. A proposal by the Pennsylvania Assembly in 1767 to levy certain duties on New England imports brought an immediate remonstrance from one "Mercator," who pointed out the great value of this trade in a communication to the *Pennsylvania Chronicle*. Lacking the "two grand staples," wheat and bar iron, New England, he asserted, had perforce to buy from Pennsylvania. For these it paid one-third in merchandise, and the remaining two-thirds in coin or bills of exchange. Altogether, Philadelphia enjoyed a favorable balance of over £52,000 annually in trade with its New England neighbors, whose vessels it would have been sheerest folly to drive away.

This extensive though little-studied coastwise intercourse had also its cultural aspects. It became the agency not only for the exchange of goods which so favored the Pennsylvanians, but also for acquaintance and familiarity among residents of various colonial ports. Much correspondence, both business and social, went on by water. Newspapers were exchanged, and journeys for business or pleasure greatly facilitated. Over a hundred Philadelphians, for instance, voyaged to Newport for summer sojourns between 1767 and 1775, there to mingle not only with native New Englanders but also with wealthy South Carolinians, Georgians and West Indians who were likewise investing the profits from commercial enterprise in a few months of expensive recreation in the refreshing Northern climate.

An expanding hinterland supplied the basis for Philadelphia's commercial prosperity. Stretching from the Delaware west beyond the Susquehanna lay a wide region of fertile farms which produced the wheat, corn, hemp, flax, beef, pork and timber products utilized by urban merchants in the export trade. From the furnaces and forges of the colony's many iron plantations came yet another article of commerce. Not only from the back country of their own province did Philadelphia merchants collect produce for export, but from New Jersey, the Delaware counties, Maryland and the Potomac Valley as well. As early as 1755 they began to gather livestock driven up the Piedmont and the Shenandoah Valley from the distant Carolina back country. After 1763, with the extension of settlement into the Juniata Valley and westward over the Forbes Road to Pittsburgh, merchants of Philadelphia and Lancaster undertook the financing of fur-trading operations as far afield as the Ohio country and the Wabash. For their part, inhabitants of agricultural regions required large quantities of European manufactured articles, which city merchants furnished to distant communities direct, or through the media of country stores or peddlers. Later, as settlement moved still farther inland, satellite towns sprang up, their shops outfitted by the wholesale dealers of the metropolis.

This inland trade of collection and distribution led to considerable travel by farmers and peddlers, shopkeepers and city merchants, and to repeated, though not always successful, attempts to improve the means of communication. After 1733 a road ran west from Philadelphia to the Susquehanna; this was later pushed down through the Shenandoah Valley and became known as the Great Philadelphia Wagon Road. By the outbreak of the Revolution, a network of passable highways covered eastern Pennsylvania, and over them, observers estimated, more than 10,000 four-horse Conestoga wagons annually made the trip to Philadelphia. The bulk of this traffic crowded the road from Lancaster, a town which, under the enterprising direction of the Shippens, Franks and Levys, became after the mid-century virtually a branch office of mercantile Philadelphia. Its "trade to this city," wrote Jacob Duché in 1771, "is very considerable . . . and is carried on by means of large covered wagons, which travel in great numbers . . . sometimes . . . there being above one hundred in a company carrying down the produce of the country, and returning with all kinds of stores and merchandize."

In the two decades preceding the War for Independence overland travel was heavy in all directions out of Philadelphia. "The roads for communication are good," reported a critical Englishman, and Governor Belcher of New Jersey boasted that his four trotters could take him easily from Burlington to Philadelphia in two hours, the road being smooth as a bowling green. Stage lines ran to New York by three different routes, and by 1767 there were three lines south to Baltimore, one to Annapolis, and another to Virginia. Under the efficient management of Benjamin Franklin the colonial post provided regular mail service north to New England and south as far as Virginia; after 1764 a letter could be sent to New York in one day and to Boston in six.

The improvement in means of travel and communication increased both tempo and volume of cultural interchange. The circulation of Philadelphia newspapers by post riders and wagoners throughout the rural areas of the middle colonies, the sale of books and pamphlets by mail order, and the general broadcasting of urban views and attitudes meant that by the decade of the seventies ideas were passing along the highroads, beating against back-country provincialism and subtly preparing the minds of embattled farmers for momentous events to come. At the same time, more extensive travel by cultivated Philadelphians, such as the tours of Henry and Elizabeth Drinker into interior Pennsylvania and south as far as Baltimore, broadened the outlook and increased the understanding of city folk, teaching them that not all farmers were the "country boobys" of popular urban belief.

The greater activity of the 1750's and after produced an expansion in the life of the town, both physical and economic. Increase of population and business demanded the development of many more urban services. To cater to the growing numbers of inhabitants and to the crowds of country people whose affairs brought them daily into town, retail shops of every description appeared, taverns multiplied, and a host of crafts and small manufactures came into being. The extent of the latter and the number of workmen they employed have not often been realized. Among the larger establishments may be mentioned the most extensive shipbuilding yards in the colonies, dozens of cooperages, fourteen rum distilleries, three steel furnaces and an anchor forge, four carriage and wagon shops, a shop for the manufacture of fire engines, Richard Wistar's "Glass-Works," and his shop for the fabrication of the famous "Philadelphia Brass buttons, well noted for their Strength." Smaller businesses of all sorts abounded, such as the mustard and chocolate works of Widow Mary Crathorne, or the shop of Anthony Vitalli, "sausage-maker, late from Italy."

In such artisans' establishments and in the retail shops a large proportion of the city's population found employ. Their proprietors, journeymen and apprentices were the "Tradesmen" or "Mechanics" whose numbers gave the middle class much of its importance in the development of the community. They prospered with the city, and grew in wealth and potential influence as their numbers increased. Below them in the economic scale was a large but inarticulate class of laborers, apprentices and servants—carters, stevedores, porters and the like—who contributed their muscles to the heavy labor and their backs to the movement of freight and shipping in the Delaware port.

To some, the incessant pulsing of trade at Philadelphia proved bewildering. "There is so many people catching at every appearance of gain," sighed the idealist Anthony Benezet in 1771. Yet beneath the apparent formlessness of the general prosperity lay a definite pattern, traceable to the able leadership of a group of daring and enterprising merchants who controlled and directed the economic life of the growing city and enjoyed the cream of its profits. They it was who owned the ships that engaged in distant or coastwise commerce and the shipyards for their building and repair, who collected the produce of farm and forest for exchange in foreign markets, who invested in iron furnaces, flour mills and distilleries, who speculated in broad acres and who dabbled in money lending. The returns from their many ventures were generous, but some of their profits were shared with lesser folk, upon whose essential prosperity the general well-being ultimately depended. Thus, though princely fortunes did accumulate in the hands of the very few, there were signs of material progress observable on every side, nowhere more concretely than in the physical development and improvement of the city itself.

When the Swedish naturalist Peter Kalm visited Philadelphia in 1749, he marveled at its rapid rise to "such grandeur and perfection" in a period of less than seventy years. "Its fine appearance, good regulations, agreeable situation, natural advantages, trade, riches and power, are by no means inferior to those of any, even of the most ancient towns in Europe." Yet at the time of his observations Philadelphia had barely begun its great expansion, and contained at the most some 1,864 houses, "the greatest part of them built of Brick . . . three Stories high, and well Sashed." By 1776, as a result of almost continuous building, a careful count listed 6,057 dwelling houses and 287 warehouses, shops and business establishments. Solomon Drowne deemed it worthy of note that only 473 new houses had been erected in Philadelphia in the year 1774.

Civic improvements were undertaken, and for the most part kept pace with urban needs. Public street-lighting was instituted in 1752, although two years before James Birket declared that as a result of private enterprise there were "few Towns if any in England that are better Illumined with Lamps, and those of the best Sort." In the sixties the streets began to be paved, so that by 1771 Jacob Duché could take pride in his city, whose tree-shaded streets were "all well paved in the middle for carriages and . . . a foot-path of hard bricks on each side next the houses." At intervals along these thoroughfares some five hundred public pumps supplied the citizens with their water, and never failed to make an impression upon visitors.

By the eve of the Revolution Philadelphia had assumed the appearance, and something of the ugliness, of any prosperous and rapidly growing city. Some of its public buildings were impressive, but most observers agreed with Dr. Drowne that "there are very few elegant Dwelling Houses here, and scarce one that may be called grand. Many appear old and shabby, and they are in general very irregular as to their Height."

The expanding city quickly overleapt its bounds, both north and south. As early as 1750 Franklin had noted the rapid building-up of the south end of the town and the fact that many of the principal merchants were moving thither to live. Both natural and artificial stimuli encouraged this suburban trend. While high real-estate prices within the city limits were driving many people to the outskirts, such shrewd operators as the Shippens and the Whartons, sensing the direction of residential development, bought up large tracts of land to the south of the city, which were soon in "very good fashion and . . . inhabited by people of circumstances." To improve land values the realtors agitated for a new market and the institution of borough government, and were rewarded in 1762 when the Assembly created the District of Southwark. With the erection of the Northern Liberties into a borough in 1771, such speculators as Michael Hillegas profited handsomely from high perpetual ground rents, although, somewhat to the disappointment of its promoters, the portion of this suburb lying closest to the city rapidly filled up with German tradesmen and artisans. The townships of Passyunk and Moyamensing were similarly absorbed into the metropolitan area of Philadelphia.

One reason why visitors noted an absence of elegant city homes is to be found in this movement of prosperous citizens into the Philadelphia suburbs. Here they could live remote from the noise and confusion of city traffic, "the thundering of Coaches, Chariots, Chaises, Waggons, Drays and the whole Fraternity of Noise" which "almost continually" assailed the ears and nerves of city-dwellers. The "lower sort" were consigned to the city proper, its older streets and shabbier houses. But even here urban wealth and civic talent left their mark with the erection of nobler public buildings as the years went by—the Pennsylvania Hospital, the new Alms House, the State House, and several fine churches.

Although the city of Philadelphia enjoyed continuing prosperity and a steady rise in the standard of living, the fruits of the community's mounting wealth were by no means equally, or even fairly, distributed. Accumulating fortunes soon permitted the transformation of the merchant plutocracy into a privileged aristocracy. Requirement of the possession of either a freehold estate or personal property to the value of £50 for exercise of both local and provincial franchise effectively limited political control of the city to men of wealth and substance. Before 1776 only about one in fifty of the inhabitants could meet the property qualifications for the vote. In addition, the municipal government was itself a closed corporation, which only occasionally admitted to its councils even so wealthy and able a member of the middle class as Benjamin Franklin. Most members of this oligarchy, as one of their number, Dr. William Shippen, Jr., freely admitted, "in many instances behaved as though they had a sort of fee simple" in their offices, and "might dispose of all places of Honour and Profit as pleased them best."

The political power of the gentry enabled it to throttle economic competition from below. City merchants made the going hard for auctioneers or peddlers who sought to undersell them, and could always keep shopkeepers in country as well as town in line with their wishes by their power to withhold or extend credit. By their steadfast opposition to relief for debtors and to any relaxation of the laws governing those unfortunates, they sowed much trouble and bitterness for themselves in the years immediately preceding and during the Revolutionary period.

On the social side, evidences of class distinctions made their appearance to accompany the widening inequalities of wealth. Quaker plainness in dress gave way before genteel, if sometimes gaudy, finery, which provided marked contrasts with the sober apparel of tradesmen and the leather aprons of working folk. To the gentry belonged the delights of suburban living or, if very wealthy, the distinction of a country seat. Philadelphia society was still fluid, of course, and such immigrant Germans as Caspar Wistar and Jacob Hiltzheimer by business shrewdness and commercial success could achieve admission to the charmed circle. But, like other aristocracies on the make, the ruling class was jealous of its none too secure position, and sought by social, economic and political exclusiveness to strengthen the barriers that divided it from those below.

Among these privileged gentlemen conservative fears naturally arose as they witnessed the growing self-confidence of the "middling sort." This group, composed of "Tradesmen" and "Mechanics," was both prosperous and increasingly numerous. Seldom wealthy enough to exercise the franchise, its members yet formed the backbone of city life and furnished leadership to the "lower sort." There were among them men and women of capacity and ambition, who not only sensed the potential power of their kind but, as they read and thought, became increasingly democratic in their aspirations. Possessing freedom of worship, they sought to eradicate monopoly and privilege in business and social life, and to exercise the political responsibility to which their collective wealth, energy and intelligence entitled them. To many of them the domination of their city by local gentry appeared as obnoxious as proprietary rule or the monarchy was later to become. From among their numbers came many a political radical, and such scholarly rebels as Benjamin Franklin, David Rittenhouse and James Cannon, who so influenced Pennsylvania's liberal constitution of 1776.

The gentry, fearing their ability and resenting their achievements, adopted toward members of the middle class a patronizing air that was poorly suited to their improving positions and demonstrable accomplishments. This attitude was recognized for what it was, and promptly resented. Wealthier tradesmen could easily detect election-time flattery. "Be freemen," admonished one of their number, "and you will be companions for gentlemen annually." By the same token they delighted in an occasional victory over their betters. The story was told with great satisfaction in shops and taverns of how Sir William Draper, K.C.B., had been defeated by a mechanic, "the hero of the Tennis Court," who "put on the appearance of doing so with difficulty," although he was heard to say "he could have done the same with the encumbrance of a wheelbarrow."

The "lower sort" or laboring class was perhaps as well off in Philadelphia as in any urban community in the world. Although in 1767 a correspondent to the *Pennsylvania Chronicle* declared one reason for the city's commercial superiority to be its "industrious labourers, whose wages are moderate, when compared with those of other American ports," there could be little real exploitation in a community where the labor shortage was nearly always acute. As a result, competent observers remarked on the large numbers of the inferior sort who strutted about town clothed in fashionable coats and "a Stock of Impudence." To Joseph Galloway, archconservative, the "Democratic notions" of middle-class and lower-class citizens loomed as a graver threat than British tyranny. Unfortunately, it was from the nether ranks of laborers and workingmen that enough urban crime originated to lend color to aristocratic fears.

Although the steady progress of the middle class, to whom the lower ranks soon learned to look for leadership, together with the intensification of aristocratic privilege, led to a definite development of class feeling in these years, Philadelphia society was growing and changing too rapidly to permit its crystallization before 1776. Something more than local issues and conditions was required before it was to break forth in violent and open antagonisms. Briefly, during the Paxton riots of 1764, the veil was drawn aside, and the two parties faced each other across a barrier of mutual hatred and distrust, but for the most part class resentments remained latent rather than active until the dawn of the Revolutionary era.

These years did, however, witness a democratic drift and the growth of a desire for self-expression from below. While no one dreamed of a classless society, republican ideas and anti-aristocratic feelings were rife. Resentment of monopoly in business and of privilege in political and social life flourished, and a literate, responsible and increasingly well-to-do people failed to see why they should continue to be excluded from exercise of the franchise. Despite the desires of gentlemen, the four decades preceding 1776 exhibited a noteworthy decline in what Daniel Defoe had termed "the Great Law of Subordination."

Two further factors conditioned social development at Philadelphia, to wit, the racial and the religious constitution of its citizenry. By the mid-century there was in the city a very large number of "lowly and poor German immigrants," for whom many of the English inhabitants entertained a "supreme contempt." This attitude was the natural expression of suspicions engendered by the presence of an alien group with its own language and customs, which resisted amalgamation by the maintenance of its own schools, churches and press, and whose general poverty made it a potential problem to the community. To some extent this condescension was extended to include Ulster Scots and "bog-trotting Teagues."

Yet by the end of the period both groups were finding their place in the Pennsylvania scheme of things, and there was probably less nativism in 1776 than in 1750. Most inhabitants would have endorsed the statement of William Smith: "We are a people, thrown together from various quarters of the world, differing in all things— language, manners and sentiments. We are blessed with privileges, which to the wise will prove a sanctuary, but to the foolish a rock of offense."

The Christian religion, in both its institutional and its spiritual forms, profoundly affected Philadelphia society in these years. Here toleration for all sects reached its colonial apogee, and as Alexander Graydon recorded in his *Memoirs*, "the puritanical spirit was unknown among us." The absence of an established church permitted the development of many denominations, and allowed great numbers of people of no faith at all to flourish happily without benefit of clergy. On the whole, the city's inhabitants, like most people of the eighteenth century, remained faithful worshipers without being deeply religious.

The primary religious development of these years was the rapid and real decline of the Society of Friends, and the concurrent rise to dignity and affluence of the Anglican and Presbyterian communions. By 1750 the Friends numbered only eight hundred families, or about 25 per cent of the city's population, and in the 1770's, according to their own historian, they embraced only one-seventh of the citizens. Reasons for this spectacular falling-off are to be found in the negative and purely defensive policy pursued by the Society, its readiness to expel members for "marrying out of Meeting," and its failure to proselyte. While under the influence of George White-field many humbler members were attracted into the newer evangelical sects, wealthy Quakers, wearying of plainness and yearning for display, went over in increasing numbers to the fashionable and ritualistic Church of England. After 1735 it is an anachronism to speak of Philadelphia as the Quaker City; the real strength of the Society lay in its rural meetings.

Numerically, the Presbyterians constituted the strongest denomination in the city. Their conservative or "Old Side" wing enjoyed the reputation, even among Anglicans, of including "some of the most substantial and sensible People of this place," among them the Reverend Francis Alison and the wealthy Chief Justice William Allen. The evangelical or "New Side" branch, under the leadership of Gilbert "Hell Fire" Tennent, gained adherents rapidly among the emotionally starved middling and inferior sorts who had been roused to religious enthusiasm by the preaching of Whitefield, but it was never so strong within the city as on the Pennsylvania frontier. With the reconciliation of the two groups in 1758 the Presbyterian Church became beyond a doubt Philadelphia's leading religious body.

After 1750, however, Presbyterianism like Quakerism had to share wealth and influence with the Church of England, which, under the skillful leadership of its clergy and aided by the strenuous proselyting of the redoubtable William Smith, enjoyed a remarkable expansion. Like wealthy Quakers, families of other dissenting sects who nourished social aspirations passed over to Christ Church, and in 1761 the fashionable St. Peter's had to be erected to serve the mercantile gentry living in the southern part of town. Though never so numerous as the Friends, Presbyterians, or even the Lutherans, the Anglicans became definitely the congregation of wealth, fashion and position.

The leading German denomination was the Lutheran, several of whose ministers in 1764, under Episcopal persuasion, nearly succeeded in merging its membership with the Church of England. Concurrently, Presbyterians were making similar overtures to the smaller body of German Reformed worshipers. Baptists, Moravians, Methodists, Roman Catholics, and about a dozen Jewish families completed the religious scene. But inasmuch as there were in the city in 1776 only eighteen churches in all, or one for every 2,200 persons, it is clear that large numbers of the inhabitants must have had no regular affiliation with any religious denomination whatever.

In this period of generally declining religious enthusiasm Philadelphia churches exercised probably more influence upon the social and political than upon the spiritual lives of their communicants. All denominations agreed upon the inculcation of a strict morality, with the result that observers found the inhabitants as a whole sober, thrifty and peace-loving. But in other respects the churches acted as social and political divisors. In general, the older English and Welsh stocks adhered to the Quaker Meeting, while later comers from England and wealthy Irish Protestants made confession of their faith with the Anglicans. The Presbyterian Church drew most of its recruits from among the Scots and the Scotch-Irish. Germans worshiped principally at the Lutheran churches; or attended the Reformed or Moravian services. National and linguistic distinctions thus tended to be maintained by religious affiliations and perpetuated through the medium of church schools. In similar fashion, although persons from all walks of life were to be found in every communion, denominational connections also carried their social implications. Wealth was largely concentrated in the hands of Friends and Anglicans; the Quaker custom of confining profitable secular business as much as possible to fellow members resulted in some bitterness on the part of adherents of other denominations, while the eyes of all regarded the Church of England as the stronghold of aristocracy.

More calculated to disrupt the local scene, however, was the competition for political influence, frequently productive of the fiercest factionalism, among Quakers, Presbyterians, and Anglicans. Control of the Assembly by Quakers led to the early formation of the Proprietary party, composed of Anglicans and Old Side Presbyterians, to oppose them. Later, as the Presbyterians increased in numbers, a struggle developed between them and the Anglicans for control of the Proprietary party. "The Presbyterians should not be allowed to grow too great," one member of the "Hot-Church party" asserted. "They are all of republican principles. The Bostonians are Presbyterians." As the controversy with the mother country approached its climax in the seventies, Anglicans and Presbyterians gradually forgot their differences, and each group furnished both leaders and followers for the American cause. Only the Friends, with their pacifist and Tory principles, kept apart from the hurly-burly of events. Until the very eve of the struggle, however, sectarian rivalries among the three faiths, intensified by social and political strivings, pervaded the whole life of the city.

The intercolonial religious revival known as the Great Awakening left a profound mark upon Philadelphia. The arrival of George Whitefield in 1739 to preach to thousands in the streets—when the churches were closed to him—resulted in a genuine upsurge of religious emotion. "Religion is become the subject of most conversations," exulted one enthusiast. "No books are in request but those of piety and devotion, and instead of idle songs and ballads the people are everywhere entertaining themselves with psalms, hymns and spiritual songs." Particularly effective was Whitefield's appeal to the middle and lower classes, many of whom belonged to no church, but who readily responded to his eloquent but simple oratory and his contempt for the formalism and pretensions of orthodox faiths. Anglicans and Quakers held aloof from the great preacher, deploring his rabble-rousing tactics, while the Presbyterians split over the issue of his evangelicalism, with Gilbert Tennent forming the second, or "New Side," church to meet in Whitefield's tabernacle in 1743.

In time the revival ran its religious course, and the enthusiasm it inspired subsided, but the eight visits of Whitefield to Philadelphia between 1739 and 1770, and the work of his followers, had lasting effects. Most important was his preaching of a social gospel, his ap-

peal to humanitarian principles, which penetrated to all sects, causing even the most conservative to join in attempts to improve the
general welfare and better the lot of the unfortunate. But his use
of the evangelical method also had its effect on older denominations, all of whom save the Quakers eventually made concessions to
its influence.

Rural parsons of the Church of England experienced a rude shock
when Whitefield, arriving for his seventh visit in 1763, was cordially
received by the Episcopal clergy of Philadelphia. For twenty-four
years the horrid spectacle of the Presbyterian split had led all Anglicans to eschew his principles, but now the Reverend Richard Peters
and the Reverend Jacob Duché were "openly preaching up to his
Doctrine and espousing his cause." It is evident that urban Episco-
palianism was moving away from practical orthodoxy, even before
the outbreak of the War for Independence. "Every means is made
use of to fill up the Churches . . . with Methodist preachers," lamented the Reverend Hugh O'Neil. "Philadelphia is well stored
with them." Even more amazing, during each visit Whitefield extended baptism to Quakers. "I suppose as Whitefield has preached
among the Church of England, presbyterian, Dutch, Baptist and
Swedes congregations," wrote George Roberts fearfully in 1763,
" 'twill not be long before he begs permission to mount our Quaker
Gallery."

Just as English Methodism made its way among the emotionally
susceptible in the city on the Delaware, so did eighteenth-century
rationalism find a home among all classes of its intellectuals. As
early as 1734 a Presbyterian minister complained that the leading
men of his church were tainted with Deism, and by the sixties the
doctrine had made considerable headway not only among upper-
class intellectuals, but among members of the artisan middle class
as well. When John Bartram was able to declare that "it is through
the telescope I see God in his Glory," his differences with the
Quaker Meeting are obvious. Even some women dared speculate
on Nature and Nature's God, inspiring from the Reverend Mr.
Duché the pronouncement that "a female free thinker is as awk-

ward and pitiable a character as can be conceived," and he thanked Heaven that he had met but few who "made any pretensions to infidelity."

"All sects of religionists compose this city," wrote Josiah Quincy, summarizing the spiritual state of Philadelphia in 1773, but "the most influential, opulent and first characters scarce ever attend public worship anywhere. This is amazingly general and arises partly from policy, partly from other causes. A man is sure to be less exceptionable to the many, more likely to carry his point . . . by neglecting all religious parties in general, than adhering to any one in particular. And they who call themselves Christians much sooner encourage and vote for a deist or an infidel, than one who appears under a religious persuasion different from their own."

Although basically life in the colonial metropolis was organized through the family and the church, the urban setting provided both the means and the leisure for citizens to combine in special groups according to their tastes or talents. At Philadelphia there existed that full and free interplay of spontaneous and responsible group association which appears to be a necessary condition to a healthy social order. For this the tavern, sometimes a much abused or underrated institution, furnished the requisite machinery. As early as 1752 one hundred and twenty licensed taverns did business in the city, and their number increased steadily until the outbreak of the war. There was a public house to suit every purse and every taste, from innumerable sailors' groggeries down by the wharves to Daniel Smith's famous City Tavern, erected and furnished after the London mode "at great expence, by a voluntary subscription of the principal gentlemen of the city," so that it was "by much the largest and most elegant house occupied in that way in America." There were also places of resort for suburban parties, such as "Vauxhall, on the agreeable Banks of Schuylkill," where Thomas Mullen solicited the custom of ladies and gentlemen in summer, a season when business was slack at his wife's Beefsteak House in town.

Such houses offered a genuine social solvent. "I dined at a tavern with a very mixed company of different nations and religions," recorded Dr. Alexander Hamilton in his *Itinerarium* in 1744. "There were Scots, English, Dutch, Germans, and Irish; there were Roman Catholicks, Churchmen, Presbyterians, Quakers, Newlighters, Methodists, Seventh daymen, Moravians, Anabaptists, and one Jew," gathered in "a great hall well stocked with flies. The company was divided into committees in conversation." Daytimes, hundreds frequented the London Coffee House at Front and Market streets, opened by William Bradford in 1754, which served as a general clearinghouse for business, news and gossip, and had for sale tickets for concerts, plays, lectures and public events of all kinds.

After the mid-century, instead of frequenting public houses indiscriminately, most Philadelphians came to have their favorite places of meeting with their cronies or business associates. The Library Tavern, near the old Union Library on Second Street, became the resort of booklovers; artists generally sought out James's Coffee House, which was run by a brother of Claypoole the painter; the Northwest Company met in "the private room" of the Bull's Head on Third Street when planning its Arctic expeditions. Most public houses of any reputation or following had their own loosely knit groups of customers, who met weekly to dine, drink, play cards or discuss, and from them developed an amazing number of social clubs of a more carefully organized type.

The formation of "Clubs, consisting of Knots' of men rightly sorted," declared a well-known clubman of the period, constitutes one of the most worth-while embellishments of civilized living. "We meet, converse, laugh, talk, smoke, drink, differ, agree, argue, Philosophize, harrangue, pun, sing, dance and fiddle together, nay we are really in fact a Club." The existence of some fifty "particular" or "set" clubs indicates the extent to which Philadelphians enjoyed such social embellishments in the years preceding the Revolution. While the bulk of them numbered only gentlemen among their members, many more of which there is no record doubtless existed for the pleasure of lower-class and middle-class groups, also rightly sorted.

These organizations fall into several types. Many of them were convivial groups meeting weekly, such as the Governor's Club, at which in 1744 Dr. Hamilton listened to a conversation on "the English poets and some of the foreign writers, particularly Cervantes . . . whom we loaded with eulogiums." Such groups furnished one means of intercolonial intercourse when distinguished visitors like Hamilton were introduced at their meetings. Then there was the "Club of 20 Young Fellows," whose rules were framed "to avoid drunkenness" and to make "Contention penal"; and "The Friends of the Young Sort," to which Quaker John Smith belonged.

Another very important and numerous category was the dining or "glutton clubs," prominent among which were the six fishing companies, which made their appearance with the founding of the Society of Fort St. David's and the Colony in Schuylkill in 1732. To judge from their records, the art of Izaak Walton had to compete with delights of the table at the meetings of these fashionable anglers. When members of the Mt. Regale Fishing Company met on June 1, 1763, George Clymer as caterer provided for the fifty-eight fishermen present a feast that would have sated twice their number. These organizations popularized such famous local dishes as cream cheese, smoked tongue and cherry pie, and of course that powerful and delectable potation, Fish House punch. Whether menus of the Liberty Fishing Company, founded in 1767, suffered greatly from the nonimportation movement we have no means of knowing. Prominent among city eating clubs was the "Beef-Stake Clubb," which met weekly at Peg Mullen's Beefsteak House, to consume that delicacy and some twenty others.

Since Philadelphians were on the whole a serious people, many clubs came to combine some benevolent, social or political purpose with the lesser objectives of companionship and conviviality. This was true of the three Masonic lodges and of the host of national societies to be treated more extensively in a later chapter. Prototype of all such clubs with a purpose was Franklin's Junto, modeled after Cotton Mather's Boston societies, and representative of their later

development was "The Society meeting weekly for their Mutual
Improvement in Useful Knowledge." At a meeting of this group
in October, 1766, Isaac Zane proposed the topic "Is it advantageous
to admit women into the Councils of State?" After an animated
and extremely serious discussion, in which it was conceded that
women have natural abilities equal to those of men, which might
be improved by education, that their lively imaginations would
"throw a subject into new lights," that their natural timidity would
make for prudent decisions, and that Queen Elizabeth had proved
an able ruler, the question was decided in the negative, on the
grounds that the use of beauty and female arts would prejudice the
public good and that active participation by the ladies in public
affairs would "destroy the peace of Families." Thus, if somewhat
vicariously, women took part in Philadelphia club life, and by 1775
the Gridiron Club had progressed so far as to give an entertainment
"in their usual frugal style" to twenty-three feminine guests.

Perhaps the most important organizations in the city were the
seventeen fire companies, which, beginning with Franklin's Union
Fire Company of 1736, had come by the seventies to involve a membership of from five to seven hundred citizens. Persons of all ranks
and nationalities joined to form these bodies. The Hibernia Fire
Company was made up wholly of well-to-do Irishmen, while the
rosters of the Queen Charlotte and the Neptune companies, which
met in St. Michael's and the Zion churches respectively, were exclusively German Lutheran. In 1760 thirty-nine shoemakers organized the Cordwainer's Fire Company, a body built on guild lines
which proved as useful for the control of unruly apprentices as of
conflagrations. In fact, convivial, benevolent or political functions
occupied the membership of all companies quite as much as the
satisfaction of the natural desire in men of all ages to attend fires.

The various companies began to co-operate with one another for
the furthering of fire protection in 1747, and in 1764 the Hand-in-
Hand, Neptune, Fame and Queen Charlotte companies joined in
electing a common president and board of managers, although each
retained its identity as an independent organization. Further inte-

gration of activities, in keeping with the social and political drift of the times, continued down to 1775.

Members of the middle class found in their clubs a vehicle for self-expression similar to that supplied by the town meeting in New England communities. So important did this function become, as awareness among tradesmen of their own peculiar interests increased, that in the seventies a society came into being dedicated specifically to the protection and furtherance of those interests. Carefully disassociating themselves from rabble elements, and emphasizing their devotion to orderly procedure, the "Tradesmen, Mechanics, etc." who formed the Patriotic Society declared its purposes to be the support of their "just rights and liberties as by law and the charter of the province established," and their preservation "against every attempt to violate or infringe the same either here or *on the other side of the Atlantic.*" Especially did they deplore the obstruction by corrupt practices of their freedom of voting at annual elections, for the prevention of which these middle-class citizens had thought it "expedient to enter into a more firm and established Union."

The subtle influence exerted by clubs and organizations on the entire social and cultural life of the city will become evident in succeeding chapters. They were powerful centers for the generation of public projects and the focusing of public opinion. When differences with the mother country began to result in popular tension, nearly "every particular club" in the city was available for political action, to "meet and carry their votes into execution."

At the time of the Stamp Act newspapers all over the colonies printed the resolutions of the Sun, Hibernia, Fellowship, Union, and Crown and Beaver fire companies to encourage home manufactures by refusal to purchase lamb (to increase the local output of wool) or to drink foreign-brewed beer. At Boston John Adams noted with relish the expulsion of "Mr. Hughes, the stamp man," from membership in the Heart and Hand. When the Townshend Acts again aroused the city in 1768, the Fellowship republished its resolves against the eating of lamb, and the Fishing Society of Fort

St. David's presented to John Dickinson, as a tribute to his *Farmer's Letters,* an address contained in a casket fashioned from "Heart of Oak." But, despite all this, local clubs were not swinging into action with the rapidity some patriots desired. On June 2 the *Gazette* carried a letter purporting to come from Lancaster, but which suggests the fine organizing hand of Charles Thomson, urging the "many small societies, companies and clubs . . . each to unite in sundry public spirited measures," for, pointed out the writer, "Is it not the *many* that spread and suggest a fashion?" In the response from the clubs that was soon forthcoming, the fire companies led the way.

When in 1774 plans were being laid for the convening of the First Continental Congress, the City Committee held a two-day meeting in the rooms of the American Philosophical Society in the State House. At that time, significantly, "a Number of respectable Inhabitants [were] called in from all Societies in Town to devise, consult and deliberate upon Propositions, to be laid before the General Meeting of the Inhabitants." What had originated as "Knots of men rightly sorted" for social and convivial purposes, after thirty years of influencing the cultural and political destinies of the city was ready, when stormy times appeared, to apply itself with secret vigor to "working the political engine." Thus not a few reluctant gentlemen were transformed into mild rebels, at the least.

In the four decades before 1776 Philadelphians fashioned a society in which men of ability and ambition could rise and flourish. A growing, grasping, expanding society, it offered to individualism a degree of free play seldom exceeded. At the same time, few communities of the age could present such golden opportunities for communion and interchange of all kinds, material, intellectual and spiritual, and a continuing sense of social and civic responsibility kept extremes of individual or plutocratic selfishness in check. A clever youngster, no matter what his breeding and antecedents, had a good chance to succeed in this community, which, despite the attempts of some to create the artificial barriers of a stratified society, was moving steadily, though perhaps unconsciously, in the direction of nineteenth-century democracy.

In this society young Benjamin Franklin found his way to wealth and fame unimpeded from his return in 1726 until 1757, when he went again to England. The city and its people offered an uncommon opportunity which none better than he was able to seize and utilize. But in so doing he was not alone. In the bustling commercial activity of the city on the Delaware its citizens displayed a material and practical philosophy of life, yet through all their actions ran a strong vein of idealism and the sense of historic mission which to some extent characterized most colonial ventures in the New World and all enlightened societies of the eighteenth century.

Both qualities, so prominent in Pennsylvania's greatest citizen, were characteristic of all its leading men, and both qualities distinguished, in many fields, their social and intellectual endeavors. Within their capital city they established a system of education and a free press to serve the complex needs of their changing times; they fostered the development of arts and literature to express the spirit of the new world they were building; they enlisted the resources of the many and the taste of the few in the enrichment of city life and the amelioration of the lot of its citizenry; and they made practical employment of community wealth and knowledge for the furthering of medical progress and scientific lore.

Philadelphia was ripe for intellectual advance just as Franklin returned to take up residence there, and when he departed in 1757, to remain abroad except for two years until after the outbreak of the War for Independence, the men he left behind were well able to carry their city along its road to greatness and distinction. No colonial city, and few in contemporary Europe, could boast the galaxy of intellectual and civic leaders produced by Philadelphia from 1740 to 1776.

Franklin was unique not in kind but in quality, not in the nature of his genius but only in its extent. He alone could hardly have made of Philadelphia the dynamic, forward-looking society it became in these years, and it is small tribute to his capacity to picture him as the ingenious manipulator of small and passive puppets among his fellow citizens. Rather, his quality looms the greater if we consider him as a leader among leaders, first among a group of able men as distinguished in their narrower fields, if not so universally capable, as he.

Succeeding pages seek to portray the accomplishments of the men and women who collectively constituted the Philadelphia mind in action. They it was who, more than any other society, brought the Enlightenment to America and there naturalized our second great stream of European thought. They, it may be said in truth, gave to the world a new American culture and Benjamin Franklin, its finest exponent.

Chapter II

EDUCATION FOR A LITERARY REPUBLIC

FAITH in the efficacy of widespread education is far older in America than devotion to any political system. A phase of the vigorous optimism that characterized a rapidly growing society, it led men to the belief that they might as readily attain mastery of the realm of the spirit and its accomplishments as they had achieved conquest of their physical frontiers. Especially in Philadelphia, which trebled its population in these years, and in less than a century had seen the building of an urban center where only fields and forests had stood before, there existed little doubt that intensification of education and diffusion of its benefits would bring glory to the metropolis and prosperity to its citizenry. For the most part this faith was implicit rather than expressed, but occasionally hopes were voiced in the emergence of a "Literary Republic," whose institutions should be "designed to make men fit and useful members" of society, and Franklin himself believed, with the "wise men of all ages," the sound education of youth to be "the surest foundation of the happiness both of private families and of commonwealths."

Yet the methods by which this great and desirable public happiness might be attained were subjects throughout the pre-Revolutionary years of much confusion and debate. Force of circumstances, and the constitution of society in the New World city, encouraged the growth of practical, vernacular education, with some emphasis on vocational, mechanical, or business training. The early preference of the Society of Friends for the practical aspects of secondary education over the more ornamental branches of higher learning gave this type of training something of the dignity of tradition in the city of their founding.

Notwithstanding the potency of these factors the old classical curriculum retained its devotees not only among professional men but with those to whom knowledge of Latin and Greek constituted the sure mark of a scholar and a gentleman, however deficient he might be in general information or ability to write his mother tongue. Franklin had wisely observed that "there is in mankind an unaccountable prejudice in favor of ancient customs and habitudes" long after their usefulness has passed. As wealth and leisure multiplied and a colonial gentry developed, an immense "snob value" came to be attached to a classical education. Even urban Quakers, noted Jacob Duché, "now think it no more a crime to send their children to school to learn Greek and Latin, Mathematicks and Natural Philosophy, than to put them to Merchants or Mechanics." Consequently, despite much learned accomplishment in these fields, the Latin and Greek languages degenerated, in Franklin's happy phrase, into "the *chapeau bras* of modern literature."

There was at the same time no lack of familiarity with the educational treatises of Milton and Locke or the theories of such Continental pedagogists as Fénelon and Rousseau, so that patronage was as readily forthcoming for the experimental as for the traditional. Thus most current types of schooling—religious, genteel, practical or vocational—enjoyed a trial in Philadelphia in these years. A sort of battle of pedagogues runs through the whole educational history of the period, with the democratic-vocational group achieving a slight advantage by the outbreak of the Revolution. The ultimate attack on the charter of the College of Philadelphia should be regarded in the light of this struggle to evolve an educational system suited to the society it was designed to serve rather than as the gratuitous interference of a political mob.

In 1740 education at Philadelphia was still overshadowed by two inheritances from its medieval past—the ecclesiastical control of learning, and the classical curriculum. Neither convention answered the needs of the growing city, with its religious heterogeneity and its practical and secular interests. Yet although private schoolmasters, unrestrained by connections with any church, had from time to time since 1720 advertised instruction in the different branches of polite or practical learning, the teaching of youth had for the most part devolved upon the various religious bodies in the town.

Local factors combined to prolong the religious control of education, even though the drift of the times was clearly in the opposite direction. The conservatism of the Quakers as a body caused them to cling to their own schools as a bulwark against changing times, and only the church schools of the various denominations seemed able or willing to supply the educational needs of poor and foreign groups. But while the number and activities of such schools showed considerable increase, new influences profoundly modified their curricula and objectives, and the proportion of students enrolled therein steadily declined.

The Quaker system of schools comprised the town's principal educational facilities in 1740. In addition a small school attached to Christ Church had been dispensing charity instruction to Anglicans since 1698. Other schools appeared to signalize the rising importance of their respective denominations as the century progressed. In 1742 both the Lutheran and the German Reformed churches, denominations that had jointly supported a primary school since 1735, achieved separate institutions for the instruction of their young. About 1745 the Moravians opened an elementary school on Race Street, while ten years later the "ignorant" Baptists confounded their critics when their Minister's Association sponsored a Latin Grammar School under Isaac Eaton, "for the promotion of learning among us."

The system of education maintained by the Quakers well demonstrates the confusion in pedagogical aims and practices that characterized the period. The original ideal of the Society of Friends had been to educate all young Quakers in the ways of temperance, morality and obedience, and to stress ultilitarian studies with a view to making useful citizens of the children of the poor. Their indifference to higher learning deprived them of the opportunity for educational leadership, even among their own members. Yet within the limits of their ideal Quaker achievement was considerable. At several places in the city they set up schools for primary instruction, whence young boys proceeded to the "Public School" for secondary training. Here the majority was probably enrolled in the "English School" where from 1742 to 1754 Anthony Benezet presided over the teaching of writing, arithmetic, bookkeeping, French and German—though "not the whole variation of the nouns and irregular verbs."

By the mid-century, however, the Overseers, influenced by the desire of urban Quakers to acquire the classical hallmarks of their increasing gentility, were tending to emphasize the work of the "Latin School" at the expense of the English department. This tendency ran counter to the views of conservative Friends, who regarded the course of study at the Latin School as neither plain nor practical, and as definitely subversive of Quaker ideals. Yet it was the means of a moderate extension of Quaker influence, for this increasing emphasis on the traditional curriculum of the English Latin Grammar School as well as the general excellence of its instruction caused prominent members of other denominations, such as the Presbyterian William Allen, Chief Justice of Pennsylvania, to enter their sons in the Friends' School. Nevertheless, despite the attitude of Overseers and public, the old Quaker predilection in favor of practical and vernacular education kept enrollment at the English School throughout the period over twice that of its classical competitor.

The Overseers shared to the full in the prevailing uncertainties of Quaker educational theory. Along with their increasingly aristocratic curriculum they retained the generous policy of free education for the poor of both sexes, and opened their schools to members of all denominations, so that many a charity student had his head as well filled with classical erudition as the paying son of some non-Quaker merchant or official. Well qualified masters, liberally recompensed, succeeded in maintaining a very high level of teaching in both schools. Anthony Benezet, Robert Proud and John Wilson were not only able teachers, but each in his way was a leader in colonial educational thought. Benezet pioneered in the education of women and of Negroes. Proud, author of a "Treatise on Education," stressed thorough knowledge of the classics as the basis for the development of habits of work, study and reflection. Historian and linguist, he was said to understand Latin better than his mother tongue.

It was the third of this trio, John Wilson, who after serious thought revealed how far the Quaker system had deviated from its original aims and who sought to swing the Friends' schools back to what had by 1768 become the American tradition in education. In despairing protest against the classical curriculum, he resigned his mastership in 1769. "The employing so large a part of your funds upon the Latin School," he wrote in able explanation of his action to the Overseers, "and the indiscriminate receiving into it all Sorts of Boys without regard to Capacity or Behaviour, appears to me a Measure extremely imprudent and such as has made me strongly doubtful whether I am not a party in a glaring misappropriation of Money devoted to charitable uses. You use Care and Caution in admitting poor children to learn English which ought to be taught to all, but little or none in admitting Latin scholars which is a Science that none ought to learn but Boys of Capacity." Latin is well enough, he thought, as training for the professions, "Doctors and Lawyers, Criticks and Commentators," or for "such as being intended for no Calling may saunter away their Time in a School with less injury than anywhere else . . . but the generality of our Youth have no great relish for such learned Trifles," and being intended by their parents for "Mercantile or Mechanick Employments," can have small use for the "uncouth Terms and intricate distinctions of dead Languages of little importance in their use and essentially different from their native Tongues."

After devoting some space to the suggestion of "Proper Studies" to replace the overemphasis on Latin, Wilson concluded on a pious note: "Instead of dissipating your Revenues in humouring the Pride

of Rich men and debauching their offspring with the rubbish of
Paganism, let it be your study as it will be your happiness to promote the increase of Christian knowledge." But his penetrating
criticisms had no effect upon the progress of Quaker education, and
he was forced to join the ranks of the private teachers in order to
put his views into practice.

The Lutherans were another denomination to undertake the fairly
complete instruction of their youth. Their problem was complicated
by the bilingual nature of their membership, and their school became the most influential of those catering to the needs of Philadelphia's German population. At first limited to elementary instruction, it began in 1769 the education of youth "grammatically in both
languages." The *Pennsylvania Journal,* reporting its graduation exercises in 1771, noted performances by the matriculants in oratory,
poetry, prose, and a "diversion" of vocal and instrumental music.

In 1773, concerned over the failure of Germans in Pennsylvania to
continue the cultural traditions of their homeland, the Lutheran
Ministerium founded "the German Seminary of Philadelphia," under the direction of two able scholars, John Christian Lips of Halle
and John Christopher Kunze of Leipsic. The curriculum presup-
posed a knowledge of reading and writing for admission, and offered instruction in geography, history, letter-writing and oratory
in German, nature study, mathematics, commerce, colonial industry,
Latin and elementary Greek. This broadly conceived plan of study,
which owed much to the liberal influence of such leading Germans
in the city as Dr. Bodo Otto and the Henry Keppeles, elder and
younger, and something perhaps to the educational ideas of Benjamin Franklin, went far beyond the needs of those training for
the Lutheran ministry. Its object, as defined in the report of its first
annual examinations, was not to compete with "the most com-
mendable of all Seminaries in America, the encreasing College of
Philadelphia," but rather to prepare German boys for entrance to
that college, where formerly, despite their monetary support, German "friends and Advocates to Learning" had been unable to secure
admittance. The business and professional value of German studies

to English-speaking people was also stressed. Educational practice among the Lutherans proved more in the spirit of the times than that of their Quaker contemporaries, and resulted in one of the best secondary schools in the Middle Colonies.

The failure of classical schools to meet the requirements of a new age, with its business and commercial opportunities, its need for trained mechanics, and its distinctly vernacular culture, cleared the way for the rise of the private school, the success of which depended on its supplying a better response to the public demand. As early as 1735, a generation before John Wilson's indictment of the Quaker curriculum, a writer in the *American Weekly Mercury* deplored the current emphasis on the study of Latin and Greek, advocating in their place instruction in English grammar, writing, arithmetic, "the excellent Art of Italian Book-Keeping," geography, chronology, history, and "above all a Good Narrative Style." "Can there be anything more Rediculous," he demanded, "than that a Father should waste his own Money and his Son's Time, in setting him to learn the Roman Language, when at the same Time he designs him for a Trade?" Twenty years later the self-taught John Bartram was voicing the usual complaint of middle-class parents when he confided to Collinson that he had no wish to see his son William, then sixteen years of age, become "what is commonly called a gentleman," but wanted him instead to have some business or calling that would enable him, with care and industry, to make "a temperate, reasonable living."

Philadelphians of the middling and inferior sorts desired their children to learn not the "most ornamental," the Latinized graces and embellishments of gentlemen, but the "most useful," reading, writing, and, if possible, how to get on in the world. For this they were willing and, in the growing and prosperous city, well able to pay.

Here was a vast field, untouched by formal institutions of learning, which private schoolmasters in large numbers hastened to cultivate. Over one hundred and twenty-five of them advertised their services in the newspapers between 1740 and 1776. While a few made a bid for genteel patronage by offering instruction in Latin and Greek or in polite accomplishments, the majority adhered to utilitarian subjects, especially practical and theoretical mathematics, surveying, navigation, accounting, bookkeeping, the various branches of science, English and contemporary foreign languages. There is no doubt that their establishments became the most popular of the city's secondary schools, nor that, in Philadelphia as elsewhere in the colonies, they trained a majority of the citizenry.

While many of the private schoolmasters, poorly qualified and financially insecure, lasted only a year or so, dropping out because of failure or of more attractive opportunities in other occupations, those who possessed training and ability stuck to their lasts and prospered. In June, 1776, Andrew Porter, who had kept a mathematical school for nine years, enrolled over a hundred students, whose fees enabled him to provide comfortable support for a growing family of seven. There was much sound learning and capacity among the private schoolmasters of Philadelphia, and from their ranks the Academy drew such able teachers as Theophilus Grew, David James Dove and Paul Fooks.

Foremost among Philadelphia pedagogues, the crotchety and colorful David James Dove had taught sixteen years in a grammar school at Chichester, England, before adventuring in the New World. Here Benjamin Franklin recognized his "unusual abilities" and secured his appointment as master of English at the new Academy in 1751. Two years later the trustees, somewhat reluctantly, accepted his resignation, because he insisted on augmenting his inadequate Academy salary by conducting a private school for girls in his leisure hours. Thereupon he opened a boarding school for both boys and girls in Vidal's Alley, where with great success he taught English "according to the most exact rules of grammar, with such an accurate and masculine pronunciation and accent as becomes its dignity." Alexander Graydon, coming as a lad from Bristol to study at this school, found that Dove had evolved a system of pedagogy distinctly his own. His "birch," says Graydon, "was rarely used in the canonical method," and boys who were habitually late for his classes were held up to ridicule by being called for by a committee of their fellow students and escorted through the streets to school with bell and lighted lantern.

Dove's growing reputation led to his appointment as first master of the Union School of Germantown (Germantown Academy) in 1761, but his imperious temper shortly involved him in a quarrel with the trustees over management, and within two years he had again resigned to open a competing institution of his own, next door to the Academy. Popular demand caused his return to Philadelphia in 1767, where he resumed the teaching of both boys and girls to read, write, cipher, and especially to "*speak* their own Language." Here he became so well established that he undertook the next year to dispose of his Germantown estate, grandiloquently described by him as "the Montpelier of America" and "a fit seat for any gentleman of taste." His school continued extremely popular until its master's death in 1769.

During the two decades of his career Dove not only taught hundreds of boys and girls from Philadelphia and its vicinity, but trained a number of able teachers who, after serving as ushers for him, set up successfully for themselves. His vigorous personality, capacity for searing sarcasm, and hatred of all learned sham made a vivid impression on his subordinates and inculcated in them a love of high standards in scholarship and teaching. He was fanatically devoted to the correct usage and pronunciation of his mother tongue, and believed oratory to be the queen of arts and sciences. After leaving Dove's school for further study at the Academy, Graydon recalled a visit from his old master to one of the classes there. Sitting in the back of the room, the old pedagogue listened to his former student's performance for as long as he could stand it, and then, "as I had an ill habit of speaking with my teeth closed, as if indifferent whether I spoke or not, he bawled out in one of his hugest tones: 'Why don't you speak louder? Open your mouth like a Dutchman —say *Yaw!*' "

At a time when qualifications for teaching were to say the least poorly defined, no one entertained a more profound contempt than did Dove for the quack schoolmasters with whom the town abounded. In 1768 he advertised for a second assistant, "who understands writing and arithmetic, and who can pronounce English articulately, and read with emphasis, accent, Quantity and pauses. But if he has not these Qualifications, tho' he should puff away in all the Newspapers in the city, and dub himself PROFESSOR and ORATOR, he will be rejected as an imposter." The shaft seems to have reached its mark among "parading schoolmasters and grammaticasters," and drew, in the usual anonymous reply of eighteenth-century controversy, a rebuke to that "ill-natured and unsociable gentleman" who so unjustly assailed the sensible and virtuous instructors of Philadelphia's youth.

Another noteworthy member of Philadelphia's teaching profession was Andrew Lamb, instrument-maker's apprentice of London, who had arrived in the New World by a sordid and spectacular route. Convicted as an accomplice of the notorious Jack Sheppard in 1724 and condemned to be hanged, he was reprieved on the ground of its being his first offense, and his sentence commuted to transportation to Virginia. There he served out his time, and after a brief stay in New York (where his son John, the Revolutionary general, was born) settled in Philadelphia in 1733. For twenty-six years in the Pennsylvania city he taught Italian bookkeeping, writing, arithmetic, and his own specialties, practical mathematics, surveying and navigation. An enthusiastic teacher, he achieved remarkable success in his use of the case method of instruction in his favorite subjects. Journals kept during an actual voyage to Lisbon, for instance, formed his texts for the study of navigation.

Lamb's reputation was second only to that of Theophilus Grew, mathematician and almanac-maker, who came to Philadelphia in 1734 from the neighboring province of Maryland. Teaching the same fields as Lamb, he enjoyed considerable patronage until his friend Benjamin Franklin had him named professor of mathematics at the Academy in 1750. This chair he filled with ability and distinction, receiving an honorary A.M. degree from the College of Philadelphia two years before his death in 1759.

Paul Fooks began his career as professor of languages at the College of Philadelphia in 1766, and, the trustees having perhaps become wiser since the Dove affair, simultaneously carried on a private school for the teaching of languages. Seeking primarily the patronage of the growing middle class, Fooks emphasized the use of French and Spanish in the West India traffic, and offered a series of practical lectures, based upon his own experiences, on the nature of trade and methods of business in the countries of the Caribbean and adjacent to the Gulf of Mexico. He by no means disdained the custom of the gentry, but felt it unnecessary to stress the polite and ornamental aspects of linguistic accomplishment in so cultivated a city as Philadelphia; even a gentleman, he thought, would find a knowledge of Romance tongues bringing him peculiar advantages in trade.

Widely traveled, and experienced in business as a notary and a translator, Fooks drew sons of both merchants and gentry into his classes. In February, 1767, young Edward Burd of Lancaster reported to his father: "I have been learning French with Mr. Fooks . . . who put me with Billy Allen and two others to begin Gil Blas, after which book we must learn Telemachus, and therefore if you have that Author without English, be pleased to let me have it." With his connections and his accomplishments, Fooks easily entered the American Society for Promoting Useful Knowledge in 1768.

Artisans, apprentices, and working people in general, while eager for the tangible advantages of education that might enable them to get ahead in the world, were as a class unable and often unwilling to attend the church or other day schools. Prompt to respond to the possibility of custom, private schoolmen began conducting evening schools for their benefit, which had by mid-century become quite common. For the most part these schools offered vocational instruction, along with English, reading, writing and grammar, to "the emulous sons of industry," but Charles Fortescue and Patrick Lenagan made a specialty of night classes in elementary Greek and Latin for aspiring "men who work."

Nearly all of Philadelphia's German population labored in the daytime, and thus had to depend upon night schools for the learning of English. For many years Godfreyd Richter taught both English and German, especially among the Palatines, and Lazarus Pine dispensed the rudiments of English in his "Englische Nacht-Schule." The real accomplishments of these schools in the service of Americanization for the first large group of our foreign-born have been generally overlooked.

In 1767 eleven "Evening Schools" jointly advertised in the press that they would open on October 12 for instruction in writing, arithmetic, bookkeeping and practical mathematics, and that "To prevent trouble, the Price will be" twelve shillings sixpence per quarter, pens, ink and fire included. Among the members of this educational cartel were two masters of the Quaker School, Todd and Dickinson, who conducted their evening classes in the Friends' building. At least five other flourishing night schools were omitted from the combine, two of them directed by Rathell and Maguire, ushers and disciples of that arch-individualist, David James Dove. More effective as producers of educational harmony than mere considerations of policy and profit were the exigencies of the Philadelphia climate, from which all schools, night or day, equally suffered. "The Schoolmasters of the City and its districts," announced the *Pennsylvania Gazette,* August 3, 1774, "on account of the extreme heat . . . have agreed on a vacation in their respective schools . . . for the mutual health of themselves and pupils."

Increasing prosperity and burgeoning local pride, coupled with the successful example of Philadelphia's private schools, were by mid-century directing the attention of forward-looking citizens toward "the Happiness both of private families and of Commonwealths" as it might be achieved by better and more general education. The new movement found expression in an unsigned letter from the pen of Benjamin Franklin, which appeared in the *Penn-*

sylvania Gazette of August 24, 1749. Franklin conceded that, the settling of new countries being so arduous and demanding a task, education and the arts had perforce to be postponed to times of greater wealth and leisure. But, he went on,

since those times are come, and numbers of our inhabitants are both able and willing to give their sons a good education, if it might be had at home, free from the extraordinary expence and hazard in sending them abroad for that purpose; and since a proportion of men of learning is useful in every country, and those who of late years come to settle among us, are chiefly foreigners, unacquainted with our language, laws and customs; it is thought a proposal for establishing an ACADEMY in this province, will not now be deemed unreasonable. Such a proposal the publick may therefore shortly expect.

Accordingly, there soon appeared Franklin's famous *Proposals Relating to the Education of Youth in Pennsylvania,* wherein he suggested that "some Persons of Leisure and publick Spirit" apply for a charter for an academy.

Franklin's plan of education, as set forth in this justly celebrated pamphlet, represented a compromise with his real views. He had observed the success of Philadelphia's private schools in supplying the kind of instruction, especially in English, wherein the church schools had proved themselves most inadequate, and had been profoundly impressed by George Whitefield's account of the school for Dissenters kept by the Reverend Philip Doddridge at Northampton, England, where the teaching of English was placed on an equal footing with that of the classics. The works of such current pedagogical theorists as Samuel Johnson of Connecticut were also familiar to him. All this coincided with the printer's own experience; despite the generally accepted excellence of the public school system of Boston, the bulk of what formal education he possessed he had received from the less classical, more mundane hand of the versatile private schoolmaster, George Brownell.

As early as 1743 Franklin had conceived a scheme for a quasi-public academy to prepare boys for business and civil life, which he believed the Reverend Richard Peters was admirably fitted to direct.

But Peters had other plans, and the times proved not yet ripe for such an undertaking. Absence of provision for the gentlemanly studies, Latin and Greek, precluded co-operation from many of the men of capacity, wealth and leisure whom Franklin had wished to interest, and outbreak of the War of the Austrian Succession put a temporary quietus to the project.

During the war years, however, the signal success of the Presbyterian Latin Grammar School at New London, Pennsylvania, established by the Reverend Francis Alison in 1743 and supported by the Old Side Synod of Philadelphia, attracted the attention of Philadelphia gentlemen, who began to desire a similar institution for their city. University men in town, such as William Allen, who had studied at Clare College, Cambridge, began to show concern lest the classical training fail to be continued in the New World. With such backing as his, classical learning, in the words of Alison, "became reputable even amongst those that formerly gave [us] the nickname of Letter-Learned Pharisees."

By the end of hostilities, then, provided the classics were given a place in his plan, Franklin could count on such varied support as that of the Episcopalians Peters and Tench Francis, the Presbyterian William Allen and the Shippen family, and James Logan, Quaker. He therefore admitted, in his *Proposals* of 1749, that though "Art is long, and their Time is short," many of the city's youth would prefer ornamental to useful training. The subjects he recommended for study were all taught by masters of private schools, and the plan to unite them all in one institution really represented no great departure from current practice.

The nonsectarian character of the Academy proceeded naturally from the varied religious affiliations of its supporters, and calls for no fine-spun theories of toleration. Upon no other basis could it have been established. Yet of the first board of twenty-four trustees, three-quarters were Anglican, and the rest, according to Franklin's description, "of moderate principles." A most significant feature of the founding of the Academy was the fact that the Society of Friends, with the notable exceptions of James Logan and Samuel

Rhoads, took no part in its establishment, contributing neither labor nor funds. In time the Quakers became actively hostile. Their diffidence stemmed in part from the nature of their own educational theories, but even more from the realization that the movement of which this institution was a product boded ill for their political influence in an environment where they were now outnumbered by Presbyterians and Lutherans, and where Anglicanism was becoming increasingly vigorous. A complex combination of social, economic, religious and political forces had awakened thinking Philadelphians to the need for the Academy, and the institution continued throughout the colonial era to be simultaneously the beneficiary and the victim of the conditions of its birth.

By August, 1750, £15,000 had been raised by means of a public subscription and a substantial gift from the city Corporation. Advocates of the scheme stressed the financial and moral advantages of education at home rather than far abroad, the desirability of training young men for civil service in a province teeming with foreigners, and the need for teachers in rural areas to replace "vicious imported Servants or concealed Papists." The possibility of money to be spent in Philadelphia by students whom the Academy was expected to entice thither from other colonies carried weight in some quarters—at least, such was the ulterior argument developed by William Allen and presented to the Corporation.

At the beginning of the new year (January 7, 1751) the Academy of Philadelphia was inaugurated with a sermon by the Reverend Richard Peters, delivered before the governor and the trustees, and classes began to be held in a warehouse in Second Street, lent for the purpose by William Allen. From these temporary quarters the institution soon moved to the building erected in 1741 for the preaching of Whitefield and a proposed charity school. This the trustees had acquired and renovated on condition that such a school be conducted in conjunction with the Academy. In 1762, for the benefit of the "many Persons at a Distance from the City" who desired their sons to "be lodged and boarded in a Collegiate way," a structure known as the New College was opened under the direc-

tion of Professor Ebenezer Kinnersley. Here Mrs. Kinnersley presided, and for the comfort of absent parents assured them that she
would send "for the smaller Boys twice every Week to have their
Heads combed," and would arrange to have their laundry sent out.

The Academy, as set up in 1751, consisted of two departments,
the English School, which was the heart of Franklin's proposals,
and the Latin School, to which he had in effect consented for the
increased support its presence might bring to the whole. To each of
the two branches he had expected the trustees to pay "an equal
regard," but from the beginning the scales appeared to be weighted
against the English School. Disregarding the social and educational
needs of city and province, the trustees made the master of the
Latin School, David Martin, rector of the institution, and voted him
twice the salary of his English colleague. Under David James Dove,
master of English, and Theophilus Grew, teacher of mathematics
and geography, the English School soon had ninety boys, whose
"performances were surprisingly good, and . . . were admired and
applauded." But Dove, as we have seen, sought more remunerative
employment elsewhere, and in 1753 Ebenezer Kinnersley, able scie-
entist but ineffective teacher, succeeded to his place.

In the face of indifference, if not actual hostility, from the trustees,
attendance at the English School declined in a single year to forty-
one scholars. For a time, in 1769, the trustees virtually withdrew
support from Kinnersley, under pretext that his department was
proving too costly. The English School survived only because "the
public was not satisfied," and because doubts of the legality of their
action "haunted the Trustees like an evil conscience."

Franklin, returning from England in 1762, was shocked by the
condition of affairs at the Academy, and took the trustees severely
to task for the partial performance of their trust. He recalled in
later years how "Parents . . . despairing of any reformation, withdrew their children, and placed them in private schools . . . and
they have since flourished and increased by the scholars the Academy
might have had, if it had performed its engagements." The course
of study stressed at the Academy led Benjamin Rush to rejoice in

retrospect that his friend David Rittenhouse had escaped the pernicious influences of an educational system designed for fifteenth-century Europe and in no way adapted to circumstances in the New World. "Rittenhouse, the Philosopher, and one of the luminaries of the eighteenth century, might have spent his hours of study in composing syllogisms, or in measuring the feet of Greek and Latin poetry." It is clear that one potent source of hostility on the part of the rank and file to the Academy and the College of Philadelphia during the Revolutionary years lay in the failure of its officers to support the educational program which had led to its founding.

Ironically enough, two remarkable appointments, for which Franklin himself was largely responsible, contributed most to this overdevelopment of the classical curriculum. Francis Alison, Presbyterian divine and the finest classical scholar in America, took charge of the institution upon the death of David Martin in 1752. Born in Donegal, Ireland, and educated at Glasgow, he was described by Franklin as "a Person of great ingenuity and learning, a catholic Divine, and what is more, an Honest Man." Since his advent to the province of Maryland in 1735, at a time when "there was not a College, nor even a good grammar school in four Provinces, Maryland, Pennsylvania, Jersey, and New York," he had devoted himself as much to the cause of education in the colonies as to the service of his religion.

The example of Alison's New London School had provided real encouragement for educational reformers in Philadelphia, and with his characteristic ability to select the best man, Franklin persuaded him to come to the Academy. More a scholar than an administrator, Alison refused the rectorship, but under his care the Latin School flourished, and its curriculum received the vigorous support so many of the trustees desired. The appointment a year later of the ardent and aggressive Anglican William Smith as rector finally cemented the supremacy of the classics. He more than anyone else, Franklin later charged, shifted emphasis from the English to the Latin School, which after 1755 was taken under the wing of the College of Philadelphia, and served as a feeder to it.

Within the limits of its curriculum, instruction in the Latin department was good, and the ushers capable, although owing to the fact that the classes of from seventy to eighty boys were often "superlatively pickle and unruly," these functionaries were changed frequently. Alexander Graydon, who spent four years in the Latin School in the sixties, was fortunate in studying under James Wilson and the poet John Beveridge, both Scotsmen.

From a pretty close application, [he recalled], we were well grounded in grammar, and had passed through the elementary books, [but after the first two years we] became possessed of liberty and idleness. . . . One boy thought he had Latin enough, as he was not designed for a learned profession; his father thought so too, and was about taking him from school. Another was of the opinion that he might be much better employed in a counting house, and was about ridding himself of his scholastic shackles. As this was a consummation devoutly wished by us all, we cheerfully renounced the learned professions. . . . We were all, therefore, to be merchants, as to be mechanics was too humiliating.

So Graydon quit school at the age of fourteen, after having read through Horace, Cicero, Ovid, Virgil, Caesar and Sallust. "A little Latin, and but a little, was the chief fruit of my education. I was tolerably instructed in the rudiments of grammar, but in nothing else. I wrote a very indifferent hand and spelled worse than I wrote. I knew little or nothing of arithmetic; that, as a branch of the mathematics being taught in the Academy after the languages."

Inasmuch as Graydon later became one of Philadelphia's men of letters, his criticisms of the educational system to which he had been exposed carry authority. The inadequacies of that system were just what Franklin's group had deplored and feared, what Bartram had not wanted for his son, and what Rittenhouse so fortunately avoided. What these educational reformers had desired was vocational training for those designing to become artisans, and a thorough grounding in mathematics, history, logic, grammar, English authors and foreign languages for boys intending to enter a mercantile life. "Thus instructed, Youth will come out of this School fitted for learning any Business, Calling or Profession, except wherein Languages [Latin and Greek] are required." At least, they will be "Masters of their own" tongue, which Graydon confesses he was not, after four years at the Academy.

The men who saw eye to eye with Franklin in this matter had no objections to the dead languages as such, but felt their study should not be forced upon those students to whom they could be of no value. The opposing view, that of the gentry and the would-be gentry, which prevailed, was nowhere better expressed than in a letter of advice written from London in 1749 by young Edward Shippen to his brother Joseph, then attending a private Latin school in Philadelphia: "If you ever travel, you'll find how men of letters are everywhere respected; you'll see the ascendancy the knowing man has over the blockhead; you'll have a friend which will stand by you when all others fail. Be a man of learning and you'll be a man of consequence wherever you go." The tragedy of the Academy, and later of the University of Pennsylvania, was that, despite much validity in both of these views, one was persistently contemned—and that, the one enjoying the greater popular appeal and support.

In September, 1751, in keeping with the provisions of the deed to the Whitefield building, the trustees opened a "Free School" for the instruction of poor children in reading, writing and arithmetic, and in 1753 the Proprietors issued a charter incorporating "The Trustees of the Academy and Charitable School in the Province of Pennsylvania." Save for a common board of trustees, the Charity School had no connection with the plan or operation of the Academy. It enjoyed a large attendance throughout the period, Provost Smith reporting an enrollment of eighty boys under two masters and an assistant in 1761.

By that year, the tenth anniversary of its opening, the Academy in all its departments numbered three hundred and ten students, all selected with scrupulous regard for the vote of the trustees (February 6, 1750) that admission should be based on "Priority of Application, without View to Sect or Party." Thus, though deviating somewhat from the educational tenets of its principal founders, the Academy had within the space of a decade achieved a definite success. Its size and liberal admission policy alone would have assured it a prominent role in the cultural life of the city.

The movement for the founding of the Academy revealed how conversant were thinking Philadelphians with the more advanced educational theories of the eighteenth century. Similarly, they shared the awakened interest of their times in the education of women, and were familiar with the current literature of the subject. Edward Shippen of Lancaster in 1765 commissioned his son Joseph to procure for him in Philadelphia "Instructions for the education of daughters (as proper, I think, for sons), by Monsieur Fénelon." The French author, who was widely read in Pennsylvania, advocated the instruction of girls in reading, writing, knowledge of their own tongue, poetry, music and painting. But the Quaker traditions of the city, which had from the first permitted to women wide freedom of activity, allowed Philadelphians to go even beyond European theory in the education of their womenfolk.

In addition to many schools teaching the subjects recommended by Fénelon, and the usual establishments of any colonial city offering courses in such polite feminine accomplishments as needlework, music, dancing, drawing, and painting on glass, young women in the Quaker city had access also to instruction in the classics, modern languages, and some of the sciences. Girls of all classes found some form of schooling available to them in Philadelphia, and a considerable number received a fine education. Collegiate instruction alone remained closed to them.

Although girls had been admitted to the Friends' "Publick School" from its earliest days, they had received instruction there in elementary subjects only. In 1754, no doubt impressed by the success of private schools for girls under such masters as David Dove, Anthony Benezet persuaded the Overseers to fit up a building in which he was soon teaching reading, writing, arithmetic and English grammar to about forty girls. Later, along with needlework, both Latin and Greek were added to this curriculum. For the most part the students came from wealthy and exclusive Quaker families—Drinkers, Callenders, Logans and Wistars—but provision was also made for the free education of a number of poor girls. Years later Deborah Logan recalled Benezet's meticulous teaching and his concern for the health and recreation of his charges. From his classes many a young woman went out to teach in some little Quaker school in the country, and one of his graduates, Rebecca Jones—"Romping Beck," her tutor called her—conducted a fashionable establishment for small children in Drinker's Alley for over twenty years. Benezet's zeal in the cause of feminine education caused him in 1767 to establish a morning school for the instruction of poor girls, which, he soon admitted, "its with difficulty I keep from being too large."

No other religious group seems to have provided more than elementary instruction for its girls, but thirty daughters of the poor were admitted to the Charity School to learn to read, write, and knit under Frances Folwell in 1753. Ten years later, when their number had increased to forty, provision for them was proving a vexatious problem. The Building Committee asserted in 1764 that "a School for Girls was never part of our original Plan," and complained that it was "unbecoming and indecent to have Girls among our Students." The trustees voted to continue the girls' school after removing it a "proper distance" from the College and Academy, but resolved in the future to admit feminine scholars only upon certificate issued by themselves.

In the field of female instruction beyond the elementary levels it was again the private schoolmasters who were the real pioneers. As usual, they taught what the traffic would bear. That it would bear considerably more than the polite accomplishments which had constituted the private curricula of the twenties is a tribute to the young women of eighteenth-century Philadelphia, and their parents. David James Dove was sufficiently astute to sense in 1751 that "the Ladies, excited by the laudable example, are solicitous that their Daughters too might be instructed in some Parts of Learning, as they are taught in the Academy." Accordingly, he opened a private school for girls, where, for twenty shillings a quarter, he offered the equivalent of secondary training, spelling, pronunciation, arithmetic, writing and accounting, "as recommended by the Universal Spectator." As Dove provided excellent instruction in response to a general demand, his school prospered. It was his persistence in this enterprise, which antedated his private school for boys by two years, that cost him his position at the Academy in 1753. Thereafter, he taught the same subjects to young members of both sexes, though "in separate apartments," and thus preserved, for those who could afford to pay for it, the curriculum Franklin had so ardently desired for the English School at the Academy.

William Dawson inaugurated night schools for apprentice and working girls in 1753, when he tactfully advertised to teach writing, arithmetic, merchants' accounts and psalmody "for the amusement of such young ladies as are pleased to employ their summer evenings in these useful and necessary exercises." This curriculum was considerably broadened in 1755 by James Cosgrove, one-time assistant to David Dove, who taught Latin and French in the evening as well. After Dove's death another disciple, Matthew Maguire, "Preceptor to young Ladies only, in the English Language, Penmanship, and Arithmetic," conducted the best female academy in town; in 1774 he added a night school for girls who could not "be spared" in the daytime, and for servant girls properly vouched for by their mistresses. Its objects he announced to be "the convenience and satisfaction of those well disposed persons who are desirous of affording their girls a necessary education (the greatest benefit, perhaps, they can confer upon them) and who do not choose they should intermix with, or be liable to the rudeness of boys, at Evening Schools."

As opportunities for schooling increased, and families from rural districts began sending their daughters to Philadelphia for their education, city matrons in need of income made a specialty of taking country girls to board. Elizabeth Drinker recorded in her diary in 1760 that Mrs. Peggy Parr "has left her Daughters in town, to go to

[Quaker] school, they board with Sally Evans, in Church-Alley."
Many Jersey Friends sent their daughters for a few winters' schooling at Philadelphia, and among such wealthy Maryland and Delaware planters as Thomas White and Joshua Fisher the custom
arose of moving the whole family into town for a portion of the
year, so that, among other things, their daughters might attend
school.

"A proper Boarding School for young Ladies is wanting in the
great City of Philadelphia," announced Mary McAllester when she
opened such an establishment with twelve students in 1767. Mary
Hay began another in the next year, but apparently neither of these
establishments lasted long, for some time later a Mrs. Rogers asserted the "long-felt need" for such facilities by gentlemen living
at such a distance "as to preclude a city education for their daughters." Accordingly, she rented a large house in Chestnut Street, engaged several masters, and promised careful attention to the health,
morals and behavior, as well as to the mental training of her girls.
Her experience in this work at New York, and the fact that several
former boarders had followed her from that city, she held to be
sufficient proof of her capacity and reputation. References from
Benjamin Franklin and Robert Morris assisted Mrs. Brodeau, from
England, to fill her Walnut Street boarding school "for genteel
young Ladies" in 1775.

What sort of education young girls received in these genteel establishments may be seen from "The Plan of an English Grammar
School for Young Misses" published by James Twifoot in 1774.
Dividing his scholars into five classes, he took them from a course
in reading and pronunciation, through grammar and syntax, to a
study of the most proper and elegant methods of reading prose.
Advanced students read poetry—Milton, Pope, Young, Thomson,
Mason and Gray. For the fourth and fifth classes the writing of
"familiar letters by way of evening exercises" was required. Writing
and arithmetic completed the program, which was to be limited to
thirty students. Matthew Maguire provided a similar curriculum
both at his public day school for girls and at his exclusive private

school, "elegantly prepared" for the reception and instruction of ten young ladies from eleven-thirty to one-thirty in the winter, and from eleven to one in summer.

Since hours at the grammar schools were not long, many girls studied special subjects with a second master. Foreign languages were popular, especially French. Paul Fooks, Lucy Brown, Ann Ball, and others maintained language schools for girls, and there were private tutors in these fields as well. Monsieur Peter Papin de Préfontaine began teaching French to young ladies in 1746, his classes meeting daily from eight to ten A.M., and again from ten to twelve, "for those who cannot get there so early." In 1773 Francis Daymon, long master of a "French Academy," offered instruction in both French and Latin at six-thirty in the morning, so as not "to interfere with the other branches of their education." To meet the needs of his students, M. de Préfontaine published in 1757 *A Direct Guide to the French Language,* and added tuition in arithmetic, "without any Hindrance to their French, at the same Price."

Young women in Philadelphia took their language studies seriously, and from the evidence seem often to have become well acquainted with a second or even a third tongue. Elizabeth Sandwith frequently stopped at the Sansom house on her way home from First Day morning meeting, to stay "till 1 o'clock reading French with Sammy," and sprinkled her journal liberally with phrases from the same language. One morning in 1724, after she had finished her French lesson, Sally Logan was called into her learned father's study to read the Thirty-fourth Psalm in Hebrew, "the letters of which she learned very perfectly in less than two hours' time, an experiment," explained her father, "I made of her capacity only, for my diversion."

The presence in and about Philadelphia of a large group of non-English speaking colonists could not fail to influence the educational picture in Pennsylvania. Out of the peculiar social, linguistic and religious conditions there prevailing arose a great scheme for charity education, which gave color to the cultural history of these years, and precipitated the most important educational controversy of colonial America.

For some years Governor George Thomas, William Allen and others had viewed with growing alarm the problems created by the large German migration into the province. In 1748 Thomas wrote to the Bishop of Exeter that he believed the Germans in Pennsylvania to constitute "three fifths of the whole People." Frugal and industrious, they contributed much to the flourishing condition of the colony, but since they spoke a strange tongue and had brought with them "all the Religious Whimsies of their country," there was real danger that during wartime they might be won over to the French. He therefore favored dispensing charity to them, probably through their many churches, "for a few years; for the nearer the several Religious Societies . . . are kept to a Balance, the less danger there will be of the Germans throwing off their allegiance to the Crown." What the Governor and others appeared to fear was the creation of a solid and unassimilated German bloc, with the pacifistic tenets of the sects, and with no share in the English traditions of the colony.

Thomas's rather vague scheme for "home missions" grew in time, largely through the efforts of William Smith, into a large-scale plan for Americanization of the Pennsylvania Germans. English schools among them and the influence of the English press were to be its principal agencies. Interest was aroused on both sides of the Atlantic, and in 1753 Governor James Hamilton, William Allen, Richard Peters, Benjamin Franklin, Conrad Weiser, William Smith and several others became the trustees in Pennsylvania to administer funds to be raised by Anglican philanthropists for the establishment and support of charity schools where German immigrants might learn not only the English and German tongues, mathematics, geography, history and ethics, but particularly "the Constitution and interest of the Colonies." Teachers were temporarily to be secured from among the poor students at the Academy who knew both English and German. A meeting at Mt. Airy, William Allen's country seat, in 1754 planned the erection of six such schools.

The two largest German groups, the Lutheran and Reformed churches, eagerly lent support to the plan, attracted by its educational and philanthropic aspects. One cardinal error, however, doomed the project from the start; no effort was made to include in its management the Quietist sects, numbering about 35,000, nor to conciliate Christopher Sower, their leading publicist. These sects naturally feared any concerted move of the organized denominations against their own disorganization. Sower, their aggressive spokesman, easily detected and perhaps magnified the political and religious preoccupations of the trustees, most of whom supported the war party, and hence opposed Quaker and pacifistic policies in the Assembly. From 1754 to 1764 Sower's Germantown press fairly creaked and groaned from the weight of the propaganda it turned out against the charity schools. Hamilton, Turner, Peters, Allen, Shippen and Franklin, he proclaimed in the columns of his *Pennsylvanische Berichte* in 1755, cared for neither the religious nor the educational welfare of the Germans, but only for the passage of a militia law and the election of themselves to the Assembly.

The trustees essayed counter-propaganda by supporting first Anthony Armbruster (1755-59) and later Peter Miller and Lewis Weiss in their conduct of a rival German press. From 1755 to 1757 the *Philadelphische Zeitung* sought to oppose the policies of the *Berichte,* and in 1755 Armbruster issued *A Brief History of the Rise and Progress of the Scheme Carrying on for the Instruction of Poor Germans and Their Descendants,* by William Smith. (Eight hundred copies in English, one thousand in German, and five hundred in German and English, distributed gratis!) But the damage had been done, and already it was too late to repair it. Germans of all groups, beginning to scent in the scheme dangers to their language, religion and institutions, joined with the Quietists in opposition. Their hostility deepened when they discovered the irregularity of outside donations, which left support of the charity schools a burden upon the Palatines. In 1759 eight schools were caring for four hundred and forty pupils, but five years later Richard Peters had to inform the

English trustees that "the Schools . . . in Pennsylvania are now at an End."

Despite many excellencies, not the least of which were the provision of well-qualified teachers, a local board of trustees and a liberal course of study, perhaps better worked out with regard for a special group and its needs than any other educational program in the colonies, the project was not soundly based. Sower was not altogether wrong in suspecting political motives on the part of the trustees, many of whom feared and resented the strength derived by the Quaker party from the German vote. Furthermore, Smith and Peters did try to promote the interests of the Anglican Church through the charity schools. The movement was unilateral, Weiser being the only German among the trustees, and he a Proprietor's man. Fought out by press and church, this *Kulturkampf*, rather than aiding the Germans in assimilating themselves to American ways, produced exactly the opposite effect, stimulating them to found schools of their own for the preservation of their language, customs and religion.

Until after the mid-century the problem of higher education was one for which Philadelphians had to seek the solution outside the boundaries of their own province. The city counted itself wealthy in inhabitants educated at ancient and respected institutions abroad. During this period some twenty-six lawyers who had studied at the Inns of Court practiced in the city, twenty-three of them natives of Pennsylvania or Maryland. Likewise, before 1765 and the opening of the medical department of the College of Philadelphia, the medical schools of Edinburgh, Leyden and Utrecht graduated many of the city's leading physicians. Nor were men of liberal training lacking; among others, William Allen had spent some time at Clare College, Cambridge; Francis Alison, Thomas Bond, William Elphinstone, the private schoolmaster, and James Wilson had studied in Scottish universities; Richard Peters had spent three years at Leyden; and William Smith had been an undergraduate at the University of Aberdeen.

The younger colleges on their own continent seem to have enjoyed small reputation among Philadelphians. One or two Yale graduates could be found among the ministry there, but until the opening of the College of New Jersey in 1746 and the attraction thither of such young Presbyterians as the Shippens, few among the city's youth patronized any colonial establishment of higher learning. In general, although the Atlantic crossing involved frequent risks and large expenditures, most Philadelphians in search of liberal or professional training undertook the trip.

With the successful founding of the Academy upon liberal and modern lines, prominent citizens, especially the university men among them, began to contemplate establishment of a college in Philadelphia. Franklin had made no mention of an institution of higher learning in his *Proposals* of 1749, but Richard Peters, in his inaugural sermon, definitely anticipated the day when the city should boast not only an academy but a college. By July, 1752, Franklin was writing to the Reverend Samuel Johnson that "We have now several young men desirous of entering on the study of Philosophy, and lectures are to be opened this week. Mr. Alison undertakes Logic and Ethics. . . . Mr. Peters and some other gentlemen [Grew and Kinnersley] undertake the other branches till we shall be provided with a Rector capable of the whole, who may attend wholly to the instruction of youth in higher parts of learning as they come out fitted from the lower schools." Thus began the Philosophy School, where, a year later, Franklin told William Smith he believed New York boys might receive satisfactory philosophical and mathematical training, since in addition to its fine teaching staff the Academy possessed a good English library and "a middling apparatus for experimental philosophy."

Both desire and material for a college being present, events of 1753 moved rapidly toward that end. Early in that year William Smith, then tutor in the family of a gentleman of Long Island, published in New York his *General Idea of a College of Mirania,* the object of which was the "making of good men and good citizens." This work corresponded so nicely with Franklin's educational ideas that he, along with Allen and Peters, procured the appointment of its author to head the Academy of Philadelphia. Smith's first visit to the Academy in June inspired some verses, printed by Franklin, wherein the new rector described the aims of his institution in terms that go far beyond the mere dispensing of a secondary training:

> To follow Nature, and her Source Adore;
> To raise the *Being,* and its end Explore;
> To center every Aim in *Common Weal;*
> In *publick* Deeds to spend all private Zeal;
> With social Toils, in every street, to glow;
> In every House, with well-earn'd Wealth to flow;
> To plant each Virtue in their Children's Hearts;
> To grace their *Infant Land* with polished Arts.

But chiefly it was Francis Alison who had "roused a spirit in Philadelphia to erect an academy, and then a college" in such men as Peters and Franklin. The appointment of Smith provided the final necessary impetus, and on December 10, 1754, he and Alison proposed to the trustees the advantages and desirability of granting degrees. They pointed out that already "one class of hopeful students has now attained to that station in learning and science, by which in a well regulated seminary, youth are entitled to their first *degree."* The trustees directed them to draw up a charter, which the Proprietors later confirmed (March, 1755), creating "The Trustees of the College, Academy and Charitable School of Philadelphia," with William Smith as provost and Francis Alison as vice-provost and rector of the Academy.

At the time of his elevation to this high post, William Smith was still under thirty years of age, and had just returned from receiving Episcopal ordination in England. Ambitious, calculating and capable, he had, shortly after his departure from the University of Aberdeen, seen his plan for promoting the parochial schools of his native Scotland thwarted by Parliamentary indifference, and had resolved to seek a field for his undoubted talents in the New World. Here he was for a time content to serve in the somewhat menial position of tutor in a private family, while on the watch for something more befitting his peculiar qualifications.

· Smith's arrival coincided with a period of educational ferment in the Middle Colonies. At New York, the long controversy that led to the founding of King's College was about to be resolved, and in Philadelphia the Academy, after two years, was already demonstrating its worth. The *General Idea for a College of Mirania,* containing as it did blueprints for an institution of higher learning adapted to the requirements of a new country, fitted too well the conditions in either place to have been the result of purely academic inspiration. In any event, the copies sent by the author to Peters and Franklin bore their expected fruit, and the invitation to head the Academy resulted.

Ability as well as disposition immediately assured William Smith a prominent role in the educational and religious life of his new home. The College and Academy proved insufficient to contain his influence, which soon extended to "all the affairs of the province —social, religious, scientific, literary and political." Philadelphia owed much to the intellectual energy of William Smith, who became a force second only to Franklin in many phases of its cultural life. Yet his increasing Anglicanism, his capacity for political and episcopal intrigue, and certain definite defects of his own character prevented his ever attaining the full importance his great talents warranted. He was able, vigorous, arrogant, dictatorial and avaricious, tactless in controversy and given to great personal bitterness when opposed. In addition, despite fine literary and scientific perceptions, he was slovenly in his person, a heavy drinker, and violent and intemperate in his personal conduct. He never inspired complete confidence in even his closest colleagues, and upon all he left the impression of artfulness and calculation in the pursuit of his own interests and advantage. On the eve of the Revolution John Adams summed up his character in a tremendous series of adjectives such as only that pungent diarist could achieve—"soft, polite, insinuating, adulating, sensible, learned, industrious, indefatigable; he has art enough, and refinement upon art, to make impressions."

". . . Soft, polite, adulating, learned, industrious . . ." The Reverend William Smith. Engraved after the portrait by Benjamin West.

The College of Philadelphia. Whitefield's Tabernacle of 1741 *(left)* and the New College designed by Robert Smith 1762. *(Courtesy Historical Society of Pennsylvania)*

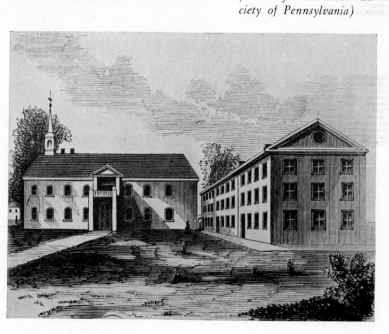

A Half-Century Before Audubon.
Marsh Hawk, painted by William Bartram at the age of 18 and engraved
for George Edwards' *Gleanings from Natural History,* London, 1758.

Smith and Alison immediately set about the reorganization of the institution under their care, bringing the Philosophical and Latin Schools under the College, and leaving to the Academy only the English and mathematical departments. In 1762 the system stood as follows: (1) the College, consisting of three Philosophical Schools and the Latin and Greek Schools and containing about a hundred students; (2) the Academy, made up of the English and Mathematical Schools and caring for some ninety students; and (3) the one hundred and twenty scholars of the Boys' and Girls' Charity Schools.

The curriculum which Smith promulgated for the College has received much praise for its breadth and social usefulness. It revealed the familiarity of both chief officers with *The Preceptor* of Robert Dodsley (1748) and the 1753 revision of the curriculum of the University of Aberdeen, but the emphasis it placed on English, history, geography and the sciences stems directly from the spirit of the place and times. The concepts that a university should offer abundant opportunity for self-development, and that social welfare rather than political expediency should motivate the pursuit of higher learning, had been practiced by the private schoolmasters, preached by Franklin and others, and adumbrated by Milton and Locke. In too large measure, however, this excellent curriculum remained an ideal rather than an actuality, for the study of the classics and classical philosophy continued to be stressed at the expense of English and the vernacular literatures, and Alison found to his sorrow little encouragement for his courses in the natural sciences.

Liberally endowed with adequate buildings, a modern curriculum, an extraordinarily able and energetic faculty, and the good wishes of all the city's leading denizens and men of learning, the College appeared destined for a happy and productive career. Such, regrettably, was not to be the case. Although the institution was honestly founded "on a coalition of all religious Societies," and its authorities kept the student body admirably free of denominational "quotas," a virus of sectarianism permeated the whole from the beginning. Consequently, since in colonial Philadelphia religious and party affiliations were inextricably intertwined, College and Academy quickly became political playthings.

Fearing just such an outcome, the Quakers had refrained from participation in the entire movement, leaving the institution largely to the management of Anglicans and Presbyterians, in whose hands it too often became an instrument of Proprietary and aristocratic interests. Yet in College as in Assembly relations were frequently strained between members of the two denominations. The former controlled the board of trustees; the latter, chief among whom was Francis Alison, "the Presbyterian Pope," dominated the faculty. Fresh from his efforts at resolving the schism between Old and New Side factions within his own church, Alison was disposed to eschew partisanship, and all the evidence shows him to have done so, but on the other hand no Scottish Presbyterian could have been expected to stand idly by while his opponents converted College and Academy into agencies for promoting the cause of the Church of England in America.

From the day of his appointment, despite much fine work performed on behalf of the College, William Smith intrigued, openly and in secret, to bring it completely under Anglican control. As a corollary, he found it impossible to keep out of local politics. As early as 1756 his patron Benjamin Franklin wrote in exasperation to Whitefield that he wished Smith would "learn to mind Party-writing and Party-Politicks less, and his proper Business more." Quakers and Germans already disliked Smith heartily for his part in the German Charity School movement, and as the Provost shortly became an open supporter of the Proprietary faction, he and Franklin soon ceased to be on speaking terms. His championship of Judge Moore in the latter's quarrel with the Assembly led to his conducting his collegiate business for a time from the Philadelphia gaol, and although such extracurricular activities resulted in his eventual marriage to the Judge's daughter, they could not but seriously affect the influence and reputation of the College.

Within the College, Smith felt his cause to be prospering, and reported in 1756 to Dr. Bancroft of London that "the Church, by soft and easy means, daily gains Ground in it." He introduced the use of the Church of England service for all public occasions, and persuaded the trustees to have printed to be used for daily prayers at the College a work compiled by a number of Anglican clergymen. Notwithstanding this progress, one clerical zealot complained that during Smith's absence in England to collect funds, College and faculty were "dwindling away . . . into a mere Presbyterian faction" whose object was to ease the Provost out of his job. "Many more Dissenters than members of our Church are bred there," he went on with his indictment, "and thus they get instead of mechanics, persons of learning for their ministers"—an observation which reveals much of the devotion to the Anglican cause to have been social rather than religious in inspiration. Richard Peters, however, explained the absence of Episcopalians from the faculty by the fact that "there is not a Churchman upon the Continent as I can hear of that is fit to make a tutor." Inasmuch as two-thirds of the trustees belonged to churches under his care, he hoped that "With care and foresight this may be set right for the future."

So far had Smith and Peters succeeded in swinging the College and Academy over to the Church of England by 1764 that both the Proprietors and the Archbishop of Canterbury, fearing an outbreak of sectarian animosities, felt it necessary to caution the trustees against too great a display of their zeal. The board somewhat disingenuously replied that "at the same Time we shew all due Regard to our national Church, we shall never violate our Faith pledged to other religious Denominations."

Success of these Anglican intrigues greatly embittered Francis Alison, who had sought to deal fairly and equally with all sects. "I am ready to resign my place . . . and retire to the country meerly thro chagrine," he told Ezra Stiles in 1766. "The College is artfully got into the hands of Episcopal Trustees. Young men educated here get a Taste for high life, and many of them do not like to bear the poverty and dependence of our ministers." Pressure of Anglican influence, he went on, leads many of the best graduates of the College to go to England to take orders, while those who do seek Presbyterian ordination can seldom pass the overdifficult examinations drawn up by ministers of that denomination who are, excusably perhaps, "inflamed with indignation against our College." Every day more Pennsylvania Presbyterians were sending their sons to "Jersey College," which "is so unfit to make scholars."

Finally, in 1768, Smith became a leader in the movement to establish an Anglican bishopric in the Colonies. To this Alison, unlike many of his faith, had no objection provided there were no "civil power annexed to it," but so reasonable an outcome would hardly have contented the Smith faction, which contemplated complete establishment. Alison's hopes after 1769 turned toward Princeton as the only bulwark against Episcopacy: "I should rejoice to see her Pistols, like honest Teagues, grown up into great Guns."

A steady crescendo of religious animosity echoed through the College in the nineteen years from its founding to the outbreak of the War for Independence. Possibly the various parties could have arrived at a peaceable accommodation but for the intransigeance of Provost Smith. His services to American education in general and to the College in particular can hardly be overestimated, but his overweening ambition to promote his denomination at the expense of all others, and within it to advance the cause of William Smith, perhaps to the extent of "a pair of lawn sleeves," very nearly nullified the effect of his good works, and of the best efforts of Alison, Franklin and the other founders. The taint of Episcopacy was on the College—a taint more social and political than religious. Politics did not enter the College for the first time in 1779; control of the institution merely passed at that time to another party.

Throughout Smith's administration the quality of the training and the standards of instruction offered by the College remained high. The rigorous admission requirements of his curriculum considerably narrowed the number of young men who could qualify for entrance, and its location in a growing city, rather than in a less distracting, more moral, rural community doubtless lost it some students. The increasing attractions of the College of New Jersey for the sons of Presbyterians also helped to keep enrollment small. Only about seven degrees, on the average, were granted annually, with none conferred in the years 1758 and 1764. Of the two hundred and ten young men who matriculated at the College from 1757 to 1776, eighty-six came from Philadelphia, and thirty-seven more from other parts of Pennsylvania. From outside the province Maryland supplied the greatest number, thirty-six, while the bulk of the remainder hailed from Delaware, New Jersey, New York and North Carolina.

In 1765 the institution increased in stature and influence by the opening of the first medical school on the American continent as a department of the College. Speaking at the Commencement of 1771, Provost Smith regarded the present situation of the College, and its development during the war and postwar years, as cause for congratulation. He emphasized that "all Branches of Science are now professed and taught in it on so liberal a Foundation, that it would be entitled not merely to the name of a College, but of an University, in any Part of the World." Philadelphians were justly proud of their College, for its graduates, equipped as they were with a training seldom equaled and hardly surpassed even in the mother country, almost without exception came to take a prominent part in the life of city and province, and some of them in the founding of a new commonwealth as well.

Failure of Provost and trustees to keep the College of Philadelphia free from sectarian bias had the effect of causing members of other denominations to look elsewhere for higher training. Certain other institutions on this continent, therefore, profited from an otherwise unfortunate situation. In the movement which led to the founding of Rhode Island College in 1764 the Philadelphia Baptist Association took the lead. The Reverend Morgan Edwards of Philadelphia played an important part in obtaining a charter for the New England institution, and personally secured a substantial part of its funds in England and America. Mounting bitterness at the High Church atmosphere of Academy and College resulted in the

increasing attendance of the sons of Philadelphia Presbyterians at
the neighboring College of New Jersey and a move to elevate its
standards of instruction. This tendency culminated in the arrival
of Dr. John Witherspoon in 1767, largely in response to the pleas
of Benjamin Rush of Philadelphia, a Princeton A.B.

Witherspoon's preaching, scholarship, and capacity for securing
funds soon satisfied even the meticulous requirements of the foremost of American Presbyterians, Francis Alison. Yet Alison, and
many of his denomination, continued in their fondness and par-
tiality for his old New London School, which as early as 1746 he
had hoped to elevate into a degree-granting institution. Situated
now at Newark, Delaware, conveniently far, it was pointed out,
from the "profligacy and vice" of the metropolis, it was chartered
by the Penns in 1770 as the Academy of Newark. Among its trustees
were Chief Justice William Allen, a founder, Vice-Provost Francis
Alison, the Reverend John Ewing and Dr. Hugh Williamson, professors, Charles Thomson, tutor, and Andrew Allen, graduate, all
of the Academy and College of Philadelphia. In March, 1772, Dr.
Williamson sailed for London to solicit funds for this school of
liberal arts and sciences, which in later years was to become the
University of Delaware.

The benefits of higher education in these years were for the most
part restricted to sons of gentlemen. Yet Philadelphia witnessed several fumbling attempts at adult education which, while they probably did not long survive, afford interesting evidence of efforts at
self-improvement among artisans and tradesmen at a time when
important events were stirring. "The Literary Republic, an institution designed to make men fit and useful members of a commonwealth or limited monarchie," opened in the bookbindery of George
Reinholt in Second Street in 1764. Here "grown gentlemen," especially among the German population, might engage in orations and
disputations in logic, jurisprudence, the law of nations, religion and
morality. This early lyceum provided other functions, such as "musical exercises and entertainments, both vocal and instrumental," a
literary club, and a German grammar school, "especially for such

as have a grammar knowledge." It even contemplated the publication of "a periodical paper . . . if encourag'd."

Six years later one Joseph Cunningham offered to the adult public, in "a large Hall," a series of timely lectures on the history and laws of England, at £1. 14s., and another, on geography and the use of the globe, at 14s. Indeed, a wide variety of lectures, especially on medical and scientific subjects, and frequent public demonstrations in mechanics and electricity, gave moderately literate Philadelphians, as the years went by, many miscellaneous opportunities for adding to their knowledge.

By the eve of the Revolution frequent communications to the Philadelphia press were dealing with the intellectual and educational needs of the middle and lower classes. One of the most interesting was an "Outline of a Scheme for the Improvement of the Philadelphia Youths," published by "Philomath" in the *Pennsylvania Chronicle* of March 5, 1772. This outline proposed a monthly meeting of young men over twenty-one years of age for the discussion of topics in the arts and sciences, and the reading of "Beautiful Parts in polite literature." Particular evenings, when visitors might be admitted, were to be set apart for orations by the members, and presiding officers were to be appointed "to see Decency and Decorum preserved." Thus, only a few years after the formation of the American Philosophical Society, an organization very like Franklin's youthful Junto was seeking to encourage similar mental recreation among the less highly trained citizenry.

The educational development of the city in these years was not without its effects upon surrounding areas and neighbor provinces. Better educational facilities in Philadelphia resulted in the advent of students from rural Pennsylvania, and from Maryland, Delaware and New Jersey. Quakers from many parts of America had long made a habit of sending their children to the superior Friends' schools of their capital city. As the period advanced and the educational supremacy of Philadelphia became more marked, a kind of educational imperialism drew young people from ever wider areas, including the Southern and island colonies, the boys to study with private masters or tutors, and later to enter Academy and College, the girls to enjoy the advantages of genteel or classical training as it could be obtained only in the metropolis.

The magnetism exerted by urban opportunities produced a very definite reaction in the efforts of such men as Benezet to strengthen and improve the education offered by Quaker schools in the country, in the rise of rural academies, usually under Presbyterian or Episcopalian sponsorship, and in the support and patronage by many of colleges located at a safe distance from the supposed pitfalls and distractions of the lustily growing city. This was the period when such suburban schools as Germantown Academy appealed to parents as safe, healthful and quiet, and when Francis Alison hoped his Newark Academy might benefit from the real hesitancy many families felt about exposing their children to the dangers of city life. Education became definitely a business in Philadelphia in these years, but it had to contend with fears and prejudices against habits of extravagance and frivolity and a "taste for high living," which residence in America's first city might inspire.

Educational progress in Philadelphia grew out of a complex of social, economic, religious and political conditions. This was an era of increasing prosperity and rapid growth, when demands for education rose along with patronage to support it. Within the city successful merchants sought the seal of genteel accomplishments on their newly achieved social positions, and prospering tradesmen reached out for means of improving their already comfortable status in a society rich with opportunity. In surrounding countrysides farmers, amassing wealth, began to desire for themselves and their sons advantages comparable to those of city-dwellers. As religious heterogeneity succeeded the earlier Quaker control, most denominations sought to extend and consolidate their influence by maintaining educational facilities for their young, and by training teachers and ministers capable of militant action, while among all sects the leavening forces of the Great Awakening brought a renewed interest in the common man, his rights, capacities and opportunities.

Finally, Pennsylvania experienced peculiar problems in the presence of a large non-English group, with its own language, religion and customs, whom education must keep from a French alliance or from falling into the hands of Papists. Whatever the reason, social, economic, religious or political, faith in the efficacy of knowledge was widespread, and the thirst for it universal.

Out of these complexities two streams of educational thought emerged. One conceived of learning as a matter of ancient knowledge and antique tongues, possession of which distinguished a gentleman from the herd and enabled him to converse with others of his kind. It was the key to past wisdom and present science, but only the better sort were fit or worthy to possess it. The other view held knowledge to be a practical tool in the hands of tradesmen and merchants, men and women, whose daily lives and mundane activities were building the new city and world in which they lived, and whose abilities and enterprise guaranteed its prosperity and increase. Such middling people wanted useful knowledge of their own society, the geography and history that produced it, the laws, natural and humane, which governed it, science to solve its riddles and avoid its pitfalls, and enough business or practical skill to achieve some independence in the midst of it. They wanted of education something to enable them to get on in the world, advance their own position, and perhaps at the same time contribute some improvement to the society that produced them. Knowledge of the classics and other purely literary accomplishments were desirable as adornments for a man's leisure time, or as a discipline for toughening his youthful capacities, but not as an end in themselves, and certainly not for a shibboleth by which genteel sheep might be separated from uncultivated goats.

The one ideal was aristocratic; the other, democratic. The one was the view of the conservative, plutocratic, generally Anglican, Tory society of Philadelphia; the other, that of the bustling, energetic, ambitious and increasing middle class, Benjamin Franklin and his group, who had a feeling for the educational needs of a democratic society, and even some sense of the cultural mission that society was to perform in the world. The one belonged to the past, to the already obsolescent classical world; the other was on the side of the future, when the ideal of free, public, nonsectarian education should become the rule.

In these years the aristocratic ideal triumphed in College and Academy, with their curricula designed for rich men's sons, and to some extent also in the schools of the Friends, who were becoming wealthy and conservative. The democratic ideal had to content itself for the most part with conquest of the private secondary schools, where people would pay only for what they wanted and masters had to offer what was most in demand. But the educational ferment of the period was such that at its close almost complete literacy prevailed in the city, and education, from being only the luxury of the rich, had become the right of the middle class and the necessity of the poor.

Here was the real revolution of the period, the opening wedge of democracy on the march. The educational accomplishments of these years were to provide the democratic base for the flowering of an indigenous culture, and the intelligent, critical and literate audience for the pamphlet warfare of the Revolutionary era. Furthermore, because the aristocratic ideal had had a shorter time to entrench itself, it was more subject to attack than in older societies, and the New World city was able to become a sort of proving-ground for radical European theories of educational reform, as well as for the practical experimentation of native thinkers. In the end, the teeming many were soon in a position to implement their resentment at the cultural exclusiveness of the few, and the Revolutionary assault upon the charter of the College thus has social and economic significance far beyond its political and factional aspects.

By 1776 Philadelphia had achieved a complete system of formal education for its better sort, practical training in the primary and secondary stages for its mechanics and tradesmen, charity instruction for underprivileged and special groups, and the hope of some learning beyond that of the schools for members of its middling and lower classes. Such hopes, ironically enough, were dashed by one of the city's leading intellectuals, who, in a grim announcement on December 2, 1776, declared it to be the opinion of the Council of Safety "that the Schools be broke up, and the Inhabitants engaged solely in providing for the Defense of this City, at this Time of extreme Danger. David Rittenhouse, V. Pres." Assuredly, pursuit of truth is among the first casualties of any war.

Chapter III

PRINTERS AND BOOKS:
THE MAKING OF FULL MEN

THE broadening of the cultural base made possible by more democratic forms of education was in part facilitated by, and in turn greatly stimulated, the activities of the Philadelphia press. Of the forty-two printers who pursued their trade in the city between 1740 and 1776, almost all played prominent and aggressive roles in the production and dissemination of enlightenment by the printed word. From their ranks, of course, came the colonies' leading citizen, in the shadow of whose pre-eminence the importance of many of his fellow craftsmen has been obscured.

Socially, politically and culturally, the printers of Philadelphia, as of the colonies in general, constituted a unique class, and yet a class that more than any other typified the spirit of their day and of the future. Skilled craftsmen, they belonged by interest and training with the mechanics and artisans. The superior education that practice of their profession required made them important members of the growing middle class, and the widening market for their wares occasioned by the increasing literacy of their times brought them material prosperity that often placed them economically at the head of it.

Many of the printers had received their training in England or Scotland, and their views were thus imperial rather than provincial in scope; in religion, they were usually to be found in the Dissenting camp, opposed to traditionalism, authoritarianism and establishment; and, as the continued existence of their profession depended upon a free press, unhampered by censorship and laws of libel, they tended to ally themselves with radical movements and later with the patriot cause. Business brought them into contact with the colonial aristocracy, whose prejudices and psychology they soon learned to divine with accuracy, at the same time that they were becoming every day more skillful in taking the public pulse, speaking for the commercial middle class, and inspiring the respect and trust of artisans and workers. They understood the art of propaganda, having had long experience in religious and social controversy before the Revolutionary movement began, and as the adult educators of their day they had already hastened the achievement of a social revolution before any political upheaval had taken place. They were known and had connections in all the colonies, were continental rather than parochial in outlook, and, before politicians or statesmen, had a sort of intuitive understanding of America's mission in the world. Above all, to the best of them printing was not only a trade, but a calling.

Two leading families, the Franklins and the Bradfords, dominated the printing trade of Philadelphia and trained most of the local apprentices in these years. William Bradford was in many respects as prominent a Philadelphian as Poor Richard. Beginning in 1742, he conducted as good a newspaper, better printed, and a superior bookstore. He established the city's leading coffeehouse in 1754, brought out two of the best colonial magazines, founded an insurance company, and became a leader in the Sons of Liberty. His aunt, Cornelia, was the first woman to operate successfully as a printer and bookseller in Philadelphia, and his son Thomas ably carried on the family tradition as bookseller, proprietor of a circulating library, and partner to his father in the printing business. For a span of one hundred and forty years, from 1685 to 1823, the Bradfords were one of the most distinguished and influential families of printers on the continent.

From Scotland came Robert Bell and Robert Aitken, and from Ireland, Andrew Steuart of Belfast and John and William Dunlap of County Tyrone; these men, with Bradford, were responsible for most of the literary output of the Philadelphia press. A Connecticut Yankee, William Goddard, gave the city its finest newspaper. Anthony Armbruster and the scholarly Henry Miller after 1769 produced in Philadelphia 54 per cent of the German imprints of the province, while in near-by Germantown the Christopher Sowers, elder and younger, accounted for the bulk of the remainder. In 1769 Goddard lent encouragement to American infant manufactures by printing his *Chronicle* on a mahogany press made by Isaac Doolittle of Connecticut, "equal if not superior to any imported," and in 1775 Enoch Story and David Humphreys began publication of the *Pennsylvania Mercury,* "the first Work with American Types," cast by Jacob Bay of Germantown. Three years earlier William and Thomas Bradford had sought to encourage their craft in rural areas by the sale of "The New Universal Portable Printing Presses."

The printing trade expanded to keep pace with the city's growth, and the eight shops of 1740 became twenty-three by the eve of the Revolution. Conservative calculation estimates the total output of the Philadelphia press from 1740 to 1776 at over 11,000 issues of all kinds; of these about 15 per cent were in the German tongue. Naturally, as in our own day, the majority of items was of an immediate and utilitarian nature, serving the commercial or political needs of the community—business and legal forms, handbills, tickets, catalogues, and various types of government printing.

A smaller, but by no means unimportant body of imprints suggests the vital role played by the printers in the cultural life not only of Philadelphia, but of the colonies as a whole. Nearly every press annually sent forth one or more almanacs—*Poor Richard's* is only the best-known—which sold widely in city and country, in rural stores in Pennsylvania, New Jersey, the lower counties and Maryland, and in the back country as far south as Georgia. In addition to their pages of needed information about the vagaries of nature, these little booklets contained the usual homely sayings and often essays of some instructive or cultural value. Armbruster's *German Almanac* for 1756, for instance, carried a very good account of the American Indians.

Religion and religious controversy provided the colonial printer with a lucrative source of income. Quakers, Presbyterians, Anglicans, Lutherans and German sectarians all had their popular divines, whose sermons were regularly published by favorite printers and eagerly read by the faithful. The 1740's witnessed a deluge of sermons from the pens of George Whitefield and Gilbert Tennent, their supporters and opponents. Religious zeal among the Germans, pietist and orthodox, accounted for many more.

Some of these theological essays dealt with doctrine and piety; almost more, it appears, with sectarian or internal controversy. Many were well written; others too often failed to rise above mere bickering and drivel. But to the people of the day this pulpit literature served a cultural purpose in presenting fodder for both mind and spirit, and in reviewing vital and current issues, as frequently political as religious, for none can tell where the line between the two may be drawn. Minds unexposed to more liberal influences became from this intellectual diet at least accustomed to the perusal of exposition and argument. A considerable number of these sermons went into second printings, and many were translated into another language, where they played their part in the interchange of cultures.

Second only to the sermons, and increasing in importance as the period advanced, were the pamphlets, floods of which poured from the presses whenever a debatable issue arose. The Great Awakening, the perennial struggle between Assembly and Proprietors, the French menace and the question of frontier defense, Judge Moore's libels on the Assembly, the Paxton riots, the debate over an Anglican episcopate and like questions, evoked arguments pro and con which Philadelphians avidly devoured in pamphlet form. Many were witty, others satirical; some were bumptious, others scurrilous; few were fair, some were dignified, and all appealed because they were partisan in a partisan age, and because they dealt with matters of immediate import and general interest. A surprising number prove to have been written in an able prose style worthy of authors who received their schooling in the golden age of English pamphleteering. They formed the editorial, or better, the columnistic writings of their day.

Constant reading of such tracts accustomed people of all classes, but especially of the middling and lower estates, to the examination and discussion of controversial issues of all sorts. It is a grave mistake to assume that the Pennsylvania audience for the great political polemics of Dickinson, Galloway, Dulany and Jefferson was confined to the intellectualized gentry. When a conservative of 1775 observed with alarm that "the mob begins to think and to reason," he was only discovering what had been slowly and inexorably developing for three decades, what the printers had long known, and controversialists had at least suspected.

The most influential of the social and cultural services performed by the printers was to be found in the fifteen newspapers issued from their presses prior to the Revolution. In 1740 there were only two weekly news sheets published in the city—Franklin's *Pennsylvania Gazette* and Bradford's *American Weekly Mercury*. Andrew Bradford died in 1740, but his newspaper, under the editorship of his wife, Cornelia, survived him by nearly a decade, while in 1742 his nephew, William Bradford, commenced publication of the *Pennsylvania Journal*. For many years Franklin and the Bradfords monopolized the English newspaper field in Philadelphia. Regarded by its publishers, Benjamin Franklin and David Hall, primarily as a business enterprise, the *Gazette* successfully straddled religious and political issues until the dissolution of the partnership in 1766, when Hall became a partisan of the Proprietary party. The *Journal,* on the other hand, had been definitely a Proprietary organ from the start. In 1767, therefore, Joseph Galloway and Thomas Wharton, desiring a newspaper for the Assembly party, set up William Goddard as proprietor of the *Pennsylvania Chronicle*. Increasing business, an ever widening circle of readers, and the insatiable demand for news in the exciting period of the seventies saw the establishment of four more English newspapers by 1776.

Thus far Philadelphia's journalistic history merely parallels that of Boston and other seaboard communities. But the presence here of a large and growing German population led to efforts to cater to their economic and political importance by means of an urban newspaper. Between 1743 and 1755 no less than five attempts to publish a German or bilingual news sheet failed, either because of the political hostility of the German public, or from inability to compete with the variously titled publication of Christopher Sower of Germantown, first issued in 1739, and sole master of the field until 1762. In June, 1755, William Smith and other supporters of the German Charity School movement purchased a press from Franklin and began publication of the *Philadelphische Zeitung,* under the editorship of Franklin and one of his partners, Anthony Arm- bruster, with the avowed purpose of counteracting Sower's inces- sant and very effective propaganda against the charity schools. This paper never enjoyed more than four hundred subscribers, while at the same time Sower's claimed a circulation of over ten times that number.

It remained for a German printer of marked ability to found a permanent newspaper for his people in the city. Henry Miller, a Moravian, had practiced his craft not only in his homeland, but in France, Holland and the British Isles. Scholar and amateur artist, he knew English as well as German, city as well as country. His *Der Wöchentliche Philadelphische Staatsbote,* inaugurated in 1762, though conducted in frank opposition to the Sowers, succeeded where its predecessors had failed because it supplied German read- ers with a better paper.

Miller had a good eye for business, and his free translation service for advertisements or news items secured him the support of many English patrons. As early as 1764 he reported that the *Staatsbote* circulated "not only through all Pennsylvania, but likewise goes to Georgia, South and North-Carolina, Virginia, Maryland, the Jer- seys, New York, Albany, up to the Mohawk River, Nova Scotia, and the West Indies," in short, wherever in the New World settle- ments of Germans, however small, might be found. The Moravian printer eagerly espoused the patriot cause, and to his paper may be attributed much of the influence that brought the Germans of

Pennsylvania and the Shenandoah Valley to the side of the revolting colonists.

Philadelphians of 1776 had access to seven newspapers. Five of them were so published that at least one came off the press every weekday morning except Wednesday; Benjamin Towne's *Pennsylvania Evening Post* appeared every Tuesday, Thursday and Saturday evening, and the *Staatsbote,* every Tuesday and Thursday. Issued in editions of from five hundred to three thousand, they constituted about one-seventh of all newspapers printed on the continent, and circulated widely, not only in town and province, but in all the colonies. Goddard of the *Chronicle* had some twenty-two subscription agents at work throughout Pennsylvania, some as far west as Carlisle and Bedford, three in Delaware, six in New Jersey, six in Maryland, and one in Virginia, while all continental and West Indian printers received copies of his paper. Bradford sent his *Pennsylvania Journal* to seven persons in Jamaica, eight in Barbados, four in Antigua, four in St. Kitts, eighteen in Dominica, three in England, and one at Bordeaux, as well as to a wide list of subscribers in the American colonies. Ezra Stiles of Newport, Rhode Island, regularly bought and read several Philadelphia newspapers. In 1765 Bradford received at one time a request to add twelve new subscriptions to the eight he was already sending by the Lancaster post to York, Pennsylvania, and in 1775 eight gentlemen of Northampton County raised a fund for a post rider "for his pains in carrying each of our newspapers from Philadelphia."

In estimating the influence of the colonial press it must be borne in mind that many more readers used the same copy of a newspaper then than now. To taverns and coffeehouses in the city, and to country stores and crossroads inns, people flocked to read the news themselves or to hear it read to them. As a practical and political force for the molding of opinion these little sheets exerted a tremendous power in both town and country. In the early months of the Revolution Lord Howe's secretary in America had to concede the "almost incredible Influence these fugitive Publications have upon the People." "However little some may think of common

News-Papers," wrote "Providus" in a *Pennsylvania Gazette* of 1768, "to a wise man they appear as the Ark of God, for the safety of the people."

These same publications, by their "fulness of general Entertainment, small bulk and price," exercised a profound influence, often overlooked, in the formation of a colonial culture. Most printers defined "general Entertainment" broadly, while adhering to the principle, now often ignored, that "generally speaking, the little concerns of individuals ought not to fill up the useful pages of a newspaper." Frequently they seem to bring a sense of cultural mission to an otherwise very practical business. William Goddard aimed to make his *Pennsylvania Chronicle* "useful, instructive and entertaining," with such success that he published far and away the best sheet in the Middle Colonies. Benjamin Towne founded Philadelphia's first evening and triweekly paper in 1775, in an effort to present by way of the public press a complete history of the commerce, politics and "Literature of the Times." As token of his sincerity he offered to publish without cost, in addition to the usual literary contributions, any advertisements of useful inventions in agriculture or manufactures.

Most publishers volunteered their columns for the support of civic and humanitarian projects. All at one time or another carried political and moral essays, often expressed in skillful and highly competent prose. Controversies on all subjects, often running tandem in more than one paper, sharpened the wits of readers, while ubiquitous advertising columns informed them of the services of schoolmasters, painters, musicians, and other practitioners of the arts and crafts. Much of the medical and scientific production of the city first reached a wider audience through the public prints.

In both consumption and production, the newspaper press stimulated the literary tastes of its subscribers. Like other colonial papers, Goddard's *Chronicle* carried frequent reprints of current English verse. Bradford's *Journal* in 1767 instituted a "Poet's Corner" for the productions of local bards, masculine and feminine, and the *Mercury* began another in 1775 which is significant for the number of pieces contributed by "females." The supplement to the issue of the *Packet* for October 28, 1771, was devoted almost exclusively to scientific or literary advertisements and contributions, including proposals for publishing several solid works in these fields and an essay on "Inducements to Natural Philosophy." Anonymous appearance in this same paper during March and April, 1772, of the "Letters of Tamoc Caspipina" occasioned much speculation as to their authorship.

Perhaps most conscious of the cultural potentialities of the newspaper was Henry Miller, who, as a patriotic Pennsylvanian and an apostle to his people, consistently employed the columns of his *Staatsbote* in an effort to foster the cultural and educational development of the province's German population. Miller hoped to promote the Anglicization of his people by his emphasis on English ways and ideas, and also to better their position in the colony by interpreting them to the larger English-speaking public. In 1762, as a contribution to solution of the language problem in business, he began the weekly publication of English lessons in his paper, and pioneered in the use of phonetics. After 1768 the *Staatsbote* carried an increasing amount of verse, chiefly of a religious nature. There is no need to explore the cultural influences of the newspapers further at this juncture, for they touched Philadelphia life at many points, as will become increasingly evident in succeeding chapters.

Philadelphia printers also pioneered in the publication of magazines. In January of 1741 appeared in close succession America's first two periodicals, Andrew Bradford's *American Magazine,* and Benjamin Franklin's *General Magazine.* Despite their prompt demise, the idea of a literary periodical carried on, and in 1757 William Bradford began issuing a really first-rate publication, the *American Magazine and Monthly Chronicle,* edited by a "Society of Gentlemen," chief among them the Reverend William Smith. With an initial subscription list of over eight hundred and fifty, this magazine might have commanded wide patronage had not its editor got himself imprisoned as a corollary to a political squabble and been forced to cease its publication after one year.

From Bradford's press also, in 1769, issued another important periodical, the *American Magazine or General Repository,* edited by Lewis Nicola, which during its brief nine months of existence was remarkable for the large number and significant quality of its scientific contributions. Outbreak of the Revolutionary War cut short the life of Philadelphia's fifth magazine of the period, Robert Aitken's *Pennsylvania Magazine, or American Monthly Museum,* launched in January, 1775, under the editorship of Thomas Paine, and terminated with the publication of the Declaration of Independence in the issue of July, 1776.

During their abbreviated lifetimes these little magazines offered a varied literary fare, often as imitative as the tastes of their readers and as unoriginal as their titles. Yet they furnish an accurate reflection of cultural fashions among a large section of Philadelphia society, and in their day provided vehicles for the publication of a considerable variety of local creative effort.

As the century advanced, book-publishing came to constitute an important factor in the printing trade. Before 1750 most books from Philadelphia presses were reprints or simple piracies of English works of a practical or religious nature. Ready reckoners, treatises on farriery, and family medical books early found an assured market. But with the development of leisure and the expansion of reading tastes, enterprising publishers, unhampered by any law of copyright, began to bring out American editions of works currently popular in England and on the Continent. Franklin reprinted *Pamela* in 1744; Bradford brought out an edition of Pope's *Essay on Man* in 1748; while from the press of James Chattin issued More's *Utopia* in 1753.

With the mounting demand for such reprints in the sixties, certain publishers began to specialize in this type of work. Between 1768 and 1776 the shrewd Scotsman Robert Bell published such standard titles as Johnson's *Rasselas,* the *Letters* of Montaigne, Robertson's *Charles V,* Sterne's *Sentimental Journey,* the first American edition of Blackstone's *Commentaries,* in five volumes, Ferguson's *Essay on Civil Society,* and Lord Kames's *History of Man.* Bradford's 1769 edition of the poetical works of Charles Churchill, issued with the co-operation of Rivington of New York, had over 2,200 advance subscribers. In 1774 James Humphreys published the first American edition of an author's collected works, those of Laurence Sterne, which he followed with four volumes of Chesterfield's *Letters.*

Among authors similarly honored with American reprints were Defoe, Goldsmith, Gray, Locke, Priestley and Young, but the reproductive activity of the Philadelphia presses was by no means limited to serious and "highbrow" literature. In response to growing interest in the theater after the successful appearance of the American Company, Andrew Steuart undertook the reprinting of popular plays for American readers. Among the eleven published under his imprint in 1762 were such ephemera as *Edgar and Emmeline, a Tragedy, The Old Maid,* and *The Double Disappointment: or, the Humors of Phelim O'Blunderoo, Esq.* Editions of current favorites on the English or American stage, works of Cumberland, Garrick or Goldsmith, found ready sale.

Local publishers also supplied the tastes now satisfied by pulp magazines or drugstore fiction with such titles as *The Man of Sensibility,* by Sarah Scott, *The School for Husbands: A Sentimental Novel, Life Truly painted in the History of Tommy and Harry,* or *Jacky and Maggy's Courtship,* while John Dunlap appealed to the worthy desire to be both entertained and entertaining with *The Wits of Westminster,* "a new Select Collection of Jests, Bon Mots, Humorous Tales, Brilliant Repartees, Epigrams, and other Sallies of Wit and Humour, Chiefly New and Original. Being an agreeable and lively companion for the parlour, or wherever such a companion is most necessary and pleasing."

The move to encourage local manufactures, though inspired by political rather than intellectual considerations, greatly stimulated the publication of American reprints. In announcing his edition of *The Vicar of Wakefield,* to the "Lovers of Literary Amusement, and the Encouragers of American Manufactures," in 1772, William

Mentz urged its purchase as a patriotic action, because it was "neatly bound," gilt and lettered, printed on Pennsylvania-made paper, and would sell for 4s, 6d., little more than half the cost of the English edition. To Robert Bell belongs chief credit for introducing to Philadelphians numbers of reprints of good current literature, in "home-made garb" at greatly reduced prices. Again, it was absence of a copyright which assisted American printers to undersell their British competitors. While the Quakers were debating the reprinting in America of works of English Friends in 1771, Anthony Benezet wrote to George Dilwyn by way of argument that "Several Books have of late been printed here, such as the History of Charles V, Tissot on health, Foundation of Laws, &c., which have sold considerably cheaper than in England."

A large part of the printers' cultural activities consisted in the publication of schoolbooks. Spread of education brought an increasing demand for textbooks, and it is probable that in actual number of copies printed this category exceeded all others combined. Edition after edition of Dilworth's speller issued from Philadelphia presses, usually in printings of from two to four thousand copies, although Dunlap published one printing of ten thousand in 1772. Between 1749 and 1766 Franklin and Hall printed 36,100 copies of their primer, and Henry Miller published a Moravian speller in frequent editions of two thousand.

Dissatisfaction with imported schoolbooks and their frequent inapplicability to conditions in Philadelphia led many local pedagogues to compile their own. Theophilus Grew was author of *The Description and Use of the Globes,* for use at the Academy in 1753, and in 1761 Andrew Steuart published Thomas Abel's *A Treatise of Substantial [sic] Plane Trigonometry, applied to Navigation and Surveying,* which was adorned with seven plates. Also from Steuart's press in 1763 came a Latin grammar for the College, which is of more than passing interest for the satirical pamphlet it evoked in criticism, *Errata, or the Art of Printing Incorrectly,* by Francis Hopkinson. This famous essay, which pointed out one hundred fifty-one errors in one hundred thirty-seven pages, so incensed the faculty that they excluded its author from musical participation in the next commencement. Peter de Préfontaine produced *A New Guide to the French Tongue* (1757), and William Thorne, writing master, compiled *A New Set of Copies . . . for the Use of Schools* (1763). J. Bachmair's German grammar passed through three editions, and Christopher Doch's famous *Schul Ordnung,* through two. Of romantic interest, at least, was David Zeisburger's *Delaware Indian Speller* of 1776.

Philadelphia early became a center of medical publication in America, and by 1776 at least eighteen important medical works had issued from its presses. Of these only three were reprints, the rest coming from the pens of local physicians. Among the more notable were Thomas Cadwalader's *Essay on the West India Dry-Gripes* (1745), Adam Thompson's *Discourse on the Preparation of the Body for the Small Pox* (1751), and *Observations on the Angina Maligna, or putrid sore throat* (1769) by John Kearsley, Jr. Local publishers also brought out in 1771 four dissertations by graduates of the first class at the Medical School.

Publication between 1750 and 1770 of about fifty pieces best classified as belles lettres, to be discussed in a later chapter, indicates that virtually any effort in poetry or prose that merited public notice found its way into print. Philadelphia letters did not lack a vehicle of expression, nor did they languish for want of public appreciation, for local newspapers willingly offered them a trial in their columns, and printers saw to it that all worthy performances were issued separately. At least one native author suffered the compliment of seeing himself pirated; Francis Hopkinson was forced to advertise in the newspapers in 1762 that Dunlap's authorized edition of his *Science, a Poem,* for sale by Dunlap, Hall, and Bradford in Philadelphia, and by Rivington in Boston and New York, had been secretly reissued by Steuart "in a very incorrect Duodecimo Pamphlet in order to undersell the first edition"—"a common trick by this printer."

Virtually all printers, whether publishers or not, conducted bookstores in conjunction with their businesses. In addition, shops devoted exclusively to the sale of books were opened from time to time, with the result that there were more than thirty such establishments in the city of the seventies, where only five had existed in 1742. The better bookshops carried fairly complete stocks of books in current demand, works published in Philadelphia and other colonial cities, maps, charts, prints, and often stationery, but the bulk of their volumes they imported from England, Germany or France. Philadelphia booksellers also sent frequent special orders to their English agents for specific works or for subscriptions to English periodicals.

Some bookshops tended to concentrate on one line of publication. James Chattin as printer to the Society of Friends quite logically lined his shelves principally with Quaker tracts and commentaries, and Sparhawk & Anderton, primarily a drug firm, displayed in 1768 "a very great choice of books adapted for the instruction and amusement of all the little masters and misstresses in America." The 1772 catalogue of William Woodhouse featured "many uncommon books, seldom to be found," while Charles Startin specialized in fine editions, Bibles, and the works of Milton, Terence, Catullus, Lucretius, Juvenal, Horace and Virgil, "printed by Baskerville, of Birmingham, and bound in an elegant manner." High prices for these collector's items enabled their purveyor to move in opulent circles, and along with such other Philadelphians as the Biddles and the Redwoods, he was an early summer colonist at Newport.

The larger firms of Aitken, Bell, Bradford, Dunlap, Hall, Miller, and Rivington maintained extensive stocks of history, biography, travel, general and polite literature, theology, jurisprudence, surgery and medicine, in addition to household works and volumes on the practical arts. In the 1770's one-fifth of the city's booksellers, chief among them Henry Miller, dealt in local and imported works in the German tongue, while other shops handled a wider variety of French titles than might be found in other colonial cities.

The problem of book-marketing is as old as the trade, and Philadelphia booksellers demonstrated considerable ingenuity in its solution. Elaborate advertisements appeared in all newspapers, listing current offerings at great length—Hall or Bradford often filled whole pages—or stressing titles on a particular subject. It was not alone to the city buyer that these notices appealed; considerable country custom was thereby attracted to the shops of Philadelphia book merchants. Edward Shippen of Lancaster maintained an account with David Hall, but for special items he was wont to commission his nephew Edward Burd, then in Philadelphia for his schooling. In response to his request for certain French newspapers young Burd wrote him in 1770: "I went to Church Alley and could not observe any Printer's Shop or Books at the Windows any where near that place except at Stewart's Old Shop, where I could get none. Mr. Hall, Mr. Bradford, Mr. Dunlap, Evitt, Sellers and Cruikshank are all without them." Marylanders found Philadelphia bookstores often more amply stocked for their purposes than those at Annapolis. "I should be obliged to you to forward any new Books or Productions of Genius to me, such as Pamphlets, &c.," the Reverend Philip Hughes of Coventry wrote to Bradford in 1768, and he concluded with the somewhat inadequate assurance, "You shall be payd with thanks."

Many in the trade sold by wholesale as well as retail, and published catalogues of their lists. James Young announced in 1772 that "Considerable allowances will be made those who may take quantities, and orders from town or country [will be] carefully and expeditiously executed," and James Chattin urged his reasonable prices upon "Shop-keepers, Hawkers, &c., who buy . . . Books to sell again" in rural communities.

Foremost among the booksellers and publishers of colonial Philadelphia was the Scotsman Robert Bell, an exceedingly witty man of "doubtful" religion, who in the sober provincial capital openly kept a mistress and fathered an illegitimate child, but nevertheless made good in business. By his production and sale of numberless current English works in cheap reprints, Bell not only taught his fellow citizens to buy and read good literature, but forced his competitors to adopt business tactics similar to his own.

Advertising was to Bell no prosaic listing of titles to be sold, but a humorous adventure, a game he played with his potential customers, bullying, flattering, cajoling, and appealing to their native snobbery. The sign before his shop read "Jewels and Diamonds for Sentimentalists," and his newspaper advertisements addressed variously the "Sons of Science," the "Sentimentalists of America," or, more inclusively, "The Lovers of literary entertainment, amusement and instruction." Announcing the third volume of Robertson's *Charles V,* Bell asserted that all gentlemen who "possess a sentimental taste" will wish to participate in this "XENOPHONTIC BANQUET" at three dollars a copy. He was a pioneer in "national" or continental advertising, buying large amounts of space in nearly every colonial newspaper for announcing his first American editions of such works as Blackstone's *Commentaries* and Robertson's *Charles V.*

Because he became the first important buyer of private libraries and dealer on a large scale in secondhand books, Bell succeeded in developing the book auction to its colonial apogee. This institution had been known in the city since 1744, but the increase in publishing activity rendered it more useful and necessary. To meet the costs of paper, binding and manufacture, a publisher had usually to print about three thousand copies of a work, and if, after a year or so, he found he had overcalculated the market, was accustomed to dispose of the surplus at auction. By selling below cost, one printer explained, he can realize "dead stock into live cash, and may again attempt the work of some celebrated author whose writings will diffuse knowledge throughout America." None knew this better than Bell, who in 1772-74 led his colleagues in an attack on the decision of the Assembly to include books along with other classes of merchandise the auctioneering of which should be confined to officially appointed vendue-masters. The fight was successful in time to permit him to dispose by his favorite method of the books of William Byrd of Virginia, of which "Perhaps as many as 40 waggon loads" were reported to have been sent to Philadelphia.

Robert Bell, however, seldom took any loss when marketing a

parcel of books in this fashion, for those who attended his sales reported he sold higher at auction than over the counter in his shop. This desire to sell at as "exorbitant a price as he could command" undoubtedly furnishes the key to the unorthodoxy of his methods. He was "full of drollery, and many, going to his auction for the merriment, would buy a book from good humour. It was as good as a play to attend his sales. . . . There were few authors of whom he could not tell some anecdote, which would get the audience in a roar. He sometimes had a can of beer beside him, and would drink comical healths. His buffoonery was diversified and without limit." With irresistible gusto he urged the public into his sales, where "the Provedore to the Sentimentalists will exhibit food for the mind, where he that buys may reap substantial advantage, because he that readeth much ought to know much."

Bell's competitors were no match for him, even the firm of auctioneers doing business under the euphonious name of Honey & Mouse. He institutionalized the colonial book auction, and more than anyone else in these years laid the solid foundations for book-publishing in America.

The purchasing of books and the building of private collections lay within the province of the rich alone, but the urge for self-improvement through reading was strong among mechanics and tradesmen, and led them to pool their resources to accomplish their desires. In the thirties the efforts of Benjamin Franklin and the patronage of James Logan had assisted a group of Philadelphia tradesmen and a few gentlemen associates to the formation of the Library Company, upon which the Proprietors conferred a plot of land and a charter in 1742. The acquisitions of this organization during its first two decades of existence reflect the primary desire of its middle-class members for serious books and volumes of instruction on a variety of subjects. Peter Kalm reported in 1748 that "there is already a fine collection of excellent works, most of them in English; many French and Latin, but few in any other language," and that in addition "Several little libraries were founded in the town on the same principle or nearly so."

Because membership in the Library Company was limited and somewhat expensive, other subscription libraries sprang up to meet the broadening demand. In 1747 a group of twenty-six professional men, tradesmen and artificers—among them Benjamin Price, attorney and possessor of one of the best law collections in the colonies, Joseph Chattin, printer and publisher, George Heap, mapmaker, William Ranstead, private schoolmaster, and William Savery, creator of exquisite furniture—opened the Union Library Company in a room on Second Street. Its first catalogue, printed by Chattin in 1754, contained three hundred seventeen titles. In 1755 this library moved to a room on Chestnut Street, and in 1759, with membership limited to one hundred and fully subscribed, it received its charter from the hand of Governor Denny. The Union's catalogue of 1765 reveals a broadening of its collection from purely utilitarian works to include such items as *Joseph Andrews, Chinese Tales,* Cibber's *Lives of the Poets, Journey from Aleppo to Jerusalem,* and finally, *How to Govern a Wife;* at least, these titles had proved so popular that the librarian had to advertise for their return in the preceding year.

In 1757 two libraries appeared to provide for would-be readers not included in the restricted memberships of the Library and Union companies. Successful artisans, mostly Quaker, made up the original forty-six who subscribed twenty shillings each to found the Association Library; included were John and Benjamin Mifflin, James and Thomas Wharton, Benjamin Betterton and Owen Biddle; also, William Bradford and David Hall, printers, James Gillingham, cabinetmaker, Christopher Marshall, apothecary, and Thomas Stretch, clockmaker. In less than ten years the limit of two hundred members had been reached, necessitating a consideration of its enlargement, and its collections, housed in a new room on Chestnut Street, totaled five hundred seventy volumes.

Only a few weeks after Quaker gentry and craftsmen had combined to father the Association, a group of "humble" men founded the Amicable Company, more nearly a workingmen's library. Too poor to assemble a large collection or to issue a printed catalogue, the members struggled along for nine years in their "Library Room" on Third Street. In 1765 these artisans somewhat expanded the original purpose of their association when at their annual meeting they treated themselves to "a lecture on Electricity, accompanied with Suitable Experiments." This departure was in a sense their swan song, for the next year the subscribers voted to add forty shillings to the value of each share to enable them to unite with the Union Library Company.

Gradual realization of the folly of maintaining a number of small libraries with similar aims and purposes came to a head about 1764, when both the Union and the Association companies were debating the enlargement of their memberships. The Union reduced the price of its shares in 1766, which enabled it to absorb the poorer Amicable Library Company, and two years later it negotiated a similar merger with the Association. Finally, in 1768-69 the Union members were asked to consider "the Utility of conveying their Estate to and becoming Members of the Library Company." Their positive action on this question resulted in the emergence of the original Library Company of Philadelphia as a single strong institution with a large membership, excellent collections and ample financial support.

With this series of mergers, undertaken because "it appeared more conducive to the interests of literature to be possessed of one large, than of several smaller collections of books," Benjamin Franklin had nothing to do, for he was throughout these years serving the colony as its agent in England. It is not fanciful, however, to regard this consolidation of libraries as part of the larger movement for colonial unity proceeding in many fields at the same time. Especially does it seem to bear an intimate relationship to the union of the two philosophical societies which was accomplished concurrently. The older of these bodies, the American Society for Promoting Useful Knowledge, met in the rooms of the Union Library Company, and certain of its leaders, Francis Hopkinson and Owen Biddle among them, were members of both. In the face of rising opposition to imperial Britain, many Philadelphians sensed the need for scrapping local differences and class prejudices, and the achievement of a single library organization was but one manifestation of the general trend.

As an independent unit the Library Company had greatly extended its influence during the decade of the sixties. In 1764, when Francis Hopkinson became librarian, the general public began to be admitted to its rooms in the State House for reading, and in 1768 reduction of the price of its shares from £21 to £10 currency made membership easier to attain. After the merger, the policy of general usefulness continued, the library rooms being kept open on Tuesday, Thursday and Saturday evenings from four until eight.

The institution remained essentially a middle-class library, its emphasis on useful and instructive rather than on merely entertaining reading; in 1764 one-half of its collection was classified as history, while works on either philosophy or theology outnumbered those in polite literature. Under the gentlemanly influence of Hopkinson, and in keeping with the drift of the times, there was some tendency to broaden the scope of the collections beyond their original utilitarian purposes, and orders for works of poetry, drama and fiction somewhat increased. Yet in 1772 the librarian told Jacob Duché "that for one person of distinction and fortune, there were twenty tradesmen that frequented this library," and of the 8,000 titles it possessed in 1774 only eighty-one were listed under the classification "Fiction, Wit and Humour." More than a trace of the "Mechanick's" influence may be seen in the fact that when in 1773 the Assembly refused permission to erect a building on the State House grounds, the library was withdrawn to Carpenter's Hall, where it was kept open daily from two to seven P.M.

The finest private library in the middle colonies, and by all odds the best in science and the classics, belonged to James Logan, who frequently permitted its use for purposes of consultation by any properly introduced citizen, and generously lent his books to such serious young students as Thomas Godfrey and John Bartram. In 1745 he housed his collection in a one-story brick building at the corner of Sixth and Walnut streets. Both building and contents he bequeathed at his death to the city, along with an endowment of £35 per annum for a librarian's salary and the purchase of books "solely . . . for the use of the public, in order to prevail on them (having such assistance) to acquaint themselves with literature." A catalogue was printed, and in November, 1768, the Loganian Library, under supervision of Lewis Weiss, librarian, was opened to the public every Saturday from three to seven in summer, "and so long as one can see to read in the Winter."

Unfortunately Logan's will had named a most incompatible group of trustees, men of such diverse views as William and James Logan, Benjamin Franklin, John Smith, Israel Pemberton, William Allen, and Richard Peters, whose political and temperamental differences led to the sad neglect of this library. To its collection of "near 3,000 volumes" few additions were made, and from it many books were stolen. Pierre du Simitière, perhaps the most consistent user of the Loganian collections, found that because the building, which was "neither elegant nor Convenient," was located close to a dusty street, its windows had to remain closed during the hot Philadelphia summer. Furthermore, it was a specialized and erudite collection, many of the books dealing with "subjects out of the reach of the generality of people." Consequently, visitors to the Loganian Library were few, though significantly Du Simitière adds, "Most of that small number [is] composed of obscure mechanicks who have a turn for mathematics."

Thus by 1770 Philadelphia possessed an excellent subscription library and a good public collection, but their contents were almost wholly in the field of serious literature, and their use confined to the masculine citizenry. Increasing leisure among certain classes in the city, especially among the ladies, and desire to fill it with light and entertaining reading, paved the way for the establishment of circulating libraries. Here booksellers dispensed to their subscribers "a considerable List of Novel Writers, whose depictive Talents," as expounded by the eloquence of Robert Bell, "tends [sic] to dignify the human Mind, by an Abundance of recreative and instructive Entertainment, calculated to guide the Youth of both Sexes through the dangerous Whirlpool of agitated Passions."

Lewis Nicola first ventured in this field, opening his New Circulating Library on Second Street in September, 1767. His rental collection contained two or three hundred volumes of history, poetry, plays and voyages, plus a recent importation of over a hundred new titles, such as *Female American, Emera, or the Fair American, Pittsborough*, Hogarth's *Cuts, with Explanations*, and *Neck or Nothing*. The library was open daily, and subscribers, by depositing £5 and paying three dollars a year, might withdraw one volume at a time. In 1769 Nicola moved to Spruce Street, in the more fashionable Society Hill neighborhood, rechristened his establishment the General Circulating Library, and announced the enlargement of his collection to seven hundred volumes and a reduction in his prices. In 1771 his library of "general Entertainment" contained over a thousand volumes, including "some few well-chosen French books." Nicola's success encouraged Thomas Bradford to open another circulating library near Second and Ann streets in 1769, which was doing a good business as late as 1773. In 1774 Robert Bell entered the field with his Universal Library in the old Union Library rooms on Third Street, introduced with the characteristic Bell flourish quoted above.

Aside from its general collections, Philadelphia acquired at least eight specialized libraries in this period. These included the fine collection of books on carpentry, engineering and architecture begun by the Carpenter's Company as early as 1736 and eventually (1771) housed in a room designed for the purpose in Carpenter's Hall, and the similar though smaller collection inaugurated by the Friendship Carpenter's Company in 1769; the library of legal works and statutes maintained at the State House after 1745 by the Assembly for the use of its members and qualified citizens; and the scientific and philosophical collections of the two Philosophical Societies, which in 1775, some years after their amalgamation, were made generally available under David Rittenhouse as librarian. Although all of these libraries were privately assembled for the benefit of their respective institutions, it is evident that properly introduced and qualified readers found no difficulty in consulting and even in some cases in borrowing their books.

In addition, three religious denominations maintained collections of books for the use of their ministry and members. The oldest of these parochial libraries was that of Christ Church, founded in 1728, greatly augmented during the years by gifts and purchases, and reorganized and catalogued in the sixties by Francis Hopkinson, its librarian. The Friends' Library, begun in 1741 and consisting mainly of bound periodicals and pamphlets, was housed for many years in the home of Anthony Benezet, but moved in 1765 to the new Meeting House at Fourth and Chestnut streets, where as a circulating library it exerted a wide influence on Quakers throughout the colonies. The Presbyterian library, under the control of the Presbyterian Ministers' Fund headed by Francis Alison, also loaned books to ministers at considerable distances from the city and to schoolmasters in country districts.

A most important group of specialized collections was devoted to education and pedagogy. A library room in the new Friends' School of 1744 housed Peter Collinson's large gift of Quaker writings as well as the classical collection later assembled and gradually augmented for use by scholars in the Latin School. A gift from Richard Peters, chiefly of titles in theology and Old English literature, was used to found the Academy Library in 1749, but later additions to this collection were so heavily classical as to inspire the heartfelt disgust of Benjamin Franklin. Whether this library was included with the later collections of the College is not clear. The College Library was initiated with a gift of books in 1762 from William Dunlap, printer, of Philadelphia, and with donations secured by Provost Smith from interested persons in England. Richard Peters and Jacob Duché, the committee on the library after 1764, so built up the collections that by 1776 the College could take pride in some 2,000 volumes.

After Dr. John Fothergill had presented a copy of William Lewis's *Materia Medica* to the Pennsylvania Hospital "for the Benefit of young Students in Physick," the staff became inspired in 1763 to plan a medical library according to "the Custom of most of the Hospitals in Great Britain," to be supported from students' fees. This collection was the first of its kind in North America, and grew rapidly, the later generous gifts of Dr. Fothergill and many Pennsylvanians soon making it really remarkable for its time. Individual accessions of importance were the medical library of Dr. Lloyd Zachary in 1767, consisting of forty-three volumes and some pamphlets, and the present by Deborah Morris of the fifty medical books acquired by her dead brother, Dr. Benjamin Morris, while a student at Leyden.

Not only did Philadelphians found libraries for their own devices, and in some cases allow their books to be loaned out of the city, but they provided the impulses that led to much general reading in rural and surrounding areas. It was the handsome gift of £500 by Dr. Thomas Cadwalader, a founder and director of the Library Company of Philadelphia, which established the Library Company of Trenton in 1750, while the Shippens of Philadelphia supplied the impetus for the founding of the Juliana Library Company by seventy-seven residents of the frontier town of Lancaster in 1759. In all, ten subscription libraries were established between 1743 and 1769 in the district from Trenton on the north to Chester on the south, many of them with the aid or the inspiration of Philadelphians. Philadelphia book merchants catered especially to the country library. William Dunlap, for instance, in his Catalogue No. 2 (1760) stressed his ability to furnish books for "all public Libraries that are already established, or those intended to be erected."

Perhaps the farthest extension of Philadelphia's bookish influence occurred in the 1740's when Abraham Redwood of Newport, Rhode Island, visited the city. Here he was so pleasantly impressed with the activities and importance of the Library Company that, according to Peter Kalm, "when he returned home he persuaded some gentlemen in that state to build a house for a library, to which he made a gift of 500 pounds sterling for books." Peter Harrison's beautiful Redwood Library in Newport owes something, therefore, to an idea of Benjamin Franklin's Junto.

Acquisition of books which, whether they were read or not, would adorn the libraries of their country seats became among the gentleman merchants of Philadelphia in these years a fashionable means of investing the profits from trade and achieving the reputation of gentility. But it appears that many of these men were genuine lovers of reading, and one or two even fell victim to the collector's disease. Wealthy Quakers, following in the footsteps of James Logan, built up remarkable collections. Isaac Norris, Sr., began to assemble books at Fair Hill as early as 1722, when he sent specially to England for a copy of *Paradise Lost*. His son, the Speaker, a man of scholarship and taste, built up this collection by careful purchase and selection. At his death it passed to his son-in-law, John Dickinson, in whose possession it met with the honest approval of critical John Adams, who pronounced it "a grand library" in 1774. Years later Dickinson presented the entire collection of "about 1,500 volumes upon the most important subjects" to the new college which bore his name.

The Quaker physician Thomas Cadwalader while pursuing his medical studies in France and England bought widely in general literature, as well as of scientific works. Friend Robert Strettel, Mayor of Philadelphia in 1749, brought together a selected little library of Greek, Latin and French literature at his Germantown estate, and the young Quaker lawyer Miers Fisher treated John Adams to a view of his collection which the Bostonian described as "clever." With Quaker booklovers, apparently, "plainness" did not extend to the purchase of books, and they spared neither effort nor expense in the gratification of their tastes.

Well-to-do Anglicans were no less active than the Friends in building up their libraries, and several of them are numbered among the earliest American bibliophiles. Joshua Maddox owned a choice collection of volumes, and when in 1745 William Peters began construction of his beautiful estate at Belmont, he erected a separate little building adjoining the mansion to house his library. His brother, the Reverend Richard Peters, possessed a collection surpassed only by those of Logan and Norris in the city.

The private library of Dr. John Morgan had become by 1774 one of the most catholic in all the colonies. In addition to its unequaled medical and scientific collections, it included works on archaeology, art, architecture, and general literature—Ariosto and Boccaccio in Italian, Hume in French, Voltaire's *Tancred,* and some Italian manuscripts. Samuel Powel's books, nearly all purchased in Europe, included works on similar subjects in French and Italian, as well as in English and the learned tongues. That Francis Hopkinson was a true booklover, his devoted services as curator of the Library Company and the Christ Church collections attest. His own library of rare and fine books so charmed certain Hessian officers that they strove to save it from destruction during the burning of Bordentown at their command in 1776.

Members of the middle class, though unable to indulge their taste for reading and acquisition to such an extent, still succeeded in building up a few large libraries and many smaller ones. Franklin's own collection is, of course, well known. That of David James Dove was large enough to require a special auction at the hands of Robert Bell in 1769, and Francis Alison's "valuable" library also went under the hammer after his death in 1780. On the eve of the War, however, the library of the relatively poor Swiss miniaturist, Pierre Eugène du Simitière, stood supreme among members of his own or of any other class. It comprised, among other things, the first important assemblage of Americana, printed and in manuscript. Its significance is sufficiently evident from the fact that it now forms the major portion of the notable collection of books, newspaper and pamphlets belonging to the Library Company of Philadelphia.

Ample evidence exists to show that books in these collections were not only carefully read by their owners, but widely lent by them as well. Indeed, much casual borrowing must have been indulged, to judge from the newspaper personals. One Philadelphian advertised in 1772, for example, that "Altieri's Italian Grammar, of an old edition, bound in parchment, was a few years ago lent to some person of this city, by a Gentleman from Jamaica, who borrowed it of the owner. As it is a book very scarce, and was purchased on that account at a very high price, and the owner having now a particular occasion for it, he will gratefully thank the person . . . for delivering it to the Printer." When Dr. Alexander Hamilton of Annapolis visited Philadelphia in 1744, he frequently borrowed books for reading in the moments when he was alone, among them *Timon of Athens,* "which tho' not written according to Aristotle's rules, yet abounds with inimitable beauties, peculiar to this excellent author."

Alexander Graydon ranged widely in his reading, and William Savery, the great Quaker preacher, confessed of his younger days that "I for many years so abused my time in reading novels, romances, plays and a variety of trumpery of this kind, that I had no relish for the Scriptures." Another prominent Quaker, John Smith of Burlington, haunted book auctions, and from the offerings of the Library Company treated himself to such varied indulgences as *Don Quixote,* Steele's *Conscious Lovers,* and *Grief à la Mode, Tom Jones, Paradise Lost,* Thomson's *Seasons,* and Anson's *Voyages.* He also withdrew "several volumes" of the works of Bayle, the skeptic, about whom he probably felt as did Friend Samuel Morris, writing in 1763 to thank a nephew for his gift of the works of Rousseau, "He's a fine writer, I wish he was as much a Christian."

One characteristic of the ladies of Philadelphia which never failed to astonish visitors from Europe was that while they possessed great beauty, natural ease, and the usual charms expected of members of their sex, "they are still anxiously attentive to the more important embellishments of the mind." Brought up among books, and permitted a good secondary education, Philadelphia women did not hesitate by continued reading to carry it to the higher levels that were formally denied them. Excluded from the masculine confines of the Library Company or the Loganian Collection, and from consultation of lawbooks at the State House or scientific treatises at the

Hospital, "female book-lovers" supplied much of the patronage for the circulating libraries that flourished in the city.

During her leisure moments Sally Wistar devoured current literature, including a number of French titles, and rejoiced when a friend sent her *Joseph Andrews, Julie Grenville, Caroline Melmouth,* and some "Lady's Magazines." Thomson's poems were the favorite reading of Sarah Eve, fiancée of Benjamin Rush, but she also enjoyed the *The West Indian,* and frequently quoted from that other "prodigious fine comedy wrote by Cumberland," *The Fashionable Lover.* Elizabeth Sandwith often spent a day "at home reading." Her taste in literature ran from Pope's *Homer* through Rabelais and other French authors, to the newspapers which she regularly perused. Many a time she "bought little Books at Rivingtons," and one of her first outings, on a visit to New York in 1760, was to "walk out" in the morning "to a Number of print-Shops and Booksellers."

The men of Philadelphia easily became accustomed to, and gradually learned to appreciate, the company of well-read young women. Occasionally one of them broke into verse "On seeing a young lady weep at reading Clarissa," or, like Amy Horner's admirer, sang praises of his lady's learning:

> You must allow that it's my duty
> To praise her sense as well as beauty;
> And, if I am inform'd aright,
> In reading she takes much delight.

At the height of the movement for home manufactures which preceded the Revolution, "Anglus Americanus" published in the *Pennsylvania Chronicle* his opinion that "could our Philadelphia ladies, who are at least equal in their endowments, both of body and mind, to those of any other part of the world, be prevailed with, instead of debauching their morals, and turning their heads with the impious rants of plays and romances," to stick, quite literally, to their knitting, America might be saved. But this gentleman was clearly in opposition to the trend of the times.

As early as 1744 young William Black of Virginia, who seems to have admired women rather for their beauty than for their wit, spent an evening along with three other gentlemen in the company of five of Philadelphia's then debutantes. After some customary polite give and take, the girls turned "artfull enough to criticising on Plays and their Authors," and poor Black and his companions soon found themselves well beyond their depths. "Addison, Prior, Otway, Congreve, Dryden, Pope, Shakespeare, &c. &c. &c., were names often in question; the words Genius—and no Genius—Invention, Poetry, Fine things, bad Language, no Style, Charming Writing, Imaginary [sic] and Diction . . . with many more Expressions, which swim on the Surface of Criticism, seem'd to have been caught by those Female Fishers for the Reputation of Wit, at last they Exhausted this Subject, and gave Time to their Tongues a little." Apparently the Virginian found it hard to take, and would have wholeheartedly concurred in the judgment of John Adams, though without his modifications in favor of some "education in women," expressed to Abigail from Philadelphia in 1776: "The *femmes savantes* are contemptible characters."

In the course of the four decades prior to 1776 Philadelphians of all walks of life, male and female, may be said to have learned to read, first for instruction, and later also for enjoyment. Spread of elementary and secondary education created an expanding market for reading matter that was assiduously cultivated by a group of enterprising printers and booksellers. Newspapers, pamphlets, foreign reprints, and books of domestic composition poured from native presses, and along with continuous importations lined the shelves of private libraries and bookstores. The range of private collections was greatly augmented by the services of subscription libraries, taverns and coffeehouses. By means of the printed word the propaganda of enlightenment reached all citizens, as would soon the propaganda for political change.

A significant feature of this development was the availability of reading matter to all who desired it, even to the inferior sort. Even laborers had leisure for reading, when such employers as Enoch David, tailor, promised in 1761 to workmen of good character "the same wages for five Days a Week as is common in the City for six." As curator of the Library Company, Francis Hopkinson was severely criticized for ceasing to leave the books in open stacks "as formerly for the inspection of all" who wanted to use them, but Francis Alison, a director, supported the new policy, contending its necessity "while we allow the whole town, and even as many strangers to attend." Apparently, at both the Library Company and the Loganian, anyone who wished to might consult the books. When officers of the former body discovered in 1748 that John Bartram could not afford £21 for the purchase of a share, they accorded him, without application, "free access to the library," and permission to withdraw books for study at his home in Kingsessing.

"The poorest labourer upon the shore of the *Delaware*," wrote Jacob Duché, with reason, in 1772, "thinks himself entitled to deliver his sentiments in matters of religion or politics with as much freedom as the gentleman or scholar. Indeed, there is less distinction among the citizens of Philadelphia, than among those of any civilized city in the world. Riches give none. For every man expects one day or another to be upon a footing with his wealthiest neighbour. . . . Such is the prevailing taste for books of every kind, that almost every man is a reader; and by pronouncing sentence, right or wrong, upon the various publications that come in his way, puts himself upon a level, in point of knowledge, with their several authors."

Chapter IV

GENTEEL VERSE AND REBEL PROSE

FROM the printing, buying and reading of books to the actual production of a native literature was a step which to an educated and successful people seemed natural, easy and attractive. Constant reading of the works of others inspired the urge to creation at home, while the surplus of both time and means, which was a by-product of economic development, provided opportunity for its satisfaction. Patronage from men of wealth was not wanting, nor a vehicle for publication in the local press, nor yet a market in the expanding reading public. A provincial society, growing up, desired expression for its increasing maturity, and hoped by successful imitation of the literary art as practiced by contemporaries in the homeland to advance indisputable proof of its own coming of age.

In addition to the impulse among leisured gentry to take up the pen in emulation of their English peers, the desire for self-expression made itself felt among the lesser and more active members of the community. The eighteenth century in Philadelphia was a period of rapid growth and flux, when old ideas were being challenged and old attachments undermined, and when new concepts, not yet wholly ripe to replace them, required publicity, elucidation and defense—in short, just the sort of age to produce a vigorous, thoughtful, expository, utilitarian literature. During the years after 1740, while the city's population trebled, its literary productivity increased perhaps sevenfold. Often slavishly imitative, occasionally really original, this literary activity accurately reflects the workings and the development of the Philadelphia mind.

The example of the mother country provided logically enough the first point of literary departure. When a colonial society has successfully mastered the physical problems of its early years and has established itself upon a workable economic basis sufficient to provide some of its members with wealth and leisure, these fortunates, groping for modes of self-expression, turn naturally to the traditions of the homeland. With understandable nostalgia they seek to perpetuate in their new country the literary conventions they knew in the old. It is to be expected, therefore, that the classical and poetical literature of Augustan England, whose leaders at this time were making a cult of stability, should find echoes on the banks of the Delaware, where there was very little stability of any kind.

Transplanted by the efforts of college-bred gentlemen among the early Quaker immigrants, the classics exhibited in Philadelphia a considerable if parasitic vitality. Aspiring aristocrats made the most of the fact that mastery of the learned tongues constituted one of the most easily detected hallmarks of gentility. Their reproduction in the New World city of the English classical grammar school betokened their earnest desire that their sons should follow in the footsteps of English gentlemen.

In the person of James Logan, educated in Ireland, classical scholarship in the colonies reached its zenith. In 1735 appeared his *Cato's Moral Distichs Englished in Couplets,* "first translation of a classic which was both made and printed in the British Colonies." Nine years later Benjamin Franklin printed Logan's edition of Cicero's *Cato Major,* a work which by 1758 had passed through four editions and various reprintings in London, Glasgow and Philadelphia. Between 1739 and 1741 Logan published in Europe three scientific treatises written in Latin, and at his death in 1751 left in manuscript a "Defense of Aristotle and the Ancient Philosophers," as well as several translations from the Greek. With a working knowledge of four ancient tongues, Greek, Latin, Hebrew, and Arabic, James Logan stood easily first among colonial classicists, the only one whose writings possessed a true validity. Latin in his day still retained much of its importance as the language of science, and was so used by him in order that his scientific papers might be read by the Dutch and other Continental scholars. Yet in his communications to the Royal Society of London, as well as in his manuscript "Essays on the Languages and Antiquities of the British Isles" he employed his mother tongue.

The defense of the ancients by the Nestor of Philadelphia marked the apex of the classical tradition in the colonies. The battle of the books had already been lost. Such gentlemen of leisure as Isaac Norris II, Samuel Powel and Joseph Wharton might wear their classical learning with familiarity and grace, and the scientists Morgan and Rush employ it for professional reasons, but in their literary use of the learned tongue scholars of native birth or later advent proved to be only pallid imitators.

William Lowry essayed Latin odes, and Robert Proud, master of Latin, Greek and Hebrew, produced some frigid verse in Latin which he always pedantically preferred to his native tongue. The migrated Scot, John Beveridge, wrote correctly but without warmth or power, and although with the publication of his *Epistolae Familiares et Alia Quaedam Miscellania* in 1764 he achieved the dubious crown of Philadelphia's leading Latin poet, he felt it necessary to accompany his masterpieces with English translations. Far more significance may be found in the four Latin theses presented by Jonathan Elmer, Jonathan Potts, Jacob Tilton and Nicholas Way as first candidates for the M.D. degree at the Medical School of the College of Philadelphia in 1771. Still, though Apollo may have become naturalized upon Society Hill, he was never really at home on Market Street.

Somewhat more successful were colonial attempts to write in the current English mode. As was to be expected, impulse for this development came primarily from those who, freed from the immediate necessity to work for a living, devoted their energies to the attempt to produce, insofar as that was possible, a replica of London society in the Pennsylvania capital. The Addisonian essay, moral or satirical, had appeared early in the columns of newspapers, and others besides Franklin had achieved real skill in this genre. Less able writers perpetuated the form throughout the period. Verse-writing, however, after a flurry of activity in the thirties, languished in Philadelphia until the arrival of William Smith in 1753.

Although born a Scot, this able and energetic man of "genius, taste and learning" held in the highest veneration everything English or Episcopalian. The Atlantic highway to Britain represented from his colonial vantage point the noblest prospect he could conceive. He was eager to fit Philadelphia into the London mold, making it the literary and artistic center of the colonies, with William Smith as a sort of Pennsylvania Dr. Johnson presiding over all. Proceeding with characteristic energy, he enjoyed a large measure of success, and by his sponsorship and encouragement of literary production among the Philadelphia gentry he built in many respects far better than he knew. From among his students at the College and the Academy he singled out those scions of Anglican families whose literary talents he detected, and with them for a nucleus surrounded himself with colonial America's first consciously artistic circle. As teacher, patron, critic and editor, and as a writer himself, Smith was responsible for an interesting literary development, of a restricted, academic, public-school variety to be sure, but none the less indicative of an earnest fumbling for a means of artistic self-expression.

The public first heard the works of Smith's fledglings declaimed at the College commencements and later read many of them in the columns of the public press. In October, 1757, "A Society of Gentlemen," one of whom was of course William Smith, began publication of *The American Magazine, or Monthly Chronicle for the British Colonies*. Printed by William Bradford, and with an initial list of over eight hundred and fifty subscribers distributed widely from New England to the West Indies, the periodical provided a far better vehicle than the university wits had hitherto enjoyed, giving them access to a larger audience and inspiring in them a more professional approach to their work. Their efforts in turn achieved for the Smith venture "the distinction of being the most vital and original literary magazine" of colonial America. When it was forced to cease publication after only a year because its principal editor had become the *enfant terrible* of Pennsylvania politics, the Provost continued to promote the productions of his protégés, first in the columns of the newspapers, and later by their publication in book form. The *American Magazine,* however, had served its purpose, for through its pages the verses of Francis Hopkinson, John Beveridge, Joseph Shippen, William Hicks and Thomas Godfrey first found their way into print.

Francis Hopkinson, son of one of the leading families of the province, had grown up in the most fortunate and cultivated surroundings that the city could afford. His father Thomas Hopkinson, sometime student at Oxford, had been successively admiralty judge and provincial councilor. Famous for his classical learning, interest in science, and conversational brilliance, the elder Hopkinson took an active part in the founding of the Library Company and served in 1743 as first president of the American Philosophical Society. It was only natural that the son should attend the Academy of which his father had been a trustee, and thence proceed to the College to receive his classical polishing under William Smith. As conventional college verse, Hopkinson's six poems published in the *American Magazine* in 1757-58 are competent and graceful, and, especially after they had evoked the praise of the cultivated Swiss gentleman Colonel Henry Bouquet, secured a considerable poetic reputation for their seventeen-year-old author.

Endowed with ample leisure and a genuine interest in literature and the arts, Hopkinson became, upon his graduation from the College in 1757, Philadelphia's first dilettante, indulging his tastes not only for amateur versemaking, but for music and painting as well. Between 1754 and 1765 he made nearly forty ventures into verse. His reputation was sufficient to lead to the pirating of his locally popular though mediocre poem *Science* by the Philadelphia publisher Andrew Steuart, to circumvent which he himself brought out a third and cheaper edition in New York in 1762. A lover and patron of the arts, witty and vastly popular not only among his own clique of wealthy Anglicans but with all groups in the city, he generously paid the price of his literary fame by the composition of numerous occasional odes and elegies. From time to time a prologue or an epilogue from his pen provided local sanction for the theatrical productions of David Douglass.

In 1766 Hopkinson went to England for an extended visit with his kinsman, the Bishop of Worcester, through whom he was able to meet and admire a large circle of current British celebrities. His introduction to prevailing artistic standards by means of the Bishop's great collection of paintings, and to London musical fashions through his kinsman's devotion to the compositions of Handel, made a definite, and unfortunately ineradicable, impression upon the eager young provincial.

Very little can be said for Hopkinson's youthful excursions into verse. His pen was facile and correct, but it lacked all touch of genius. Like that of his contemporaries, it flowed in serious, conventional and imitative vein, with small trace of the puckish humor which as wit and man about town he allowed to play continuously on all aspects of the life about him. Even in so praiseworthy an attempt to capture the picturesque qualities of aboriginal life as *The Indian Treaty* (1772), he could not escape the shackles of convention forged by early training and his English sojourn. His introduction here of a dainty imprisoned shepherdess among the dusky braves crouched round his imagined council fire reveals the intellectual and artistic astigmatism of Hopkinson as a serious poet. But his saving common sense, as well as the vein of native humor he was unable to deny, impart to *Dirtilla,* another poem of the same year, a new maturity developing to replace his collegiate enthusiasms.

After his return from England Hopkinson seems gradually to have realized that his lyric note was feeble and that his strength lay in other fields. He was a man gifted with a lively sense of the manifold absurdities of existence, for evidence of which he had to seek no farther than his own mirror. "He is one of your pretty, little, curious, ingenious men," John Adams reported to Abigail. "His head is not bigger than a large apple. . . . I have not met with any thing in natural history more amusing and entertaining than his personal appearance; yet he is genteel and well bred, and is very social." Such a person could hardly have gone long about Philadelphia taking himself overseriously and mouthing correct and tragic poetry in the company of Smith's handsome young men.

Instead he turned to the satirical essay, a medium in which he was soon to excel. His political allegory, *A Pretty Story,* which ran through three editions in 1774, revealed a writer who, in an attempt to escape from slavish attachment to English models, employed his undoubted talents of ready expression and agile wit upon native materials for the solution of pressing local problems. Several of Hopkinson's contributions to Aitken's *Pennsylvania Magazine* of 1775 show his considerable skill in handling a number of well-differentiated characters within the narrow confines of the essay form.

Francis Hopkinson made substantial contributions to the literary and artistic life of his native city. As musician, artist and book-lover as well as writer, and as encourager of artistic activity among his contemporaries, he exerted no inconsiderable influence. He was the sole member of the Smith coterie who had the courage to strike out and experiment in ways of his own, and the only one politically venturesome enough to ally himself with the patriot cause. With no other guide than his own healthy instincts, he abandoned the imported fashions and humorless self-importance of his literary companions. Perhaps only the lack of inventiveness which kept him strait-jacketed within the forms of the Addisonian essay prevented his development as one of America's early novelists.

James Parker's *New American Magazine,* which hitherto had held "but small traffic with the nymphs of *Helicon,*" received in 1760 the first lyrics of another seventeen-year-old poet, Nathaniel Evans. Fear lest "this new world ne'er feel the muse's fire" had impelled young Evans to

> . . . wake the rural reed
> And sing of swains whose snowy lambkins feed
> On Schuylkill's banks with shady walnuts crown'd,
> And bid the vales with music melt around.

The result, while without any especial beauty or originality, exceeded in abundance of classical allusion anything yet produced in the provincial capital, and was quite sufficient to procure him welcome into the circle of William Smith as a budding genius. Here he blossomed forth in a series of verses whose principal merit was to demonstrate his conception of poetry as a highly esoteric art and his conviction that Philadelphians should sing as much as possible like their English predecessors. His sponsor secured publication of one of his dialogues and an ode in the *London Advertiser* in 1763. A trip abroad to take orders, and the long return passage with Elizabeth Graeme as a fellow traveler, with whom he began a poetical correspondence, further convinced him of his mission as a conventional singer in the New World.

Evans's first act upon his return in 1765 was to arrange for the publication of the *Juvenile Poems* of his late friend Thomas Godfrey. His own poetical labors were cut prematurely short by failing health. Shortly before his death in 1767 he confided his papers to his two greatest literary friends and encouragers, Miss Graeme and Provost Smith. True to his trust, Smith secured seven hundred and fifty-nine subscribers for his 1772 edition of Evans's collected *Poems on Several Occasions*. Verbally graceful and metrically correct, though completely lacking in fire or imagination, Evans's work has this importance, that in it as a serious poet he transferred his imitative allegiance from Pope to Collins and Gray. He thus anticipates some aspects of the Romantic period to come.

Of the other young collegians sponsored by William Smith, three deserve mention here. Jacob Duché attempted poetry, but shone principally as an Anglican pulpit orator whose fervor surpassed both his invention and his capacity. Handsome in person and charming in manner, he found his chief role in his ardent admira-

tion for the achievements of his friends and in spreading their
literary fame at home and in England.

Thomas Coombe won his spurs as commencement poet in 1767,
and was further bound in devotion to the muse by his friendship
with Oliver Goldsmith, attained when he went "home" for orders.
His London sojourn was most satisfying to a provincial; in 1769
reports reached Philadelphia coupling his fame with that of Benjamin West and announcing that Mr. Coombe is "in great vogue
as a preacher here being engaged for no less than six Charity
Sermons." His devotion to Goldsmith was lifelong, and he commissioned Franklin when in London to keep him supplied with
the latest editions of his idol's works. In 1775 Coombe published
Edwin, or the Emigrant, an Eclogue, written as a sequel to *The
Deserted Village,* in strains, says Tyler severely but not unjustly,
"melodiously mixed of Goldsmith and water."

Joseph Shippen contributed some poetry to Smith's *American
Magazine* in 1758, but as a Princeton graduate, a Presbyterian, and
above all a not-too-serious practitioner of the art of versifying, he
seems to have rotated on the periphery of the Smith circle rather
than at its center. His *Glooms of Ligonier,* a popular ballad of
love and war, enjoyed a vogue in the sixties, as did also the deft
and witty compliments he paid to Philadelphia femininity in
Lines Written in an Assembly. But Shippen had no single-hearted
devotion to literature. To the glamour and polish imparted by the
Grand Tour he added the distinction of military experience under
Forbes and of public service as secretary of the province. Marriage
to Jane Galloway in Christ Church completed his translation into
the society that counted. Scholarly, with a talent for light verse and
a taste for the arts, Shippen retired to his country estate in 1773.

Among the pieces submitted to the *American Magazine* were
four anonymous odes and pastorals in derived classical form which
William Smith was delighted to print. "Nature seems not to have
designed the father for a greater mathematician, than she has the
son for a poet," he declared when in September, 1758, he revealed

the author to be Thomas Godfrey, Jr., twenty-two-year-old son of the famous though lowly glazier. Upon finishing his schooling at the age of thirteen young Godfrey had desired to become a painter, but his family, "not having the same honourable idea either of the profession or its utility," apprenticed him instead to an "ingenious" watchmaker. Godfrey hated his apprenticeship, and spent his spare hours reading and writing, or in the company of the limner John Green, "who was his sole acquaintance and friend."

At the expiration of his indentures, disgusted with the business of watchmaking, Godfrey joined up as lieutenant with the Forbes expedition to Fort Duquesne, with the interesting and entirely sound idea of finding in the provincial West materials suitable for poetry. The verses he left behind, which were those published in the *American Magazine,* he regarded as frankly experimental. But Smith and his group immediately took him up as one who shone "far above the common herd of versifiers, and others, too commonly honoured with the appellation of Poets." The Provost tutored him privately at the Academy, and young Benjamin West painted his portrait.

From Dunlap's press in 1762 came *The Court of Fancy,* a long poem written before 1758, in which Godfrey openly admitted his indebtedness to Chaucer and to Pope, but which Smith insisted exhibited "all the spirit of true *Creative Poetry."* After his military excursions into western Pennsylvania the young poet sought fortune in North Carolina, and while there in 1759 completed his well-known experiment with the dramatic form, *The Prince of Parthia.* In this highly classical performance he was perhaps influenced by the recent College presentation of *The Masque of Alfred,* as rearranged by William Smith and including some music by Francis Hopkinson.

Godfrey died in 1763, only four years after completion of the work by which he is best known. In posthumous tribute his friend and admirer Nathaniel Evans published with Henry Miller in 1765 *Juvenile Poems on Various Subjects, with the Prince of Parthia. By the late Mr. Thomas Godfrey, Junr. of Philadelphia.*

To which is prefixed Some Account of the Author and his Writings. Godfrey's final triumph occurred when the American Company produced his tragedy at the Southwark Theatre on April 24, 1767.

The verse of Thomas Godfrey has been the subject of much undiscriminating praise both from his own contemporaries and from modern critics who have ignored the author's own admissions as to its imitative and experimental nature. In his earnest seeking for mastery of his craft, his sincere search for sources of poetic inspiration, his workmanlike trial of various artistic forms, and his temporary surrender to the influence of fashionable if not altogether happy literary conventions, he suggests the development of another and greater poet, John Keats, whose career his own strangely parallels even to the denouement of an untimely death. In his own day Godfrey was belabored for insufficient classical learning, which to the modern reader will hardly seem a fault. *The Prince of Parthia* is a not unworthy addition to the small catalogue of experiments with classical drama in the English tongue. The blank verse is competent, often genuinely inspired, and the incorporation of some really graceful lyrics betrays a familiarity with the use of song conventions in English drama. The introduction of rhyme tags to indicate the termination of an act is sufficiently skillful to suggest that the writer might have handled the rhymed couplet successfully. Not so happy are his use of epithet, his insufficient characterization, and the devices to which his adherence to classical rules compelled him.

The small body of Godfrey's completed work reveals signs of true imaginative power which, added to his extremely correct verse, might have enabled him to develop into a poet of some consequence could he have divested himself of conventional influences. Coming as he did from the artisan class, with a touch of genius, an urge to write, and a willingness to find inspiration in the American scene, he might well have become an earlier Freneau. But he himself would have had to find the answer to his problems, and one may well question if the sincere though stultifying patron-

age of the College gentry did not do Thomas Godfrey more harm
than good.

Provost Smith and his little group of academic versifiers wanted
to establish in colonial Philadelphia a school of poets to compete
eventually on equal terms with bards of the mother country.
At the same time they sought to stimulate an interest in music
and the other arts. They determined to civilize the aborigines, both
red and white. But their ideal was moribund from the start, for
it was the dream of a few aristocrats and ill-suited to the genius
of a rising democracy. Their utterances bore small relation to the
teeming new world that surrounded them. Even when they de-
scended from poetry to polite prose, as did Jacob Duché in his
Letters of Tamoc Caspipina (1774), contemporaries deemed the
result, like his sermons, "flowery and flimsy."

Everyone in the circle seemed to have suffered by his pilgrimage
to England; only Godfrey, fortunate in his humbler circumstances,
remained at home. By limiting artistic attention to the Anglican
gentry, serious, conservative, self-important, and consciously attempting to soar to Parnassus from Society Hill, they completely
overlooked the vitality and promise of life around the Market Place
in High Street. In the course of time these literary anachronisms
followed the logic of their stars and chose the side of political conservatism in the parlous days about to dawn. Only the lowly born
dissenter, Godfrey, possessed genuine inspiration, and Hopkinson
alone a capacity to strike out along new lines. The contribution of
these young men lay not in their writings, but in planting amid
new colonial surroundings an interest in literature, and in the
example they furnished to other men of wealth and leisure by their
patronage of the arts.

As a result of the accident which made Nathanial Evans and
Elizabeth Graeme fellow travelers on the long voyage from England, and which produced their "discreet flirtation in verse," the
College wits became associated with a larger and slightly more
catholic group of local literati. A full-blooded Scotswoman, daugh-

ter of the Anglican physician Dr. Thomas Graeme and grand-daughter of Sir William Keith, Elizabeth Graeme moved by in-heritance and upbringing in the leading social and intellectual circles of the province. Carefully educated and mentally alert, at once romantic and witty, she was also considerable of a blue-stocking. Yet her undoubted literary talents might never have been discovered had not her fiancé, William Franklin, succumbing to the characteristic weakness of his family, lost his virtue in London and brought their engagement to a summary end by his marriage to another in 1762. To piety and poetry Elizabeth turned for con-solation, writing much herself and inspiring the youthful James Young to translate some of the Psalms "into Dutch Rhime." But, as she underwent the customary "decline," her family sent her for a change of scene to London in the party of Richard Peters in 1764.

Her sojourn in the mother country had somewhat the aspect of a social and literary triumph. "She sought, and was sought for, by the most celebrated literary gentlemen . . . in England," testified Benjamin Rush. Through Peters she met, among other celebrities, Dr. John Fothergill and members of the Penn family, and formed a friendship with Laurence Sterne which, Rush related, had its beginnings in a stagecoach. A special audience with George III, who was reported to have shown himself unusually gracious, crowned her English visit.

Restored in health and inspired by the literary society she had experienced, Miss Graeme returned home upon the death of her mother to preside over her father's house and to devote herself to further writing. Circulation of a manuscript journal of her London experiences among members of the local gentry soon gained her considerable literary reputation, which was further enhanced when it became known that she was at work on a metrical version of the Psalms. She also translated Fénelon's *Télémaque* into English verse —which she frequently revised—composed much occasional poetry, and wrote a mass of very fine letters to her personal friends.

As mistress of her father's home, Miss Graeme entertained lav-ishly and, with the example of London literary gatherings in mind,

"All eye, all ear, and all grasp." Elizabeth Graeme, artist unknown.

(Courtesy Historical Society of Pennsylvania)

"One of your pretty, little, curious, ingenious men . . ." Francis Hopkinson in conversation with a lady (possibly Elizabeth Graeme), from Benjamin West's sketchbook.

(Courtesy History Society of Pennsylvania)

Bluestocking and Dilettante.

Schoolmaster David Dove, from Benjamin West's sketchbook.
(Courtesy Historical Society of Pennsylvania)

Broadside blast against Dove, probably by Isaac Hunt.
(Courtesy Library Company of Philadelphia)

"Squire Lilliput, Professor of Scurrility."

succeeded in assembling about her colonial America's first salon. At her Saturday soirées during the winter appeared at one time or another most of Philadelphia's literary set, of both sexes, and "all strangers of note." Presbyterian Dr. Rush remembered, somewhat lyrically:

These evenings were, properly speaking, of the Attic kind. The genius of Miss Graeme evolved the heat and light that animated them. . . . She soon discovered, by the streams of information she poured upon her friends, that she had been "all eye, all ear, and all grasp," during her visit to Great Britain. . . . One while she instructed by the stores of knowledge contained in the historians, philosophers, and poets of ancient and modern nations, which she called forth at her pleasure; and again she charmed by a profusion of useful ideas, collected by her vivid and widely expanded imagination, and combined with exquisite taste and judgment into an endless variety of elegant and delightful forms. Upon these ocasions her body seemed to evanish, and she appeared to be all mind.

Even after all necessary deductions have been made for the effusiveness of Dr. Rush, it still appears that Elizabeth Graeme could hold her own with any literary man in the city, and that only Hopkinson and Godfrey surpassed her. Her verse is equal to the best of Evans and Coombe, and her wit superior. While her translation of *Télémaque* fails to do justice to the original, it represents a really massive performance for any English-speaking woman of her time, and shows her tough-minded enough to attempt a major undertaking in another language. A true citizen of the republic of letters, she succeeded in bringing together at her evening gatherings a literary circle not exclusively confined to the "Hot-Church party." But though fairly catholic in talents and interests, all her habitués were agreed on one point, that Philadelphia society should be molded on the English pattern, deriving its tone from gentlemen of letters and leisure who alone were qualified to represent it—a sort of "speaking aristocracy in the face of a silent democracy."

Elizabeth Graeme was by no means the only feminine applicant for citizenship in the literary republic. A good education, topped off with continual reading of English poetry and fiction, stirred the fancies of many a young bluestocking, and resulted in a mania for literary expression among the ladies of Philadelphia. It became indeed quite fashionable for aristocratic young women to devote their leisure to the composition of verses, many of which found their way into the columns of the newspapers, where they provided pleasant if somewhat saccharine antidotes to the usual political diatribes and conventional moral essays.

Most of this feminine output was of course in a naïve, romantic vein, with here and there a didactic note, as in the "Ode on the Evil of Pride, by a Female Hand," printed by the *Pennsylvania Journal* in 1758. From the number of poems so published it appears that many readers in both town and country delighted in such flights of fancy as the verses of "Daphne,"—"Gentle Cupid," and "Indeed, Sir, not I"—appearing in the *Pennsylvania Evening Post,* or the "Ode to Health, written during the Indisposition of Miss —," and "Amintor to Daphne: an Elegy," contributed by a young lady from distant Bedford to Bradford's *Pennsylvania Journal.*

Daughters of city Quaker families seem to have had an especial fondness for this sort of intellectual diversion, and a surprising amount of verse was the product of their pens.

> Such quick regards his Sparkling eyes bestow:
> Such wavy ringlets o'er his shoulders flow,

sang Elizabeth Drinker of her young husband, and inserted the couplet in the matter-of-fact record of her own day-to-day existence. The poetry of these aristocratic young ladies is not unlike that of their sophisticated brothers. Its only significance lies in the evidence it supplies of their desire for self-expression, and of the existence of a newspaper public that would read the result. Probably Philadelphians took an indulgent pride in the fact that their genteel daughters could make such use of their expensive educations.

The finest product to come from the pens of Philadelphia women writers is to be found in the journals that, like their young English contemporaries, they faithfully kept and widely circulated among their friends. Here the girls speak naturally in their own persons, with little self-conscious adherence to literary artifices they have been taught to admire and imitate. These journals, therefore, present a far truer picture of the minds and lives of young Philadelphia women of good families, and as both literary and social documents make far better reading than their attempts to soar on the conventional wings of song. Particularly is this the case with Quaker girls, who enjoyed wide latitude in their comings and goings, and traveled extensively throughout the colonies.

Perhaps the best of the travel diaries, the journal kept by Hannah Callender for the years 1758-59 (the very years, be it noted, when William Smith's young collegians were striving in the pages of the *American Magazine* to present evidence of the intellectual and artistic maturity of America) demonstrates the developed taste and capacity for its expression possessed by one well-educated Philadelphia Quakeress at the age of twenty-one. Especially in her account of a journey to New York are her observations keen and accurate, her judgments of people and places fair, and her entire outlook far from provincial, but even on shorter visits in pleasant country houses near at home she reveals the liberal tastes and catholic interests that characterized the best of urban Quakers.

The same naturalness and vivacity inform the journals of Sarah Eve and Sally Wistar, and through them all runs a pleasant vein of spontaneous humor. In their straightforward simplicity lies much of their charm. "Don't call me a country girl, Debby Norris," pouts Sally Wistar. "Please to observe that I pride myself on being a Philadelphian," and that a residence of ten months "in the country has not changed me." The value of educational training and social living in the growing city is everywhere evident in these pages, which suggest that when the young ladies of Philadelphia followed their instincts instead of current fashions, the results not only equaled the work of their gentlemanly brothers, but compared favorably with the informal literary productions of their sisters in the homeland.

The failure of Philadelphia's literary aristocrats lay in their lack of sensitivity to the trend of their times. Because their utterances bore small relation to the life about them their efforts had a false and artificial ring. Blind to the strength of the native strain that was already leavening colonial thought and making the colonial mind a thing apart, they would have done better, perhaps, to have confined their admiration of current English literature to reading and discussion. Philadelphia in the late fifties, when these well-meaning gentlemen founded their school, afforded no place for a contemplative literature reflecting the stability of upper-class Britain in the days of Walpole. Its young society, the mushroom growth of barely sixty years, was restless, lusty and dynamic. While busy erecting within the span of living memory a bustling commercial city on the shores of the Delaware, it had had neither time nor inclination to develop a settled aristocracy to whom the traditions of a classical training had been for generations a part of its life-blood, and no reason to respect the rules of taste and manners which governed the compact, cultivated society of Georgian London.

The instability of rapid growth characterized these years in Philadelphia. Two wars brought to the city the uncertainties and convulsions that all wars entail. Hoary religious and social standards disappeared, or became subject to searching question and analysis. This New World society was evolving novel political doctrines, and on both society and politics the New Science had its effect. Everywhere the eighteenth century was a period of transition, but nowhere, perhaps, was the transformation so rapid and so conscious as in Penn's city, nor the impact of its new philosophies upon members of all classes of such catalytic importance.

The vital writings of Philadelphia, as of colonial America at large, composed a literature of action, integrated with contemporary life in all its aspects—religious, economic, social and political. Influenced by the spread of democratic education and by the growth of empirical science, the form of this literature could hardly be other than an exact and vigorous prose. Beginning about 1735, a literature of purpose, as opposed to that of contemplation, took shape and gradually developed, in tune with the logic of events, into the mature expression of an active, growing and practical society. In the columns of newspapers and magazines, in pamphlets and in occasional books, Philadelphians gave publicity to new ideas, argued old positions, and took sides over important issues, local or cosmic. Slowly but definitely they developed their capacity to reason in speech and print and their ability to give concrete expression to the thinking of their society.

Most significant and compelling in its own day, and most interesting to ours, if only for its final flowering in the debate over Parliamentary prerogative and ultimately colonial independence, was the literature of controversy. Religious division over the issues of the Great Awakening, which dated at Philadelphia from the coming of George Whitefield in 1739, produced a flood of sermons and pamphlets attacking or defending the new faith. With its individualizing and democratizing of religion, and its nondenominational appeal to the masses, the movement contained implications which went far beyond mere questions of ecclesiastical procedure. Thus what began as a religious issue broadened, under stress of vigorous and usually acrimonious debate, into discussion of many problems of social and political import. In keeping with this drift, the writings of protagonists assumed an increasingly secular tone, religious controversy shaded imperceptibly into social and political argument, and frequently the religious question was lost sight of altogether.

The two wars, 1744-48 and 1754-63, bred a complication of issues which necessitated a re-examination of opinions and realignment of forces on matters of defense, Indian policy, and relations between Assembly and Proprietors. Peace in 1763 brought no respite to the pens of controversialists, as the Paxton riots and the movement for establishing an Anglican bishopric in America revived social and religious animosities, while the ground swell of opposition to new Imperial policies gradually swept all provincial controversies into a continental tide of Revolution.

The controversial literature of this period of change and strife constituted the overwhelming mass of the nonpractical output of the Philadelphia press, the great expansion of which was largely owing to increased activity in this field. Improving facilities for education steadily widened both the circle of readers and the number of those capable of appealing to their hopes and prejudices by means of printed argument. Each succeeding incident brought discussion pro and con, and new writers entered the lists as time passed, old quarrels merged with new, and issues became increasingly complex.

With the passage of years these writings exhibit a definite development in the techniques of controversy. They proceed from the narrowly ecclesiastical arguments of the 1740's to include discussion of broad human problems, so that by the late fifties the secular note has drowned out the religious in all save Pietistic writings, and social and political aspects predominate in most expositions of denominational questions. In style the authors become less ponderous and more direct, their vocabularies escape from the mazes of clerical patter into the concrete clarity of everyday speech, while their wits, made sharp by experience in argument, become in both attack and defense more skillful. The polemics themselves advance from crudely composed briefs for the day, concerned with a single specific issue and characterized by much personal abuse and frequent scurrility, to the cogently reasoned, polished and dignified presentations of first principles by such later penmen as John Dickinson, Joseph Galloway and James Wilson. The humorless bludgeoning of opponents by earlier controversialists recedes before the more sophisticated development of pungent sarcasm and eventually of shrewd satire and graceful wit.

The public also matured, its critical faculties sharpened and its tastes improved by the weighing of local arguments and the reading of similar productions from the pens of English authors, until it demanded writings comparable with the best the mother country could offer. Philadelphia scribblers, because in these years they were forced to write better and think more clearly, became vastly more entertaining and effective, and received thereby a valuable appren-

ticeship in one technique of revolution. Much of what they produced may be dismissed as of small artistic value. Its bulk is impressive as a reflection of the public interest, and because out of this
abundant sowing a few major figures were produced whose writings contributed by logical steps to the making of the great political
literature of the Revolutionary era.

The first notable controversialist in the city was Gilbert Tennent,
who as champion of the New Side Presbyterians came boldly to
preach in this stronghold of Old Side conservatism. A great pulpit
orator of the emotional type, he never was known "to daub with
untempered mortar." Such sermons as *A Solemn Warning to the
secure World, from the God of Terrible Majesty, or the presump-
tuous Sinner Detected* (1740) and *The Terrors of the Lord* (1749),
though smoldering with brimstone and sulphur, were ably composed and widely read. Tennent's hot-gospeling somewhat sim-
mered down as he came gradually to favor the reuniting of Presbyterian factions, and in 1744 he preached a sermon on *The Necessity of Studying to be Quiet and Doing our own Business*. This
noble sentiment did not, however, restrain him from participation
in another type of controversy, and his sermons directed against
the Quakers for their opposition to Franklin's proposals for defense,
*The Late Association for Defence encourag'd, or the Lawfulness of
a Defensive War*, passed through two editions in 1747. Indeed, as
religious and political issues became increasingly intermixed, many
a controversial pamphlet was authored by a politician in clerical
garb.

In the middle years of the period this tendency was best illustrated by the Reverend William Smith, politico under the surplice
par excellence. His own attempts at belles lettres rang as false as
those of his disciples. Pragmatic Philadelphia had small use for the
religio-philosophical reflections of his lovelorn Hermit on the banks
of the Schuylkill. Poesy and the romantic essay were not his forte,
but controversy was. He had all the love of battle, zeal for a cause,
and inability to concede any virtue in his opponents required of a
good pamphleteer. Enlisting in the Proprietary ranks, he began his

onslaught on the Quaker Assembly for its indifference to frontier defense with *A Brief State of the Province of Pennsylvania* and *A Brief View of the Conduct of Pennsylvania,* both published in London in 1753. These pamphlets revealed him to be an agile and learned partisan, well able to wield statistics in support of a position as effectively as Franklin himself. He also wrote ably in defense of the German Charity School movement, although here his propaganda proved too late to be effectual.

In 1757 Smith embarked upon a larger project with his *American Magazine and Monthly Chronicle,* the ostensible purpose of which was "to give persons at a distance a just idea of the public state of these *American* colonies, or to give one colony an idea of the public state of another" by means of reports of American and European affairs, essays, poetry, and a philosophical miscellany. In large measure the magazine achieved this objective, and its services in the cause of polite literature have already been noted. But founded as it was "in the center of the British Colonies" at Philadelphia, "a city that has an extensive commerce and immediate communication with all other settlements," the periodical provided an excellent vehicle for propaganda, and Smith employed it in relentless attack upon the Quaker program of peace at any price. His political writings and activities caused him to be twice jailed within a year after establishment of the magazine, and resulted eventually in cessation of its publication, although it was the only periodical in America to enjoy financial success before the Revolution.

In his partisan writings William Smith demonstrated outstanding abilities as a controversialist, clothing his brilliant special pleading in the garment of a vigorous and effective style. Unfortunately, his intemperate advocacy of causes that had small chance of success, his blindness to certain forces that were shaping the society in which he lived, his devotion to the Proprietary and to establishment of Episcopacy in the colonies, as well as his ubiquitous underlying concern for his own personal advancement, nullified the force of his vision of the real need for political and religious unity in the face of the French menace. He acquired from such writings a considerable fame in England, and both the *London Magazine* and the *Monthly Review* frequently recommended the results of his authorship to their subscribers. "Our readers," pointed out the editor of the *Monthly,* August, 1775, in a notice of Smith's famous sermon on *The Present State of American Affairs,* "are not unacquainted with the abilities of this American orator."

Spectacular events of the 1760's intensified the social cleavage in Pennsylvania, first noted in the alignment over the Great Awakening, and widened by the political struggles of the war years. Failure of the Quaker Assembly to provide military protection for the frontiers, especially during Pontiac's Rebellion, left Scotch-Irish and German settlers there a prey to the "barbarous cruelties" of the savages. Early in 1764 a mob of exasperated frontiersmen from the vicinity of Paxton fell upon and massacred a band of Christian Indians at Conestoga Manor and then marched in force on Philadelphia to demand redress for their grievances. In the terror that heralded their approach even the Quakers took up arms in self-defense.

A committee of clergymen and four members of the Assembly, headed by Franklin, met the rioters at Germantown and persuaded them to disperse, but it was evident that they had been "invited and encouraged by many considerable persons in Philadelphia." The general antagonism of democratic and poorer elements toward the smug selfishness of urban gentry expressed itself in sympathy with the grievances, if not the actions, of the harassed frontiersmen. Discontent was widespread, and uneasiness remained. The literary expression of the strained and varied emotions inspired by the Paxton affair constituted the greatest pamphlet controversy prior to the Revolutionary debate.

Proponents of all factions, Quaker, Presbyterian, Anglican and Proprietary, rushed into print to attack or support the Paxton Boys. Franklin, speaking for the Assembly, "our weak government," in *A Narrative of the Late Massacres in Lancaster County,* skillfully described the proceedings of the rioters as "unpopular and odious." David James Dove, defending the Paxton Boys in *The Quaker*

Unmask'd, inquired "whether the Affection which some Principals of that Sect have shewn to Indians, and the great Care they are now taking of them, can possibly be owing to the Charms of their Squaws, to any particular Advantage that may arise from their Trade, or perhaps from the Use that may be made of them to asperse the Proprietaries?" The Quakers, of course, did their utmost to demolish Dove, and a deluge of writings of all sorts, prose and verse, ensued.

In time the controversy, which had originated in questions of frontier defense, merged in the more general issue of the virtues or weaknesses of the Proprietary government. Franklin asserted, in *Cool Thoughts on the Present Situation of Our Public Affairs,* that "the political body of a proprietary government contains those convulsive principles that will at length destroy it." He was ably answered by Hugh Williamson, professor of mathematics at the College and an ardent Presbyterian, who in his three *Plain Dealer* papers claimed he could see no advantage in a change from "Proprietary Slavery to Royal Liberty." What we need, he declared, is to advance from "Quaker Slavery to British Liberty." Williamson further accused Franklin, in *What is Sauce for the Goose is also Sauce for the Gander,* of having deserted the interests of the frontiersmen for reasons of his own political advancement.

So deeply did the schism cut into popular feeling and prejudices that reason soon gave way to bitterness, satire to personal abuse, and good taste to outright scurrility. Perhaps the most effective and interesting of the combatants was the redoubtable pedagogue David James Dove. The tempestuous schoolmaster had already scored several direct hits with literary weapons upon urban gentility. In *A Fragment of the Chronicles of Nathan Ben Saddi* (1758), which purported to have been published at Constantinople in the year 5707, he produced a political satire of considerable merit on the arrest of William Smith and Judge Moore by the Assembly; this he followed with the vulgar and comical *Labour in Vain: or, An Attempt to Wash a Black-Moor White.* At about the same time, in *The Lottery* and *The Academy Garland,* two bits of Hudibrastic verse, he squared his account against the College by maintaining that even educational lotteries were "manifestly no better than public frauds." He was probably also the author of *The Manners of the Times* (1762), which in rhymed couplets very much in the manner of Dryden lampooned members of fashionable society, both male and female, who, coddled in the luxury and idleness of city life, strove only "to avoid that greatest Evil—Sober Thought." Alexander Graydon later described his famous teacher as "a dealer in the minor kind of satirical poetry. To him were attributed some political effusions in this way, which were thought highly of by his party, and made a good deal of noise."

Dove, a sort of Vicar of Bray in politics, had been successively at odds with the College, the Proprietary party, and now at the time of the Paxton affair with the Quakers. *The Quaker Unmask'd* thus aroused the greater resentment, as it was directed against his former associates. His effectiveness as "Poet Laureate to the Proprietary Party" brought down upon his head the Irish wrath of Isaac Hunt, self-constituted defender of Benjamin Franklin's reputation. Failing to accomplish very much by his scurrilous assault upon the Presbyterians in *A Letter from a Gentleman in Transilvania,* Hunt turned loose upon Dove a torrent of personal invective and abuse remarkable chiefly for its coarseness and vulgarity. But the irascible scholar he rechristened Squire Lilliput, Professor of Scurrility, proved well able to take care of himself, and in the literary sense gave fully as good as he received.

Both disputants resorted to broadsides, which in verse or pictures were hawked in taverns, barbershops and other public places, so that a large and rowdy audience was made party to their quarrel. Dove frequently embellished his poetic broadsides with little etchings or cartoons which were "as free and vigorous as any of Gillray or Rowlandson." Despite much talent for obscenity, Hunt came off rather badly in this paper war, but his libelous productions do suggest an interesting contrast with the pretty poetry of Leigh Hunt, his son.

Since the contents of the Paxton pamphlets were very nearly as picturesque as their titles, the affair provided Philadelphians with much sensational reading. More than that, however, as the incident uncovered deep social and political antagonisms, the literature it produced ran the gamut from personal abuse to thoughtful exposition of political views. Thus more than any previous controversy it provided wide experience in pamphlet warfare, a sort of dress rehearsal for the Revolutionary debate.

By the time the British Ministry exposed itself and its policies to attack by its passage of the Sugar and Stamp acts, it is evident that Philadelphians, both authors and readers, had completed their apprenticeship in the school of political controversy and were well prepared for the elevation of political discussion from the field of local animosities to the higher plane of broad principles. John Dickinson had undergone this sort of training, and his *Farmer's Letters* mark the final maturity of this genre of writing. Others in the city, Joseph Galloway and James Wilson among them, showed a similar capacity for pamphleteering which transcended the local issue and attained the dignity of political philosophy. In the field of personal and emotional appeal Tom Paine, master of that art, had the example of earlier work to build upon when he arrived on the scene in 1775. And it was of course Benjamin Franklin who brought this controversial style to a degree of perfection unsurpassed in English letters even during the great age of political pamphleteering. His achievement was in no small measure owing to the fertile field and competent support or opposition provided by his Philadelphia contemporaries.

Although the pamphlet was the principal vehicle of controversialists and satirists, the newspapers too proved useful for their purposes. Frequently short essays or letters to the editor opened up a debate or served to prolong discussion of the views of pamphleteers. Newspaper columns contained enlivening comments on current fashions and morals and provided the chief avenue of publication for female verse-writers and essayists. Indeed, should a woman venture into the field of social or political comment, the newspaper offered her only opportunity for expression. The gentle lady Hannah Griffiths shared so ardently in the Quaker dislike of Benjamin Franklin that, while in justice she praised his stove and his electrical experiments, she sturdily deplored in verse his political maneuvering:

> Oh! had he been wise to pursue
> The Track for his Talent designed,
> What a tribute of praise had been due
> To the teacher and friend of mankind,
>
> But to covet political fame
> Was in him a degrading ambition,
> For a spark which from Lucifer came
> Had kindled the blaze of sedition.

All controversy was of course not religious or political; it could be social or moral, or consist merely in gentle satire on the manners of the times. In this field too the weekly press played its part. The inveterate verse-writing of Philadelphia ladies produced a genuine literary controversy in the *Pennsylvania Chronicle* in 1772. Among gentlemen of education, complained "Misericordis," verse-making has become enough of a vice, but now "among Ladies of high and low degree, many are more eager to mix the ingredients of a little piece of this manufacture, than to mix the ingredients for a pudding. If *Miss* can put a few words into a properly dull order, and can string a few more, so that the two sets may jingle—lo!— she is a poet in a moment." Though he liked *good* poetry well enough, the effusions of "Miss Sappho Hexameter" were more than he could stomach.

In "Amicus Musarum" the ladies found a champion who enjoyed the female poetasters and had never heard that the making of puddings was a suitable occupation for ladies of high degree; his readers were left to infer that bad verse is perhaps less dangerous than an unsuccessful pudding. "Iambicus" also came to the support of the ladies, while "Misericordis" persisted in his sour stand, and the whole little tempest had no appreciable effect on female literary output. Such efforts as "The Beechen Shade" and "Reflections on

Reading Paradise Lost" by "Ariminta of Philadelphia" continued to appear in newspaper columns with their usual regularity.

Between the newspaper and the pamphlet stood the magazine, "being the taste of the age," which as it sought to be a "true miscellany" frequently included comment on matters currently agitating the public mind. With the cessation of Smith's *American Magazine* in 1758 the city lacked a periodical until Lewis Nicola began publishing *The American Magazine: or General Repository* in 1769. Widely distributed throughout the colonies from Halifax to Savannah, this periodical clearly reflected the growing secularism of its times by its emphasis on scientific developments, discussions of theories of government, and expression of the emerging spirit of opposition to Imperial measures. Within its pages comments on the decadent aristocracies and current inhumanities of Europe, served up in the form of history or biography with moral conclusions, elbowed aside the religious articles of earlier magazines.

Following the decease of Nicola's miscellany after nine issues there occurred another hiatus in periodical activity until the announcement by Robert Aitken of his intention to publish "original American productions" in *The Pennsylvania Magazine, or American Monthly Museum* beginning in January, 1775. His desire to eschew all controversy in its pages, because he was "na a fechting mon," seemed hardly capable of achievement when he hired the recently arrived Thomas Paine to be its editor and made Dr. John Witherspoon of the College of New Jersey a principal contributor. During the year 1775 Paine increased the number of subscribers from six to fifteen hundred and his prospects for a successful periodical seemed bright, but the war put an end to *The Pennsylvania Magazine,* as to so many of the city's cultural activities, in July, 1776.

Out of the prevailing mood of social satire came colonial America's first truly native drama. In 1767 the American Company announced that on April 20 it would perform the new comic opera, *The Disappointment, or The Force of Credulity,* by Andrew Barton, which by a curious train of circumstances had become, even before

its presentation, the talk of the town. Its true author, Thomas Forrest, was a dashing youth of twenty, associate of gay John Reilly
and one of a coterie of young men about town all of whom were
much given to practical joking. The piece joyfully satirized the
foibles of a credulous group of middle- and lower-class Philadelphians who had embarked on an absurd get-rich-quick scheme for
recovering the hidden pirate treasures of Kidd and Blackbeard. This
foolish passion for "digging" was an old one, toward which as
early as 1729 Franklin had directed one of his little essays. Among
citizens lampooned in the play were Anthony Armbruster, the
German printer, and Swan the hatter, who appeared under the
name of Raccoon.

Forrest originally wrote the play for the amusement of his companions, who found the joke too good to keep to themselves, so
that soon a considerable demand arose "from all ranks of people"
to see the work and have it published. This the author was at first
reluctant to permit, having but a modest opinion of its dramatic
worth. Eventually he consented, but wisely, because of the abundance of local allusion, had it brought out in New York. His reasons for publication he defined as an impulse to contribute to his
city's entertainment, his desire to correct "the infrequency of dramatic composition in America," and the hope to discourage "the
foolish and pernicious searching after supposed hidden treasure."

The Disappointment may be regarded as marking the beginning
of the American drama. Though described as comic opera, it is in
reality broad farce with occasional dramatic lyrics interspersed. It
employs a local setting and burlesques local characters humorously
and effectively. Quite properly, considering the cosmopolitan audience of Philadelphia for whom it was written, this play introduced the first stage Irishman, German, and Scot, with their respective dialects, some twenty years before Royall Tyler first made use
of the stage Yankee in *The Contrast*. John McPherson reported that
copies of *The Disappointment* were "very well rec'd by the people
here, who found no fault in it." Difficulties in the way of its theatrical presentation, however, soon arose. "This Play never was acted

here," McPherson went on, "the opposition to it being so great as
not to admit of it. Racoon [Swan] swore that it might begin in a
Comedy, but that he would make it end in a Tragedy." So despite
the demands of many in the city who wanted to witness this "very
popular drama," Douglass withdrew the piece, and in order to hold
his audience substituted another work of local composition. Yet it
might have been more in keeping with the Philadelphia scene had
the first production in this country of a play by an American author
been this novel burlesque by Thomas Forrest, rather than the conventional performance of Thomas Godfrey's frigidly classical *Prince
of Parthia.*

Despite the fact that Pennsylvania was less than a century old in
1776, events and changes had crowded in upon the inhabitants of
its principal city so rapidly as to cause men to remember and speak
of olden days even while the first person born within its bounds was
still alive. Furthermore, that they had been building a new state
and a society rich in hopeful possibilities seemed obvious to many
and worthy of description. Jacob Duché lamented in 1771 the want
of a good history of his province. "I wish to see a regular, sensible,
and well written history of Pennsylvania, from its first settlement
. . . which might comprise an interesting account of the labours of
its venerable founder, the progress of Commerce, of Arts and
Sciences, the gradual improvement of taste and manners, and the
rise of various sects of religion." His desire embraced the three cardinal features of a then new conception of historical writing: the
idea of progress, so dear to the eighteenth century, the striving for
accuracy in the critical handling of materials, and the widening of
historical horizons to include not only the chronicle of political
events but what we today call social and cultural history as well.
No son of Pennsylvania achieved in this period the synthesis
sought by Duché, but several citizens undertook works which were
to contribute to its later accomplishment. Charles Thomson's *An
Enquiry into the Causes of the Alienation of the Delaware and
Shawanese Indians from the British Interest,* published in London in

1759, was so scholarly a contemporary account that in the hands of later historians it attained the validity of a source. It was written, however, from a strongly pro-Quaker point of view, and its intense partisanship has been amply demonstrated by careful comments, based upon documents to which the author had no access, entered by Thomas Penn on the margins of his own copy.

Provost Smith made an admirable excursion into contemporary history in 1765 with his *Historical Account of the Expedition against the Ohio Indians, in the Year 1764. Under the Command of Henry Bouquet, Esq.* This work shows skill in the assembling and citing of materials, and gains much from the maps and vignettes beautifully executed by Thomas Hutchins and ably integrated with the text. Immensely popular, the *Account* was reprinted at London, Amsterdam, and Paris, and its French translator, C. G. F. Dumas, praised it as *"Un ouvrage rempli de goût, de sentiment et de vues, écrit et imprimé originairement en Pennsylvanie (naguère un Désert) à réellement de quoi piquer la curiosité."*

More in the vein of modern historiography was the work of collecting sources for a history of Pennsylvania begun by Caleb Pusey about 1682, and continued by David Lloyd, Isaac Norris II, James Logan, and finally by John Kinsey, "who in connection of several others, his friends, revised them." Unfortunately this splendid collection fell into the somewhat inadequate hands of schoolmaster Robert Proud, who completed therefrom his ponderous *History of Pennsylvania* before the outbreak of the Revolution, although it did not see publication until 1798.

A monumental enterprise was begun in 1770 when the Reverend Morgan Edwards published the initial volume of his *Materials towards a History of the American Baptists,* planned to comprise twelve volumes. Regarding himself only as a "compiler," Edwards conceived his work in the spirit of a true scholar and historian, asking in his preface for criticisms and emendations, and expressing the hope that his labors might serve to unite the various branches of his faith into one great religious body. Only one volume of this ambitious undertaking, the one dealing with Pennsylvania, was issued before the war.

Philadelphians could not by 1776 point to any great and distinctive achievement in the field of historical writing, but they had amply demonstrated the emergence of the historical spirit even in their very youthful society. Such a spirit can hardly be regarded as a sign of decadence or of nostalgic attachment to a glorious past, but rather as evidence of awareness of success achieved in a notable experiment and worthy of being recorded. Like John Winthrop, whose *Journal* began with his departure from England, these men were thoroughly conscious that they constituted a part of history in the making, and that their daily actions contained significance not only for themselves but for future generations.

In such a spirit did the Swiss miniature painter, Pierre Eugène du Simitière, begin his great collection of materials on the American Revolution immediately upon his arrival in Philadelphia in 1766, at a moment when the movement was just getting under way. The remarkable list of newspapers, pamphlets, and other materials covering the whole course of the Revolutionary movement assembled by this one relatively poor and obscure man evoked the honest astonishment of John Adams in 1774. The modern scholar feels an equal admiration for the broadly cultural conception of history underlying their collection. As a contemporary observer Du Simitière sensed that the American Revolution marked the beginning of a new epoch in human history, and that therefore its story should be written in terms far more inclusive than the chronicle of past politics.

To another great body of practical literature Philadelphia writers made signal contributions in the years before the Revolution, and thereby laid down the foundations of a literary tradition that still flourishes in their city. The combination of careful description of existing facts and exact concepts with a romantic vision of the expanding limits of human knowledge which the best scientific writing demands made a particular appeal to the Philadelphia mind and character. In the field of medical writings Dr. John Morgan's

Discourse upon the Institution of Medical Schools in America
(1765) is outstanding for clarity of literary expression and logic of
scientific argument. Morgan had able colleagues, also competent
with their pens, in Doctors Thomas Cadwalader, Adam Thompson and Thomas Bond. Dr. John Kearsley, Jr.'s, *Observations on
the Angina Maligna* achieved the distinction of threefold publication, in Lewis Nicola's *American Magazine,* in the *London Magazine* for 1769, and separately in pamphlet form.

Morgan himself, a booklover and collector of artistic masterpieces,
could on occasion turn his pen to other uses. In 1765 the trustees
of the College awarded him the gold medal donated by John Sar-
gent, Esq., London merchant and Member of Parliament, for the
best dissertation on "The Reciprocal Advantages of a Perpetual
Union between Great Britain and Her American Colonies," which
he won over the halfhearted competition of Francis Hopkinson and
the partisan effusions of Isaac Hunt. The author of this thoroughly
mercantilist argument, it is interesting to note, was later Surgeon-
General to the Continental Army.

Other scientific writings demonstrate the universality of New
World scholarship and the ability of Philadelphia writers to speak
an international language. Much of the best of eighteenth-century
scientific output appears in the personal letters of that epistolary
age, and it was by means of private correspondence with their
English contemporaries that a surprising number of papers and
observations by Philadelphia scientists reached the *Philosophical
Transactions* published by the Royal Society of London. Letters
from Franklin to Peter Collinson, for instance, first conveyed the
knowledge of the famous "Philadelphia Experiments" in the field
of electricity to the philosophers of England and the Continent.

The books of Philadelphia scholars also commanded a wide
audience—John Bartram's *Observations . . . in his travels from
Pennsilvania to Onondaga, Oswego, and Lake Ontario in Canada*
(London, 1751), his *Description of Florida* (London, 1766, and
twice reprinted by 1769), and Lewis Evans's *Geographical, Historical, Political, Philosophical and Mechanical Essays,* issued in

two parts in 1755 and 1756. Finally in 1771 came the notable volume of *Transactions* published by the American Philosophical Society, containing chiefly local contributions, printed by Bradford on Pennsylvania-made paper with plates engraved by Henry Dawkins, a thoroughly native Philadelphia product, but one which received the ungrudging and admiring accolade of scientific scholars everywhere. Much of its contents, however, had already reached an American audience through appendices in Nicola's *American Magazine.*

It was in this field that writers of eighteenth-century Philadelphia achieved what the Smith circle had hoped and failed to do. In their scientific scholarship they found themselves not champions of an obsolescent classical tradition, but completely at one with the spirit of their age and of the future. Speaking from the fullness of knowledge and absorbed in the value of the work they undertook, they were free of the apologetic imitativeness and stilted self-consciousness of their more purely literary contemporaries. By their contributions to scientific knowledge and the literary form in which they were expressed Philadelphians demonstrated the intellectual maturity of their society and their own ability to consort on equal terms with scholars and literati of the Western world.

Philadelphians were groping for means of self-expression in these decades of transition and social confusion. Two strains of writing therefore developed: the aristocratic attempt to reproduce the classical and aesthetic conventions of old Europe, and the practical, useful, unconsciously democratic writings which sprang from the contemporary life of Philadelphia and the colonies.

The great majority of citizens, as in all ages, doubtless preferred such sensational reading as *The Life and Confessions of Herman Rosencrantz: executed in the City of Philadelphia, on the 5th day of May, 1770,* for counterfeiting, which ran through two printings of two thousand copies each in a single month; or, among the better sort, "A Splendid Edition of a New Work, entitled *The American Genealogist:* in which a particular account will be given of the origin, progress, intermarriages, etc. of most of the considerable families in America." What really mattered, however, was the fact that a large minority of Philadelphians of all ranks were accustomed really to read and think, and that some few of them wrote.

The problem facing the gentry who sought to reproduce English literature in toto in the New World was that America and not England was their home. Nor did the sending of every incipient writer that appeared among them back to the mother country for incubation necessarily hatch a literary genius. American life had diverged sharply from the English; an American language and American orthography were already developing, along with an American as opposed to a British point of view. The native literature of a people growing up under such conditions had to be American, not English. What the American writer needed was to avert his attention from the examples of the Old World, and, as the eighteenth century itself would have phrased it, to seek a return to nature. The compositions of the College wits were definitely not natural to the American scene.

Europeans of the eighteenth century wished America well and wanted it to be a success. They delighted in such themes as the Noble Savage and the Good Quaker, but the local gentry seemed to find cause for shame in the fact that the Savage knew no Latin and that rhymed couplets failed to come naturally to the Quaker. While they were seeking to do away with such crudities by the importation of an alien culture they overlooked the fact that the brave new world about them was already developing its own more fitting modes of expression. The many Scots who came to share with Englishmen and Irishmen in the city's cultural life sensed this dichotomy, and for the most part enlisted their considerable talents with Franklin and his tradesmen associates in the creation of a realistic literature.

The literature of action thus evolved was concerned with the description of conditions and the presentation of facts, and with the inculcation of a native philosophy and a homespun point of view. It was, therefore, a valid literature, "called out," in the words of Emerson, "by the necessity of a people." It trained Philadelphians in a way of thinking which carried on through the Revolution and passed into the American tradition. Utilitarian though it was, it formed a foundation upon which later imaginative writing in America could be built. With its emphasis on practicality and purpose it kept civilization in transit, bringing the philosophy of the Enlightenment to colonial Philadelphia where it could be reshaped to fit the demands of a new country which owned no hereditary aristocracy. There also it combined with the strain of Puritanism inherited from the seventeenth century to flow into the main stream of American habits of thought.

Even to its practitioners the functions and achievements of this practical literature were not clear, and they shared with their politer brethren in the cultural confusion of the period. In 1769 one "Timothy Sobersides" cautioned readers of the *Pennsylvania Chronicle* lest in their zeal to promote home manufactures they overlook the nine muses, hitherto known in Philadelphia only by "hear say," since "it does not appear that any of those *Lovely Personages* migrated with our Ancestors in the early days of peopling this Continent from Europe." He devoutly hoped that "we shall no longer be so entirely beholden to the Mother Country, as we have hitherto been, for all the articles of *Poetical Haberdashery;* but that we may, at length, become able to furnish ourselves with a sufficiency of *sing-song,* the produce of our own *labour* and *Industry*." However, in his desire for

> A Bard, who, in the nick of time
> Stands forth to vindicate in rhyme
> Your life, your liberty and fame . . .

he completely ignored the possibilities of a vigorous and splendid native prose from the pens of a Franklin, a Morgan, a Dickinson and a Paine.

Chapter V

THE ARTS MOVE WESTWARD

"THE Arts delight to travel westward," Franklin, writing to Polly Stevenson in 1763, observed in his favorite strain. "After the first cares for the necessities of life are over, we shall come to think of the embellishments. Already, some of our young geniuses begin to lisp attempts at painting, poetry, and music."

By temperament and training Franklin was perhaps less qualified to render judgments in aesthetic than in other matters, but his universality of interest kept him aware of the advances made by his countrymen in the artistic as well as the practical and scientific aspects of intellectual endeavor. Always, at home or abroad, he eagerly collected the evidences of such progress. He could receive with satisfaction, therefore, the report of Charles Willson Peale from Philadelphia in 1771 that "The people here have a growing taste for the arts, and are becoming more and more fond of encouraging their progress amongst them," for his common sense undoubtedly told him that any art to flourish must enjoy two sources of continuous nourishment—the vitalizing interest of the many, and the generous patronage of the few.

Both factors were present in Philadelphia after the mid-century. While common men as usual sought beauty or entertainment to enliven their daily lives, gentlemen of wealth and leisure began to desire the artistic habiliments of the English gentry. In their search for social diversion and distinction these gentlemen discovered the value of the beautiful and the sublime. As soon as wealth permitted they replaced their homespun embellishments with "European Goods fit for the Season," even though the quality of the local product was becoming increasingly fine and was to prove extraordinarily durable.

Impressed by the rococo self-assurance and well-regulated splendor of Georgian England, colonial aristocrats turned with all the imitativeness of true provincials to the current English mode for a set of artistic standards. Even Franklin, who with his boundless faith in the future of the New World was still no great critic of the arts, felt that the colonies, which had not called in vain upon Britain for military defense, would do well to look to her also for aesthetic improvement. So the arts came westward, in a wave which very nearly drove back the already flowing rivers of colonial effort, and the resultant undertow symbolized the confusion of artistic thought which arose in the minds of eighteenth-century Philadelphians.

Few could detect that behind its glittering façade of rules and formulas English taste had begun to decline, and that such an era of decaying standards provided the perfect opportunity for men of genius, even colonials, to strike out on their own. In Philadelphia the realities of New World conditions would in any event have produced a new set of artistic conventions or some modification of the old. Here, though the artist might borrow the English form, he must revitalize it with Philadelphia substance; like literature, the arts had to learn to speak in a language Americans living in America could understand. The Pennsylvania capital, which already provided an audience and patronage for the arts, was in the process of proving that the Muses might find a comfortable home even in a democratic society. From its humble and middle-class ranks it was producing men and women who possessed the fire and capacity to interpret their society to itself—if only those at the top could be persuaded to lend an ear. "For," as one clairvoyant gentleman observed, "notwithstanding the great quantity of Chaffe visible in our Streets, yet there is some powerful weighty wheat that is covered in that heap."

These years witnessed the transplanting and early growth in Philadelphia of the arts of the drama, music, painting and the minor crafts. But the soil was not the old soil, and the fruit possessed a different flavor and texture from the English product. In painting the difference was the greatest; in the theater, least.

In 1729 a pious citizen had exulted in the *American Weekly Mercury* that in Philadelphia there were "no Masquerades, Plays, Balls, Midnight Revellings or Assemblies to Debauch the Mind or promote Intrigue." But he reckoned without the erection of the new Christ Church, symbol of the leavening effect of social as well as religious Anglicanism upon rigid Quaker discipline.

The first appearance of a professional "Company of Comedians" in the city undoubtedly resulted from encouragement by members of the Anglican gentry, whose sons had for some years, as a part of their educations, been engaged in the production of amateur theatricals. "You acquaint me of your acting a play last Winter to the Satisfaction of all Spectators," wrote Edward Shippen from London in August, 1749, to young James Burd. "I am glad that *Spirit is kept up,* because it is an amusement the most useful of any to young People, and I heartily wish it would spread to the younger Sort, I mean School Boys," for it inculcates "Grace of Speech and an elegant Pronunciation," and "emboldens a Lad and rids him of his natural Bashfulness. I feel more concern on account of the Education of Youth in my own Country than ever I did. . . . How much we are excelled by those in Europe!"

To young Shippen's elders, however, it was probably the entertainment rather than the pedagogical aspects of the theater that appealed. When the Murray-Kean company began its professional season at William Plumstead's warehouse on Water Street, they joyfully ignored the scorn and maledictions of Quakers and Presbyterians alike, and flocked to witness productions of *The Beaux' Stratagem, The Fair Penitent, George Barnwell, Richard III,* and other London successes. The stage fever even penetrated the homes of the Friends. John Smith was much distressed to learn one August day in 1749, on dropping in to drink tea with his friend Peacock Bigger, that the latter's daughter was one of a party of young Quakers "who were going to hear the tragedy of Cato. It occasioned some conversation, and I expressed my sorrow that anything of the kind was encouraged."

Quaker and Presbyterian opposition to playhouses was in no sense silenced, however, and early in the new year it consolidated its forces to rid the city of the "Company of Comedians." On December 3, 1749, William Allen notified the Corporation (with Benjamin Franklin present) that certain persons "intended to make a frequent Practice" of acting plays, which, he feared, "would be attended with very mischievous effects, such as the Encouragement of Idleness and drawing great Sums of Money from weak and inconsiderate People, who are apt to be fond of such kinds of Entertainment tho' the Performance be ever so mean and Contemptible." Bound by the Corporation "to their good Behaviour," the players concluded, in February, 1750, that the city of New York would afford them a more receptive audience.

In view of growing wealth and increasingly secular tastes, the theatrical appetites whetted in 1749 could not long be denied. After a four-year lull several Pennsylvania gentlemen, pledging themselves to forestall Quaker opposition, persuaded the Hallam troupe, recently from London and now in New York, to make an appearance in Philadelphia. Governor James Hamilton granted Lewis Hallam permission for his company to perform, provided they "offered nothing indecent or immoral." Franklin's *Gazette,* which only a month before had carried a vicious attack upon the stage, now announced with a flourish that on April 15 the London Company had played *The Fair Penitent* and *Miss in Her Teens* "before a numerous and polite Audience, with universal Applause." This left it to his competitor, William Bradford, to gratify Friends and Dissenters by the publication of a mélange of extracts directed against the theater and "Recommended to the perusal and serious Consideration of the Professors of Christianity in the City of Philadelphia."

This time, however, religious opposition proved insufficient to oust the players. Instead, they acquired an ecclesiastical champion in the Reverend William Smith, who not only consented to a benefit performance for the Charity School, but sanctified the occasion by his own presence. In all about thirty performances were presented this season at Plumstead's warehouse, which had been entirely remodeled for the purpose, fitted with galleries, pit and stage, and equipped "entirely new, extremely rich, and finished in the highest taste."

Although not until after the fall of Quebec did the players again visit Philadelphia, Thespis managed even in their absence to maintain the foothold she had gained in the city. Provost Smith encouraged theatricals at the College, and during the Christmas holidays of 1757, despite the Gallic peril, students gave several performances of Thompson and Mallet's *The Masque of Alfred* (1751), served up as "an oratorical exercise by a Sett of Young Gentlemen." Franklin's *Gazette* accorded these performances the fullest report yet received by a cultural event in the colonies; the issue of January 20 reprinted William Hamilton's Prologue and two columns of extracts from Act I, while the two succeeding numbers contained excerpts from Acts II and III. Smith gave the theater further support in his *American Magazine* in the following year, predicting, "who can tell but the coming generation may have theatres by law established, and grow as fond of actors and actresses, *men and women singers,* as the polite, well-bred ladies and gentlemen of the beau monde in Britain: of whose follies, as well as fashions, we are the most humble, zealous mimics."

In 1759 the players, now under the direction of David Douglass, erected a new theater, its scenery painted by the local artist William Williams, in the fashionable Society Hill section of the city. From that date until the last pre-Revolutionary performance in November, 1773, Philadelphians were able to enjoy several seasons of the finest repertories the contemporary British theater had to offer. As many as forty different plays, most of them well selected, with an equal number of farces or musical afterpieces, were presented in a single season; included were some thirteen works of Shakespeare, usually, it must be confessed, in the diluted versions of Thomson, Dryden, Cibber or Garrick.

By 1767 Douglass had decided to keep his troupe permanently in the Northern Colonies, shrewdly renamed them "The American Company," and built a new and better theater on Cedar Street in Southwark, just south of the city. The six-o'clock exodus from the city on play nights came to be a gay and splendid sight, the gentry in their carriages, the lesser folk on foot, picking their way along the new footway specially laid to protect ladies' slippers and their escorts' hose from Fourth Street mud, and all disappearing within the "Temple of Satan" to claim the seats their servants had been holding for them since four o'clock, while local Dogberrys struggled to circumvent gate-crashers, or strove to suppress disorders resulting from the successful performance of this unpopular duty. At this Southwark Playhouse Douglass sought to signalize his complete identification with the New World scene by his presentation of Godfrey's *Prince of Parthia* on April 20, 1767.

Playgoing Philadelphians quickly developed a set of critical standards for application to their own theater. Long readers of dramatic literature, and now no longer either shocked or amazed by the spectacle of actual presentation, they began to discuss the merits of individual plays and the performances of the players. With a view to improving the public "Taste of both Plays and Players," one writer to the newspapers recommended to the actors a more prudent choice of pieces, and the abandonment of their practice of altering the author's lines, a custom "universally condemned by all Men of Sense." "Uncle J. S. made me a present of a Ticket to see the Play," Edward Burd wrote to his sister. "Mr. Hallam is the best Actor according to the Common Opinion, but I am fonder of Mr. Allen. Miss Cheer and Miss Wainwright are the best Actresses."

Some gentlemen had attended the theater in London, and were fond of displaying their cosmopolitanism. "Critic," in a *Pennsylvania Gazette* for January, 1767, regretted that Hallam, "genteel in his Person and Actions," seemed unable to follow the example of Garrick and "speak plain English. There is no necessity of destroying the least articulate Beauty of Language, thro' Fury, Eagerness or Passion." Young Hallam had evidently been treating his Philadelphia audiences to a bombastic sample of the current oratorical style of acting. But "Critic" felt better about Miss Wainwright, who had a lovely voice, and Miss Cheer, who never loses "the Sweetest Accent, or faulters in the Clearness of Expression," he found to be "one of the best Players in the Empire." This sort of comment annoyed a correspondent to the next week's *Gazette*. Why compare Hallam to Garrick to his certain disadvantage? And what does "Critic" mean by "one of the best Players in the Empire"? In the opinion of this writer, members of the American Company deserved commendation within reason, but "in the eyes of Gentlemen and Ladies of Taste, who have seen a Garrick and a Cibber," to liken them to the most eminent in their profession is to do them a grave disservice.

Newspaper debates over the merits of dramatists followed those concerned with the capacities of their interpreters. "Eugenio," who knew his plays though he eschewed the theater, asserted in the *Chronicle* that even *Cato* contained a moral flaw in that it countenanced suicide. "Shakespeare's Plays are esteemed the apex of dramatic composition. And yet every man who reads Shakespeare, cannot but acknowledge, that his sublime flights of poesy scarcely atone for the low droll and buffoonery with which his best pieces abound." It would be difficult to cite a piece of criticism more perfectly in accord with eighteenth-century conventions of taste.

Although playgoing enjoyed increasing popularity among all ranks, the wealthy effectively sought to affix the badge of fashion to their favorite diversion. As the theater achieved respectability the snob value of being seen at a play became almost equal to the pleasure of seeing it. Ecclesiastical approval was conferred on the American Company in 1767 with the publication of *True Pleasure, Chearfulness, and Happiness. With some Remarks on the Theatre. Addressed to a Young Lady in Philadelphia,* probably by that clerical devotee of the drama, the Reverend William Smith. Secure in the patronage of homespun aristocrats, the players themselves ceased to be "rogues and vagabonds," and attained a gentility of their own. Local gentry took occasional part in dramatic or musical productions at the Southwark, and contributed at least one professional recruit to the American stage. This was a Princeton student named Greville, "of a good family in South Carolina," who, lapsing into debt at college, forsook Calvin's *Institutes* for the sock and buskin. His appearance in *The Prince of Parthia* added yet another native element to that occasion. "The People in general here rather pity than condemn him," reported young Edward Burd, who evinced a considerable interest in his career.

The actresses of the American Company seem to have been generally charming and discreet. At least one of them overtook her patrons on the social ladder by an alliance with the nobility when in August, 1768, Miss Margaret Cheer was married in Maryland to the Right Honourable Lord Rosehill. The next month the *Chronicle* announced that "the Right Honourable the Lady Rosehill (late Miss Cheer) has engaged to perform with Mr. Douglass in the Theatres of Philadelphia and New York, for the ensuing Winter, at a Sum much above Ten Pounds per Week and a Benefit." With a titled beauty with a fine voice for a star, at a salary equal to about $250 a week in modern money, it is small wonder the season was a success, or that such young blades as Alexander Graydon seldom missed a performance. This affair seems to have encouraged a scion of the Maryland Hamiltons to propose marriage to the beautiful Miss Betsey Richardson of the American Company in 1773.

Gradually the theater became integrated with the life of upper-class Philadelphia. In 1769, while the American Company was fulfilling an engagement in New York, students at the College undertook to supply their place. During May and June, on seven different occasions, such plays and operas as *Love in a Village, The Beggar's Opera, Folly on Both Sides,* and *The Musical Lady* were read and sung at the College or in the Assembly Room in Lodge Alley, for the benefit of "the Lovers of Elocution." The study of oratory and declamation by means of the drama became sufficiently popular to be promptly taken up by the private schools. A public declamation of the tragedy of *Cato* by students of Joseph Rathell in April, 1771, attracted an audience too large to be accommodated at his school. He therefore hired the Assembly Room for a second performance on April 18, added some other pieces and a musical interlude, and charged half a crown admission to defray his expenses.

When the players were in town, the importance of their performances as social events increased. Editor Goddard, in discussing the coming opening night performance of *The Tempest* in January, 1770, spoke of the "general Impatience among all Ranks of People for its Performance, it is imagined there will be a crowded Audience; A Splendid Appearance at the Theatre Tomorrow, will not only reflect Honours on our Taste, by patronizing one of the Chef d'Œuvres of that Immortal Genius, but be some Compensation to the Players." Production in Philadelphia in 1769 of Dibdin's *The Padlock,* within a year of its first night in London, reveals how closely colonials kept in touch with theatrical developments abroad.

Unfortunately this latter occasion, described in glowing terms by one "Philo-Theatricus" who could hardly conceal his satisfaction at the "most crowded and brilliant Audience," was marred by the presence of "Some Ruffians in the Gallery, who so frequently interrupted the Performance, and in the most interesting Scenes." Carpenters, masons and tailors, he went on, who pay only three shillings for admission, have no license to be outrageous, and when they persist in making a disturbance by calling for songs not listed in the playbill the management should employ constables to take them off to the workhouse. A British official, William Eddis, also found the "Sons of Liberty" in the gallery a "nuisance."

Such comments by its aristocratic patrons explain much of the second wave of opposition to the stage in Philadelphia, which was less religious than social in character, and which, though temporarily dormant, was by no means satisfied. Many of the thrifty middle class—carpenters, masons and tailors—resented the ostentatious gentility of the theater, quite as much as, in their capacities of Quaker, Baptist, or Presbyterian, they deplored its supposed effect on morality and religion. By the eve of the Revolution this secularization of anti-stage feeling was complete, and opposition to the theater had become almost wholly social and economic.

Religious groups, led by the Quakers, had forced the comedians from town in 1750. Caught off guard in 1754, they had been unable to organize rapidly enough to make their displeasure effective, and in any event, the French War precluded theatrical performances in Philadelphia for a time. But when Douglass and his company came to Philadelphia in 1759, the forces of righteousness were ready for them. Quakers, Presbyterians, Lutherans and Baptists simultaneously petitioned Governor Denny and the Assembly to prevent the erection of a playhouse on the grounds that the presentation of plays would prove "subversive of the good Order and Morals" of the community.

The Quaker-controlled Assembly responded with an act "for the More Effectual Suppressing and Preventing Lotteries and Plays," the preamble of which rehearsed all the stock objections urged against the theater since the days of the Roman stage, that "the weak, the poor and necessitous have been prevailed upon to neglect their labor and industry and to give extravagant prices for their tickets, and great numbers of disorderly persons have been drawn together in the night to the great distress of many poor families . . . and grievous scandal of religion and the laws of this government." This emphasis on the police problem created by the existence of a playhouse, on the threat it represented to public order and morals rather than to religious orthodoxy, though somewhat new in the Quaker capital, found considerable justification in the past history of the stage both in England and in America.

There was, in addition, a political motive behind the Assembly's action. Provost Smith, patron of the theater and sworn enemy of the Assembly, was at this time in England seeking redress for his recent imprisonment at its hands. By prohibiting lotteries, then one of the chief sources of income for the Academy, the Quaker legislators hoped to procure his overthrow, or at least his serious embarrassment. This partisan measure they shrewdly combined with legislation for suppression of the theater, in order to secure the backing of dissenting groups. Governor Denny, however, told the Council that the "Prohibition of plays was a most unreasonable restraint . . . from taking innocent diversions." He so altered the law that it could not take effect until January 1, 1760, thereby giving the players opportunity to get their season started "By Authority," while the Privy Council was disallowing the measure. Thus the fate of William Smith became coupled with that of the Philadelphia stage, and both survived through the maneuver of Governor Denny.

The erection of the Southwark Theater by Douglass in 1767 coincided with the movement for economy and retrenchment inspired by the unpopularity of the Townshend Acts, and universal emphasis on the current shortage of a circulating medium led to arguments of the deleterious economic consequences from spending money on these "lawless vagrants." "A false Taste of Pleasure" might unhappily prevail, and the attention of unwary youth be distracted from "Employments by which they may become useful Members of Society." As usual, the opposition regarded playacting as "an Inlet to Vice and Degeneracy," and only as a sort of afterthought stressed its possible effect upon religion.

Occasional outbreaks of disorder at the Southwark Theater, continuing throughout the period, provided some vindication for the middle-class antagonism to the theater as a "publick nuisance." In 1772 Douglass posted £10 reward for the apprehension of those levelers who had broken open the gallery doors and sought to democratize the playhouse "by carrying away the iron spikes which divide the galleries from the upper boxes." In addition to the scheduled play, a truer drama of social division between box and gallery was often enacted at the Southwark.

The achievement of the theater in colonial Philadelphia was considerable. By presenting on the shores of the Delaware several seasons of current English repertoire the American Company kept colonials abreast of one stream of contemporary cultural effort. Competent critics pronounced the work of the players to be excelled only by those on the London stage, and in later years Graydon asserted he believed they had not been improved on in America. One of them, John Palmer, proved in the London theater from 1761 to 1798 to be "one of the best general actors it ever had." As a force for improving diction and encouraging the study of public speaking in the schools the theater performed a distinct service to a community threatened with inroads from dissonant dialects and a foreign tongue.

By disarming much of the conventional criticism against it the theater helped to lessen local prejudices and to liberalize the provincial point of view. The highly respectable behavior of members of the American Company belied the moral charges of its critics. Its actors moved easily in the best circles of colonial society and became themselves genteel. Its actresses did not take lovers; instead they married, and married well. Above all, with the vogue for good entertainment, Philadelphians received instruction sweetened with diversion, and achieved enjoyable participation in one phase of Western literary development.

Unfortunately, however, the drama proved a social divisor. An aristocracy on the make cannot refrain from ostentation and display, and the public performance of plays afforded it an excellent opportunity for both. At the same time, to the powerful middle class, also on the make and increasingly devoted to the "Republican virtues," the theater became a symbol of all it detested and found antagonistic in its self-styled betters. When the radicals at the First Continental Congress, after having first decided to convene in Carpenter's Hall —meeting place of carpenters, masons and tailors—included in the Continental Association a provision for the closing of all theaters, they well knew they were playing to the galleries with certain dramatic effect.

Still another contribution of the American Company to the cultural life of the city was the stimulus it provided to the appreciation and performance of sophisticated music. Such a development had, however, to be predicated upon the existence of an audience in whom a love of music was at least latently present. Although other communities on the Atlantic seaboard earlier became musical centers—Boston, for instance, was as far ahead in sacred music as was Charleston in secular during the first half of the eighteenth century—a genuine interest in music did exist before the coming of the players in 1759. By the end of the period, with its cosmopolitan population and its varied musical background, Philadelphia had overtaken its sister communities to both north and south and had seized the lead in the encouragement of this art.

An incipient interest in secular music and its performance which had begun in the thirties had been checked by the denunciations of George Whitefield, who could detect in the Scriptures justification only for devotional hymns. Yet even the great evangelist could not wholly prevent the music-loving Germans from introducing vocal and instrumental exercises into their worship. In 1740 Christ Church, Old Swede's and the Moravian Meeting alone in the city possessed organs, but during the next decade these instruments were installed in the Lutheran churches of Germantown and Philadelphia, as well as in the Roman Chapel, where a fine choir developed under the leadership of a cultivated musician. Congregations were learning to sing in tune, in parts as well as in unison, from the hymnals of Watts and Wesley, and by 1763 a Presbyterian felt that it was doctrinally safe to publish *The Lawfulness, Excellency, and Advantage of Instrumental Musick in the publick Worship of God.*

Following the lead of Germans and Anglicans, other religious groups introduced more music into their churches, whereby the city's population grew to share in and appreciate the great devotional music of their age. By 1774 it appears that every denomination save the Friends employed an organ in its services, and that most were making a real effort to beautify and enrich their rituals therewith. On October 7, 1772, at a charity service at Christ Church, Francis Hopkinson directed the performance of "several pieces of solemn Church-Music, and particularly a Grand Chorus from the celebrated *Messiah* of *Handel.*"

Few aspects of Philadelphia life so impressed John Adams in 1774 as the music of its churches. Philadelphia preachers may have seemed inferior to the Boston connoisseur, but he was obviously captivated by the "soft, sweet music" at the Moravian evening lecture. He found the singing at the Methodist Church "very sweet and soft indeed"; at Christ Church "the organ and a new choir of singers were very musical"; but at the "Romish Chapel," where the chanting was "exquisitely soft and sweet," Adams reported "the scenery and music are so calculated to take in mankind, that I wonder the Reformation ever succeeded."

From old homes in England, Scotland, Ireland and Germany immigrants brought their popular airs and folk songs, and, if the Quakers disapproved of music, it must be remembered that they made up a constantly shrinking minority of the population. Continuous use among the common folk preserved the traditional balladry, and new verses, sentimental or satirical, were set to old tunes and printed on broadsides to be hawked through town and country. Armbruster and other printers found ready sale for such items as "A New Song. About Miss Ketty, leaving the Country, to the Tune of Derry down, down, down, Derry down." The mounting opposition to the mother country demonstrated the vitality and adaptability of the folk ballad with the appearance of numerous political songs, set to the tunes of Derry-down or Hearts of Oak. The climax of this political balladry on the one side was John Dickinson's stirring *Liberty Song,* set to music by Francis Hopkinson, and on the other, the bantering verses of the Philadelphia Tory Joseph Stansbury:

> Friends push round the bottle, and let us be drinking,
> While Washington up in his mountains is slinking.

In fact, the circulating bottle at city pubs served as baton and tuning fork to lead many into song, and for gentry as well as common folk the tavern often became a musical center. At David Lockwood's as far back as 1744 could be heard a "Musical Clock," which played "Sonatas, Concertos, Marches, Minuets, Jiggs and Scots Airs," composed by "Corelli, Alberoni, Mr. Handel and other great and eminent Masters of Musick," while lodgers at a near-by house could listen to the more spontaneous performances of the traveling

Virginian, William Black, who, rising often at five in the morning, was wont to amuse himself with fiddle and flute until breakfast time. "Singing and fiddling at midnight" were not unknown in the Quaker capital. Alexander Graydon and Ebenezer Kinnersley, Jr., belonged in the late sixties to "a large bottle association." Here young Kinnersley, who had the "knack of being gross without being disgusting, and consequently, of entertaining a company sunk below the point of Attic refinement," was always found ready and willing to sing, usually with the accompaniment of his own violin, "to the exquisite delight of his hearers."

The activities of gay British officers were also set to music, such as the winter excursion engineered by Alexander Macraby in 1769: "Seven sleighs with two Ladies and two men in each, preceded by fiddlers on horseback, set out together . . . on the roads, to a public house a few miles from town, where we danced, sung and romped and eat and drank, and kicked away care from morning till night, and finished our frolic in two or three side-boxes at the play." Sometimes informality had to yield to dignity, even in tavern festivities. On April 30, 1773, Josiah Quincy of Boston was present at Bryne's Tavern, where he "Feasted with the Sons of St. (alias) King Tammany. Three French horns, bassoon, three fiddles, etc., before and after dinner."

Feminine lovers of music, of the better sort at least, could hardly frequent city public houses, but they found a share in the singing traditions of the town when local Macaronis and young British officers made serenading the vogue in the years just prior to the Revolution. "The manner is as follows:" wrote Macraby, "We, with four or five young officers . . . drink as hard as we can, to keep out the cold, and about midnight sally forth, attended by the band, march thro' the streets, and play under the window of any lady you choose to distinguish; which they esteem a high compliment. In about an hour all the blackguards who sleep upon bulks, with gentlemen of a certain profession are collected round, drawn by that charm which soothes a savage breast, and altogether make it extremely agreeable in a fine frosty morning."

Why this "silly custom" of serenading? demanded in the pages of the *Chronicle* one sleepy "Anti-Serenader," who failed to understand why young blades employed music, which was supposed to soothe passion, when their object was obviously to rouse it. Yet even he, along with "all the blackguards," doubtless joined the rest of the citizenry to line the curbs of High Street on those occasions when one hundred and sixty Masons paraded with a band "gayly" playing the "Entered Apprentice's Song," or turned out for fireworks "with musical accompaniment" presented by the "two Italian Brothers" for several performances in 1768 and 1769. He may in passing have tossed a few pennies to the two hand-organ men, or to George Pyke, whose barrel organ played songs, hymns, a pair of pieces by Handel, and *Rule Britannia;* and he may have witnessed the tragic occurrence when "an Old Blind Harper," familiar on Second Street, striking out at several boys who were tormenting him with their teasing, accidentally killed one of them and was in consequence committed to gaol. Between the rush of ships sliding down the ways, and the rattle of farmers' carts going to and from market, the sounds of singing and street music were often heard in pre-Revolutionary Philadelphia.

This varied musical background, together with the example set by some of the recently arrived immigrants, especially Germans and Scots, in the realm of musical accomplishment, led many inhabitants to seek instruction in different branches of the art. Also, to the gentry and many of the middling sort, familiarity with some instrument came to be regarded as an essential part of a proper liberal education. The existence of some thirty-odd music teachers in the city during these years is sufficient evidence of the widespread desire for musical instruction.

John Beals, netmaker, led this host by offering in 1748 to teach "Young Ladies, or others . . . the Violin, Hautboy, German Flute, Common Flute, and Dulcimer, by note." Ten years later, driven to misogyny by the elopement of Hannah his wife, he directed his advertisements exclusively at the stronger sex. Here he had been anticipated by Robert Coe, who, in undertaking to teach the German flute by an easy method, announced that "as some Gentlemen are afraid to undertake it by Reason of its taking more wind than they can well spare," he had invented a mouthpiece, made of either tin or silver (for middling or better purses), which "does not in the least alter the Tone of the Flute, but does the same as if blown by the nicest Lips." In time, under tutelage of numerous accomplished Palatines, the German flute became the favorite instrument of Philadelphians. John Stadler performed excellently on the flute, and acquired so fine a reputation as a teacher in Philadelphia and New York that Councilor Robert Carter called him to his Virginia estate, Nomini Hall, to instruct his children. Here lonely Philip Fithian grew quite fond of "this good German," with his great ability, "simplicity and goodness of heart."

Voice teachers also flourished in the Pennsylvania city, and singing schools taught choral music and the popular and agreeable art of psalmody. The Evening Singing School conducted by Mr. Garner at the Christ Church schoolhouse became so popular that in order to preserve his promised strict decorum among youth of both sexes its director was forced to exclude from attendance at its meetings all save the parents or guardians of his pupils. After 1760 aspiring musicians in Philadelphia could obtain instruction in virtually any known instrument, and receive expert voice culture either individually or at a singing school.

More than two-thirds of these teachers, who at day or night schools did much to stimulate love of music and its performance in the city, were Germans, Italians or Scots, and one of them may well be regarded as the founder of formal music in the Middle Colonies. James Bremmer, kinsman to the Scottish music publisher, Robert Bremmer, and author of *Instructions for the Sticcato Pastorale,* came to Philadelphia late in 1763 with an already established reputation as a composer and as master of the harpsichord, violin, and other instruments. He opened a school near the Coffee House to teach harpsichord and guitar to young ladies, and these instruments plus the violin to gentlemen of the town. Sally Franklin, who had begun study of the harpsichord in 1758, was transferred to

Bremmer when her father wrote from London in 1765 to recommend him highly.

At this time the foremost native musician in the city was the versatile Francis Hopkinson, who as organist, first at St. Peter's and later at Christ Church, was well acquainted with Bremmer's various compositions for the harpsichord—"Trumpet Air," "March," "Lesson," and "Lady Coventry's Minuet." Seeking out the Scotsman, Hopkinson became his fast friend and most prominent pupil, a combination which proved extraordinarily happy, for it brought to the middle-class artist the support of a local aristocrat of wide influence, and subjected Hopkinson's real talent for musical composition to the discipline of an experienced master. By the time of Bremmer's arrival Hopkinson had already written and set to music *My Days Have Been So Wondrous Free,* the first secular composition of note in the colonies, and had published *A Collection of Psalm Tunes,* including some of his own, for use in Anglican churches. Together the accomplished Scot and the talented young Philadelphian raised the music of the United Churches to a very high plane, Hopkinson himself carefully instructing the children in psalmody. In 1764 at the Assembly Room, with the capable assistance of his student, Bremmer inaugurated a concert series for seventy subscribers, which ran from January until May, and proved so popular that a second series was undertaken in the following winter.

In these developments the importance of Francis Hopkinson lay in the link he furnished between the professional interests of his master and the nonprofessional appreciation by his friends among the laymen. His energy rounded up both amateur and professional performers for Bremmer's concerts, and secured the fashionable attendance of the gentry. Indeed, Bremmer made no attempt to continue the concert series after his student's departure for England in 1766. But Philadelphia music profited in other ways from Hopkinson's English visit. In London he purchased a harpsichord for Elizabeth Graeme, and large quantities of sheet music, including compositions by Palma, Vinci, Arne, Pepusch, Giardini, Handel,

Purcell, Corelli and Geminiani, for Bremmer and himself. Bremmer's careful instruction had equipped him to make good use of his new experiences for the development of his musical taste, and through the offices of his host and kinsman, the Bishop of Worcester, he was given opportunity to hear Handel's "Messiah and other solemn Pieces of Music performed by the best Hands." When in 1767 Bremmer himself returned to England for a stay of several years, Hopkinson had well prepared himself by study and travel to undertake direction of Philadelphia's musical life. In less than five years the Scottish composer and music master had, in the best of his students, laid the foundation for a musical tradition in the Pennsylvania capital.

As early as 1739 Franklin had carried Corelli's sonatas and Geminiani's concertos in stock at his printing office, but spreading interest in music called into being shops specializing in the sale of sheet music and musical instruments. In 1759 Michael Hillegas, sportsman and general merchant, advertised to sell a harpsichord, a violoncello, English and Italian violins, and imported flutes of Italian manufacture, as well as an "Assortment of Music of the best Masters," books of instruction, ruled paper for musical composition, songbooks, cantatas, sheet music and violin strings. Himself a musician, Hillegas continued throughout the period to be the largest music-dealer in the city. In 1774 he offered a very extensive stock of musical publications, as well as spinets, pianofortes, clarinets and organs, and such incidental equipment as strings, wires and reeds. But the widening market brought him able competitors, among them Martin Foy, who sold instruments exclusively, and was probably the first American dealer in Cremona violins.

These shops also carried the works of local composers, such as James Lyon, whose *Urania* (1761) was described as the "first Attempt of the Kind to spread the Art of Psalmody, in its Perfection, thro' our American colonies." The reputation gained by Francis Hopkinson from his hymn collection of 1763 resulted in a commission from the Dutch Reformed Church of New York for an English version of their Psalms, which was published in 1767, and both in that year and in 1774 there appeared new and enlarged editions of Lyon's *Urania*. Also for sale, as the Revolution approached, was a plentiful crop of political songs and ballads, such as Tom Paine's *Death of General Wolfe,* "set to Music by a Gentleman of this country." Demand was such that stocks often ran low: "I have tried several places to get you the song you wrote to me for but could not," reported John McCalla to a student friend at Princeton in 1772.

Introduction of music into the churches and its increasing practice among the citizenry induced local artisans, many of them Germans, to undertake the manufacture of instruments. Although the surly braggart Gottlieb Mittelberger declared in 1750 that "in the capital city, Philadelphia, no music is made either in the English or German Churches. . . . I came to the country with the first organ," several fine instruments had already been constructed by Gustavus Hesselius, the portrait-painter, John S. Klem of Dresden, and David Tannenberger. Klem was so well known for his craftsmanship that several years earlier he had built organs for churches in New York and distant Charleston. On first listening to the splendid tones of the organ built by Philip Fyring for St. Paul's Church in 1762, the visiting Charles Willson Peale paid tribute in verse to a fellow artist:

> Whilst Organ's dulcet Notes the Breast inspire
> With true Devotion and a sacred Fire:—
> Thy Name, O Fyring, thy deserving Name,
> Shall shine conspicuous in the Roll of Fame.

By 1772 many sorts of instruments, including flutes, guitars and violins, were made and sold by Peter Young and Jacob Anthony. Hesselius, Klem, Tannenberger, Young and John Berendt all made spinets and harpsichords, and in 1775 Berendt, "Schreiner und Instrumentmacher," notified all "lovers of music in Philadelphia" that he had "just finished for sale, an extraordinary fine instrument, by the name of Piano Forte, of Mahogany, in the manner of an harpsichord, with hammers, and several changes."

While common folk fiddled and sang, many of the gentry studied music seriously and mastered difficult instruments. Organs could be

Christopher Meng, painted by his son John.

(Courtesy Historical Society of Pennsylvania)

"The Temple of Satan." The Southwark Theater, erected in 1767.

(Courtesy University of Pennsylvania)

The old South Street Theatre.

A Thwarted Artist.
Self-portrait of John Meng, aged 19.
(Courtesy Historical Society of Pennsylvania)

found in most genteel ménages, and occasionally also in such middle-class homes as that of Christopher and Catherine Meng, whose son John so loved music that he painted his own portrait with a piece of sheet music held prominently in the right hand. Music cut gently through sectarian lines, for one day the Moravian minister discovered that ardent Anglican, "pretty Mr. Duché," sitting at his organ and playing a Moravian hymn—"and he sung it finely at the same Time." Music had social charms as well, which led Mr. Duché and his lady often to join another young married couple around the harpsichord, while the hostess played and sang a sentimental piece of local composition:

> Oft shall Schuylkill's rocky shore,
> With her waving woods around,
> Thy fond name repeating o'er
> Strive to swell the pleasing sound.

More pleasant to modern ears, perhaps, would have been the "low and sweet" tones of Colonel John Reid, best flute-player in the city, whose tunes Graydon complained were too much "overloaded with variations." Even Presbyterian scruples broke down before the sweet attractions of harmony. Philip Fithian, while a student at Princeton, had his friend Dr. John Beatty of Philadelphia copy out for him "the notes of the variations of lovely nancy" and send them over by the stage wagon. His mild heresy was completely overshadowed by the action of Nassau Hall itself when it imported "a band of music from Philadelphia" to assist "in making all agreeable" at the commencement of 1773.

The gregarious nature of this, the least intellectual of the arts, led naturally to the organization of musicales by the gentry. A music club under the leadership of Tench Francis had given exclusive little concerts at the Assembly Room in 1739 and 1740, until Whitefield's condemnation forced it to seek sanctuary in private homes. Here, however, the pleasant tradition was kept up, and in 1744 William Black of Virginia and Dr. Alexander Hamilton of Annapolis, both being properly recommended, attended an evening at this "Musical Club." "I heard a tolerable concerto, performed by a harpsichord and three violins," recorded the Maryland physician without enthusiasm. "One Levy there played a very good violin; one Quin bore another pretty good part; Tench Francis played a very indifferent finger upon an excellent violin. . . . We dismissed at eleven o'clock, after having regaled ourselves with musick, and good viands and liquor."

Musical soirées, attended by Richard Bache, Charles Batho, David Franks, Michael Hillegas, and the Reverend Richard Peters, and meeting at the homes of Francis Hopkinson, Dr. Adam Kuhn or John Penn, became popular in the latter part of the period. Penn found Batho, who was a dealer in dry goods, an honest fellow who occasioned "much discord in our small concerts." Chief among these "Philo-Musical Merchants" was Michael Hillegas, gentlemanly son of a German immigrant, and later first Treasurer of the United States. That he was a "great musician" was the honest judgment of John Adams in 1775, who found he talked "perpetually of the forte and piano, of Handel, etc., and songs and tunes." Music may have been his stock in trade, but it was also his love.

Prompted no doubt by Francis Hopkinson, students at the College founded the Orpheus Club in 1759, while proceeds from a benefit performance by the Douglass Company of *George Barnwell,* with entr'actes of concert music by several local gentlemen, enabled the institution to purchase an organ. Thereafter, as the *Gazette* reported, it became possible "to render the Entertainment of the Town more compleat at Commencements and the public Occasions in our College." Finest of these by far was the really remarkable performance of choral and instrumental music for the benefit of the Charity School, conducted by James Bremmer in April, 1765, "to the Satisfaction of a polite and numerous audience." The College of Philadelphia also far outclassed Princeton (with its band hired from Philadelphia) by adding to the usual church music at its commencement of 1773 the stirring and martial airs of the Royal Irish Regiment Band.

Always alert to contemporary developments on the English stage, the American Company introduced the ballad opera to Philadelphia audiences in the winter of 1766-67. During this and four other seasons before the war the city enjoyed performances of current London's most popular operas. Dibdin's *The Padlock,* first produced late in 1768, was played in Philadelphia November 6, 1769; his *Lionel and Clarissa* of 1768 appeared on local boards in 1772. In the Misses Cheer, Storer and Wainwright, and Messrs. Woolls and Hallam, the troupe possessed a group of singers whose voices were admirably adapted for comic opera, but it was at first considerably restricted in its operatic performances by the want of an adequate orchestra. Within a year or two, however, some of the local gentry felt sufficient mastery of their instruments to be willing to take their turn in the pit, and in 1769 Douglass announced that "the Orchestra, on Opera Nights, will be assisted by some musical Persons, who as they have no View but to contribute to the Entertainment of the Public, certainly claim a Protection from any Manner of Insult." There is no record whether the Sons of Liberty in the gallery, because of their common love of music, were persuaded to spare the musical gentry below.

In an age when the music of Italy was conquering all of western Europe, it was fitting that the outstanding musical genius of pre-Revolutionary Philadelphia should have been a native of that country. Signor Giovanni Gualdo, musician and wine merchant, came to Philadelphia from Italy via London in 1767. Fortunately for the future of music in the Pennsylvania city, his wine cellar led him into bankruptcy, and in order to recover himself financially he announced the opening of his music store on Front Street in February, 1769. Here he sold violins, guitars, mandolins, spinets, clavichords, the ever popular German flutes, and a variety of stringed instruments. He employed a staff of able repair men, a German musician who taught violin, cello and the French horn, and a servant boy to copy music for anyone desiring "a particular sonata, trio, duet, solo, minuet or country dance," without having to buy the entire book. Gualdo himself undertook to compose or adapt music "for every kind of instrument, as usual." In September he advertised that he would accept "a few" gentlemen and ladies as students of the flute, violin, guitar or mandolin. Here was a complete musical service which more than rivaled that of the well-established and widely connected Michael Hillegas.

A child prodigy furnished John Gualdo with opportunity to enter the concert field. In October, 1769, he directed a performance of vocal and instrumental music at the Assembly Room, "for the Benefit of a little Master, not seven years old," who gave an appreciative audience "a specimen of his early abilities." Whether because sentimental interest in the antics of precocious children had already become a part of the American character, or because he offered free dancing after the performance, the affair was so successful as to inspire the Maestro to more ambitious undertakings.

On November 16, 1769, he presented and directed "after the Italian Method" the first American composer's concert. Divided into two acts, the program opened and closed with overtures by the Earl of Kelly; the Misses Hallam and Storer and Mr. Woolls of the American Company sang such popular numbers as "Vain is Beauty, gaudy Flower," and "The Spinning Wheel"; Mr. Hoffman, Jr., played a clarinet solo, and Mr. Curts a sonata on the harpsichord. The remainder of the bill consisted of music composed and played by the director. In Act I "little" Master Billy Crumpto's violin was featured in a trio; Gualdo himself played a solo in one of his own concertos; and the act ended with a "new Symphony after the present taste" of his own composition. Act II included Gualdo's new violin concerto with solos, and one of his compositions for the mandolin.

Enthusiastic reception of this concert, in which the combination of composition and performance by native talent supplied pleasant flattery for local pride, encouraged Gualdo to propose a biweekly series of concerts to be held at Mr. Davenport's on Third Street. He addressed his prospectus to "the Philo-Musical Ladies and Gentlemen," who, he hoped, would assist him by lending their new music and their services in the orchestra. The series opened on November 30, 1769, in an atmosphere of "Decency, good Manners and silence" at Davenport's Hall. Here ladies seated upon chairs and gentlemen on benches listened to programs made up of the works of recent and contemporary composers, the Stravinskis and Sibeliuses of their day: "the Vocal Music by Messieurs Handel, Arne, Giardini, Jackson, Stanley and others. The Instrumental Music by Messieurs Geminiani, Barbella, Campioni, Zanetti, Pellegrino, Abel, Bach, Gualdo, the Earl of Kelly and others." The entertainment was of high quality, for Gualdo placed his own works in excellent company.

A second subscription series followed in the winter of 1770. In these concerts Gualdo made use of all known instruments, including the clarinet, which, invented about 1750, was still rarely played in Europe. He wrote a considerable amount of original music, composing six new minuets for the ball which followed his holiday concert of December 27. Gualdo's final concert took place on February 8, 1771. He had never satisfactorily recouped his losses, and financial worries added to an amazing amount of hard work finally unbalanced his mind. He died insane sometime in 1772.

"Music is at present in a very deplorable condition here," wrote Francis Hopkinson sadly to John Penn in October, 1771. "Sigr. Gualdo lies in Chains in one of the Cells of the Pennsylvania Hospital, and poor Batho was kill'd a few weeks ago by a fall from his House. Except Forage and myself I don't know a single Votary the Goddess hath in this large city." In this judgment Hopkinson was unnecessarily despondent, for even as he wrote a concert was preparing, and he himself assisted in the performance of the "Hallelujah Chorus" at Christ Church the following year. Music had taken root in the people, and there were among them enough accomplished gentleman performers to supply all the instruments needed for an orchestra. Inspired by Hopkinson, taught the rudiments by Bremmer, and welded into a trained and disciplined group by Gualdo, the colonies' first genuine conductor and composer of orchestral music, these gentlemen could now carry on by themselves.

When Provost Smith was making arrangements for the funeral of General Richard Montgomery in February, 1776, he wrote to

Jasper Yeates at Lancaster, asking him to send Eberhart Michael to Philadelphia immediately to take part in the services, adding that "Messrs Bremmer, Peters, Bache, Hare, Hillegas, Franks, and all the gentlemen in Town, who are able, will assist in the music." Two violinists, all he now needed, he could procure from New York. The situation was much like that in a small city of today, when amateurs from chamber-music groups combine with a few professionals to make up the augmented orchestras required by a special occasion. These men for the most part passed through war and revolution, and because love of music had already been planted in their city, were able to revive it in the new republic.

In contrast with the theater, music, which knew no nation and no class, was a cultural force making for social unity in Philadelphia. Its increasing use in religious worship democratized the art by allowing the whole congregation to share in it, and in an age of sectarian tension churches found in their musical programs a common factor. On the secular side, the music of Italy attained a popularity analogous to that which it enjoyed in Europe, but its practice was limited to no national or social group. Such middle-class teachers as the Scotsman Bremmer and the German John Stadler instructed the gentlemanly Hopkinson and Hillegas and such ladies as Mary Hopkinson and Elizabeth Graeme. Levy the Jew, the Irish Quin, and the German Schneider played together with English and native-born gentry, under the direction of John Gualdo, a Catholic from Italy. The draper Batho and the Governor John Penn met regularly to play concertos, and, on another plane, at taverns or "bottle associations" a man's ability to sing or perform was his only necessary passport to a merry company. Only an occasional Quaker, like John Smith who denounced the performance of *Cato,* remembered the contempt of the *Dunciad*—"Lo! a harlot form soft sliding by"—when the opera first made its appearance in Philadelphia. The increasing number of music-lovers rather found beauty in all varieties of musical performance, and in them too a lasting joy.

As life along the Delaware became more settled, the effort to enrich and beautify it led naturally to a development of the pictorial and graphic arts. This movement, too, was limited to no one class. All strata of society shared in the patronage of art, though the size of one's pocketbook might determine the nature and extent of one's interest, and its actual practitioners were in general recruited from the sturdy and growing middle class.

Color was the common heritage of all citizens of eighteenth-century Philadelphia. The natural setting of their city, in a verdant countryside between two lovely rivers, gave a warm tonality to the background of their daily lives. The soft browns and grays of Pennsylvania fieldstone punctuated the rural scene, and city streets were lined with the sightly red and black Flemish bond of well-proportioned brick façades. Color pervaded the interiors of these homes—the woodwork painted red, blue, green or pink-tinted gray, and as the period advanced the walls hung with papers of brilliant design, flowers or chinoiserie, while hangings progressed from the rich deep tones of damask to the gayer hues of printed chintz. In dress a brightness unknown today prevailed, in male and female fashions alike, gayest among the gentry, but shared in part by artisan and working classes, while commercial life was enlivened not only by colorful displays of merchandise in shop windows, but by many a painted sign hanging into the street from a finely wrought ornamental bracket, a form of commercial art combining usefulness and beauty to an extremely successful degree.

As surplus wealth accumulated, and its possessors began to investigate the more purely decorative aspects of the graphic arts, acquaintance with the produce of English and Continental craftsmanship resulted as usual in the desire for its possession or imitation at home. Fortunately, perhaps, for the birth of an American tradition, the years following the accession of Queen Anne in England were a period of crystallizing rather than developing taste. With the onset of decadence which follows closely on the cessation of progress, English art was in no position to furnish a strong example to the provinces, however desirous they might be of imitation. Left comparatively to themselves, therefore, the colonies succeeded in developing a set of standards which partially answered their artistic needs. Indigenous habits of truthful recording and sincere if clumsy realism became sufficiently rooted by the mid-century so that even the English success of Benjamin West, and the host of European influences which were the result of larger spending and wider travel, could not entirely dislodge them.

Philadelphians made their first acquaintance with the arts, outside of those employed in their own homes, through the popular European prints imported by various booksellers. Engraved views of cities, mezzotints, cartoons, "perspective views of Gentlemen's Seats," maps and "history pieces" found a ready market, first with the gentry, and later among all classes. In 1762 Robert and Thomas Kennedy opened a "Print-Shop" at Second and Chestnut streets, known in 1770 as the "Sign of the West's Head," which dealt exclusively in such by-products of European art as paintings on glass, maps, pictures and prints by wholesale and retail. The Kennedys carried "Glazed Pictures in the present English taste . . . amongst which are, scriptural, historical, humorous and miscellaneous designs," ranging in cost from forty-two shillings to £3 6s. In 1768 they added a patriotic note by featuring "elegant gardens, landscapes and AMERICAN VIEWS, fit for Gentlemen FARMERS," who were known to be "lovers of art and their country." Their 1770 stock they claimed to be the "best ever imported, and equal to any thing in the world"; it included prints of the most important paintings extant in England, suitable for hanging on walls or in "the cabinet of the curious," and selected by "the famous Mr. Ben. West of this city, now history painter to the king."

In the seventies four other print shops competed with the Kennedys for the patronage of such inveterate print-buyers as Elizabeth Drinker and Hannah Callender, who, as soon as Friend Sansom had returned from England, rushed posthaste to his house "to see Sammy's Prospective Views." At the gallery of Nicholas Brooks each importation was "exhibited in a convenient room, where all gentlemen and ladies who delight in the fine arts, and the copyists of nature are invited to regale themselves" with such masterpieces as cartoons after Raphael, the "Four Seasons" of Rosalba, landscapes, sporting pieces, sea pieces, and "the passions of the soul, as they are expressed in the human countenance by Le Brun." Landscapes by Zacharilli of London, a set of heads by Holbein and an oil copy of his "Mary Queen of Scots" made up part of the large stock at John Winter's shop on Arch Street.

While casual buyers of all ranks made purchases in these shops for the adornment of their homes, others began to assemble collections. Many colored prints, sepia washes, and ink drawings from the Italian masters were acquired by Francis Hopkinson, who made a present of eleven of them along with a little book of sixty caricatures to Pierre Eugène du Simitière in 1765. At this time the insatiably curious little Swiss, eking out a small competence as a miniature-painter, began his truly remarkable collection, which by the end of the year numbered 326 items. Included were prints of Watteau, Boucher, Borghum, Guercino, Panini, Mantegna, Raphael and Caravaggio, ten of those "passions of the soul," and five of the battles of Alexander, *les plus grandes,* engraved by Van Gunst after paintings by Le Brun. He also possessed eighty-three prints of birds, plants and animals, some etchings, a "Holy Family" by Poussin, and twelve landscapes by Sebastian Le Clerc. That such a collection could be brought together in the New World city within a single twelvemonth is tribute to the improved public taste to which print and picture shops were catering.

The creative impulse which had found means to express itself in literature and music was not for long satisfied to enjoy the graphic arts solely through the medium of engraver's copies. Economically conditions were propitious, for one could make a living by the brush so long as the ever increasing number of shops needed signs, and there is no record that any artist ever starved in a draughty garret in colonial Philadelphia. Manufacture of signs made possible a transition from house- and ship-painting to the more artistic craft of limning. The painting of tavern signs especially gave scope for imagination and individuality; the artist could provide a "Bottle and Glass" for John Dudley's mead house on Society Hill, or a "Harp and Crown" for Mrs. Steven's thoroughly respectable establishment on Third Street, while there was opportunity for a portrait on boards of Benjamin West for Kennedy's Print Shop. By Matthew Pratt the trade of sign-painting was raised to the level of an art, and his work excited comment and admiration.

When mounting wealth and self-esteem made it desirable to the gentry to have their portraits painted, and their improving taste required that the job should be professionally done, the limners were ready with their services. During this period some thirty-six portraitists, native or foreign-born, practiced in the city of Philadelphia. No preconceived theories of art motivated these painters. In their businesslike approach to their craft they felt no need to indulge in any self-conscious mannerisms or to set themselves apart by a Bohemian mode of existence. Nor were they hampered by the desires of their patrons, whose principal wish was for a faithful likeness of their persons. Even growing wealth and pride and the sense of approaching gentility failed to destroy the earlier spirit of plainness and the respect of self-made men for the democratic virtues, or to alter their middle-class preference for truthful reproduction to the fashionably aristocratic deceptions of current English portraiture. Painter and sitter were perhaps closer in point of view, and more in accord as to the usefulness and purpose of their art, than ever again.

As a result, colonial "face painting" reveals a conscious frankness and a spontaneous realism. Honest craftsmanship produced faithful delineations, not only of person but of character and spirit, which, taken collectively, represent a portrait of a society hardly equaled anywhere outside the American colonies. Much of the work was unschooled and poorly executed, but to the emergence of one or two real artists the lesser efforts of many daubers must always contribute, and Philadelphia in these years uncovered its full share of native genius.

The 1740's saw the beginnings of a native tradition in painting, as well as in its patronage by local citizens. Gustavus Hesselius, trained in the eclecticism of the Swedish school, readily adapted himself to the utilitarian exigencies of Pennsylvania conditions. Pleased with his work in copying family pictures in 1735, Thomas Penn paid the Swedish artist £16 for two portraits, the earliest on record, of Delaware Indian chiefs. The "Crucifixion" painted by Hesselius for the Catholic Church attracted wide attention when exhibited at his shop in 1748, and greatly impressed John Adams when he came to town for the meeting of the First Continental Congress. The early work of Hesselius, coupled with visits by the Newport painter, Robert Feke, in 1740, 1746 and 1750, when he painted members of the Shippen, Willing and Francis families, provided both stimulus and examples for many aspiring young men. The latter events excited even the curiosity of Quakers, and in 1750 William Logan and John Smith one day after dinner paid a visit to "Fewke's the painter's, and viewed several pieces and faces of his painting."

It remained, however, for men of lesser talents but greater ability for organization to gather about them what may be termed the Philadelphia school. In 1743 James Claypoole, scion of an early Philadelphia family, opened a shop in Walnut Street, where he sold books and "most Sorts of Painter's Colours, ready prepar'd for Use and neatly put up in Bladders." Claypoole himself undertook "all Sorts of Painting and Glasing," but gradually progressed from "Painter in general" to limning and the taking of views. In 1749 he took as apprentice his nephew, Matthew Pratt, "for 6 years and 8 months," and trained him so thoroughly that in 1758 Pratt "began to practice portrait painting," meeting "with great encouragement, having full employ, and much to my satisfaction, making money fast, with the approbation of every employer."

As Claypoole's own work grew more absorbing, the "Oil and Colour Shop at the Sign of the Golden Ball" in Chestnut Street, kept by Christopher Marshall, became the gathering place of local and visiting artists. Here in 1762 Charles Willson Peale, who had journeyed up from Maryland, came to purchase supplies. Amazed at the extent of Marshall's stock and not knowing what to buy, he took refuge in Rivington and Brown's Book Store, where he purchased *The Handmaid of the Arts,* the only art book in stock, with a view to finding help with his colors. More useful, perhaps, was his meeting with a man named Steele, member of an Eastern Shore family, who had studied painting in Italy. This "eccentric" habitué of Rivington's shop, who was wont to entertain all comers "by the hour," took the young Marylander to his studio, where Peale was greatly impressed by a self-portrait of the artist, which, though the face revealed a "penetrating earnestness," was fearfully colored "a purple red and the middle tints of a blueish tinge."

On the advice of Mr. Steele, Peale went to call on James Claypoole. The older artist generously showed him his work, including his portrait of Miss Wrench of Maryland, who later became Mrs. Claypoole. This alliance brought Mrs. Claypoole's sister, Polly Wrench, and her friend Laetitia Sage to Philadelphia, where both engaged in miniature-painting. Polly was a handsome girl, brilliant in conversation, and a sweet singer to her own accompaniment on the guitar. Not liking to stare into gentlemen's faces, she confined her painting to the features of ladies, until Dr. Rush's brother Jacob led her to the altar and relieved her of the embarrassment of this method of making a living. Miss Sage, who had taken lessons in miniature-painting with Charles Peale, also gave up her professional work when in 1772 she married his friend Henry Bembridge, himself just returned from artistic triumphs in England. Another member of the Maryland group was the amateur landscape-painter John Beale Bordley, who spent most of his winters during the 1770's in Philadelphia with his friends the Cadwaladers, and who was well known in the Claypoole circle. Peale, too, joined this group regularly after 1769.

Sometime or other all the painters of the Middle Colonies visited the city to purchase materials from the shops of Claypoole or Marshall. Not far from Marshall's, on Chestnut Street, was the Sign of the Hogarth's Head, which its occupant, William Williams, one of the most important of Philadelphia's foreign-born limners, made a center not only for painters, but for practitioners of all the arts.

For Williams, a Welshman, who had arrived in the province about 1750, was a true virtuoso, giving lessons on the hautboy and the German flute, as well as in drawing and painting in oils, and serving, on occasion, as stucco-worker, architect and landscape gardener as well. In 1759 he demonstrated the union of arts he so well exemplified by painting the scenery for the Society Hill Theatre. At his house a music teacher conducted a flourishing singing school, and in 1760 and 1763 George Deissenberg, one of the city's finest musicians, took rooms there.

Very little is known of Williams's own work. His portrait of a "Gentleman and His Wife" shows a familiarity with the conversation pieces of Hogarth and Devis, while his interest in the theater seems to be reflected in the picturesque, almost melodramatic backgrounds he provided for his full-length likenesses of such characters as the printer David Hall and Benjamin Lay, the eccentric Quaker preacher. The latter portrait, considerably to the surprise of her absent husband, was acquired by Deborah Franklin.

As was the case with Claypoole, Williams's influence upon the young men of Philadelphia was more significant than his own artistic work. In 1756 Benjamin West, then eighteen years of age, established himself professionally in the city under the patronage of Provost Smith, who undertook to supply the defects in his backwoods education by private tutoring at the Academy. It was Williams who gave the young artist his first instruction in painting, as well as his first sight of a work in oils by a professional. At this time, too, West saw the works of Feke, whose treatment of drapery made a lasting impression on his style, of John Hesselius, inferior son of a talented father, and of John Wollaston, "the almond-eyed artist" from England, then at work in Philadelphia, and also an influence upon the embryo "American Raphael."

Through West and Williams, and probably also through Henry Groath, popular Swedish painter of miniatures, who entered his son John in the Academy in this year (1756), artistic talent at the College and the Academy was brought into contact with the professional circles of Williams and Claypoole. Along with his taste for collecting, Francis Hopkinson combined a love of color and an interest in drawing, the most lasting evidence of which lies in the fact that he supplied the design from which the legendary Betsy Ross constructed the original banner of the thirteen revolting colonies. Other enthusiastic amateurs of art were Hopkinson's classmates, Samuel Powel and John Morgan, the latter eventually becoming one of Philadelphia's foremost collectors.

Young John Green, son of a dry-cleaner, and Henry Bembridge, well-born youth of considerable talent, were both students in the Academy in 1754, when a German immigrant named Creamer was giving instruction there in "some kinds of Painting." Also in the Academy at this time was a young man who, while he chafed at enforced study of the dead languages, displayed great talents for both drawing and botany. Before leaving school in 1756 William Bartram had already begun to make drawings of American birds for the English ornithologist George Edwards—drawings which place him first, and by no means unworthily, in the American tradition of Wilson and Audubon. The community of artistic feeling between academics and professionals found expression in the publication in Smith's *American Magazine* of 1758 of Hopkinson's "Verses Inscribed to Mr. Wollaston" and William Hicks's lines "Upon Seeing the Portrait of Miss xx—by Mr. West," while young Thomas Godfrey, himself a thwarted painter, celebrated more than generously the art of his "sole acquaintance," John Green, in "A Pindaric Ode on Friendship."

The decade of the 1750's was the seedtime of Philadelphia painting. Always profitable, limning, like medicine and the law, achieved a greater respectability with its wider patronage and its practice by sons of gentry as well as of tradesmen. No longer could fathers and mothers regard art as a base and unremunerative calling for their sons, as had the parents who apprenticed Thomas Godfrey to a watchmaker or who nearly quenched the fire of John Meng. Instruction in painting became part of a polite education, and young women unable like the Misses Wrench and Sage to take up the painting of miniatures found less satisfactory avenues of artistic expression in the art of painting on glass, learned at one of the city's many drawing schools, or in the production of such elaborate pieces of needlework as the lost pair of green silk garters ("on one Garter is worked in Gold Letters, La Constance; on the other, est ma Loy,") for return of which a reward of £3 was offered in 1763. Painting attained general popularity when middle-class families like the Franklins had portraits taken of the elders and miniatures of the children by such artists as Feke, John Hesselius or Henry Groath. Franklin even told Lord Kames with some amusement that he knew of "some eminent Quakers [who] have had their pictures privately drawn, and deposited with trusty friends" for safekeeping.

During the course of this decade some dozen painters, professional and amateur, were at work in the city. By James Claypoole, William Williams, Marshall's paint shop, and the College, they were brought into close association with one another as was no other artistic group in the colonies, and, comparatively free of foreign influences, they worked out for themselves what here as elsewhere was becoming the New World tradition in art.

The portraits of John Meng of Germantown, who insisted on continuing with his painting despite the parental pressure which forced him into a trade, well illustrate this trend. His few extant works show him to have been, though apparently untutored, a youth of undoubted talent. A "Kit-kat nicely painter," he took great pains with costume and revealed a remarkable instinct for characterization. His portrait of his father depicts in the frank vernacular of the colonies the German stolidity and unsympathetic stubbornness which led him to deny his son the pursuit of either music or painting as a profession. With Meng's death in the West Indies at the age of twenty the city lost a painter whose early work was rich in promise.

Just as the Philadelphia school seemed on the verge of genuine accomplishment an unfortunate mutation occurred. In 1759 Chief Justice William Allen sent his son John and his nephew, Colonel Joseph Shippen of the Pennsylvania militia, to Leghorn, where he hoped they might open up a commercial connection while absorbing cultural experience on the Grand Tour. With them went young Benjamin West. The eight or nine portraits he had executed by this time, together with his very interesting sketchbook containing drawings of David James Dove, John Green, Francis Hopkinson and Thomson (the barber of Forrest's *The Disappointment*), convinced local connoisseurs that West was the possessor of talents which could be improved by study abroad. Consequently, the Allens and a New Yorker named Kelly put up the money to finance his travel in the Allen entourage.

The young men carried letters of introduction to Sir Horace Mann, British resident at Florence, who received them graciously and recommended to their attention "a Collection of some of the greatest Rareties and pieces of Antiquity in all Italy." West parted from his companions at Florence, and went on to Rome and worldwide fame. "My God, how like a Mohawk warrior!" exclaimed the young Pennsylvanian, to the delight of Italian society, when first taken to see the "Apollo Belvedere." Under tutelage from Raphael Mengs and the influence of Johann Wincklemann, however, he soon lost the profound instinct for the perfection of the natural which underlay his spontaneous observation, and, abandoning his native realism, began the attempt to improve on vulgar nature according to the rules of contemporary neoclassicism.

After four years of study in Rome, during which time he was supported by William Allen, Samuel Powel, Governor Hamilton and Joseph Shippen, "the American Raphael" went to London "with a great character as a Painter." Here, introduced to eminent personages by Samuel Powel, and praised by Wilson and Reynolds, his popular success was immediate. As early as 1766 a critical pamphlet addressed him thus:

> Thou long expected, wish'd for Stranger, hail!
> In Britain's bosom make thy loved Abode.
> And open daily to her raptured Eye
> The mystic wonders of thy Raphael's school.

When at a later date West became the favorite painter of George

III and succeeded Sir Joshua Reynolds as head of the Royal Academy, colonial Philadelphians reflected with pride that such an exotic had been produced from the virtues of their frontier soil.

Benjamin West's success was London's gain, but it was a greater loss to Philadelphia than the removal of its most technically perfect painter. With his departure the local school largely broke up. Wollaston moved southward to become "painter in ordinary" to the gentry of Virginia, and Williams journeyed to the West Indies, whence he did not return until 1763. By that time pride in the local boy who had made good, the confidence that his success inspired, and the desire for emulation among artistic aspirants were attracting the best of local talent to Italy and England. When Peale first visited the city in 1763 he found only Steele and Claypoole still at work. Matthew Pratt, who in addition to his marked success as a painter had married money, departed for England as the escort of Miss Betsy Shewell, whom he had aided to elope from her family so that she might marry Benjamin West in London. Pratt spent two years in England, painting and studying with his famous countryman. To Italy the next year went Henry Bembridge, to study with Batoni and Mengs, and to strike up a profitable acquaintance with James Boswell. Maryland gentry, sensing the real genius of Charles Willson Peale, sent him to study with West in 1766.

Meanwhile more and more sons of wealthy Quaker and Anglican families were following the example of John Allen and Joseph Shippen in spending a Wanderjahr abroad before settling down to the confinements of mercantile life. Francis Rawle, Thomas Mifflin and William Bingham were but a few of the young men who sailed for Italy and, after a visit there, followed the traditional route across the map of Europe, through France to London. From Naples in 1764 Dr. John Morgan wrote to Colonel Shippen that he and Samuel Powel were witnessing the very scenes enjoyed by Allen and Shippen four years before. Everywhere we go, reported Morgan, such people as Sir Horace Mann, James Byers, the connoisseur, and Abbé Grant speak of "the repute you give America."

The fact that it was on the whole easier to meet and mix with English notables in Italy than at "home" no doubt played a part in this rush abroad for culture, which, while it broadened the young provincials in the sense of enlarging their social experience and making them familiar with other lands, too often served to overlay their instinctive good taste with a rage for bad imitations. Powel and Morgan, for example, visited Herculaneum and the Tomb of Virgil, viewed and criticized all the works of old masters in Italian galleries from Venice to Naples, and took a course in antiquities with James Byers at Rome. They purchased art books, prints, drawings, copies, and one or two old masters; they collected objets d'art by the trunkload, and very nearly fell in love with the beautiful artist Angelica Kaufmann, who later sent Morgan a portrait of herself in payment for medical attention for which he had refused a fee.

Such eager young collectors began the pillage of Europe which was to become a nineteenth-century mania, and which, whenever in the history of America it has been indulged, has resulted in obscuring the value and merit of native art and in degrading the local artist. This mistaken faith in Old World canons had much the same retrograde effect upon the art of colonial Philadelphia as when in the nineteenth century it caused the real vitality of Thomas Eakins to be ignored because his style was not that of contemporary Frenchmen. When these graduates from the Grand Tour returned to their native shores, they furnished their homes with Italian antiquities and filled their gardens with neoclassic statuary, sought to elevate the tastes of their less fortunate townsmen, and in general set themselves up as connoisseurs and critics. Colonel "Joe" Shippen even presumed to advise West of his artistic shortcomings. "I am very sensible of my own wants in regard to painting," the successful artist of inferior birth replied suavely in 1763. "Your useful hints upon this subject I take in the kindest part . . . I value them as much as if they came from Mings [sic] himself."

The lull in artistic interest and activity lasted for nearly a decade, during which time other Pennsylvania-born artists than West, working in foreign lands, were reflecting credit on their native city. Matthew Pratt executed a number of profitable commissions at Bristol, and was made a member of the Incorporated Society of Arts after the popular exhibition there of his "American School" in 1766. Notwithstanding these triumphs, he chose to return to Philadelphia, resuming his "professional line" at the corner of Front and Pine streets in 1768. At his studio arrived shortly the Reverend Thomas Barton, who "came purposely to introduce me to Governor Hamilton, Governor Johnson [of North Carolina?], Mr. Jno. Dickinson, Mr. Samuel Powel, and all the Willing family, the [Anglican] clergy, etc., among whom I met with full employ for two years." With his fine individuality of style and a nice sense of color and composition, Pratt, in such later works as his portrait of Dr. John Cochran, is shown to have developed into a portraitist of no little distinction.

In 1772 another Philadelphian, Henry Bembridge, also returned out of preference to his native land. His full-length portrait of the Corsican patriot Pasquale Paoli, commissioned by Boswell and painted while in the island, had evoked praise from the Grand Duke of Tuscany, and had drawn "abundance of fashion" to the exhibition of the Free Society of Artists in London in 1769. Critics judged he had posed his subject gracefully, and had "finished the face in a masterly manner." In 1770 Bembridge exhibited a portrait of Franklin at the Royal Academy. West wrote of him to Francis Hopkinson, "You will find him an ingenuous artist. . . . His merit in the art must procure him great encouragement and much esteem." Asthma soon took him south to Charleston with his bride, the miniaturist Laetitia Sage. There the Italianate style of this capable painter met with a cordial reception and enabled him to pursue his profession "with Reputation and Success."

The return of Pratt and Bembridge, with their European reputations, to join the local landscapists Isaac Beston and Alexander Stewart, the miniaturists Du Simitière, Richard Collins, William Verstile and Laetitia Sage, and the amateur artists John Beale Bordley, Francis Hopkinson, who had turned to pastels, and the printer Henry Miller, who was also an accomplished water-colorist, made of Philadelphia the most active artistic center in the colonies. Moreover, generous patronage by its traveled cognoscenti gave it the reputation of a provincial Rome, and painters of other cities were drawn thither by commissions or by desire to view its fine private collections.

Charles Willson Peale, having had enough of the mother country, commenced his annual visits in 1769, settling permanently in the city in 1774. His painting of the Cadwalader family, executed there in 1772, demonstrates the straightforward informality of his developing portrait style. Patience Wright came over from Bordentown in 1769 to exhibit her "clever portraits modelled in wax," before moving on to New York and London and a wider career as spy for patriot interests in the Revolution, while her sister, Mrs. Rachel Wells, drew large crowds for over three years with her waxworks of Chatham, Franklin, Mrs. Catherine Macaulay, and a "thief pilfering a miser." John Adams found genius as well as taste in this exhibition, but his considered judgment on the art of Mrs. Wells was that it would "make but little progress in the world." Also a visitor to the city in these years was Cosmo Alexander, teacher of Gilbert Stuart.

By far the most important artistic pilgrimage of the period, however, was that of John Singleton Copley, who in September, 1771, sufficiently overcame his phobia against travel to spend a week in Philadelphia, because he believed it to be "a place of too much importance not to visit." An introduction from General Gage procured him admission to the collection of William Allen, and here the lonely young artist was genuinely thrilled by his first view of paintings from the Old World. He "saw a fine Coppy of the Titiano Venus, and Holy Family at whole length as large as life from Coregio, and four other small half lengths of single figures as large as life, one a St. Cecilia, an Herodias with John the Baptists head, Venus lamenting over the Body of Adonis and I think a Niobe, I cannot be certain." The Venus and the Holy Family he thought the finest coloring he had ever seen.

Yet, despite the merits he found in the Italian masters, could Copley have but known it, there was nothing in the stylized flattery of contemporary British portraiture to compare with the best of his own work. In his painting of Mr. and Mrs. Thomas Mifflin, executed probably in New York at about this time, colonial portraiture reached its zenith.

There is cause for abundant irony in the reflection that Copley's visit to the most artistically active city in the colonies, his sight of the "very great and Elegant" paintings in Philadelphia collections, and the urgent advice of Thomas Mifflin, William Allen and others were probably deciding factors in inducing the reluctant artist to set out for European travels and an English career. "These Gentlemen [are] the first in America for fortune and Character," he wrote to Henry Pelham, with the awe in which he always held success in other fields than his own, "and highly distinguished for their love and Patronage of the Polite Arts and who have it very much in their power to do . . . a kindness either here or in Europe." In view of the long and continuous prodding of Sir Joshua Reynolds and Benjamin West, and with letters of introduction from Dr. John Morgan, written at Mifflin's request, to Sir John Dick, Sir Horace Mann, Abbé Grant, Isaac Jamineau, and James Byers, wherein he was described as "the best Painter that has ever performed in America, without excepting our American Raphael," how else was he to decide?

Copley's advisers meant well, thinking it an "Honour to America" that it could produce such a genius without "the assistance of able Masters." So they sent him to Guido and Guercino, to Rome for classical seasoning, and to London for a brief success and long years of disappointment. Peale, a far stronger personality, and his colleagues Pratt and Bembridge, seem to have sensed that their destiny lay with the rising democracy of the colonies. Peale became the "Artist of the Revolution," and both the others supported the patriot cause. Copley, a lukewarm Tory, fled to Italy and artistic ruin when he cut himself off from his native land.

The artistic activity which took place in Philadelphia in these years was the result of the natural urge for expression among a relatively free and prosperous people, and should occasion neither wonder nor apology. Its purpose was to furnish yet another demonstration of the social and intellectual maturity of the colonial way of life, and to enable colonial society to escape from the humiliating parent-child relationship to a spiritual status more nearly equal to that of the mother land.

There existed considerable confusion as to the methods by which these twin objectives might be attained. Some felt the colonies should receive their artistic conventions complete from the mother country, that England, with some help from western Europe, should set the tempo and the tune, and that colonial artistic output should be as nearly as possible an echo of that of contemporary London. But there were others whom instinct and experience told that America was already developing its own way of life, as different in social aims and economic aspirations as in geography from that of the mother country, and was, from the essence of those differences, capable of distilling its own forms of artistic expression.

Whatever the methods or the aims, the experience of these years in Philadelphia clearly demonstrated that the arts could flourish in a democratic society, that its broad spread of education and abundance of economic opportunity did, in fact, furnish an extremely hospitable atmosphere for their development. Furthermore, in an age when aristocratic taste was on the decline, it was the energetic and growing middle class that produced both new ideas and men capable of giving them expression. Like the rest of colonial America, the society of Philadelphia was predominantly middle-class, and in general its artists and musicians were recruited from that increasingly important body.

Within the various fields of art the accomplishments were unequal, depending upon whether the native or the borrowed note was dominant. The theater, for instance, owed little to colonial Philadelphia; nor, indeed, except for the entertainment involved, did colonial Philadelphia owe much to the theater. Both the plays

A London Sensation in 1769.
Pasquale Paoli, the Patriot, by Henry Bembridge.
(From Boswell's *Account of Corsica,* 3rd ed., London, 1769)

Caricature of Henry Bembridge by his friend Patch.
(*Courtesy Medici Society and Hale, Cushman & Flint, Boston*)

presented and their interpreters, with a few unimportant exceptions, remained completely English throughout the period. The social conventions followed or introduced by the theater were all British, and it thus became the particular possession of the most Anglophile elements of Philadelphia society, and ultimately the butt of attack from emergent patriotism. Music became somewhat better acclimated. Though there was little native composition and the works played were still those of European masters, performers, adapters, teachers, directors, and listeners, and even makers of instruments belonged to the local scene, and the universality of both participation and enjoyment caused it to become well integrated with the life of Philadelphia.

The art to attain most complete naturalization in these years was painting. Here both the artist and his subject were usually colonials, and both conformed to already established native traditions and local taste. Both taste and tradition reached their height in the decade of the fifties, when numbers of local artists were perfecting themselves technically with little reference to British conventions or European theories. In the history of American art, the English success of Benjamin West, while gratifying to colonial pride, may be regarded as an unfortunate accident from which it required more than a century to recover. More immediately, that success led directly to the artistic tragedy of Copley, a somber drama that was often to be repeated in the national period.

Practitioners of the arts, as we have noted, came largely from the middle class, and interest in their accomplishments was fairly well distributed throughout the population of eighteenth-century Philadelphia. But there was another factor without which the arts in this period could not exist, that of generous and often disinterested patronage. There had to be a class of men whose cultivated tastes and surplus wealth enabled them to attend the theater, purchase tickets for concerts, sit for their portraits, and even to finance the education and training of young men of talent. Their mansions provided work for craftsmen, especially painters, cabinetmakers and silversmiths, their social life made patronage for actors and musicians, and their families furnished custom for teachers of the arts. They supplied the aristocratic patronage necessary to art even in a democratic society, and their existence, in numbers sufficient to leave their impress, is an index of how far that society had developed. To this group of gentlemen, therefore, our attention must now be turned.

Chapter VI

GENTLEMEN OF LEISURE AND CAPACITY

"You may depend upon it," asserted William Allen in 1760 of his native province of Pennsylvania, "that this is one of the best poor Man's Countrys in the World, and agrees very well with English Constitutions." Its capital city, the Chief Justice might well have added, proved equally agreeable to the constitutions of all nationalities, and afforded to a man of property the greatest rich man's opportunity in the Western Hemisphere. The truth of the latter proposition none knew better than he.

A number of great fortunes had their rise in Philadelphia in the expanding though fluctuating prosperity of the years from 1740 to 1775. Commerce and privateering, land speculation and the fur trade accounted for much of the new wealth. Some there were who declared that to be a "man of business" was "the only road in Pennsylvania to honours and distinction." Yet during and after the last French war the very presence of wealth and the increasing complexity of trading operations called into being a series of new and exceedingly profitable professions. The growing dignity and importance of these callings in time raised many of their practitioners to an equal or higher plane, both economically and socially, than that occupied by the commercial magnates.

Chief among these was the law. In 1740 the Philadelphia bar was far from distinguished, but by the decade of the seventies training at the Inns of Court and abundance of new opportunities had done their work. With the ability, learning and success of such men as

John Moland, Andrew and William Hamilton, Tench Francis, Joseph Galloway and John Dickinson the fame of "the Philadelphia lawyer" became firmly established. The rise of the medical profession was as spectacular as that of the law, and in some respects even more worthy of comment, as a later chapter will make evident. Similarly, certain members of the skilled crafts, particularly those requiring the infusion of some artistic capacity, such as architecture or silversmithing, achieved both reputation and fortune, moved in the same circles with the merchant princes, and were regarded by all as the founders of professions. Meanwhile the clergy, especially the Anglicans, prospered with their churches and, while holding their own professionally, contrived even to better their social standing. Preachers of all sects, as Anthony Benezet observed, loved "to live delicately and ware soft raiment."

There thus arose in Philadelphia a group of well-to-do mercantile and professional families, for the most part Quaker or Anglican, who by the careful pyramiding of their interests and astutely arranged intermarriages consolidated their riches and position and gradually coalesced into a distinct upper class. Within this circle there was ample leisure, for the eighteenth-century merchant or professional man was less tied to his countinghouse or office than his counterpart today. Possessed of wealth, political power, social prestige and freedom from practical worries, members of this newly formed plutocracy quite naturally sought to ape the manners, interests and ways of living of contemporary aristocrats in the mother country.

Such successful merchants as Chief Justice Allen and William Coleman "in a great measure got out of trade" to live on invested capital, their incomes derived from local rents, lotteries or South Sea annuities. Scions of the second generation, such as Francis Hopkinson and James Hamilton, lived as gentlemen on inherited wealth, while Joseph Galloway was only one of many who frankly assured their gentility by marriage with young women of fortune. As contemporary comment on this last tendency Jack McPherson sent the following "humble imitation of the Newspapers" to a friend in New Jersey in July, 1770:

Last Thursday evening was married John Dickinson, Esq. of this City, Author of the Farmer's Letters, to the aimiable Miss Polly Norris of Fairhill, only surviving daughter of the late Isaac Norris, Esq. deceased. . . . She is a young lady endowed with every qualification requisite to make the marriage state happy, with a fortune of £50,000 (some say £80,000) sterling.

Their fortunes assured, Philadelphia's "gentlemen of distinction" proceeded to surround themselves and their families with the amenities becoming to their class. Their manner of living steadily improved throughout the period, although persistence of Quaker traditions coupled with the economic uncertainties of the war years restrained them from a too elaborate display of elegance. A good badge of a man's social and financial status being the sort of house he lived in, many hastened to remodel, enlarge and improve their homes. A successful "She Merchant," Elizabeth Paschall, announced in the *Journal* in 1746 her intention "to take down and Rebuild the house she now lives in," and more than one commentator as the period advanced observed that such operations were becoming a fashionable vice. "Building is one gulph of expence scarce fathomable," wrote "Antigallican" in 1757. "Additions, alterations, decorations are endless. 'Tis one eternal scene of pulling down and putting up."

Despite all this activity, Philadelphians were slow to develop an elegant town architecture for the reason that, never really removed from the soil themselves, they fell easy prey to desire for the most important outward sign of English gentility—broad acres and a country house. Moreover, to the natural aspiration and fashionable taste for country living was added the need to escape from the unbearably humid heat of the Philadelphia summer with its attendant yellow fever and smallpox. Nature as much as fashion dictated this earliest large-scale exodus from an American city. Accumulated wealth made it possible, and the country round about Philadelphia became dotted with lovely estates which strove to challenge the similar places of old county families or newer Whig grandees in the mother land.

With surprising rapidity much of the ostentation and snobbery of contemporary English gentry appeared among its New World imitators. In an effort to cement their imperial social connections wealthy Anglicans and Quakers began to summer at Newport along with royal officials from Carolina and the West Indies. Arrival of such celebrities as Sir William Draper, K.C.B., or Lady Gordon caused many a flutter among these embryo aristocrats. They fawned on "Walter Irvine Ogelvie Graham, Esq: of the antient families of Montrose, Monteith, Findlater, Airly, Dundee, Preston, Banff, Braco, Innergularity, Carnonflie, Banas, Norton, Conyers, Forglen, etc., in Scotland, from Drummadd-Major, near Enniskillen, Ireland: but last from South Carolina," and were well taken in by the Princess Susanna Carolina Matilda, Marchioness of Waldegrave and own cousin to the Queen of England, until she was revealed to be plain Sarah Wilson, former maid to one of the Queen's waiting women, and now serving a sentence of transportation to the New World for theft of some of the royal jewels.

These same purse-proud gentry patronized Miss Cheer of the American Company until she became Lady Rosehill; then, they adored her. For such as they Quakerism appeared too austere and too spiritual, and many drifted out of Meeting into the Anglican faith with its fashionably deistic doctrines, elaborate ritual, and consequent social prestige. By 1760 the belief was widespread that one might be a "Christian in any church, but could not be a gentleman outside the Church of England."

With this shift in moral emphasis some scions of Quaker families went to the dogs completely. In 1770 Samuel Coates sent William Logan, then in London, a gloomy account of the activities of twelve young Quakers with whom they had formerly been schoolmates. Young Coates was neither a Jeremiah nor a prude, but his story speaks for itself. "Poor P. S. . . . drinks very hard. . . . John Cameron, John Relf, John Baily, John Marsh and Dan Wistar are broke," having either dissipated their inheritances or failed in trade.

The Meeting is disowning many for sottishness and immorality, and has condemned "D. W." for keeping game cocks to the value of £25. Furthermore, the gentleman last named "is said to give a Girl £50 to strip Stark naked before him."

While such actions were sufficient to rouse fierce resentment among the lower orders of Philadelphia's citizenry and to give demagogues cause to rant, they were the extravagances of a very few. Vulgarity, licentiousness and waste are excrescences endemic to a leisure class, and that of Philadelphia, though it produced much solid substance, real accomplishment, and devotion to the public service, was no exception. After the manner of its time it was worldly, but apparently not so blatantly so as it might have been. Said Josiah Quincy in 1773, after condemning the lush living of Carolina planters: "The Philadelphians in respect of the bounty and decency of table are an example to the world, especially the American: with the means of profusion, they are not luxurious; with the bounties of earth and sea, they are not riotous; with the riches of commerce and industry they avoid even the appearance of epicurean splendor and parade."

Enough remained of the old Quaker love of plainness and of the pioneer emphasis on the virtues of industry and frugality to prevent the mere selfish enjoyment of wealth and leisure from becoming wholly respectable. Moreover, to the omnivorous needs of the new country for labor and development were being added in these years new conceptions of the humane duties of gentlemen and of the possible perfectibility of the human race under guidance from enlightened aristocrats. A sense of the responsibilities not only of wealth but of position was growing up, along with the conviction that men endowed with "capacity and leisure" should employ their capacities not only for the enrichment of their leisure but for the amelioration of society as well.

So members of that fortunate class in Philadelphia devoted years to unselfish public service, even though like William Allen they found it an unpleasant burden. They held innumerable trusteeships in hospitals, libraries, charitable foundations and insurance companies. They patronized education, music and the arts, often supporting the artist or, like Samuel Powel, assembling good collections of paintings and objets d'art. They experimented with the new agriculture on their country acres, and by their application and scholarship made considerable contributions to the sciences, especially to medicine. Furthermore, the mere development of their wealth and taste contributed to the economic and artistic enrichment of the city, for catering to their needs and fancies supported architects, gardeners, workers in precious metals and cabinetmakers, and the town or country houses they erected, with their libraries, gardens and art galleries, became the show places of all British America.

Foremost among the earlier generation of Philadelphia aristocrats was William Allen, Chief Justice of the Province of Pennsylvania, whose active life spanned the entire pre-Revolutionary period and whose interests and activities epitomize all that was best and most valuable in the emergent New World aristocracy. His public service began in 1727, when he was a young man of twenty-three and his native city was barely a generation old, and lasted for half a century. His career thus parallels that of his great contemporary, Benjamin Franklin, and as the life story of a member of a privileged minority presents interesting comparisons and contrasts with that of the ambitious and accomplished tradesman.

Though possessor of inherited wealth, Allen was for much of his life an active businessman and speculator, and contributed in his own person and accomplishments as well as in the almost dynastic marriages of his progeny to the elevation and consolidation of the class of which he was one of the earliest representatives. Forgotten by posterity because he espoused the losing side of conservatism in the War for Independence, and quietly ignored in the *Autobiography* because of the personal dislike and political antagonism of its author, William Allen was throughout these years the true Maecenas of Philadelphia and a fine example of the type of aristocrat its young society could on occasion produce.

Born in 1704 to a wealthy and influential Presbyterian family of Scotch-Irish origins, Allen was one of the first young Pennsylvanians to be sent abroad for his education. In 1720 he was entered at the Middle Temple, and later became a pensioner of Clare Hall, Cambridge. Finally in 1725, accompanied by a manservant, he rounded out his gentlemanly training by what he called "my Travels to France, etc." In 1727, shortly after his return to take over the administration of his deceased father's estate, he entered upon his career of forty-nine years of political service to his city and province. He represented the city in the Pennsylvania Assembly until 1739, meantime serving a term as Mayor in 1735. From 1741 to 1750 he occupied the office of Recorder, a post which he relinquished upon becoming Chief Justice of the province.

During King George's War William Allen was strongly opposed to the passive Quaker policies and prominent among those who demanded a vigorous defense for the colony. Soon he had become the leading representative in the province of the Proprietary interests, and inevitably, as the breach widened between Proprietor and Assembly, found in Benjamin Franklin his principal political opponent. A loyal Pennsylvanian, however, he stood stanchly for the maintenance of colonial rights until the moment of final revolt. He opposed both the Iron Act of 1750 and the Revenue Act of 1764, and seems to have been a chief factor, through his friendships with Lord Shelburne and Isaac Barré, in securing postponement, for one session of Parliament at least, of passage of the Stamp Act. He resigned from the office of Chief Justice in 1774, but continued for two years longer as member of the Assembly from Cumberland County, which he had represented since 1756. Shortly before the outbreak of hostilities he supplied the Pennsylvania Council of Safety with cannon shot from one of his iron furnaces. But as a man in his seventies, all of whose life had been spent as a British subject and whose extensive property gave him a considerable stake in the status quo, he could not bring himself to accept the idea of colonial independence.

"A man of wit and pleasantry," known with affection and respect as "the great giant," William Allen served his city and his native province generously and well. His bitterest opponents in the Assembly had to admit his fairness on the bench and the truth of his assertion that he had "never desired office . . . but served from a sense of duty." Even his greatest enemy, "the grand Incendiary Franklin," was mindful of the fact that as Chief Justice he devoted his entire public salary to various charities. In the end, what his traducers resented was his probity and his influence. More than once Franklin, Galloway, and their cohorts felt his strength, as in the case of the newly elected German who on being asked his sentiments by another Assemblyman replied, "I tinks as Mishter Allen tinks, be dat as it vill."

For many years Allen combined business with politics, and building on the considerable property left him by his father, amassed the largest fortune in Pennsylvania. The firm of Allen & Turner was extremely successful in its commercial ventures, particularly in trading during King George's War under flags of truce. A part of its profits were invested in a rum distillery, a copper mine and several iron furnaces. South Sea stocks, loans at interest, and especially local real estate absorbed much of Allen's capital; his Pennsylvania landholdings were extensive, and in New Jersey he owned 30,000 acres. In 1753, when he retired from trade, he carefully transferred much of his wealth into easily convertible forms, so that it is probable that no one in America commanded more mobile capital than did he.

As a person of wealth and leisure, cultivated and cosmopolitan, Allen turned readily to the life of a country gentleman. He forsook his town house on Water Street for the rural comforts of his seat at Mt. Airy, where with his wife Margaret, daughter of Speaker Andrew Hamilton, he was accustomed to entertain lavishly. Here too he busied himself with raising "Colly Flower" and "every sort of Cabbage that is esteemed to be very good" in his famous kitchen garden, while pressing upon his sons and daughters "among other lessons . . . that of Frugality and Oeconomy." Yet he exemplified no narrow practice of these virtues. His chaise and chariot had long attracted attention, and after 1761 his coach, drawn by four black horses and driven by an accomplished English whip, carried its owner in state unequaled down Germantown Road to the city. Their wealth, education and social eminence enabled the four Allen boys to marry well, and secured the brilliant alliances of his daughters, Ann to John Penn in 1766, and Margaret to James de Lancey, horseman and cockfighter of New York, in 1771.

The life of a politician, gentleman farmer and socialite did not preclude the genial and corpulent Mr. Allen from participation in many other phases of local activity. One of the principal organizers and first Grand Master of St. John's Lodge of Philadelphia in 1732, he became in 1750 Provincial Grand Master of the Freemasons. Daniel Fisher from Virginia was duly impressed on June 24, 1755, by "the Greatest Procession of Free Masons to the Church and their Lodge in Second Street that ever was seen in America. No less than 160 being in the Procession in Gloves, Aprons, etc., attended by a band of Music." Well in the forefront marched William Allen, preceded only by "a Sword-bearer with a naked sword drawn."

His wealth Allen placed often at the disposal of his province. In 1729 he advanced funds for the purchase of the lot on which Andrew Hamilton, his father-in-law, built the Pennsylvania State House, a loan for which he was not reimbursed for over thirty years. On another occasion, when Governor and Assembly were hopelessly deadlocked over a revenue bill, Allen personally underwrote a large portion of the Proprietary's tax in order that the province should not be without adequate defense. In 1764 he headed a list of leading citizens who sought to encourage home industries by the erection of a "Linen Manufactory," and in 1765 he founded, at his "Great Grant" on the Lehigh, the town which now bears his name.

Concern over the absence of suitable educational facilities in his native city led to Allen's hearty concurrence in Franklin's proposals for the foundation of an academy. His gift of £75 was the largest donation from any of the trustees, and it was at his suggestion that the city corporation was persuaded to make its handsome contribution to the project. Allen was chairman of the committee to secure the use of Whitefield's Tabernacle for the Academy, and when that building was found not yet ready for occupancy contributed the use of "a large house" of his own on Second Street for its early classes. The four Allen sons all attended the Academy and the College, and their father was an active and regular attendant at trustees' meetings until the year before his death in 1780. His general interest in education led to his promotion of the movement for German Charity Schools and to his service, under the terms of James Logan's will, as trustee of the Loganian Library. That interest, combined with his devoted Presbyterianism, produced his continued care and attention for Francis Alison's school at New London, Pennsylvania. Allen was instrumental in bringing the Presbyterian scholar to Philadelphia, and he freely lent his influence for the securing of the charter which transformed the New London School into the Academy of Newark in 1770.

Allen's desire to promote the welfare of his community caused him also to patronize liberally such individuals as seemed to him worthy. By no means the least among the beneficiaries of his intelligent interest and generosity was Benjamin Franklin, who in 1727 had been proud to reckon Judge Allen among his "acquired friends." This friendship may have assisted him to secure his contract for the public printing, which he obtained through the influence of Speaker Hamilton. The ambitious printer and the merchant-politician collaborated on numerous public projects. They were fellow members of St. John's Lodge; together with others they superintended the taking of the first Philadelphia census in 1749; and Allen's influence with Lancaster farmers measurably eased Franklin's task of collecting wagons for Braddock's army in the spring of 1754. Success of Franklin's academy scheme owed much to the purse and prominence of William Allen, and the two were further associated, though from slightly different motives, in the movement for German charity education.

In 1753 Franklin reported to William Smith that Mr. Allen had ordered six copies of his *College of Mirania,* and cautioned Smith to supply himself with letters of introduction to the Justice should he venture to Philadelphia. "If you are more noticed here on account of his recommendation," your highroad to success will be so much the easier. Franklin well knew the value of Allen's patronage, which at this very time was procuring his appointment as Deputy Postmaster General for the Colonies, although he did not know that the Judge had offered also to go his bond for the office. Sensibility of his influence, as well as a certain affectionate respect, can be detected in a letter written to Richard Peters the next year in which Franklin recommends the abilities of schoolmaster William Elphinstone, who can teach "even a veteran Scrawler to write fairly in 30 Hours. . . . P. S. I have heard our good friend Mr. Allen sometimes wishing for a better Hand; this may be a good Opportunity for him to acquire it easily. His Example and yours would be the Making of the Artist's Fortune."

Other able young Philadelphians owed their start in life to the influence and generosity of the Chief Justice. Funds put up by him financed much of Dr. John Redman's European study, and a credit of £100 from the same source enabled Ralph Ashton to "improve himself by tending the Hospitals" of London. Having in the journey of his son and nephew to Italy in 1760 immeasurably contributed to the vogue of the Grand Tour, he willingly furnished traveling colonials with letters of introduction to his fellow Cantabrigian, Sir Horace Mann in Florence, who as willingly obliged by seeing to it that the young men met the right people and became acquainted with the artistic treasures of Italy in the right way.

Perhaps Allen's greatest service to the artistic education of his countrymen was his establishment, with the aid of his brother-in-law, James Hamilton, of what amounted to a drawing account for the impecunious Benjamin West, lest "such a Genius should be cramped for want of a little Cash." West always spoke with feeling of "Mr. Allen . . . the principal of my patrons," and when Charles Willson Peale arrived at his London studio in 1766 bearing a letter from Allen, West told him "it was the best that could be brought him." Another young colonial of promise, John Morgan, paid tribute in 1761 to both Allen and Hamilton, "from whom I have received so many favors."

A considerable portion of Allen's substantial fortune was devoted by him to charity. In 1750 he became a trustee and a heavy contributor to the newly founded Pennsylvania Hospital, and in 1766 he personally subscribed £50 for relief of the poor in Philadelphia. Always a generous supporter of the First Presbyterian Church, he donated a large sum to Francis Alison's Fund for Presbyterian Poor Widows and Orphans, and later assumed the management of its accounts. Much of his private charity, however, carried no advertisement. Hearing in 1759 of the needs of John Monkton, who thirty-four years before had been his servant for a few months in France, he instructed his London agent to make the man a payment of ten guineas. A fitting conclusion to a long life of humane activity was the clause in his will providing for the manumission of his slaves.

Allen shared with the best of eighteenth-century intellectuals an eager desire for useful knowledge that was not satisfied with mere kindly interest and financial support. He read widely in the classics and in scientific works, and numbered such natural philosophers as John Bartram and Cadwalader Colden among his friends. In a belated attempt to locate the ever receding Northwest Passage he headed the organization of two Arctic expeditions under Captain Swaine in 1753 and 1754. He was greatly interested in Dr. John Morgan's project for a Medical Society in 1765, offering some excellent advice which might have been accepted with profit, and he was one of the first members of the revived American Philosophical Society in 1768. His patronage of art was twofold, manifesting itself in his pecuniary support of Benjamin West and in the fine collection of paintings, chiefly copies of Italian masters, which made his town house a Mecca for visiting artists. His love for the older cultures of Europe was continuous from the time of his youthful travels to the day of his death.

Despite business and political success, however, and a life filled with activity in the affairs of men, Allen's real devotion was to the soil. One of the first colonials to become thoroughly acquainted with the revolution in English husbandry, he eagerly read all new treatises on the subject, which he had forwarded to him from London as they came off the press. In 1770 he sent to England for a seed drill and horse hoe "with directions how to use them." "Very few persons in this Country have made more experiments in the farming way than I have, and, in this latter Stage of my Life, my Books, and my little Farm are great part of my Amusement." Here speaks the true country gentleman. Gifted, intelligent and humane, honest, generous and affable, William Allen was a credit to his community and well deserves to be remembered as leading patron of the arts and sciences and first gentleman of Pennsylvania.

In his devotion to the country way of life Allen was typical of his time and locality. Already Philadelphians were manifesting that preference for gardens and orchards, for country amusements in a rural setting, that has characterized them throughout their history and that resulted during the eighteenth century in the most nearly perfect replica of English country life that it was possible for the New World to produce.

In the move toward country living the Quakers led the way. Grantees of the choicest parcels of land round about the city and the first of its inhabitants to amass considerable fortunes, many of them easily followed the example of James Logan at Stenton by opening up country estates in the 1740's. Most of these early places were mere "Plantation Houses," located not far from the city and having few or no bedrooms, because their owners would rather drive the short distance back to town than risk a night in what they regarded as the unwholesome "vapours" of the country air. At best they served as week-end lodges or as retreats from the city during recurrent smallpox scares. They were plain and informal, built for comfort and simply furnished. "Our tables and chairs that do not meet with approval," wrote one Quaker matron, "have been sent to the country."

Gradually some Friends, especially those of an earlier generation who were growing old and withdrawing from business, began to retire permanently to their estates and set up as country gentlemen.

Isaac Norris, upon inheriting Fairhill, left town in 1743 to live "downright in the country way," surrounded by his family, his orchards and flowers, and his books. In 1746 John Smith purchased a large property at Point-no-Point (Richmond), which he proceeded to develop into a lovely seat, its plants and flowers selected with the advice of John Bartram and cultivated by a gardener who commanded a salary of £30 a year.

Alone among these early country houses James Logan's Stenton possessed any architectural distinction. Built near the Wingohocking Creek and approached by a long avenue of stately hemlocks, the house in its simple proportions and quiet beauty reflected the placid classical tastes of its owner. Such places as Whitby Hall or Elizabeth Paschall's Cedar Grove were the result of building on to earlier one- or two-room houses and reveal a consequent commingling of styles. With all of them, in the decade of the forties, solid comfort rather than rural splendor was the touchstone.

Yet country living in the vicinity of Philadelphia never exceeded the sophisticated heights it attained at one of the earliest country seats. This was Graeme Park, situated at Horsham in Bucks County more than twenty miles from the city, and owned by Dr. Thomas Graeme, whose wife had inherited the estate from her father, Sir William Keith. Here a severely plain great house of local stone, surrounded by gardens, lakes, and vistas of carefully planted trees and shrubbery, groves well stocked with wild life, and meadows dotted with picturesque though useful sheep, provided for the princely hospitality of Dr. Graeme and his talented daughter a background more nearly approaching the seventeenth-century ideal of English country living than was ever achieved by plantations on the Ashley or the James. Of its three-hundred-acre deer park, one of the few in America, its owner wrote, "If you consider it as a place of beauty and ornament to a dwelling, I venture to say that no nobleman in England but would be proud to have it on his seat."

Graeme Park was unique, but other landowners, nearer the city and on a more modest scale, were striving for and discovering the same rural delights. When Nicholas Scull and George Heap published their *Map of Philadelphia and Parts Adjacent* in 1750 this country way of life had so far developed that the area from Chestnut Hill to Point Breeze and from the Delaware west of the Schuylkill to Cobb's Creek appeared well filled with the names of country estates.

After 1755 several new influences combined to produce a noticeable change in the style of country life. With the new commercial prosperity, somewhat expanding in the glow of wartime profits, some Philadelphians became very rich. Abundance of opportunity enabled recently arrived Scots and Irishmen to pile up fortunes, and as their Anglicanism began to carry social implications many prosperous Quakers forsook the plain faith of their fathers for the more fashionable communion. Young Samuel Powel was only one of the more spectacular converts by this route. Out of plutocratic beginnings a colonial gentry was growing up. Class distinctions being implicit in the idea of an aristocracy, wealthy Philadelphians now consciously sought to set themselves apart from their fellows as men of taste and elegance, as arbiters of society and patrons of the arts, and as exponents of gentle living. Into this aristocratic ideal the half-town, half-country way of life of the eighteenth-century English gentleman fitted with beautiful ease, and Philadelphians, though they still sought relaxation and comfort and a refuge from hot weather epidemics, began to indulge a new and expensive luxury in their rural seats.

Although wealth lay at the base of this new display of elegance, the shift in genteel tastes was significantly molded by the increasingly intimate contacts of the gentry with England and the Continent, especially with Italy. As sons of important merchants completed their local education at the College their parents sent them "home" to Britain, to take orders in the Anglican Church, to read law at the Inns of Court, or to study medicine at Edinburgh or London. Upon termination of such graduate study many spent a year in travel on the Continent. Even where no professional training was contemplated it became usual for Philadelphia businessmen, quite frequently Quakers, to grant their sons a year or more in England

and Italy to increase both their mercantile and their cultural experience.

The young Quaker Francis Rawle seems to have initiated the Philadelphia custom of making the Grand Tour in 1748. In that year also Edward Shippen, studying at the Middle Temple, allowed himself time for "seeing all the curiosities." But the great impetus to Italian travel occurred in 1760, when Chief Justice Allen arranged "Letters of Credit" for his twenty-one-year-old son John, who had "an Inclination to see a little of the World." Thus provided, John Allen sailed for Leghorn with his cousin, Colonel Joseph Shippen, to spend "a few months in Italy" and thence to travel through Switzerland and France to London. In a bit of youthful special pleading the boys had stressed the opportunity their travels might afford for the opening up of trading connections at Leghorn, but the Judge shrewdly observed that they chiefly wished "to have the pleasure of visiting the different parts of Italy," a desire with which, in view of his own early experiences, he was probably fully in sympathy. The Wanderjahr took on additional significance when Allen announced that he was sending to accompany the members of his family Benjamin West, "a young ingenious Painter, of this city, who is desirous to improve himself in that Science, by visiting Florence and Rome."

The benediction of the city's richest citizen, the successful achievement of a European reputation by Benjamin West, and the widespread interest in all things Italian inspired by the collections of curiosities which Colonel Shippen sent home to Pennsylvania rendered the Grand Tour almost a necessity for fashionable young townsmen henceforth. In the sixties Samuel Powel and Dr. John Morgan were off to Italy to inspect the works of the great masters and to study the antiquities of Rome. Quaker Thomas Mifflin and Anglican William Bingham soon followed suit. To Rome also went Henry Bembridge for lessons in painting from Raphael Mengs. James Hamilton made three extended trips to England, and along with William Allen, Richard Peters, Dr. Thomas Bond and Benjamin Franklin was responsible for the introduction of many young colonials (among them Francis Hopkinson, the junior Allens, Morgan, Powel, and Benjamin Rush) to those who counted in the public and social life of both England and Scotland.

During these years it is clear that more young men from the Quaker city undertook a sojourn in the mother country than from any other part of the American colonies, and that the scions of Philadelphia wealth and gentility were almost alone among their New World contemporaries in making the Grand Tour. Travel across the Atlantic was very nearly continuous, with such items as the following, from the *Chronicle* of October 26, 1767, frequent in the press: "Last Friday, arrived the Ship Pennsylvania Packet, in nine weeks from London," bearing as passengers the Honorable James Hamilton, Mr. Samuel Powel and Mr. Francis Hopkinson. When John Adams first ventured out of his own bailiwick to attend the First Continental Congress in 1774, he was struck by the contrast between the want of art and address in his fellow Bostonians and the "freedom of ease and behaviour" of the "nobles of Pennsylvania." He concluded that the lack of the "exterior and superficial accomplishments of gentlemen" among his countrymen was owing to the "little intercourse we have with strangers, and . . . our inexperience in the world." By comparison, as the result of constant travel and association with social and political leaders in many lands, Philadelphians had acquired the easy and cosmopolitan manners of gentlemen anywhere.

Under stimulus from the new wealth and the wider ideas induced by travel, the country way of life developed from a means of escape from either the discomforts of the city or the pressure of affairs into something good and positive in itself. In the sixties the area around Philadelphia became the setting for more fine estates than could be found elsewhere on the continent. In keeping with this trend the simple family dwelling of earlier days gave way to the mansion house of the pre-Revolutionary country gentleman, acquiring dignity and architectural distinction, and reflecting to an extraordinary degree the tastes and interests of its owner. To their preoccupation with music and the theater and their patronage of education, literature and painting these gentlemen of leisure and experience now added an intelligent and very personal interest in the style and process of building. To this end they either became amateur architects themselves or, more usually, commissioned master builders to construct homes for them in accordance with their own ideas or what they had seen on their travels. Thus they sponsored not only the building of elaborate town houses wherein earlier Quaker simplicity gave way to the new elegance of the Georgian, but also the evolution of the now famous mansion-house architecture of suburban Philadelphia.

Despite the desire of Philadelphia gentlemen to approximate as closely as possible the country-house life of old England, the homes they built were less slavishly copied from English prototypes than might have been expected. One reason for this was the comparative absence of professional architects from the vicinity of Philadelphia until the latter years of the eighteenth century. The master craftsmen employed to plan and build these houses were practical, honest workmen, middle-class and usually Quaker in origin, who were untroubled by the academic temptation to divorce design from construction and whose natural good taste and inherent sense of proportion had not become overlaid by the Italianizing influences of a Grand Tour. Sensibly they made use of native stone and locally baked brick and of the woods indigenous to Pennsylvania—oak and white pine—while their English contemporaries were insisting upon marble and other exotic materials, and they saw eye to eye with their patrons in their steadfast refusal to sacrifice the convenience so much desired by this comfort-loving gentry to any rigid and academic definition of Palladian symmetry. The result of these influences was to give their work, however closely the design may have been inspired by a manor seen in Kent or a villa outside of Rome, the effect of a new and indigenous architectural form. Such a result was possible because the great age of Philadelphia building occurred before the decadence of the Georgian style had fully set in.

Into the country houses the carpenter-architects built sets of forms and proportions taken directly from books of orders and designs imported from England. But the result was no pallid copying. These buildings exhibited a creative strength derived from the inspiration of the individual craftsman. Far from any masters, and faced by new problems of materials, climate and function, the colonial carpenter-architect had to be willing to experiment, and his combinations and modifications of designs produced a living if eclectic architecture.

Virtually every suburban dwelling reveals some departure from the rules of the manual, some artistic gamble in either structure or decorative detail, that was often surprisingly successful. The entrance hall of Samuel Morris's Hope Lodge is lighted by unusually placed corner windows and its front door protected from the weather by an unsupported "Germantown hood." At Stenton, despite the textbook regularity of the façade, a generous porch is appended in the rear for use and comfort, and its outbuildings straggle casually down one side of the garden. Only occasionally, as at John McPherson's Mt. Pleasant, were logic and nature compressed into the limits of a magnificently regular and grandiose scheme. What these craftsmen, and their employers, principally sought was the marriage of the structure with both its natural and its human surroundings, the adaptation of the academic to its setting and its function.

The lifelong devotion of the Pennsylvania gentry to comfort and convenience may well have seemed barbaric to the Englishmen of these years who were building their houses to impress their neighbors and to exhibit to the county. In the New World houses were not only to be seen but to be lived in, and the Philadelphia builder had therefore to provide first for comfort and only secondarily for the spectacular architecture so much sought after in Britain. Embellishment, too, had to yield to convenience, so that even where interior decoration became most intricate, as with the elaborate carving and plasterwork at Belmont, it was in no way permitted to interfere with the comfortable living arrangements of the owner.

Accumulating wealth and sophistication did, of course, produce a few magnificent show places copied almost verbatim from the examples of the academics. Hence the earlier and simpler country style of Pennsylvania, as exemplified in Hope Lodge (1723), Stenton (1728) and Woodford (1756), remains more pleasing and seems more satisfactorily indigenous than the elaborately formal Mt. Pleasant (1761), for all its dignity and elegance, or the monumental if chilly Palladianism of William Hamilton's Woodlands (1770). In most cases, early or late, local master builders succeeded by their willingness to ignore the rules in favor of their own imaginations in achieving a noteworthy synthesis. They breathed life into the dead forms of the manuals by means of their active and vigorous concepts of function, structure and materials. To such men as these tradition was servant rather than master, and their buildings seem to exhibit the restlessness so characteristic of the society they were designed to house.

Among these master artisans the professional spirit had been a long time growing, and in both their individual and their corporate capacities they left a lasting mark upon the face of Philadelphia. In 1724, "for the purpose of obtaining instruction in the science of architecture," the house carpenters of the city had formed the Carpenter's Company of the City and County of Philadelphia, which by 1752 had become sufficiently strong to absorb a competing organization that had been pursuing a rival existence for a number of years. In 1769, however, a real schism occurred. Differences about the wisdom of increasing the fee for membership, as well as over methods employed for the measuring and valuing of carpenter's work, proved impossible to resolve, and dissenters withdrew to form the Friendship Carpenter's Company.

Both organizations accumulated good libraries of engineering and architectural books. By reference to these, and by discussion at their meetings, they elevated the professional status and encouraged the professional spirit of their members, many of whom developed from competent artisans into accomplished master craftsmen and builder-architects. These men were responsible for many of the public buildings of Philadelphia and, by the commissions they received from the gentry, for the mansion-house architecture of the city and surrounding countryside as well. At least three of them, all of whom happen to have been Quakers, achieved real distinction in their work.

Samuel Powel the elder, known as "the rich carpenter," became the first of Philadelphia's operative builders. At his death in 1756 he owned a large amount of city real estate, comprising over ninety houses and a large landed property. His construction operations caused him to be eulogized as a "Publick Benefactor to this City . . . being a Man remarkable for his Care in promoting Regularity in the Buildings thereof." He was also an example of how the exercise of honest craftsmanship might in eighteenth-century Philadelphia be made the road to wealth and social position, for it was the fortune he accumulated that enabled his grandson, also Samuel Powel, last Mayor of colonial Philadelphia, to live lavishly and travel widely without the necessity to work for a living.

Powel belonged to the earlier generation of Philadelphia capitalists, and his period of activity preceded that of any large-scale public building in the city. But the working years of his junior, Samuel Rhoads, spanned the entire pre-Revolutionary period and touched the public architecture of Philadelphia at many points. Rhoads, also a Quaker, practiced as builder, architect and engineer, and had a well-rounded interest especially in the technical aspects of his profession, being numbered among the members of the original American Philosophical Society and the friends of Benjamin Franklin.

As one of the managers for the Pennsylvania Hospital Rhoads drew up the ingenious and monumental design for its buildings in 1755. His plan, which made use not only of his own engineering and artistic experience but also of the advice of doctors concerning the requirements of a hospital, called for the erection of two lateral wings joined by a larger central building, each unit to be architecturally symmetrical and functionally complete in itself, and the three, when completed, to form an harmonious whole. Thus, according to the plan which permitted the erection of the building a third at a time, only the east wing was constructed in 1755. The whole design, as recorded in James Claypoole's "Perspective View," was on a larger scale than anything hitherto attempted in the colonies, and required until well after the Revolution to bring to final completion.

Rhoads also served as a manager of the new Alms House in 1766-67, and may well have had an active part in the planning of that structure. Similarities in its design with the general scheme for the Pennsylvania Hospital tend to confirm this, while certain details, such as the arched colonnades which formed a covered walk, suggest some European travel on the part of the architect. Rhoads was vice-president of the American Philosophical Society, experimented with several kinds of fireproof roofing for the possible benefit of his city, and acted from time to time as consulting engineer for the province. While Mayor of Philadelphia in 1775 he served as architect on the committee for erecting a district Court House and City Hall adjacent to the State House.

It was however the Scottish Quaker, Robert Smith of Glasgow, who became most eminent in his profession and shared with the amateur Peter Harrison of Newport the distinction of evolving a style of architecture in many respects definitely indigenous to the colonies. In him the unornamented functionalism apparent in the public buildings of Samuel Rhoads reached its complete development. Especially was he responsible for the first, and probably the most valid, American style of college building.

Upon recommendation of Dr. William Shippen, Sr., Smith received the commission to design Nassau Hall and the president's house for the College of New Jersey at Princeton, after which, in 1761, he prepared plans for the "New College" building at Philadelphia. Success with these educational structures apparently attracted the attention of the Reverend Morgan Edwards, who may have consulted him concerning the building problems of the new College of Rhode Island. Whether or not Smith actually designed the "college edifice" in Providence, he was in correspondence with its builders, and Nassau Hall at Princeton clearly furnished the pattern both for the Rhode Island structure and for Dartmouth

Hall at Hanover. Hence for four out of the nine collegiate institutions in the American colonies Robert Smith furnished, if not the actual plans, at least the style of the building.

Smith also designed for other than academic purposes, and the public architecture of Philadelphia owed much to his talents in the years prior to the Revolution. He served as master carpenter on the Alms House job in 1766-67, so that, in view of the imperfect separation of functions between builder and architect, he as well as Samuel Rhoads may have contributed something to its design. He both planned and superintended the building of Carpenter's Hall, completed in 1771, and in 1773 he designed the Walnut Street Prison, finest structure of its kind in colonial America. Despite the sectarian bitterness which flourished in the city, three denominations seem to have chosen Robert Smith to plan their churches. Possibly with the aid of Dr. John Kearsley, accomplished amateur who had shared in the designing of Christ Church, he produced his masterpiece in St. Peter's in 1758. In 1761 he was the architect of Old Pine Presbyterian Church, and most authorities agree he also designed the fine edifice of the Zion Lutheran Congregation. In 1771 he was entrusted with rebuilding the steeple of Christ Church.

When Smith turned to the construction of domestic dwellings he shared the weakness of all builders. Franklin, writing from London in 1765, was considerably annoyed that his new house had not been completed earlier and his Deborah able to move in. "The Architect of Philadelphia," as Smith came to be known, enjoyed to the full the pleasant life of those who became his patrons, and managed to combine in his one person the character of artist, scholar and bon vivant. For himself he built a fine house on Lombard Street, which sheltered his excellent library of architectural books, and he maintained in addition a country place which was the scene of frequent convivial meetings with Jacob Hiltzheimer and his Jockey Club associates. Smith even designed a wooden bridge with stone piers to be thrown across the Schuylkill, which would have rendered his estate and those of other gentlemen on the west bank much more accessible, and which only its great cost seems to have deterred the Assembly from building.

As an important member of the American Philosophical Society Smith had his serious and scholarly side, and despite social and financial success he never drifted far from his associates of the Carpenter's Company. Though his patronage came largely from the gentry, he himself in the stirring events of the seventies remained loyal to the "Mechanicks." His politics, like his architecture, were native. Plain, overly severe, and tending to repetition as his buildings may have been, yet with their simple lines, dignified proportions and ample fenestration they were admirably adapted to the public purposes for which they were designed. His treatment of the Georgian style kept continually in mind the logic, function and convenience of the structure to be built, and never surrendered to the elaborateness and overornamentation that weakened the latter stages of that style in England. Robert Smith made a considerable artistic contribution to his city and bequeathed to America its most satisfactory style of college architecure.

Changing tastes and the wealth to gratify them invaded Philadelphia houses in these years, and the interior decoration of plutocratic homes further distinguished their owners' way of life from that of the growing middle and artisan classes. Though even near the end of the period Jacob Duché could still observe that Philadelphia houses remained in general "plain, but not elegant, for the most part built upon the same plan, a few excepted," he was forced to add that they were "furnished with some taste, and neatly decorated within." That characteristic of the Philadelphia gentry persisted which had caused its earlier Quaker representatives, while clinging to their simplicity of dress, to invest considerable fortunes in fine and heavy plate, so that behind traditionally plain façades the interiors of both town and country houses gave increasing evidence of accumulating wealth, the vagaries of fashionable taste, and the influence of European travel.

Gradually the wainscoting, carved or paneled and made from

fine woods, that had constituted the principal interior finish of earlier houses gave way before the use of other and often flimsier materials, as enthusiastic young men, full of new ideas of decoration, returned home from the experiences of their Grand Tour. As early as 1763 Robert Smith had in his employ one James Clow, "Stucco-worker," who made "ornaments for ceilings, consisting of foliage and festoons of fruits and flowers." Peter Biggs, "late Mason to the Earl of Essex," made "all sorts of Marble Chimneys and Bath Stoves, very beautiful and convenient for burning coal," while John Webster equipped houses with "the best and newest invented Venetian Sun Blinds . . . stained any colour." Imported scenic wallpapers became so popular that by 1769 Plunkett Fleeson was advertising Philadelphia-made "American Paper Hangings" equal to any brought in from England, as well as "Paper Mache, or raised paper mouldings for hangings, in imitation of carving."

Stuccowork was used in conjunction with wood-carving for the interiors of John McPherson's show place, Mt. Pleasant, while at Belmont, mansion of the Peters family, the parlor boasts an elaborate plaster ceiling consisting of a design of musical instruments in high relief which must surely have been the work of an accomplished artist in the medium. All in all, ample demand soon existed for the skills of such London trained architects as William Williams, who in 1773 advertised to work in the "new, bold, light and elegant taste, which has lately been introduced by the great architect [Adam] of the Adelphia Buildings . . . and which is now universally practised." While elegant taste was not necessarily good taste, practical as well as fashionable considerations explained the preference for stucco over paneling in its lower cost and the belief that it offered greater resistance to fire. Writing in 1771 to Samuel Rhoads concerning the problem of fire protection for the city, Franklin remarked, "I am glad to hear that you have good Workmen in the Stucco Way, and that it is likely to take the place of Wainscot." Aesthetic judgments, however, were never the forte of that philosopher.

A similar transition in taste from simple beauty of line to elabo-

rate elegance of decoration occurred in the furnishings which filled
the homes of the merchant gentry. The outfit of Ann Allen at the
time of her marriage to John Penn in 1766, provided by her Chief
Justice father on a scale befitting the social and financial status of
both families, illustrates this new elegance. Ann Allen had an interest in houses and their decoration, both for herself and for her
friends, that would in a later day have enabled her to set up in
business and make a comfortable income, and the furnishings
selected for her own use comprised the finest that taste or fashion
could demand. Her use of "Elegant cotton" and "India Chintz" for
hangings and the appearance of the very newest of green-and-white
worsted curtains in her parlor shows her completely abreast of
contemporary fashion; only in her formal dining room were the
windows hung with the traditional damask. Her furniture, nearly
all in the Chippendale style, was in "the newest and most elegant
taste," and included two settees, twelve chairs and a fire screen in
"burnished gold."

The bulk of this furniture was probably of local manufacture.
With the continuous building of country places, some far out "Paoli
way, others up Schuylkill Banks," in addition to the houses most
of the same people maintained in town, large numbers of cabinetmakers were finding ample market and encouragement for their
work. Also these craftsmen became to some extent beneficiaries of
the nonimportation movement of the sixties which impelled the
gentry, in order to avoid charges of extravagance, subservience to
the ministry and lack of patriotism, to patronize local workmen,
many of whom were of course ringleaders in the opposition by
"Mechanicks" and others to regulation by the mother country. Samuel Morris wrote to his nephew, Samuel Powel, in 1765, warning
him against bringing home too much European furniture. "I have
heard the joiners here object this against Dr. Morgan and others
who have brought their furniture with them." However, a tactful
pampering of local prejudice was not entirely without compensation, for Morris hastens to add that "Household goods may be had
here as cheap and as well made from English patterns."

The skill of the Philadelphia cabinetmakers from 1740 to the Revolution surpassed that of any others on the continent, save possibly the Goddards and Townsends of Newport. Unlike the architects and the painters, however, the cabinetmakers largely failed to develop a style of their own, and in the main devoted their remarkable craftsmanship to the production of imitations or elaborations of the work of the current London favorites, Chippendale and Hepplewhite. From Chippendale's *Director,* a copy of which was owned by the Library Company as early as 1762, and from the manuals of Mainwaring and Langley, they took designs which they interpreted liberally and sought to naturalize to the uses of Philadelphia. In this they enjoyed rather less success than the architects who employed the same technique. Rather, in attaining "the greatest degree of elaboration and ornamentation in American furniture," they seem to have weakened the original design, overlaying and obscuring it with a profusion of truly beautiful wood-carving. Of their workmanship no criticism need be made, and perhaps in matters of design they had to surrender too much to the whims of their customers.

The elaborate Chippendale pieces of William Savery, the simpler, more faithful reproductions of Thomas Tufft, the chests by Jonathan Gostelowe with their ornate hardware, and the masterpieces in mahogany by James Gillingham and Benjamin Randolph brought high prices in the local market, rendering their creators financially secure and socially important. These master craftsmen held local political offices, joined library companies and fire societies, and in general participated in the active life of the growing city. They took great pride in their work, and along with other artisans many of them chose the radical side when the time of political division arrived. Randolph was an active patriot, and Gostelowe served first as commissary officer and later as major of the artillery in the Continental Army.

Like their fellow artists the portrait painters, the cabinetmakers assumed no self-conscious airs about the special dignity of their profession. All of them, from Benjamin Randolph down, made coffins, repaired furniture, recaned old chairs, and did all sorts of odd jobs. Thomas Tufft, when making a wedding outfit like that of Deborah Norris of Fairhill, supplied not only highboys and card tables, but kitchen furniture, ironing board and rolling pin as well (and received better prices for such small services than his famous competitor, William Savery), while Randolph, whose exquisite pieces formed a fitting background for many of Charles Willson Peale's portraits of Philadelphia worthies, was also responsible for the sash for the new Alms House.

Men of wealth likewise furnished patronage for local silversmiths, especially as in the days before the existence of banking facilities the most usual method of conserving money free from fluctuations in its value was to put it into plate. Thus the silversmiths occupied a position socially superior to that of other skilled artisans; they were regarded as artists and bankers, never as mere mechanics. The daybook of a Quaker silversmith, kept from 1745 to 1748 probably by Joseph Richardson, reads like a social directory of contemporary Philadelphia. Powels, Pembertons, Willings, Mifflins, Norrises, Callenders, Duchés, Morgans and Allens, among others, brought him their precious metals for conversion into plate.

Wealthy Quakers admired fine workmanship, but demanded simplicity of design. This called for real skill in the art of silver-smithing, since incidental decoration, however intricate, could not be depended upon to mask any slight deviation from purity of line and fineness of balance. In this work of simple perfection Richard-son and his sons came to excel. Products from the workshop of the Anglican Philip Syng, such as the inkstand he created in 1752 for the Pennsylvania State House, were more elaborate and ornate, but no less expert in execution.

Philadelphia's leading silversmiths amassed considerable wealth, and became themselves prominent as patrons in the city's religious and civic life. Richardson took active part in the founding of the Pennsylvania Hospital, and helped in 1756 to organize the Friendly Association, for which he made medals and ornaments for presenta-tion to the Indians. David Hall was secretary of the fashionable

Heart-in-Hand Fire Company. Philip Syng, a member of Franklin's Junto and coworker with him in his electrical experiments, served as junior warden of the Masons and on the vestry of Christ Church, was one of the original trustees of the College, and became first treasurer of the united American Philosophical Society in 1769.

The gentler, more gracious living of the sixties and seventies owed much to the importation of foreign influences, or, as a less sympathetic contemporary described it, to "the evil Itch of over-valuing Foreign parts." The newer homes of the gentry in both town and country, their interior embellishments and the life they housed, all bore witness to the tendency to abandon the sincere if sometimes primitive work of native inspiration in favor of the baroque taste of eighteenth-century Europe. The popularity of European travel enormously facilitated this conquest of the rich by imported fashions, but the nature of that conquest was considerably affected by the personalities and interests of the returning graduates of the Grand Tour, who were its principal instruments.

Typical and best of Philadelphia's cosmopolitan gentry was young Samuel Powel, third of the name, inheritor of one of the city's largest fortunes and its last Mayor under the British allegiance. In him the benefits of inherited wealth, superior education and ample leisure, the experiences of extended travel and the effects of changing tastes produced a rounded, urbane and cultivated citizen. No one better than he illustrated the process, at once broadening and softening, of refinement and sophistication, and the shifts in temperament and interests, which members of his class had undergone since the days when William Allen was a young man. Because he was only one, though perhaps the most prominent, among this younger generation of aristocrats, his career, in many respects remarkable for a colonial, deserves some passing attention.

What was probably the largest Quaker fortune in Pennsylvania had been amassed by Samuel Powel, "the great builder," and his son of the same name. At the latter's death in 1759 possession of more than ninety city houses and a fine country estate near Gloucester, New Jersey, passed to the third Samuel, then a student at the College. Upon graduation from that institution with its second class in 1760, this youth, so well endowed with property, education and leisure, found ready welcome among a group, made up principally of young Quakers, who called themselves the Society Meeting Weekly in the City of Philadelphia for Their Mutual Improvement in Useful Knowledge. Powel, however, desired more of improvement than his native city seemed to afford, and before the year was out he sailed for England to begin a quest for European culture and experience that was to last for seven years. In London he slipped easily into the pleasant life there awaiting the gently bred young colonial with ample funds. Among his compatriots temporarily established in the mother capital he found William Logan, the younger William Shippen, and especially his friend John Morgan, who had come abroad for medical study.

Although he reported from London that "All our Americans are jolly," Powel remained mindful of the responsibilities laid upon him by the possession of great wealth. He was already bearing a portion of the expenses of Benjamin West at Rome, and when Provost Smith arrived in 1762 to collect funds for the College, Powel with Morgan, his fellow alumnus, entered heartily into the project. In February, 1763, while in Scotland soliciting for the College, both young men were presented with the freedom of the city of Stirling. Later in the same year Powel, along with Smith and John Inglis, a trustee, received an audience with the King. "His Majesty kindly asked me some questions about our college and the success of our collection," reported the Provost, "and also received Mr. Inglis and Mr. Powel very graciously. I had almost got the latter dubbed a Knight, but we thought it would be idle, and considered a design to separate him from his old friends the Quakers of Philadelphia." Morgan, himself an Anglican, was at work on his friend's religious affiliations, and the Provost was content to wait.

When West arrived from Italy in September "with a great character as a Painter," Powel procured him the introduction to the Penns which launched the "American Raphael" on his notable career. West's portrait of Powel, probably made at this time, shows an elegant young Quaker in red coat and ruffles, holding in one hand the plans of what was soon to become Philadelphia's finest town house. "Indeed, your house is so finely situated that it looks like the habitation of a Turkish Bashaw," George Roberts wrote him from the spot ". . . the front wall being very high from the street . . . and the enclosure, the parade of a Seraglio,—'tis the noblest spot in the city—don't you wish to see it?" But Roberts sent also an account of the Paxton riots, and Powel replied that he and Dr. Morgan had been "lolling in the lap of ease and revelling in scenes of another nature. Italia, muse of the softer arts, has detained us from mixing with the turbulent throng."

In 1763 Powel had joined Dr. Morgan in Paris for a year's Grand Tour of the Continent. Moving south through France, they called at Verney, where Voltaire received them on the steps before his house and introduced them to his guests with impressive rhetoric: "Behold, two amiable young men, lovers of truth and enquirers into nature. They are not satisfied with mere appearances, they love investigation and truth and despise superstition." From this triumph they passed on to Turin, where they were presented to the Royal Family of Sardinia and received permission from its head to view the fortifications. At Leghorn they joined the suite of the Duke of York, with whom they journeyed to Florence and Rome. Here they experienced the kindness of the Abbé Grant, Judge Allen's friend Sir Horace Mann, and most of the English gentry resident in Italy. Their obvious eligibility secured them invitations to numerous gay balls and parties and to share many a box at the opera.

Modern Italy, to the eager-eyed young Philadelphians, seemed in many respects inferior to what they had known at home, but they agreed that "as to the grandeur of the ancients, from what we can see of their remains, it is most extraordinary. Arts with them seem to have been in a perfection which . . . could not be imagined. Their palaces, temples, aqueducts, baths, theatres, amphitheatres, monuments, statues, sculptures, were most amazing. The soul is struck at the review, and the ideas expand." From Milan and Venice to Naples and Rome they viewed Italian art with thoroughness, faithfully recording their observations in journals. Soon they were setting themselves up as connoisseurs. The sculptures at Loretto they found admirable, but the paintings "not remarkable," and one of them said to be by Raphael they were convinced was merely the work of a student. They were charmed by the "Liberality and Modesty" of Guido Reni, and while the Laocoön was human, the Apollo Belvedere, far from resembling a Mohawk warrior, they pronounced "divine."

At Rome the illness of the lovely Angelica Kaufmann and the already considerable medical reputation of Dr. Morgan combined to bring about a meeting and a friendship based on mutual admiration. Here also they joined Messrs. Apthorp and Palmer in a "Course of Antiquities" under the direction of James Byers, who had made a small fortune by instructing wealthy Englishmen in classical archaeology. The avid students assiduously took notes, copied inscriptions, and carefully noted the data for computing the proper size of columns. Through the good offices, no doubt, of Byers and the Abbé Grant, both Powel and Morgan became members of an organization of English and Italian cognoscenti, the Arcadian Society of Belles Lettres of Rome.

From this profusion of delightful paganism they came at last to an audience with the Pope, who, wrote Powel, "condescended to converse familiarly with us." The varied experiences of five years in foreign lands, coupled with Morgan's persuasions, gradually broke down Powel's wavering Quakerism. In 1765, when the companions had got back to England loaded with the artistic and intellectual booty of their travels, Morgan wrote home to the Reverend Richard Peters that upon his return to his native city his friend would seek baptism in the Church of England.

In the autumn of 1767 Samuel Powel returned to Philadelphia, perhaps in order to be present at the marriage of his sister Sally to Joseph Potts, which took place in January of the next year. Miss Sally Powel, reported Goddard of the *Chronicle,* was a young woman whose virtue and good sense reflected more luster on her

character than "the Fortune of 20,000 £ which she actually pos-
sesses," a summary of her qualities which leaves the reader wonder-
ing if she was very homely. The eager young Quaker who had
left Philadelphia seven years before graced the occasion with the
polish born of his European experiences; how far he had traveled
was soon demonstrated when shortly he was baptized by the city's
most fashionable prelate and became a communicant of St. Peter's
Church.

He now set himself up in the splendid town house which had
been long awaiting him on Third Street, and which he proceeded
to fill with the plunder of his foreign journeys—fine imported furniture brought home despite his uncle's warnings, original canvasses
and careful copies of old masters, marbles, statuary, and a profusion
of objets d'art—while into its extensive formal gardens went costly
Italian statuary and other exotic furnishings. Magnificence and
delicacy combined in the mansion's lovely music room; concerts
and audiences worthy of it must have been elegant indeed. To this
house in August, 1769, Samuel Powel brought the former Miss
Elizabeth Willing as his bride.

Despite long expatriation and the foreign tastes acquired during
his travels, Powel, once back in his native city, quickly adjusted
himself to the life of the provincial capital. Surrounded by old
friends and new, he easily followed their example in his willing
assumption of the civic responsibilities his wealth entailed and his
acceptance of work of a "social contexture." Immediately on changing his denominational allegiance he volunteered his services as a
trustee for administering the Episcopal minister's fund. Along with
Charles Thomson and Dr. Morgan he infused new life into the
old improvement society, which in 1768 became the American Society held at Philadelphia for Promoting Useful Knowledge. Of
this reorganized body he was vice-president when union with its
rival produced the American Philosophical Society. His interest in
the arts, fostered by his European experiences, he continued in the
varied roles of connoisseur, patron and practitioner. His collection
of paintings and reproductions testified to his knowledge and ap-

preciation, and he was himself an accomplished silhouettist. His important patronage assisted Matthew Pratt, returning from London in 1768, to establish himself as a portraitist in Philadelphia. He was a member of the Hand-in-Hand, by 1770 less a fire society than a fashionable gentleman's club, and in 1773 he became a trustee of the College.

Although "never politically inclined," Powel was chosen to the Common Council of Philadelphia in 1770. Four years later he served his city as alderman and in 1775 became its last Mayor under its colonial status. He continued in office under the new government, for unlike William Allen, whose career his so much resembles, he adhered to the patriot cause. Despite his thorough inoculation with foreign ideas and an alien culture, and despite his conversion to the religion of fashion and officialdom, the Quaker strain remained strong in Samuel Powel. In the end his native loyalties proved sufficient to overcome his "London tricks and St. James customs," and he was throughout a generous participant in the duties of public life.

The real triumph of the Grand Tour appeared in the pursuit by Philadelphia socialites of two extremely sophisticated hobbies—the acquisition of galleries filled with collections of paintings and antiquities, and the rage for elaborate formal gardening. Both were activities open only to men of wealth, and both were in some measure dependent upon foreign inspiration and influences.

Yet the irony of these developments lay in the scarcely noted fact that in the very years when cultivated and traveled Philadelphians were assiduously emulating the Continental tastes and fashions indulged by English gentlemen, the American colonies of England were producing materials for the fashions of the future. Already England was depending upon the brush of Benjamin West, Pennsylvania-born painter, to establish its artistic independence of the traditions of the Continent and its parity with its artistic output, while the great importations of American shrubs and shade trees, many of them supplied by John Bartram of Kingsessing, were effecting a revolution in English gardening, preparing the way for the transformation of the Dutch formal garden into the studied irregularity of the age of Shenstone and Horace Walpole. The cultural influences of their native land upon the mother country passed quite unnoticed by Anglophile colonials.

The tastes which led Powel to collect evidences of his cultural and artistic experiences abroad were shared by most of his traveling and many of his stay-at-home contemporaries. In earlier years the art of painting had been valued chiefly for purposes of record, and family portraits by native or visiting limners to adorn the walls of town or country houses had fulfilled the artistic interests and requirements of their owners. But as their travels began to afford Philadelphians a larger view of the great arts of modern France and ancient Italy, such simple satisfactions no longer sufficed. In contemplation of the relics of the ancient world or of the works of Raphael and Titian young men forgot their Protestant prejudices and opened their minds to both the pagan and the Catholic. Like the English gentlemen they encountered on their travels, they too fell easy victims to the collector's disease. Such souvenirs as were transportable they must have for their homes—if not in the original, then in the finest of copies their money could procure.

The first notable art collection in Pennsylvania was that assembled by James Hamilton for his estate at Bush Hill. It began in the forties with the acquisition of a "St. Ignatius" by Murillo, purchased at the sale of a captured Spanish prize; even privateering, it seems, had its cultural aspects in the eighteenth century. Hamilton added to his treasures in the course of his frequent journeys abroad. In 1745 he acquired two fine historical tableaux by Richard of Paris, one representing "The Atonement" and the other, the "Elevation of Proserpine," and by 1763 he had bought, in the words of Du Simitière, *"quelques bonnes peintures copiées par un nommé West,"* among them Titian's "Venus" *("toute nue!")* and Annibale Caracci's "Venus Lamenting over the Body of Adonis."

Later buyers of art in Philadelphia owed much to the industry of Benjamin West. Many of his copies went into the collection of

Judge Allen in payment for earlier financial assistance. Thus Allen too owned the Titian "Venus," as well as Correggio's "Holy Family" "as large as life," Guido Reni's "Herod and John the Baptist," Guercino's "St. Peter and St. Paul," a fine Giorgione, and several other copies from Italian masters. To Colonel Joseph Shippen, confident critic of the arts, West sent his copy of Raphael Mengs' "Holy Family," and the fine collection of paintings placed by William Hamilton in his magnificent country seat, The Woodlands, in 1774, was in part selected by the former Pennsylvanian. Allen's son-in-law, John Penn, brought together at his new mansion, Lansdowne, a "Collection of Paintings, which is very great and elegant," and William Peters furnished the large hall at Belmont with paintings and statues in bronze.

These collections their owners generously opened to local painters, to gentlemen and their families, and to such properly introduced visitors as John Singleton Copley and his half-brother, Henry Pelham. Parties of young Quakers were among the most frequent visitors to Bush Hill. In 1759 Francis Rawle, Elizabeth Sandwith, and some half-dozen of their friends "view'd the Paintings," and on another occasion Hannah Callender's party admired the collection, "particularly a picture of St. Ignatius at his devotions, exceedingly well done." It speaks much for the broadening effects of cosmopolitan influences and foreign travel upon the cultural life of pre-Revolutionary Philadelphia that a young Quakeress of twenty could voice appreciative criticism of a piece of Roman Catholic art seen in the home of an Anglican gentleman.

Foremost among Philadelphia collectors was Dr. John Morgan, who while in Italy had employed one Companions to make his copies. Among works he thus obtained were Albani's "Bacchus and Cupid," a "Judith with the Head of Holophernes," a Venetian female mask, a "Venus, Cupid and Nymph," and a "Piping Boy." He purchased more than fifty cartoons and drawings, including "a rare Vandyke," Veronese's "Christ and the Publicans," Titian's "Europa and the Bull," Domenichino's "St. Jerome," Michelangelo's "Day of Judgment," and two cartoons by Raphael. His plates included the plan of a country house, a section of a church, two rural scenes, a "Prospective of Trevi," and a temple design by Mansart, while among his library of art volumes he possessed Vignola on architecture and a manuscript treatise on painting by Paulino.

Back in the colonies, Dr. Morgan achieved the reputation of "a great Lover of and a judge of Painting." John Adams, dining with the "ingenious physician" in October, 1774, greatly admired the intricacy of "some curious paintings upon silk which he had brought from Italy." Two months later Henry Pelham confessed himself even more impressed by the "clever Coppys" of old masters in Morgan's collection, and so pleased with his "Original Portrait of Angelica [Kaufmann] painted by her self" that he asked to take a miniature of it. Writing to Copley, then in Italy, he urged his half-brother to keep up his correspondence with the doctor, "as he is a man of consequence in the Literary World." Dr. Morgan, Thomas Mifflin, William Allen and James Hamilton were not only patrons and buyers of art but scholars and connoisseurs as well. Pelham remembered as the highlight of his visit to the art center of colonial America the "three hours very entertaining and instructive Conversation on painting and the Arts" he enjoyed with Governor Hamilton and Judge Allen, "who had been in Rome."

Another item of fashionable baggage brought home by Samuel Powel and his returning countrymen was the rage for formal gardening in the Continental manner, which was in these years sweeping through the big estates of France and England. The imported seed fell on good fertile native soil, for Philadelphia had early become a city of gardens.

From the time of the Founder patches of vegetables and fruit trees in the rear of the houses had been a feature of the town, and as people moved out into the country the cultivation of orchards and vegetable gardens developed on a considerable scale. The pride and joy of William Allen in his "Colly Flowers" was characteristic of his horticulturally-minded contemporaries. When Roxbury, at the Falls of the Schuylkill, was placed on the market, its owner made much of its orchard of 1,500 grafted fruit trees "of as curious a collection as perhaps in America," among them apples, peaches, pears, plums, cherries, apricots, nectarines, figs, almonds, English walnuts and "Illinois nuts"; also, its strawberry and asparagus beds, raspberry, currant and gooseberry bushes, and "a fine parcel of grape vines and Espalier fruit." At Peel Hall William Dowell devoted more than an acre to asparagus beds "well manured." Hannah Callender described her father's "Richmond Seat" as "a little romantic rural scene," its fences covered with honeysuckle, and the kitchen and flower gardens separated from one another by low hedges.

In time the enthusiasm of returning cosmopolites infected this pleasant art, and in the effort to emulate things seen abroad gardening in both town and country became elaborated and formalized, the result to be enjoyed mainly by the eye, or by the eye of one's neighbors, and most of the backbreaking work turned over to a professional gardener. It was not even necessary to have traveled to know what was going on in the great estates of the Old World. The taking of "prospective views" of gentlemen's seats began in England about 1725, and the results were eagerly purchased as soon as they became available in Philadelphia, where they soon constituted a large part of the stocks of print shops. As early as 1749 citizens were flocking to performances of "the Philosophical Optical Machine" which showed representations of St. James' Park, Vauxhall Gardens and Walks, and famous country estates of old England, and whose operator declared it offered the safest, cheapest and easiest way of traveling, with all the satisfactions and none of the fatigues or hazards of a tour.

Thus by actual or vicarious experience Philadelphians learned of the splendors of formal horticulture, which they sought to reproduce with all embellishments. So successful were they that by 1768 Kennedy's Print Shop on Second Street was carrying "American Views of elegant gardens and Landscapes," and Pierre du Simitière and Charles Willson Peale were engaged in making views and perspectives, not only of public buildings, but of near-by country estates.

Men of taste and fortune made a cult of formal gardening in these years. Thomas Mifflin surrounded Fort Hill, his "grand, spacious and elegant house" just above the Falls of the Schuylkill, with such extensive gardens that in 1773 he had to build a special windmill to pump sufficient water for them. A strong interest in the art of landscaping led Captain Charles Cruikshank, a wealthy Scot, to purchase Clifton Hall on the west bank of the river in 1761 and proceed to lay out the grounds in the "newest taste." The garden was set on three terraced levels, its walks lined with box; the Captain's own hothouse supplied it with plants, and in a special private garden he erected his bath. The gardens at Belmont were planned with the mansion's great hall as a pivot. Hannah Callender's description of them in 1762 reads like a page from an English garden manual.

The doors of the house . . . admit a prospect of the length of the garden over a broad gravel walk to a large handsome summer house on a green. From the windows a vista is terminated by an obelisk. On the right you enter a labyrinth of hedge of low cedar and spruce. In the middle stands a statue of Apollo. In the garden are statues of Diana, Fame and Mercury with urns. We left the garden for a wood cut into vistas. In the midst is a Chinese temple for a summer house. One avenue gives a fine prospect of the City. With a spy glass you discern the houses and hospital distinctly. Another avenue looks to the obelisk.

Classical statuary, Chinese temples, labyrinths, obelisks, avenues and vistas—all the conventions of English formal gardening were to be found at Belmont.

Across the river was Fairhill, the Norris estate, unquestionably one of the show places of colonial America. Begun in the old-fashioned style with emphasis on orchards, lawns, and avenues of willows, it passed by inheritance to John Dickinson in 1770 and under him came to embody all the current fads of landscape gardening. In 1773, though he had visited most of the great plantations of Virginia and the Carolinas, Josiah Quincy considered Fairhill superior to anything he had ever seen. He concluded that, considering "the antique look of his house, his gardens, green-house, bathing-house, grotto, study, fish-pond, fields, meadows, vista, through which is a distant prospect of Delaware River, his paintings, antiquities, improvements, etc., in short his whole life," John Dickinson ought to be the happiest of men.

Nearer the city than most lay the great estates of Governor Hamilton and the Proprietors. Bush Hill, located north of Vine between the present Twelfth and Nineteenth streets, and encompassing about one hundred and fifty acres, had been laid out by Speaker Andrew Hamilton in 1740 and passed by inheritance to his bachelor son James, the Governor. At one end of a long avenue of tall shade trees stood the mansion house with its "very splendid and grand apartments magnificently decorated and adorned with curious paintings, hangings and statuary, and marble tablets." At the other lay the formal gardens, their parterres and flower beds intersected by graveled walks, their alleys bordered with clipped hedges of boxwood. Though familiar with the beautiful gardens of Newport estates, those of the Malbones, Redwoods and others, Ezra Stiles when he came to Bush Hill in 1754 admired its "very elegant garden in which are seven statues in fine Italian marble curiously wrought." Another visitor, Miss Alexander of New York, was most impressed by the "fishing house" which stood "romantically in a wood over the Schuylkill on a projecting rock."

The Proprietor's estate of Springettsbury, which lay half a mile to the west and bordered on the Schuylkill, was less extensive, but its gardens, under the management of James Alexander, were "laid out with more judgment," and its small brick house enjoyed a two-mile-long vista. The estate boasted "a pretty pleasure garden," graveled walks ornamented with a variety of evergreens and shrubs, spruce hedges cut into various figures, "a small wilderness," several groves, and "a neat little Park, tho' . . . there are no Deer in it." The whole formed in the opinion of Stiles, who believed with John Evelyn that uniformity glutted the eye and choked delight, "the most agreeable variety, and even regular confusion and disorder." To Daniel Fisher of Virginia what "surpassed everything of the kind I had seen in America was a pretty bricked Green House, out of which was disposed very properly in the Pleasure Garden a good many Orange, Lemon, and Citron Trees in great perfection loaded with abundance of Fruit." Stiles also observed some lime trees. Poor Alexander suffered from the rabble who "Pilfer'd" from his exotic trees, seldom leaving enough of their fruit to ripen so that he could make up his hoped-for annual shipment to the Penns in London of three dozen of each variety.

While most of these beautiful gardens existed only for the enjoyment of owners and their friends, Bush Hill and Springettsbury were open to visitors, and at either place there might frequently be found "a large company, much at their ease, very sociable." Other estates, and their mansion houses, were sometimes opened to the gentry, and such young people as Hannah Callender visited place after place, much as Jane Austen's heroines toured the seats of rural England.

For townsmen who did not wish to go far afield there were Israel Pemberton's gardens, laid out in pleasing uniformity, "with walks and alleys nodding to their brothers, and decorated with a number of evergreens, carefully clipped into pyramidal and conical forms." Here Elizabeth Drinker often joined her Quaker acquaintances for a walk at sunset, and even the blasé young Graydon admitted "the amenity of the view usually detained me a few minutes." Just south of the city "Commons" on Tenth Street in 1773 Daniel Duchemine took over George Emlen's estate, Lebanon, which he converted into a teahouse for visitors to the Hospital and Alms House. Here those of humbler circumstances, not able to visit gentlemen's seats, had opportunity to enjoy the gardens. "At six with Miss Ruth Webster, Her Sister Althee, and Betsy and Polly Armitage," wrote Philip Fithian in April, 1774, "I walked to a lovely Garden near the Hospital call'd Lebanon, drank some Mead and had a most agreeable Ramble."

"The country round this [city]," observed the Scottish traveler Patrick M'Robert in 1775, "is very pleasant and agreeable, finely interspersed with genteel country seats, fields and orchards, for several miles around, and along both the rivers for a good many miles." Though only some dozen of these estates were as elaborately laid out as those just described, less pretentious places were numbered in the hundreds. The care demanded by these glorified acres gave rise to a new and profitable profession. James Alexander was the first professional gardener of whom there is any record, and the results of his labors at Springettsbury surpassed anything in the neighborhood with the possible exception of Fairhill. As the period advanced newspapers carried frequent advertisements by Scots gardeners seeking positions, or by gentlemen desiring their services. In 1766 John McPherson of Mt. Pleasant, "the most elegant seat in Pennsylvania," advertised for a head gardener who could be well recommended for honesty, sobriety and industry, unmarried, and "of proper Resolution, Direction and humanity to command several other servants under him."

For many years Christian Lehman maintained a twenty-acre orchard and large seed garden in Germantown. From his nurseries in 1766 he supplied gentlemen's gardens with "Most Sorts of curious Fruit trees . . . English double Hyacinths, Tulips, and other flowering Roots, with most sorts of flowering Shrubs and a Number of young Catalpar Trees," and urged his patrons to call for their "flower Roots" before the middle of October. So intensively did Philadelphians pursue their horticultural avocation that Bradford's *Journal* of March 15, 1770, contained a special advertisement of books on "Farming and Gardening," and J. Russell, the Boston auctioneer, announced in its issue of July 26 his vendue of a choice lot of one hundred orange and lemon trees and "a few" fig and cork trees "in excellent order." For those who could not like Governor Hamilton decorate their homes and gardens with statuary of Italian marble, Bartholomew and Lucas Florin, Swiss craftsmen, made plaster of Paris figures, in "full stature" or busts, "likewise Birds and many other Sorts of Ornaments . . . for ornamenting Garden Walks."

Out of the country way of life came the development of sporting activities and other forms of outdoor recreation, which like country living itself followed the current English mode. In 1766 seventy-one "Gentlemen of the Turf" organized the Jockey Club, whose annual race meetings drew entries from all colonies from New York to Virginia and attracted the presence of such ardent worshipers of horseflesh as Colonel George Washington of Virginia, Samuel Galloway of Maryland (owner of the great "Selim"), and the Manhattan De Lanceys to witness the running of "the City Plate." If donning a pink coat and riding to hounds made an English gentleman, then many Philadelphians could qualify through membership in the Gloucester Hunting Club (1766), earliest in the colonies and said by some to have been "the first fox-hunting club in the world." At its meetings Squire Western might have found boon companions in Jacob Hiltzheimer and his cronies, who frequently after a hunt at Darby "got decently drunk," even though their grooms "could not be accused of the same fault."

Pennsylvania ladies imitated their British sisters by driving out daily for tea or to take the air in their "elegant carriages." Indeed, the increasing use of vehicles not only rendered social life more mobile and varied, but furnished a not inaccurate indication of their owners' financial status as well. Writing to inform his father of the birth of his soon-to-be-famous daughter Peggy, Edward Shippen, Jr., seemed almost to take more pride in the prospect that "it is but staying a few years longer before I ride in my Coach."

A former Philadelphian, James Ralph, had once told Englishmen in London that "no man can properly be styled a gentleman who has not made use of every opportunity to enrich his own capacity and settle the elements of taste, which he may improve at leisure." Citizens of his native town strove valiantly in these years to translate that precept into practice, seeking in all fields those amenities and advantages which were rightly considered the attributes of gentlemen. They pursued education in the arts and graces of polite society at home, in England, and on the continent of Europe. They introduced gentility even into their relations with the Deity, many Presbyterians and Quakers forsaking their original allegiance for more elegant and fashionable communion at Christ Church or St.

Peter's, while those who remained true to their old faiths became considerably less austere than in earlier years. Observing the Friends in 1774 Silas Deane remarked that "indeed the younger and politer part of that profession in this city are not distinguishable, but in very few particulars, from other people." By erecting country homes and city mansions, assembling libraries and art collections, attending concerts and the theater, sitting for their portraits, and having their sons and daughters instructed in a variety of genteel accomplishments, these plutocratic gentlemen succeeded in setting themselves apart from common ways of life, while at the same time they furnished substantial patronage and increasing encouragement to the practitioners of many arts.

All these efforts had as their ultimate objective the fastening of English standards of taste upon the aristocratic life of eastern Pennsylvania. Here local gentry found themselves considerably aided by the physiography of their section. Since except for its rage for sport the ruling class of eighteenth-century England was "urban in its inclinations," composed as it was increasingly of recruits from the expanding world of trade, Philadelphia was the most natural place for an attempted reproduction of the life of that class in the New World. In climate, terrain and produce the rolling, fertile lands of eastern Pennsylvania more closely resembled the mother country than did low-country Carolina or tidewater Virginia, and the country estates around Philadelphia, with their English or Scottish head gardeners and white servants, their groves, parks, stables and kitchen gardens, bore far greater likeness to an English country ménage than did extended and isolated plantations manned by gangs of black slaves.

For dwellers in this pleasant region Philadelphia provided an urban focus, and the wealth that supported both country living and town amusements came from sources similar to, often identical with those of mercantile London. Presence of a prospering metropolis in the midst of country much like parts of England and possession of the greatest amount of mobile wealth in the colonies made it possible for Philadelphians to combine the season in town with

"The Great Giant."
First Gentleman of
Pennsylvania, William
Allen, by Benjamin
West.

(Courtesy Curator of Independence Hall)

"London Tricks and St.
James Customs."

Samuel Powel, last Mayor
of colonial Philadelphia,
probably by Benjamin
West.

(Courtesy Samuel Powel, Providence, R. I.)

A View of the House of Employment, Alms-house, Pennsylvania Hospital, & part of the City of Philadelphia

The Social Conscience of Philadelphia in Brick and Stone.
(From Woodbury and Morton: *History of the Pennsylvania Hospital*)

residence in the country more nearly under English conditions than anywhere else in the New World. And just as families in distant counties made periodic journeys to the capital for a taste of court society, many of the Maryland gentry, sensing this similarity, were drawn within the orbit of the Philadelphia way of life.

Enjoyment of their wealth and leisure in the patronage of the arts and the cultivation of English taste did not prevent merchant grandees and professional leaders from contributing heavily in money, thought and services to the enrichment of their city's life. While these New World aristocrats may have agreed wholeheartedly with James Ralph's admonitions to self-improvement, many of them also accepted the dictum of another fellow townsman, Dr. Benjamin Rush, that "Every man is public property. His time and talents—his youth—his manhood—his old age—nay more, his life, his all, belong to his country." Some of them, it is true, were content to remain mere idle rich, impregnated with snobbery or indulging in such extravagances as the one-time schoolfellows of Samuel Coates. But many more accepted the responsibilities that possession of wealth imposed. They served in the public offices of their city and province, in the administration of economic activities and the employment of the citizenry. They proved public-spirited in the furtherance of educational and civic enterprises, and extraordinarily generous in their support of public and private charities.

In their admiration of current standards of English taste, often crystallized to the point of decadence, these gentlemen may have mistaken the direction of their own destinies, and in their desire to transplant those standards to the New World they were so out of step with the trend of their times as to have small chance of success. When the hour came for making the difficult choice between England and the colonies, quite a few found it impossible to abandon their inherited ways to follow the uncharted paths of revolution. Some remained loyal to the Crown. Others, such as Graydon's friend, Mr. John Ross, "who loved ease and Madeira much better than liberty and strife, declared for neutrality." But many more stood forthright for the patriot cause, and helped, albeit often unwittingly, to usher in a social revolution that was in time to threaten their privileges and their very property.

Philadelphia never developed a ruling clique so compact and self-contained, so devoted to the status quo, as the arbiters of taste of Augustan London. Even the most lordly of its gentry never divorced themselves completely from the vital forces of the community in which they lived. Few possessed the arrogance of self-made men, and many realized how recently they had risen from the ranks in a city rich with the same opportunity for others. Ambrose Serle found to his dismay that even the most ardent Tories "had been tinctured with the Notion of the vast Consequence and Power of America." Moreover, the custom of their times demanded that "gentlemen of capacity and leisure" use their capacities during their leisure for something more than their own idle enjoyment. Having succeeded economically by the acquisition of fortunes, they were expected to devote those fortunes and the leisure they made possible to contributions and services to the society that had afforded them such a chance. This many "men of distinction" in Philadelphia earnestly did. We have seen them as patrons of the arts. Succeeding chapters will reveal them as active humanitarians and as students and encouragers of the New Science. In such men as these middle-class Benjamin Franklin found in his youth models upon which to pattern his own later activities.

Chapter VII

THE SOCIAL USE OF THE FAVORS
OF PROVIDENCE

THE Enlightenment, along with its faith in the power of reason and its belief in the possibility of progress, brought also to Philadelphia the new concern for unfortunate humanity which was their natural corollary. In Penn's city, eighteenth-century humanitarianism combined with the charitable tradition of the Quakers and with certain factors indigenous to all New World societies to produce an interest and an accomplishment in movements humanitarian unsurpassed in any other community of the age.

With the secularization of society and the intensified interest in the individual and the humane, human life in the eighteenth century came to enjoy an increased valuation. If humanity were to be remade by thinking and brought to new levels of perfection by the exercise of reason, then man himself was worthy of being saved from the indignities of poverty, illness, social injustice and misfortune. As curiosity about human society resulted for the first time in adequate information concerning social ills, the conviction arose that such conditions constituted not only a reproach to man's intelligence, but a barrier to the progress in which all believed. Existence of human misery offered a direct challenge to current theories of perfectibility, and the application of reason to the study and amelioration of social conditions appealed to the scientific temper of the times.

While the contracting of ecclesiastical activities, income and influence placed much of the problem squarely on the doorstep of the growing, materialistic, secular society, the accumulation of wealth in private hands, which was one of the first fruits of emergent capitalism, furnished machinery for the social control of matters formerly left in the hands of the church. At the same time, the economic restlessness and expanding activities of the eighteenth century accelerated the growth of a vigorous middle class which possessed in happy combination the wealth, energy and social conscience to deal with the problem of the less fortunate. In contrast with previous periods of history, the eighteenth century made such advances in the discovery and alleviation of human suffering as to lend reality and justification to the label "The Age of Benevolence."

At Philadelphia, where, as has been pointed out in other connections, there existed a high degree of sensitivity to the intellectual currents of the times, this humanitarian leaven was at work. The New World offered an excellent proving-ground for the doctrine of perfectibility, and Philadelphia itself afforded remarkable exemplification, in material things at least, of the idea of progress. In the short span of a single generation Penn's town had grown to be one of the important cities of the British Empire, and men whose original capital had consisted of their tools or their native wit had become wealthy and influential. Amid material growth unknown in other parts of the world, and amid fairly general prosperity for the ambitious and the energetic, the existence of poverty stood out as a conspicuous badge of public shame. Moreover, many immigrants had come to Pennsylvania in the belief that its new society would correct inequalities and imperfections from which they had suffered in older countries, and the continued toleration of social injustices constituted a denial of their dearest faith.

Local factors also animated the drive against poverty and suffering which became so notable a feature of the city's life after the mid-century. The New World, with its need for labor and development, placed greater value on the individual than did older societies with their crowded labor markets and poorly distributed populations. The economic folly of permitting this limited labor supply to become depleted through unnecessary hardships was as obvious as the crime of allowing hunger and want to flourish in the midst of such abundant opportunities. Furthermore, there was here no callous aristocracy holding inherited ideas that poverty was inevitable and beggary the just reward for the sins of the "disorderly poor." Human memory, though short, could still recall too many instances of local success from humble beginnings.

Despite unprecedented growth, the city did not become so large that rich men could avoid learning of the lot of the less fortunate, and thoughtful men were shocked by what they learned. So a people who because of the evidences of progress they saw about them could hardly doubt the truth of the doctrine of perfectibility refused to subscribe to the axiom that because wealth accumulated men had to decay. The facts of their experience from living in a land of plentiful opportunity and great natural riches laid upon even the most practical of them a grave responsibility to aid the unfortunate and remove the causes of their plight, for society's good and for their own.

There was also, in the New World as in the Old, the approach to the problems of poverty and distress by means of religious organizations. Throughout the history of Protestant humanitarianism the Quakers have stood pre-eminent in this field. From the days of William Penn the Society of Friends had furnished ideas, funds and leadership for the care of the unfortunate in Philadelphia, and they continued throughout the colonial period the most prominent and active group in the struggle for social welfare. But they also furnished impetus and example to energetic and devoted workers from other sects, and the magnitude of their services should not be allowed to obscure the accomplishments of others.

The effects of poverty become more acute with the concentration of populations in cities, and it was fortunate that the humanitarian teachings of George Whitefield and his followers, with their emphasis on individual human dignity, took root in the years about mid-century when Philadelphia was experiencing its greatest growth. Whitefield dramatized the problem of the poor, calling attention to their need for alms, education, sympathy and understanding. He laid responsibility directly upon the individual, talking his way into pockets as zealously guarded by practical common sense as those of the young Franklin, but he also aroused all religious groups to the necessity for charitable action by preaching that compassion for one's fellowmen might be truer religion than the ritual of formal worship.

In time, not only professional churchmen but members of the gentry and prosperous tradesmen discovered that their community had genuine social problems to be faced, as preachers and printers told them of the increase of the poor and destitute, the plight of the sick and the insane, and the horrible conditions that faced the foreign immigrant. "I would sooner give up my interest in a future state," wrote the scientist, David Rittenhouse, "than be divested of humanity—I mean that good will I have to the species, although one half of them are said to be fools, and almost the other half knaves." This humanitarianism found expression in churches and in clubs, founded as often for convivial as for charitable purposes, and in the use of new methods borrowed from England or Scotland, often before they had enjoyed any widespread application there. In general this was not an age of public concern with the problems of poverty, and the conception of corporate responsibility for the alleviation of distress, beyond ridding society of the most obvious threats and nuisances, was slow in developing. The charity of the eighteenth century was largely a movement of private interests, though occasionally the outraged conscience of the community was able to force action by constituted authorities.

Within these limits eighteenth-century Philadelphians accomplished much for the alleviation of poverty, the elimination of beggary, and the care of the sick, the aged and the insane. So well did they build that young aristocrats as they traveled "home" with more frequency, forgetting perhaps the graver problems of older societies, were sincerely shocked at the sight of Old World conditions. What he saw near Derry, Ireland, stunned and horrified Francis Hopkinson in 1766. "All along the Road are built the most miserable Hutts you can imagine, of Mud and Straw, much worse than Indian Wig Wams, and the wretched Inhabitants go scarce decently covered with Rags.—The Poor here are numerous and very indigent indeed." He felt a sense of pride in the fact that few poor in his native city lacked the "Necessaries of life." The young Englishman Alexander Macraby found Philadelphia in 1770 "far beyond the inhabitants of any other part of the continent in public spirit," and four years later John Adams, while maintaining that "Philadelphia with all its trade, wealth and regularity, is not Boston," had grudgingly to acknowledge its pre-eminence in "charitable, public foundations."

Prior to 1732, the dispensation of charity in Philadelphia rested mainly in the hands of the Quakers, who, since their religious convictions barred them from many avenues of public service, tended to concentrate their energies in the struggle for social betterment. The Friends' Meeting cared privately for its own poor throughout the colonial era; in 1729 it erected an Alms House on Walnut Street, where poor families were assured the novelty of privacy by their assignment to separate apartments. But the Quaker belief in the close interdependence among individuals composing any social group led to the extension of their charity to include the entire community. So effectively did Quakers implement their belief in action that in the early decades of the century the Corporation of Philadelphia was largely able to abdicate its public duty in the care of the city's poor, and as late as 1724 Christopher Sower could write that "there are people who have been living here for 40 years and have not seen a beggar in Philadelphia."

When in the twenties the expansion of the city and the coming in of Scotch-Irish and German immigrants made public action on the problem of poor relief imperative, it was largely Quaker pressure on Assembly and Corporation that produced results. In 1732 the Commonalty erected a brick Alms House, containing an infirmary for the indigent sick and special apartments for the insane, and providing for the healthy poor facilities for work. The institution was admirably conducted under supervision by Overseers of the Poor, appointed by the Mayor and Common Council. Unfortunately, it soon proved inadequate as ensuing years of growth and upheaval created unprecedented problems which the Corporation, restricted in its powers and always dilatory, regarded with almost criminal neglect.

The enormous accretion of population in Philadelphia after 1740 —some 200 per cent in thirty-five years—would have produced a host of problems even in normal times. But conditions were hardly ever normal in this period, which opened with a four-year depression, moved on through two wars and their subsequent periods of deflation, and terminated in social and political revolution. The combined wealth of the citizenry mounted geometrically, but its distribution became increasingly unequal as real poverty appeared to counterbalance the accumulation of large fortunes. Furthermore, Philadelphia became in these years the first seaboard city to experience large-scale immigration, especially of foreign-language groups, as incoming Germans and Scotch-Irish swelled the steady trickle of English newcomers to the proportions of a deluge. To local and foreign-born poor were added during the last French War a large body of transported Acadians, and a considerable refugee population from exposed and undefended frontiers.

Care of the unfortunate became an onerous burden even to such benevolent Friends as John Smith, who recorded in his diary in January, 1748, "It is remarkable What an Increase of Beggars there is about town this winter,—many more than I have before observed, and I have not yet sent any away Empty handed." The quiet generosity of the Quakers must certainly have proved insufficient to cope with this acute situation had not the Great Awakening become transformed at about this time into a great popular movement, with the compelling voice of George Whitefield inspiring in persons of all sects and classes emotions of compassion for their less fortunate fellowmen.

Taxation for poor relief remained small throughout the period, and the privately organized charities of the city were hardly equipped to deal with emergency situations. Until the outbreak of the Seven Years' War city authorities managed to muddle through by resorting, in times of extreme need, to special collections to supplement their inadequate funds. During the bitter winter of 1741, for example, such a "drive" netted £204, which was laid out in food and firewood for needy families. Division of responsibility for public charities between the Corporation and the Overseers of the Poor rendered action slow and frequently ineffective. Moreover, both bodies clung resolutely to the harsh Elizabethan conception of philanthropy, which, motivated by fears of disorder and vagrancy, made no attempt to deal with the causes of poverty.

Fortunately, in unusual situations which strained or baffled the charitable agencies of the time, the citizens of Philadelphia, either singly or in groups, showed themselves ready to come to the aid of their unfortunate fellow townsmen. When in the autumn of 1755 some four hundred and fifty Acadian exiles were debarked at the city, the harassed Overseers of the Poor could do no better than house them in ancient and miserably inadequate army barracks. Enemies and Catholics, these miserable expatriates were objects of fear and suspicion, and but for the efforts of Anthony Benezet, schoolteacher and reformer, their lot might have been tragic indeed.

This Philadelphia Quaker of French ancestry easily obtained from a Provincial Council delighted to be relieved of the problem of the "French Neutrals" authorization to act in their behalf. After assiduous solicitation of funds from all and sundry, Benezet secured from Samuel Emlen, a wealthy Friend, the use of a piece of property on Pine Street, and was able to build thereon a row of one-story houses to shelter the exiles. "He appeared almost their only friend," wrote Deborah Logan, "gave liberally of his own, solicited alms for others in their behalf (to which he endeavoured to turn the attention of the government,) and gratuitously educated many of their daughters" in his school for girls. Every year he carried their case to the Assembly, often with small success. This bewildered and homeless people of an alien faith received its only extensive sympathy from the Quaker son of a French Huguenot, who initiated among his coreligionists in America the great Friendly tradition of nonpartisan relief to the civilian sufferers from war.

Deplorable conditions, quite beyond the capacities of existing agencies to deal with, arrived with the decade of the sixties. By 1764 the increase in the number of poor was "tremendous," as post-war deflation produced widespread unemployment. "Scarcity of money" followed the cessation of large expenditures for the army and the funding of provincial currency, while new revenue laws and restrictive regulation by the British Government, which rendered commercial ventures "very dull as well as very precarious," caused numerous failures in business. To the large numbers of local poor who had thus to be cared for were added in these years hundreds of refugees fleeing from the rising fury of Pontiac's braves along the Pennsylvania frontiers. In the wholly inadequate Alms House five and six beds were crowded into rooms measuring ten feet by eleven, while further accommodations had to be set up in a near-by church.

In the face of this crying need it was again the quiet persistence of Quaker pressure which forced the reluctant and parsimonious Assembly to act. The Grand Jury, the Pennsylvania Hospital, and especially the influence of wealthy and prominent citizens were enlisted in their philanthropic crusade. Finally in 1766 they wrung from the Assembly a law which authorized the mortgaging of the old Alms House to finance the construction of a new one, and provided for the erection of a workhouse in which vagrant strangers and "certain Disorderly Persons" might be put to labor by the city authorities.

The major provision of the act, however, was the incorporation of "The Contributors to the Relief and Employment of the Poor of the City of Philadelphia," Southwark, Moyamensing, Passyunk and the Northern Liberties, a body organized principally by Quakers, and consisting of 417 subscribers to a fund for the erection and support of a building to promote industry and frugality among the poor. Merchant princes contributed generously to this enterprise, Quaker Joseph Wharton giving £80, Chief Justice Allen, £50, and

Benjamin Chew, £50. Many smaller gifts came from artisans and laborers, and the first year's collections, ranging from five shillings upwards, but averaging from £5 to £10, amounted to over £1,852. The sympathy and generosity of Philadelphia's citizens, large and small, outran that of their government, and society's unfortunates received needed relief only when the humanitarianism of the Society of Friends compelled the Assembly to empower a group of private individuals to act in the emergency.

The Managers of the Alms House set to work with considerable energy, and in October, 1767, opened the new Bettering House, located on Spruce Street between Tenth and Eleventh. "One of the principal Ornaments" of the city, "being a very pretty building and in good Taste," it was built of brick, and consisted of a two-and-a-half-story main structure flanked by two wings, each having a square tower four stories high. Around the inside of the wings ran a covered piazza where inmates might walk in bad weather. The building had a capacity of five hundred persons, and immediately received the 284 recipients of public charity from the old Alms House. Not quite half of these were employed in spinning, sewing, washing, or picking oakum, which nearly met the expenses of their food and clothing. Children, expectant mothers, blind persons and over a hundred unemployables made up the remainder.

The Bettering House was supported in part by taxation, but chiefly by charitable contributions, and under the able stewardship of such Quaker managers as Jeremiah Warder, William Fisher, Stephen Collins and Henry Drinker it sheltered from three to four hundred inmates throughout the remainder of the colonial period. Generous financial assistance from the citizenry, especially in the form of special gifts, enabled it to expand its services yearly. Five city fire companies united to present it with a fire engine, and the Union Fire Company contributed forty fire buckets as well. A donation of £243 in 1770 was used by the institution to supply many of the poor with firewood. As early as the winter of 1768, when already there were 368 inmates at the Bettering House, city authorities reported the annual burden of beggars had noticeably decreased.

The variety of charity dispensed by the Managers of the Bettering House and their success in ministering to the needs of all classes of indigent persons became soon a source of pride to public-spirited Philadelphians. For the aged and infirm, fallen women and unemployables, the institution provided an adequate and humane home. Its services to the insane and the sick poor will be discussed in another connection. In 1768 the Managers employed a schoolmistress to instruct in reading the sixty orphans housed there, and by 1774 they were supporting two schools. A surplus of funds usually made possible some out-relief to supplement the work of the Overseers of the Poor in that department of public charity. Nowhere in the then world, perhaps, did the indigent receive more efficient and generous treatment. Items for tea, coffee and chocolate, and even for playing cards and tobacco, occur in the Alms House accounts of its expenditures. Cleanliness and neatness characterized the building, and the gardens surrounding it excited the admiration of the city's many visitors, who seemed glad to pay the fee of one bit that was charged for a visit to the institution.

One of the most sincere compliments ever paid the generosity of Quakers came from the pen of a critical Connecticut Yankee who in 1774 inspected the Bettering House under the guidance of the Quaker rebel Christopher Marshall. "It vastly exceeds all of the kind in America put together," wrote Silas Deane, "and, I guess equals in its institutions any thing in Europe. . . . This house, I judge, must have cost forty thousand pounds, and the annual support of it amounts to ten thousand. . . . Nothing that serves at once to alleviate the wants and distresses of age, sickness and poverty is unattended to." But what most amazed this product of the Town Meeting was that "all this is done by private donation, and chiefly by the people called Quakers . . . yet, as if these people determine to outdo all the rest of the world, they never permit any of their own poor to be sent there, but support them in a neat house by themselves."

In contrast to other public enterprises in the city, and in common with most of its charitable undertakings, this movement for the humane care of the poor produced no individual leaders of prominence. It was definitely a group movement, largely of Quaker inspiration, and the Friendly desire for anonymity prevailed. The idea germinated no doubt in the Philadelphia Monthly Meeting, and to it the bulk of the credit should be assigned.

Often the press was influential in uncovering conditions calling for charity and in inspiring private action to deal with them. In 1762 both the *Gazette* and the *Journal* publicized the labors of public-spirited men in each ward in collecting funds with which to purchase fuel for the needy. Hall of the *Gazette* pointed out that many of the poor, who "thro' the high Price of Fire-wood . . . and the present Severity of the Season, are reduced to great Extremity and Distress," richly deserved the "compassion" of their more fortunate neighbors. In 1770 the *Chronicle* lent its support to a similar private collection for the same purpose. The high cost and contracting supply of firewood in these years brought ever increasing hardships to the poor, and caused George Emlen at his death in 1776 to bequeath a large fund to the Managers of the Bettering House and to the Pennsylvania Hospital, to be expended by them in providing fuel for needy families.

Cheap fuel was by no means the only necessity of the Philadelphia unemployed in the years of distress following the last French War. The *Gazette* of January 24, 1765, quoted an essay from the *Spectator* in an effort to stimulate a public subscription for "the many poor Families in, and about, this City, who are, in a great Measure, destitute of the Common Necessaries of Life," and reminded its readers of the success of the fuel collection of 1762. The result was the organization of a sort of Friendly Aid. At a public meeting held at the Court House two residents from each city block were appointed to take subscriptions for a charity fund, and a committe of five citizens was named to distribute the proceeds. This movement attracted favorable attention and finally imitation in New York, where similar conditions prevailed among the lower classes.

The spirit of compassion became widespread in these years. The many charity sermons of George Whitefield raised substantial sums

for use of the hospital or for the poor of the city. Benefit performances to aid the needy were given by the players of the American
Company, and by various music and dancing teachers whose philanthropic impulses were one with their desire to quiet moral and
theological objections to their arts. In November, 1772, "the original
American Rider," Jacob Bates, gave an exhibition of his equestrian
skill on upper High Street, proceeds of which he donated for the
relief of the poor during the coming winter.

A growing concern with the problems of society led to the extension of philanthropic activity beyond the bounds of city and province. The Philadelphia Monthly Meeting conducted a subscription
for the general relief of sufferers from the disastrous fire at Charleston, South Carolina, in 1741, and voted special gifts to Quakers who
had been rendered homeless, and Philadelphians of all groups contributed to the raising of the large sum of £1,212 which was sent
to the Selectmen of Boston to aid fire sufferers there in 1760. There
was ample precedent and tradition for the generosity with which
Philadelphians came to the aid of their New England compatriots
when the closing of the port of Boston brought distress and threat
of famine in its wake.

The whole civic and social experience of Philadelphians had
shown them that "In Nations . . . men form themselves into Cor-
porations and other Societies for promoting some particular Good
which either had not or could not be so well provided for by the
Publick acts of the Community." With the increasing organization
of business, social and intellectual life into clubs and societies, the
spirit of association invaded the realm of philanthropy as well. Indeed, throughout the eighteenth century the taste for club life and
the growing humanitarianism reacted constantly upon each other
in a fashion that was stimulating to both.

The movement for the founding of friendly societies among Scottish nationals, begun by them in London in the mid-seventeenth
century, had by 1740 spread with them to Boston and Newport in
New England, and to Charleston in South Carolina. The number

of Scots settling in Philadelphia after that date greatly increased, and in 1749 a group of them, with characteristic clannishness and benevolence, formed the St. Andrew's Society at Philadelphia in Pennsylvania for the purpose of aiding "our country people here in distress." Promoted chiefly by Doctors Thomas Graeme and Adam Thompson, and by the printer David Hall, the Society flourished. Twenty years later 67 resident and 147 honorary members were contributing to its funds, by means of which "many hundreds" of unfortunate Scots in the New World had been granted assistance.

The St. Andrew's Society combined social with charitable activities, meeting quarterly for important dinners which soon took on the proportions of banquets. So nearly was sociability driving out benevolence that canny members in 1765 secured passage of a bylaw that thereafter only "a cold supper for 10 or 12 persons" with no liquor would be served, and that the bill should be brought in at eleven o'clock. Such outstanding presidents as Dr. Graeme and Provost Smith enabled the Society to perform much admirable charity throughout the period, until in August, 1776, its meetings were discontinued because of "the convulsed and unsettled state of the times."

Other national groups soon emulated the organization and work of the Scots. By 1759 weekly gatherings of Gentlemen of the British Society, the Hibernian Club, and another Scot's Club were meeting "cheerfully" to receive "their worthy friends and countrymen" in the British Punch House on Water Street. Conviviality rather than charity motivated these assemblies for many years, but eventually two of them developed into organizations similar to the St. Andrew's Society. In 1762 the St. Lewis Society met quarterly at its "lodge," and seems to have combined fraternal with benevolent activities.

The dire plight of many Palatine immigrants offered a real field for charitable activity, especially to those of German origin or parentage. Living-conditions on immigrant vessels were often so deplorable that a recent scholar has found them comparable to the worst evils of the Middle Passage. Overcrowding, bad food or com-

plete lack of it, prevalence of disease and an appalling rate of
mortality led Germans in Philadelphia to seek legislative redress in
1749. Though they wrung from the Assembly in the following year
a law prohibiting the overcrowding of passenger ships bearing immigrants, accommodations continued neither wholesome nor comfortable, and the plight of the poor Palatine when he arrived, pen-
niless, friendless, half-starved, and fit only to be sold for a period
of servitude, was terrible to contemplate.

In 1764, under leadership of the wealthy merchant Henry Keppele,
a group of German residents meeting at the Lutheran School in
Cherry Street organized the Deutschen Gesellschaft von Pennsylvanien, whose specific aims were to secure passage of more stringent
legislation affecting living-conditions on immigrant vessels, and to
assemble food, clothing and money for the relief of needy Palatines
already in town. In 1765 the Assembly met some of their demands,
and by August of that year the Society could boast that the new
and stricter laws of Pennsylvania were already causing ship captains
to disembark their passengers in other colonies—*"Die erste Frucht
der Teutschen Gesellschaft."*

The Society also sought to render legal aid to those whose humble
station and inability to speak or understand English placed them at
a disadvantage or in danger of exploitation. When Johann Zimmer-
mann and his wife complained that one of their countrymen, the
prominent merchant Matthias Koplin, refused them their freedom
dues at the expiration of their indentures, the Deutschen Gesellschaft took the matter to court and secured an order directing him
to pay the couple £5. Relief to poor Palatines was a continuous
function of the Society. As its activities increased, the organization
purchased a lot and was drawing up plans for the erection of a
building when the outbreak of hostilities forced the project to be
postponed.

Genuine need for assistance among their nationals in the city,
and the tendency among all groups to band together as parlous
times approached, produced a new crop of national societies in the
seventies. The Hibernian Club of 1759, purely a convivial organiza-

tion, may have continued into the next decade; for instance, on March 17, 1769, "a number of Sons of St. Patrick" met at dinner to celebrate the anniversary of their patron in "chearful mirth and jollity." Not until 1771, however, did "twenty natives of Ireland and sons of natives" form the Society of the Friendly Sons of St. Patrick of Philadelphia for the Relief of Immigrants from Ireland. Though the membership included only three Roman Catholics, one of them, Stephen Moylan, became its first president.

Despite the fact that Englishmen in need of aid probably outnumbered those of any other nationality in the city, they were the last to receive assistance from an organization of their own countrymen. The British Club of 1759 seems not to have survived, for in 1770 Alexander Macraby wrote to his brother, "Would you think that in a city with 20,000 [sic] inhabitants we should find difficulty in collecting 20 native Englishmen to celebrate St. George's day yesterday?" The party was finally arranged only two days before the event. "We met at a Tavern, stuffed roast beef and plum pudding, and got drunk, *pour l'honneur de St. George;* wore crosses and finished the evening at the playhouse, where we made the people all chorus 'God save the king,' and 'Rule Britannia,' . . . and in short conducted ourselves with all the decency and confusion usual on such occasions. My head aches plaguely!" Apparently all theatrical disorders were not confined to Sons of Liberty and the 3-shilling seats.

Two years later Macraby would not have found such difficulty in observing the birthday of England's patron saint, but he might have had to do so more decorously. By that time the efforts of the Reverend Richard Peters, Dr. John Kearsley, Robert Morris, Father Robert Harding and other prominent gentry had resulted in the formation of the Society of the Sons of St. George, Established at Philadelphia, for the Advice and Assistance of Englishmen in Distress, with a roster of eighty-five members. So numerous were the English poor and so crying their needs, especially among the families of weavers and other artisans, that in October, 1773, the Society published in both the local and the British press an appeal for contributions to a permanent fund from which small weekly payments might be made to deserving families or individuals. For reasons not at all clear there arose about 1774 another organization calling itself the Society of Englishmen and Sons of Englishmen, Established at Philadelphia, for the Advice and Assistance of Englishmen in Distress, which, considering the similarity of titles, may well have consisted of dissatisfied or dissident members breaking away from the Society of the Sons of St. George. In all events, the activities of both were brought to a close by occurrences of the year 1775.

As the most cosmopolitan of colonial cities, Philadelphia constituted a peculiarly fertile field for the formation of these national societies, and their role in the years preceding Independence has a considerable social significance. Their preservation of the tribal loyalties of the Old World, which might at first glance seem to offer a resistant to the emerging spirit of the New, supplied instead another element in the creation of a new and American society. Within each national group all ranks and interests—gentleman, artisan and laborer—whose paths in their home countries might never have crossed, achieved, if not friendship and intimacy, at least a sympathetic understanding based on the powerful though accidental bond of common homeland and common national traditions. Such vertical democratization within the group was a necessary prelude to horizontal fusion in the melting-pot of New World society. In their care for their less fortunate countrymen, which was reason and excuse for their existence, the clubs contributed to the New World ideals of opportunity for all and faith in the future, while through correspondence with similar groups in other colonial communities—Boston, New York and Charleston—they became an important intercolonial interest and a factor in the burgeoning patriotism of the American colonies.

This nascent American spirit, robust and democratic, inspired citizens of native birth to found an organization of their own on the national pattern of the English, Irish and Scots. The Philadelphians, observed an English official in 1771, "have likewise a Saint, whose history . . . is lost in fable and uncertainty." For some years native-born Americans had been wont to symbolize their rising community of interest by wearing a piece of buck tail in their caps on May first in honor of "King Tammany," the Delaware chieftain who had concluded the legendary treaty of Shackamaxon with William Penn. In 1772 the *Chronicle* reported that on the current May day "a number of Americans, Sons of King Tammany, met . . . to celebrate the memory of that truly noble Chieftain," and expressed the hope that "a Society may be formed of great *utility* to the Distressed; as this meeting was more for the Purpose of promoting Charity and Benevolence than Mirth and Frivolity." On May 1, 1773, the King was canonized, when over a hundred Philadelphians, including most of the local Sons of Liberty, formed the Sons of St. Tammany. Though the drinking of patriotic toasts gave its meetings something of a political flavor, the new Society performed important charitable services in the community.

Other secular organizations concerned themselves with the business of charity, as the sympathies of the age expanded to embrace the needy everywhere. The "assisting such of their members as should by accident be in need of support, or the widows and minor children of members," had been one of the principal objectives for the founding of the Carpenter's Company in 1724. A similar motive led to development of the Society for the Relief of Poor and Distressed Masters of Ships, Their Widows and Children out of the Sea-Captain's Club in 1765. Five years later, with a membership of over two hundred and a capital stock of £1,094, this organization received a charter from the Assembly, and with the constantly increasing funds at its disposal soon proved to be one of the most active benevolent institutions of the city.

The charitable activities of such occupational groups belonged to the medieval guild tradition, but the proposals of the Philadelphia Society for Annuities for the Benefit of Widows, Children and Aged Persons struck a more modern note. Its articles, as explained by Matthew Clarkson, clerk of the Philadelphia Contributionship, in 1772, provided for the payment by the subscriber of from 15 shillings

to £3 annually during his lifetime, with the consequent assurance
to his assigns of an annuity of three and one-third times the yearly
rate. Though carefully worked out, the scheme seems to have come
to naught because of the outbreak of the war, but it is nevertheless
highly significant as the earliest public annuity plan in America
and as a measure of the alertness of men of property to insurance
developments in other parts of the world.

Most religious denominations recognized the principle of association for charitable purposes in these years. Churches continued to
dispense much general benevolence and to take up collections for
use in specific emergencies, but in addition they formed special
organizations to provide for the needs of particular groups within
their memberships. As early as 1717 the Philadelphia Synod had
instituted a Pious Fund for the relief of widows and orphans of
Presbyterian ministers. By 1754 the difficulties of the more poorly
paid among his brother clergymen in attempting to provide security
for their dependents inspired the Reverend Francis Alison to propose adoption of the Scottish plan for their support, whereby each
minister contributed £2 or £3 yearly "to a fund from which his
widow would receive an annual payment of five pounds." Under
the able management of William Allen the Presbyterian Minister's
Fund was incorporated in 1759. In 1761 it undertook administration
of the Pious Fund as well, and soon boasted a capital of £11,000.

The prosperity of this "first incorporated insurance company in
America" led to the formation of a similar corporation for the benefit of Anglican clergymen, after earnest advocacy by the Reverend
William Smith, in 1767. In 1770 the Moravian Church extended its
benefit program so that the relicts of all members might receive assistance from the Brotherly Association for the Support of Widows.
Absence of such provision for members of the Church of England
was remedied in 1772 by the will of Dr. John Kearsley, who bequeathed a fund for the founding of Christ Church Hospital and
the support therein of "ten or more poor or distressed women" of
Anglican faith, supplying them with "meat, drink and lodging, and
the assistance of persons practicing physick and surgery."

Throughout the colonial era religious bodies showed a praiseworthy concern for the physical necessities of the unfortunate. Only toward the end of the period did they come to the realization that many of the "inferior sort" remained outside the ministrations of organized religion, and turn their attention to the problems of spiritual poverty. Gradually the social and political implications of the Great Awakening combined with the growing sentimentalism of the age to call attention to the existence of a wide-open field for "home missions."

Concern over "the prevalence and daily increase of vice and immorality of every kind, . . . too evident to escape the notice of the most superficial observer," led a number of prominent citizens of the Middle and New England colonies, meeting at New York in 1773, to found the American Society for Promoting Religious Knowledge among the Poor in the British Colonies. In Philadelphia the Reverend James Sprout of the Presbyterian Church and the printing office of the Bradford family were designated to receive gifts from local well-wishers to the new organization, whose object was the purchase and distribution of Bibles and books of piety among the uninformed though literate poor. The American Society was modeled after existing English and Scottish associations of similar purpose, but even the most sanguine of its promoters could hardly have foreseen the number and vitality of the descendants this first Bible society in the New World was one day to produce.

Problems of poverty and ignorance were by no means all that faced the humane Philadelphian in these years. While one current of the humanitarian movement was merging with the romantic sentimentalism of the latter years of the century, another owed much to the scientific spirit which was also a product of the Enlightenment.

As Philadelphia became a populous commercial city many conditions arose that science, especially medical science, might hope to correct. Epidemic sickness, the bane of seaport communities, occupational illnesses, and diseases induced by poverty kept pace with the growth of population and of need, and far outran the meager facilities existing for their care or alleviation. The poor who fell ill languished for want of care—indeed, absence of proper nursing and medical attention was not confined to paupers—while miserable souls afflicted with mental disorders were either tormented by ignorant keepers, who kept them locked up and chained, or allowed to wander about the streets "to the terrour of their neighbours." Furthermore, with the growth of Philadelphia's medical profession, the local problem was augmented by the coming in for treatment of persons from country districts and neighboring towns, and for them too lodgings and nursing were difficult to obtain.

Though there were many devoted and brilliant men among the city's doctors, a number of them products of the best training the Old World afforded, it was not until Dr. Thomas Bond, himself a graduate of Paris hospitals, returned to England for a visit in 1748 that the example of the English hospital movement began to make itself felt in America. At this time the old Alms House, built in 1732 and "by no means fitted for such Purposes," constituted Philadelphia's only refuge for the sick poor and the demented. In the recently established institutions he visited in England Bond was impressed with the vastly improved methods of caring for the sick, and especially with the successful record of Bethlehem Hospital in curing "above two thirds of the Mad People received." The need of his home city for similar institutions was too obvious to be missed, and upon his return to Philadelphia Bond immediately proposed the establishment of a hospital "for the reception and cure of poor sick persons, whether inhabitants of the province or strangers."

Until he thought to enlist the promotional genius of his friend Benjamin Franklin, Bond's proposal met with popular indifference and distrust. However, that ever skillful manipulator employed the columns of the *Pennsylvania Gazette,* his "usual custom in such cases," to good effect, and succeeded in so playing public and Assembly against each other that he obtained from the one a large popular subscription and from the other a generous grant. Late in life Franklin remembered that of all his "political manoeuvres" none gave him such solid satisfaction as this, but he clearly stated that inspiration and initiative belonged to Dr. Bond.

In 1751, when £4,750 had thus been raised, the "Contributors to the Pennsylvania Hospital" were incorporated by charter and authorized to choose annually a president and a board of managers. The institution was a private undertaking, and its contributors— 693 of them by 1776—though largely Quaker, came from all faiths and all ranks of society. Chief Justice Allen led the list with a gift of £250 and the promise of £12 annually as long as he lived. Israel Pemberton, Joshua Crosby and Governor Hamilton each subscribed £100. Middle-class citizens generously emptied their purses, James Chattin, printer, Matthew Clarkson, mapmaker, James Claypoole, limner, Joseph Johnson, tinman, and Robert Smith, master builder, subscribing £10 each. Humbler folk also did their bit, such working people as Dennis Dougherty and his wife Mary contributing £1 apiece, and Mary Thrasher, 6 shillings. Matthias Koplin, a pious though eccentric German, convinced by the account in Sower's newspaper that the institution was "not likely to become such a Hospital as I have seen and known in Germany, where great sums of alms were collected and ill-used according to the affection of the masters of the Hospital," donated a small piece of land for its use. By 1754 the Managers could truthfully report that "few of the Wealthy, or those of a middling Rank, failed of contributing according to their Circumstances."

Not waiting for the erection of its fine building designed by Samuel Rhoads, the Pennsylvania Hospital opened on February 6, 1752, in a house on High Street rented from Judge Kinsey. Its facilities were offered, on either a charity or a paying basis, to lunatics and to all sick persons except incurables and those with infectious diseases. Several hundred patients received care and treatment here before the east wing of the new structure was put to use in December, 1756.

Rhoads's plan provided for the most modern type of hospital building then known. The ground floor housed a walking gallery and apartments for lunatics, and was equipped with bathing, heat-ing and sanitary arrangements and with ventilators to expel foul air. Nowhere in the Western world were such comfortable accommodations and enlightened care provided for the mentally ill, whose usual lot was a cold and filthy pen. Male medical and surgical patients were accommodated on the second floor, and women on the third. Open fireplaces and ventilators were also provided for the wards, which were supplied from an apothecary shop, a kitchen and offices. There was a parlor for the reception of visitors, and for use by the staff an excellent medical library was soon assembled.

As the Pennsylvania Hospital acquired fame throughout the colonies, not only for its architectural splendors and well-arranged interiors, but for its excellent medical record, visitors flocked to inspect it as one of the sights of the locality. The Managers finally established a fee of one Spanish dollar for the gratification of such curiosity, whether morbid or scientific. "Traveller" complained in 1771 that, considering one might visit English institutions for only three shillings, this charge was far too high "for a very slight and cursory view of a few coloured prints, and . . . waxen figures" and sight of some lunatic patients. "Citizen," however, retorted that payment of this fee enabled one to see "as fine a set of paintings as were ever in America," inspect the fine work of the hospital, and do good to humanity. Dr. Robert Honyman, an Aberdeen graduate, when he visited the place in 1775 found the hospital overrated, its wards crowded, dirty and poorly ventilated, but he was definitely in the minority. Most visitors, among them John Adams, received a most favorable impression of the "social Use of the Favours of Providence" made by Philadelphians by means of this institution, finding it a worthy and successful enterprise, and one likely "to open a Door of Ease and Comfort to such as are bowed down with Poverty and Sickness."

Better than the reports of any sightseers as a recommendation was the hospital's actual record. As the reputation of its staff and their services grew, patients came to the institution from all parts of the province, and from New Jersey, Maryland and Virginia. In the period from its opening to 1777, out of 8,831 admissions to its medical and surgical departments, it reported 4,440 complete cures and only 852 deaths. Its death rate was thus but a fraction of that in London and Paris hospitals, where the number of patients lost during the same period was staggering. The staff continually emphasized the need for "pure, fresh air," and was wont to condemn English institutions on the ground that not one of them was "constructed upon proper medical principles." Behind the Hospital lay an ideal of social purpose and the hope that it might become "a means of increasing the Number of People, and preserving many useful Members to the Public from Ruin and Distress." Legacies, contributions and voluntary services came steadily from the citizens to assure, in the words of Dr. Rush, that "The Pennsylvania Hospital is as perfect as the wisdom and benevolence of man can make it."

Throughout this period the healing work of the Pennsylvania Hospital was supplemented by that of the Philadelphia Alms House. The latter institution had from the time of its opening in 1732 provided apartments for the sick and the insane among the city's poor, and after 1751 Dr. William Shippen the elder received a salary for his medical services to the inmates. With the erection of the Bettering House, the Contributors took steps to make the institution a complete hospital as well as a house of alms and employment. In May, 1770, Doctors Thomas Bond and Cadwalader Evans were each voted £50 a year for their services as visiting physicians, and two years later the distinguished doctors Adam Kuhn, Benjamin Rush, Samuel Duffield and Gerardus Clarkson were added to its staff.

In addition to the types of cases treated at the Pennsylvania Hospital, the Bettering House accepted incurables, sufferers from certain infectious diseases such as smallpox, and maternity cases; in fact, its lying-in department was the best in the city. Not only "an Asylum for the poor, old, and emaciated, as an Alms House," declared its Managers when requesting a further appropriation from the Assembly in 1775, the Bettering House "is likewise really and fully an Hospital, in every sense of the word, and perhaps more extensively so than any other Institution on this Continent." In its maternity ward "upwards of 30 poor destitute women in a year are

carefully delivered and comfortably provided for in that extremity."
As a foundling hospital the institution annually housed and educated more than fifty orphans. The Managers also took pride in its
services as an inoculation hospital, as a result of which twenty poor
children were at that very moment "all happily coming through the
Disease under Inoculation. . . . In fine," they concluded, "it is a
Hospital for Curables and Incurables of all ages and sexes, and in
every Disease and Malady, even to Lunacy and Idiotism, to a considerable degree."

Even beyond the walls of Hospital and Alms House, efforts to apply the scientific and medical knowledge of the day to problems of
public health went on. Throughout this period citizens continued
to be alarmed at the ravages of the smallpox. Out of 1,344 recorded
deaths in 1773, over 300 resulted from this infection. Mortality from
smallpox was greatest among the children of poor folk, who either
could not afford inoculation or were ignorant of its advantages. In
London as colonial agent in 1759, Franklin had persuaded Dr.
William Heberden to write a pamphlet on the success of inoculation in England and America, with instructions for performing the
operation in one's own home. Printed in London, with a four-page
preface by the American, 1,500 copies were sent to Philadelphia for
free distribution by David Hall. The authors hoped thus to quiet
certain clerical objections to inoculation, and at the same time to
circumvent the barrier of its cost by enabling poor people themselves
to provide such immunization for their children.

Despite considerable publicity throughout the colonies, the success
of this idea hardly measured up to the hopes of its sponsors, but
ultimately there resulted from the campaign to secure inoculation
for the poor an organization devoted to that purpose. Its twelve
managers, among whom were the Quakers Thomas Wharton and
Jacob Shoemaker, collected a substantial fund from the citizens of
Philadelphia with which in February, 1774, they rented a room in
the State House. Here every Tuesday morning applications might
be received and arrangements made for the performance of the
"operation" by Doctors Moore, Kuhn, Kearsley, Duffield, Clarkson,

Thomas Bond, William Shippen, Jr., or Benjamin Rush, each of whom donated his services.

Success of this organization, which enjoyed the compliment of imitation elsewhere in the colonies, led to further suggestions for the increase of population by preventing its "destruction." Deaths by drowning being frequent with the growth of Philadelphia's water front, attention was called to the increasing use of artificial means of resuscitation, and a correspondent to the *Pennsylvania Packet* in March, 1775, suggested following the successful example of Amsterdam and London by formation of a Society for the Recovery of Persons Supposed to Be Drowned. Philadelphia, he maintained, should "step forward, the first trading city in America, and stretch forth her saving hand."

Enlightened public opinion had by 1776 combined with the one important scientific profession of the day to provide for the poor of Philadelphia as fine medical and surgical care as the knowledge of the age could command. At a time when the medical needs of the poor were becoming more clamorous, owing to the growth of population in urban proximity, subject to the periodic epidemics of all eighteenth-century seaports, and exposed to all the ills attendant on poverty, unemployment and seasonal hardships, Philadelphia supplied a set of services unsurpassed in any other community of its day, and indeed, in proportion to the size of the place, seldom equaled. In turn, the advantages to the community, to the colonies as a whole, and to science itself were considerable. The contribution of the two hospitals to the clinical practice of medicine and the growth of scientific experience will be discussed in another connection. It was, however, from the humanitarian impulses of eighteenth-century Quakers and their fellow townsmen that Philadelphia became and was to remain one of the great centers of medical practice and training in the United States.

The effectiveness with which citizens of eighteenth-century Philadelphia brought their consciences to bear on the problem created by another type of social casualty rendered their city for many years pre-eminent in the fields of penal experiment and practice. Influenced by the social theories of John Bellers, the Society of Friends had in 1722 secured the erection at Third and High streets of a fine stone prison which housed debtors in one of its two connecting buildings and criminals in the other. This was a model penal institution for its times; nowhere else in the colonies was a practical distinction maintained between the two categories of prisoners, and in no other prison was so much care given to the provision of fresh air and facilities for exercise.

Until the close of the last French War this building seems to have been well run and adequate for the town's needs. But the depression of the sixties, which followed the collapse of the war prosperity and the tightening of commercial restrictions, and which affected the town's entire economic life, disrupted its penal system as well. Increase of business failures and in the number of attendant lawsuits soon filled the old prison to overflowing with insolvent debtors. So deplorable was the lot of these unfortunates that the *Pennsylvania Journal* solicited the assistance of the charitable by announcing in March, 1763, that contributions for the relief of inmates would be gratefully received by John Mitchell, keeper of the prison. In January, 1766, the continued "wretched condition of debtors now in gaol, without food or Raiment in this rigorous season," caused Joseph Garner, music teacher at the Christ Church School, to conduct a benefit concert, the dollar tickets for which netted a considerable sum for the purchase of "such Necessaries the unhappy Sufferers stand most in need of."

Gradually, as they witnessed the confinement for small obligations of many hitherto honest and respectable neighbors, Philadelphians came to the realization that imprisonment for debt was a social as well as an economic problem. Despite some economic recovery, conditions at the prison did not improve. In 1767 "G. E." published in the pages of the *Pennsylvania Chronicle* an account of Philadelphia's imprisoned debtors, to whom, as their total allowance for food was but two pennies a day, scraps taken from the tables of even "the middle rank," let alone the wealthy, would seem a feast.

Addressing the "female sex" with particular eloquence, the writer pointed out that the city which boasted the finest market in America ought to feel shame that so little of its produce reached the prisoners.

"C. D.", in the *Chronicle* for January 22, 1770, went further, advocating a change in the laws with respect to imprisonment for debt. Many in the prison, dependent "solely on the donations of a few sympathizing inhabitants," had been from six to twelve months destitute of necessities. Some wretches lingered in gaol until death brought relief, two such cases having only recently occurred. What was needed, he maintained, was action by the Assembly, especially in the extension of greater leniency to debtors. That this analysis was not incorrect was emphasized by a report the following December that there were in the prison over fifty debtors, "most of whom are Strangers, destitute of any Provision made for their Releasement, and under long Confinement,—a Circumstance well Worthy of the Attention and Humanity of the Legislature."

Though legislative action was not forthcoming in these years, the imprisoned debtors were not without their active supporters. Private individuals or groups assembled food, bedding, wearing apparel and firewood in increasing amounts for distribution at the prison. Frequent charity sermons raised sums for the prisoners, and in 1769 debtors confined "in No. 9 and 10" announced in the *Chronicle* their gratitude for contributions from "the Young Gentlemen of a School." In March, 1772, a number of Irish gentlemen contributed £30 for prison relief, and the next year "unfortunate Natives of England" in the debtors' department received a generous donation from the Society of the Sons of St. George. At this time also, a "Considerable Number of the most indigent of the confined Debtors" published their thanks to the Sons of St. Tammany for gifts of food and beer.

Humane and sympathetic persons who went to the city prison to minister to the needs of debtors could hardly avoid noticing the even more deplorable conditions obtaining in the criminal department. The harsh penology of the times paid them little heed, however, until the death of a prisoner from starvation in 1770 brought about a legislative investigation. The committee appointed by the Assembly reported that of the thirty-two men and twelve women confined in the city gaol, most had been tried and sentenced, and many had already served out their punishment. Two men had been detained long after their fines for petty larceny had been forgiven; Peter Kearns, for four years, because of his inability to meet the gaoler's fees, and John Harrison for three, because he couldn't furnish security for good behavior demanded by the sheriff, who thought him a dangerous character. The committee found many of the prisoners "almost naked and without Shirts" or bedding. One blanket had to serve two inmates, and only funds raised by a charity sermon had made their inadequate purchase possible. Three more deaths from starvation in March, 1772, focused public attention on these outrages and secured authorization in the next year for the erection of a new prison and workhouse at a cost of £25,000.

Robert Smith designed the new prison, which was opened on the corner of Walnut and Sixth streets in 1775, with the avowed purpose of providing better conditions for the health and comfort of the inmates. Dr. Honyman, one of its first visitors, reported it to be "the largest building for that purpose I ever saw. It consists of a Body and two wings; two stories high besides a Cellar story. . . . It is built of rough stone, and all the apartments within are arched with Brick." There were eight large rooms on a floor, with two windows in each. Dark cells for solitary confinement were provided in another structure standing in the prison yard. Separation of debtors from criminals was still maintained, and improved facilities for the accommodation of both made the Philadelphia prison, by the standards of its day, a remarkable institution. Thirteen years of publicity and agitation had finally resulted in the erection of a place of confinement unequaled in England or America.

There was as yet no liberalization of the law of imprisonment for debt, and no one seems to have thought of making the whole cost of providing warmth and nourishment for prisoners a public charge. Thus, two of the chief causes of want and suffering during imprisonment remained untouched. Private charity was still the sole dependence of criminal or debtor for any comforts beyond the barest necessities of life. Friend Richard Wistar, for instance, was accustomed to have soup prepared in the kitchen of his own home and thence delivered to the inmates of the gaol. In 1776 such spasmodic and undirected activities were finally systematized in the Society for the Relief of Distressed Prisoners, whose members daily for nineteen months, until the British took possession of the city, trundled closed wheelbarrows bearing the legend "Victuals for the prisoners" about the streets from house to house.

Social concern in the colonial era progressed sufficiently to provide private organizations to lessen the miseries of those who had become entangled in the regulations of political society. Reform of the laws that put them in gaol, especially those permitting confinement of the person of a debtor, had to await the radical provisions of the Pennsylvania Constitution of 1776. By the outbreak of the war, however, Philadelphians had already manifested their deep concern over the problems of penology that was again to flourish when hostilities should have passed away.

Perhaps Philadelphia's principal contribution to the "Age of Benevolence" was its crusade for humane treatment of the Negro. Quaker emphasis on the dignity of the individual and the essential brotherhood of man had early focused the attention of Friends on the question of human bondage. In 1688 Francis Daniel Pastorius and his neighbors of Germantown had protested to the Yearly Meeting "against the traffic of menbody," charging that "Quakers do here handel men as they handel the cattle" in Holland or Germany. By 1696 the Meeting had begun to urge its members to cease importing slaves and to accept as men rather than as chattels those they already possessed. A Quarterly Meeting for Negroes was instituted in the city, and Friendly interest in both the material and the spiritual welfare of the black population continued throughout the period intense and fruitful.

The infectious humanitarianism of the Society of Friends spread in time to the city's other religious bodies. The "numerous" black communicants of Christ Church had by 1744 become so "desirous" of religious instruction that the Reverend Robert Jenney applied to London for a catechist for them. All denominations showed concern at the plight of the blacks during the economic depression of the sixties. Charity sermons "in Favour of the distressed Black Inhabitants" preached in most of the city's churches on Sunday, August 4, 1763, were followed up by a house-to-house canvass for funds for Negro relief. Evangelical interest in the souls of black folk reached a peak in 1775 when the Presbyterian Synod undertook consideration of a plan to send two missionaries to Africa. That nothing came of the scheme is but another indication of the blighting effects of the war.

The education of young Negroes had always interested the Quakers, who occasionally admitted a few of them to the Friends' Public School. In numerous letters, and in his tract, *All Slave-Keepers Apostates* (1737), Benjamin Lay had advocated instruction of blacks in reading, writing, and the principles of religion. George Whitefield believed Pennsylvania the most likely province on the continent for the establishment of a Negro school. "The negroes meet there with the best usage," he wrote to the Society for the Propagation of the Gospel in 1740, "and I believe many of my acquaintances will either give me or let me purchase their young slaves at a very easy rate." Anthony Benezet, as a part of his response to the challenge of the whole slavery problem, started in 1750 an evening school for black children, which for twenty years he conducted in his home and supported out of his own purse. In 1770 he finally persuaded the Friends to assume responsibility for this work by undertaking a free school for Negroes in reading, writing and arithmetic. This school proved an extremely popular Quaker charity, receiving frequent generous donations from wealthy members.

Impressed by the labors of Whitefield and Benezet, Benjamin Franklin in 1758 approached the Bray Associates of London on the subject of education for Philadelphia Negroes. In November the Associates authorized the Reverend William Sturgeon of Christ Church, Philadelphia, to employ a schoolmistress to teach thirty young blacks "to Sew, Knit, read and work." A year later this school numbered sixty—thirty-six boys and twenty-four girls. Franklin gave the project his continuous support, and Francis Hopkinson and Edward Duffield, who became trustees in 1766, proved extraordinarily faithful and efficient in their stewardship. The school flourished until the outbreak of the War for Independence interrupted its activities.

The Society of Friends at Philadelphia was the first organized body in the world to take action against the slave trade. In 1712 it memorialized the London Yearly Meeting to consult with Friends in other colonies for the purpose of forming a united front against the traffic in slaves and the holding of blacks in unlimited bondage. At home Quaker influence in the Assembly secured the levying of high duties on the importation of slaves. Testimony in Meeting, combined with the powerful effect of Ralph Sandiford's fiery and eloquent *Brief Examination of the Practice of the Times* (1729), twice printed by Franklin and distributed gratis by the Quakers, caused the gradual withdrawal of Friends from active participation in the trade, and left the Meeting free to concentrate its pressure upon members who bought slaves imported by others.

Fresh from Barbados in 1735, the zealous and eccentric Benjamin Lay, himself a former slave trader, sounded a clarion summons to righteous battle with his *All Slave-Keepers Apostates,* two hundred and seventy-one pages of explosive testimony against this "filthy leprosy . . . so hurtful to religion and destructive to government." Lay's methods were as sensational as his titles; once, at a meeting, he dramatically ran a sword through his coat and drew it forth bathed in blood (it had punctured a filled bladder concealed beneath his clothing), shouting as he did so, "Thus shall God shed the blood of those persons who enslave their fellow creatures!" By such theatrics was the groundwork laid for the services of Benezet and Woolman.

With the declaration that the distinction between slavery and the slave trade constituted "a Plea founded more in Words than Supported by truth," Schoolmaster Anthony Benezet began in 1750 his long and effective war upon slavery itself. Endeavoring in his school to free the blacks from the shackles of ignorance, he sought with voice and pen to strike off their physical fetters as well. In Philadelphia's literature of protest his antislavery writings, contained in his voluminous personal correspondence, in countless articles for almanacs and newspapers, and in numerous pamphlet publications, enjoy a prominent and well-deserved position. His first important piece of writing, *An Epistle of Caution and Advice Concerning the Buying and Keeping of Slaves,* published by the Yearly Meeting in 1754, demanded a definite stand by the Society against the importation and purchase of Negroes. From New Jersey came substantial support for his cause with the publication of *Some Considerations on the Keeping of Negroes* by his friend John Woolman. Ferment ripened into action when in 1758 the Yearly Meeting urged all members to free their blacks, and appointed Woolman head of a committee to prosecute the work.

Thus encouraged, Benezet continued his literary crusade. Newspaper notices of the sale of Negroes newly arrived from Africa, "who have had the Small Pox," had henceforth to compete with the productions of a master of publicity. Sower's press brought out in 1759, and again in 1760, Benezet's *Observations on the Inslaving, Importing and Purchasing of Negroes.* Two years later appeared his *Short Account of That Part of Africa, Inhabited by the Negroes. With Respect to the Fertility of the Country: the Good Disposition of Many of the Natives, and the Manner by Which the Slave Trade is Carried On.* Advocating recourse to legislation, Benezet proposed to end outright the importation of Negroes and to declare free, after a stipulated period of service, those already in bondage. Dunlap had to issue three printings of this work within two years. The Ephrata Brethren published a German version in 1763, and editions appeared in both London and Dublin in 1768. It was very probably a reading of this pamphlet that caused Edward Physick to propose on September 3, 1762, that the Junto debate the question "Is it a good Policy to admit the Importation of Negro Slaves into America?"

Wide discussion had by now aroused the inhabitants, not only of

Philadelphia, but of the colonies at large, to the evils of the slave trade. But Benezet advanced beyond even the colonial point of view with *A Caution and Warning to Great Britain and Her Colonies, in a Short Representation of the Calamitous State of the Enslaved Negroes in the British Dominions,* wherein with impressive clarity and logic he set forth the inconsistency of human slavery with the precepts of Christ. Two thousand copies of this work were sent for distribution to London Quakers with the request that they have it reprinted. This they did in 1767. In that year also a second Philadelphia edition was issued, and later a French translation appeared.

The appeal to the humane instincts of Philadelphians made by Benezet and Woolman, who stressed the natural and moral rights of the blacks, and the economic argument against the slave trade as set forth by Franklin and others, caused a fusion of the question with the whole Revolutionary movement, just as at a later date abolition was frequently associated with larger programs for the radical reconstruction of society.

In the heat of the discussion occasioned by passage of the Townshend Acts the Philadelphia press still carried many items concerned with slavery. Goddard reprinted in his *Pennsylvania Chronicle* of May 23, 1768, materials on the unjustifiable evils of the "Guinea Trade." In November an "Anti-Slave Trader" demanded that "every government on the continent, and in the islands, absolutely prohibit the importation of slaves." Moreover, he proposed the freeing of every black born in America, and a petition to the Crown for the establishment of a colony in "the new lands to the Southward," whither these free Negroes should be sent at government expense when they reached a suitable age. "One step farther would be to emancipate the whole race," restoring thereby the liberty unjustly withheld. Colonials carelessly lay themselves open to charges of barefaced hypocrisy, who publish abroad their "grievances" against Britain, while at the same time they do nothing to rectify this "ignoble practice of slave-keeping." About this time Francis Alison protested indignantly to his friend Ezra Stiles the fact that Yale students were publicly defending slavery. Such proceedings, he feared, would bring down upon the unhappy colonies the full weight of Divine wrath.

Meanwhile, Anthony Benezet continued his labors. At Philadelphia in 1771, and the next year in London, he published his most ambitious book, *Some Historical Account of Guinea . . . with an Enquiry into the Rise and Progress of the Slave Trade,* which was to have sensational results in the movement against the traffic. It so influenced John Wesley that the great evangelist freely plagiarized from it in his *Thoughts on Slavery* (1774). In 1773 Dr. Benjamin Rush, the Presbyterian physician who had become Benezet's most important convert, published anonymously at the latter's suggestion his stirring *Address to the Inhabitants of the British Settlements in America upon Slave-Keeping,* written to accompany a petition requesting the Assembly to increase the import duty on black slaves. This pamphlet drew considerable fire from proslavery advocates, in such arguments as *Personal Slavery Established,* and *Slavery Not Forbidden by Scripture,* and in a long newspaper defense which quoted the book of Genesis to adduce divine sanction for white supremacy and to silence those "who will not allow that God formed them [the blacks] with horses, oxen, dogs, etc., for the benefit of the white people alone . . . to labor with their other beasts in the culture of tobacco, indigo, rice and sugar."

Rush followed his original pamphlet with a *Vindication,* and Benezet saw to it that both were circulated throughout the colonies and in England. "I think the Phisition has handled the subject of slavery in a masterly manner," wrote Robert Pleasants of Virginia upon receipt of the two tracts, and though the Royal African Company will hardly applaud his efforts, he "will receive . . . the approbation of Juditious sensible men." Dr. Rush, George Bryan and others worked fervently with Benezet to muster public opinion for an intercolonial movement against the slave traffic and the holding of black men in bondage. "Great events have been brought about by small beginnings," wrote Rush to Granville Sharp in England in 1773. "Anthony Benezet stood alone a few years ago, in opposing negro slavery in Philadelphia; and now three-fourths of the province, as well as of the city, cry out against it. I sometimes please myself with the hopes of living to see it abolished, or put upon another footing in America."

Frequent kidnaping of free Negroes, manumitted by their Quaker owners, and their resale in Southern colonies led Benezet to seek concerted action against this abuse. In 1775 he founded the Society for the Relief of Free Negroes Unlawfully Held in Bondage, which, while not strictly an antislavery organization, certainly constituted the first "Freedman's Bureau" in America. The culmination of the pre-Revolutionary agitation against slavery occurred in 1776 when, directly as a result of Benezet's continuous pleadings, the Society of Friends agreed to censure and disown all members who persisted in the holding of slaves.

Unlike other aspects of the Enlightenment in Philadelphia, the humanitarian movement despite its many phases produced few outstanding personalities. The towering figure of Anthony Benezet, whose name indeed became synonymous with fervent activity on behalf of his fellow men, constituted the one notable exception. A familiar experience in Philadelphia, said Benjamin Rush, was the sight of this benevolent French Quaker hurrying from house to house, a subscription paper and a petition in one hand, and in the other a pamphlet on the evils of the African slave trade and a letter, addressed to the King of Prussia, on the unlawfulness of war. Professionally an educator, pioneering in the teaching of women and Negroes, he was the friend of Acadians and Indians, the sworn enemy of traffic in human beings and of war.

Benezet's whole life was consecrated in a relentless struggle against "whatever has a tendency to abridge the comforts, increase the sorrows, or endanger the safety of men." His *Thoughts on the Nature of War,* written to promote the cause of peace in 1766, he reissued ten years later to emphasize the fact that "the consequences of war, when impartially examined, will be found big, not only with outward and temporal distress, but also with an evil that extends itself into the regions of eternity." With characteristic directness he sent copies to Henry Laurens, president of the Continental Congress, and to Frederick the Great of Prussia. His interest in the welfare of the aborigines, and his horror at the consequences of their extravagant intemperance, produced his pamphlet *The Mighty Destroyer Destroyed* (1774), in which he compared the havoc wrought by liquor upon the individual with the ravages of war upon society—both brought poverty, pestilence and death.

Composed always in the heat of the moment, his voluminous writings were frequently marred by haste and carelessness, but their passionate sincerity and fervor inevitably commanded attention. Numerous reprintings abroad and translations into French and German attest not only the intercolonial but the international extent of his influence. Anthony Benezet was America's first great humanitarian reformer, the epitome of all that was comprehended in the phrase "the good Quaker."

By the close of the third quarter of the eighteenth century the most significant humanitarian achievements of the Enlightenment were to be found in the American colonies, and especially at Philadelphia, their capital city. While the movement embraced both sides of the Atlantic, and speculation and sermonizing were rife in Europe as in America, it was at Philadelphia, more than anywhere else, that practice kept pace with theory. Here men generally accepted the proposition that poverty, disease and cruelty were intrinsically bad and socially inefficient, and that all were anachronisms in a community where progress was a demonstrable fact. Existence of such deplorable conditions was contrary to right reason, and through reason translated into action they could and must be eliminated. If, as Chief Justice Allen maintained and nobody really disbelieved, Pennsylvania was the best poor man's country in the world, then poverty and inhumanity had no place there.

Although the Age of Reason may have caused a falling off in piety among most organized religious groups, their faith in a creative social gospel intensified under the influence of George Whitefield and the leadership of good Quakers. Also, the administration of charity was no longer confined to sects and denominations. When agencies of government demonstrated unwillingness, indifference, or lack of authority to cope with social problems, citizens, especially the Quakers among them, took matters into their own hands, utilized their free press to turn upon these problems the searchlight of publicity, and effectively employed the voluntary association for achievement of their solution. By either religious or secular means inhabitants of eighteenth-century Philadelphia expended remarkably large amounts of time and money in the interests of those upon whom fortune had failed to smile.

Philadelphia life had, of course, its seamy side, but the increasing number of those who made the eradication of its inhumanities their immediate concern somewhat justified the emerging French legend of *"l'Age d'Or de Pennsylvanie."* As wealth accumulated and the acquisition of information via press or travel improved, it was not easy for the prosperous man to avoid his share of responsibility for the misfortunes of others. The practical concern of citizens in a democracy with the problem of poverty and the social conscience called into being by the Great Awakening merged also with the growing sentimentalism of the later years of the century, so that there were many in the city to whom suffering and cruelty in any form became anathema.

By 1775 this militant sympathy was being extended even to the cause of dumb beasts, and Aitken's *Pennsylvania Magazine* carried an article on "Cruelty to Animals Exposed." At this time cockfighting enjoyed such popularity among the gentry that the elegant James De Lancey was induced to bring his famous bantams over from New York for an intercolonial match. The glib and graceful lines addressed by Francis Hopkinson to the Manhattan sportsman, while primarily for humorous effect, reveal a timely concern over the barbarity of the "cruel Sport."

> Think'st thou that Heav'n was to thy Fortunes kind,
> Gave wealth and Pow'r, gave an immortal Mind,
> With boasted Reason, and a ruling Hand
> To make thee first Cock-Fighter in the Land?
> With crimson Dye our blood shall spot thy Fame,
> And Chickens yet unhatch'd shall curse D[e Lancey]'s Name.

Philadelphians did not need to read Rousseau and Cowper in order
to experience sentiments of pity for man and beast. The greatest humanitarian crusade of the age, the attack upon slavery, had its incep-
tion on the New World side of the Atlantic, as Philadelphians saw
only too clearly the results of their own inhumanity to man.

In Philadelphia the rise of humanitarianism both contributed to
and benefited from the growing spirit of the New World. As sympathy expanded to embrace not only the particular unfortunate but
misery and injustice in general, as new philosophies and the new
religion merged with social and economic needs to endow the individual with dignity and his sufferings with horrible significance,
and as compassion that was romantic and sentimental combined
with knowledge that was practical and sometimes scientific, the
movement became increasingly democratic in its implications. It
impressed the resources of the wealthy, to be sure, but no one can
read the list of benefactors to such enterprises as the Pennsylvania
Hospital without being struck by the number of small contributors.
A very little of worldly prosperity, it seems, was necessary to create
a sense of responsibility toward those less favored.

The movement was popular in composition and collective in expression. In it men clearly demonstrated the powers they were
beginning to find in organization—the strength that lay in union—
so that with the possible exception of Anthony Benezet no one
character overshadowed his neighbors in humane endeavors for
society's good. The humanitarian movement proved a unifying factor
that cut across the social divisors of the age. Despite the bitter partisan and denominational controversy that characterized these years,
men of all classes, sects and political beliefs showed a signal willingness to forget private animosities in the prosecution of a worthy
cause. This experience in co-operation was to pay dividends in the
decade of the seventies, when much the same types of association,
sometimes even the same organizations, that had proved useful in
the fight against social injustice were to be employed in the larger
struggle against injustice to a people as a whole.

Chapter VIII

THE MEDICAL PROFESSION: A COALITION
OF ABLE MEN

WHEN Dr. Thomas Bond appealed to Benjamin Franklin in the year 1751 for assistance in promoting his project for the establishment of a hospital in Philadelphia—a proposal which, "being a novelty in America, and at first not well understood," had up to that date met with little success—the city was already enjoying the services of a medical faculty not inferior in numbers, training and capacity to that of any contemporary community of comparable size and wealth. Its medical demands were those of any city of its day—care of the poor whose illness made them a direct charge upon the community, palliation of chronic ailments and the infirmities of old age, reduction of the number of days lost from productive labor because of sickness, surgical patching up of casualties from accidents, and alleviation, to whatever extent possible, of recurring epidemics of infectious diseases and "summer fevers." However limited may have been the assistance that medical science in its then state of development could offer in these contingencies, it was possible for experienced doctors to practice in such a community with profit and prestige, and so they had been doing, with varying degrees of skill, for many years.

In February, 1752, a group of such doctors, who had recently given "a demonstration of their Skill and Abilities in Anatomy, Operations, Dressings, and Bandaging before the Managers," assumed direction of the newly opened "Infirmary, or Hospital, in the manner of several lately established in Great Britain." With this event, the fruit of Dr. Bond's inspiration and labor, the performance of physic and surgery came of age in Philadelphia, ceasing to be an art practiced by individuals and attaining the dignity of a profession.

The medical knowledge and surgical skill, the high standards of practice and instruction, and the fine sense of professional responsibility of one outstanding man had largely rendered this development possible. Dr. John Kearsley had come to Philadelphia in 1711 and, ardent Anglican though he was, began successfully to compete for fees with the Welsh Quakers who had hitherto monopolized the practice of physic in the town. A liberal education acquired in England soon placed him in the forefront of the town's civic leaders, while his splendid medical training easily gained him pre-eminence in his profession.

With typical eighteenth-century virtuosity Kearsley was not only a doctor but scientist, artist and politician as well. A vestryman of Christ Church, he was the principal architect of its lovely edifice, and years later shared with Robert Smith in drawing up the plans for St. Peter's, while his long service as Assemblyman naturally secured him a place on the committee to superintend the erection of the State House. During his leisure the Doctor made notes on his observations of comets and eclipses, which by the good offices of his friend Collinson of London were published in the *Philosophical Transactions* of the Royal Society.

Yet it was in his capacity as a professional physician that Kearsley left the greatest impress upon the life of his adopted city. In addition to the daily exercise of his skill, he was able by observation, practice, and the use of his pen to contribute to the advance of medical knowledge in Philadelphia. As early as 1731 he and a number of his students (Zachary, Cadwalader, Sommers, Thomas Bond and William Shippen) set a public example by submitting themselves to inoculation for smallpox, and twenty years later he was able to record with some pride that it was "myself, who was the first that us'd Inoculation in this Place."

His interest in and advocacy of this highly controversial operation, as well as his own natural contentiousness, involved him in much literary argument with his medical contemporaries. In *A Letter to a Friend* (1751) he charged that Dr. Adam Thompson's *Discourse on the Preparation of the Body for the Small Pox* (1750) betrayed that author's lack of acquaintance with those authorities whose "Rules of Practice in a Science" cannot "be prostituted to the vain Chimeras of a doubtful Hypothesis," and insinuated that Thompson's liberal use of "Catholic Bark" was "the common Refuge of Ignorance." Kearsley's style reflected both the writer and his age, for medical controversy in the eighteenth century was characterized by a ferocious dogmatism in which no reputable scientist would today indulge. Later, in an open letter to Thompson in the *Pennsylvania Journal,* he made a partial apology, expressing regret that the feelings of the Scottish doctor had been wounded by the exchange.

Many leading physicians, including Dr. Alexander Hamilton of Annapolis, upheld Thompson's advocacy of mercury and antimony as preparatives for inoculation, and Kearsley himself ultimately condoned their "mild" use. He was also the first of a long line of Philadelphia physicians to make a study of the ravages of yellow fever. In 1742 he wrote a critique of the work of Dr. John Mitchell on the Virginia epidemic of 1740-41, pointing out the differences in its symptoms appearing among Pennsylvania victims at the same time. This paper remained in manuscript but may have furnished the basis for the appendix to his *Letter to a Friend,* which presented "some Practical Hints relating to the Cure of the Dumb Ague, Lung Fever, the Bilious Fever, and some other Fevers, incidental to this Province."

Thus in a very real sense John Kearsley was the founder of the medical profession of Philadelphia, marking out the lines of its future development, and devoting his talents without stint in many fields of public endeavor. He introduced a method of immunization from one of the most dreaded diseases of his age and inaugurated the study of a plague that was to remain for some time the city's greatest curse. He pioneered in the publication of his scientific findings, and assumed leadership of one side in the chief medical controversy of his day. But his principal contribution to the medical development of his community lay in the thorough fundamental training and desire for further scientific education and research imparted by him to a group of young men, his students, who in the year 1752 constituted the foremost medical coterie in the thirteen colonies. Indeed, by the time of the founding of the hospital their youth, energy, and splendid training were already beginning to eclipse even the capacities of their sixty-eight-year-old mentor.

Up to this time the sole means of securing a medical education in America was by apprenticeship to a practicing physician or surgeon. Here a lad spent his time compounding medicines, running errands, making fires and cleaning offices, serving in general as "servant, coachman, messenger-boy, prescription-maker, nurse and assistant surgeon." Between such menial chores he might read a few medical books, learn to bandage and to hold instruments, and pick up what knowledge he could from observation and from such lessons as his master chose to impart. The better master physicians were much in demand and parents paid high fees to secure admission of a son to their households. One of the most popular was Kearsley, who in the course of thirty years of exacting practice took to live with him as house pupils and apprentices a number of young men of good families and divers faiths, and so trained them that their later achievements in the field of medicine were in almost every case remarkable.

As master Kearsley revealed none of the qualities that as Assemblyman had rendered him so popular that he was often "borne from the Assembly to his own home on the shoulders of the people." His training was exhausting and his discipline strict. To his students he appeared a harsh and slavish taskmaster, whose "morose and churlish temper," Dr. John Bard remembered, "banished all cheerfulness and social converse from his pupils, and rendered him an unpleasant companion." Yet while these scions of the gentry chafed under his stern regimen, they imbibed from their mentor the spirit of scientific inquiry and a thirst for further knowledge.

Young men of means, they were able to follow out his suggestions, and almost to a man they crossed the Atlantic in search of the best the medical profession of the Old World had to offer. Lloyd Zachary led the way in 1723 with a three-year sojourn in England. Shortly afterwards, Thomas Cadwalader became the first native Philadelphian to attain a European medical degree, graduating from the University of Rheims, and afterwards studying surgery in London under William Cheselden. Thomas Bond acquired much of his surgical knowledge at the Hôtel Dieu in Paris, and his younger brother Phineas studied at London, Leyden, Paris and Edinburgh. To Edinburgh as well went Cadwalader Evans, while John Kearsley II and John Bard also pursued further study abroad.

Thomas Cadwalader, progenitor of one of Philadelphia's most aristocratic families, was the first of Dr. Kearsley's pupils to achieve professional eminence. Armed with his French medical degree and his London surgical experience, he returned to the Pennsylvania capital about 1730, and there began a series of anatomical lectures for the benefit of local practitioners. Among his most regular listeners was William Shippen the elder, who alone of Kearsley's famous students did not go to Europe for graduate study. Shippen, however, made himself proficient in chemistry and natural philosophy, and soon became, under Cadwalader's tutelage, a skillful surgeon. Dr. Cadwalader moved to Trenton about 1740 and practiced there for a decade, though he regularly spent a part of each year at his country seat on the Schuylkill, and retained his active interest in the Library Company of Philadelphia, of which he had been a director.

In 1745 from the press of Benjamin Franklin came Dr. Cadwalader's *Essay on the West-India Dry-Gripes: with the Method of Preventing and Curing That Cruel Distemper,* wherein he demonstrated this colic to be caused by drinking a punch made from Jamaica rum which had been distilled through leaden pipes. Apparently the paper resulted from some professional controversy over the causes of the "dry-gripes," for a somewhat acid preface, soon to be suppressed, claimed that neither thirst for fame nor expectation of profit but only desire to be of public service impelled the author to publish. A second, more amiable foreword generously acknowledged the assistance and additional material contributed by Dr. Adam Spencer and "his Trouble in revising this Essay."

"I have long been of the opinion," wrote Dr. Cadwalader, in thus inaugurating local medical publication, "that 'tis the duty of Physicians frankly to communicate to the World any particular Method of treating diseases, which they have found to be successful in the course of their experience, and not generally known or practiced by others." To this end he printed with the *Essay* a careful account of an autopsy performed in April, 1742, on the body of a woman afflicted with *mollites ossium*. The paper was well received, attracting attention abroad as well as in the colonies, and as a result the drinking of rum punch was somewhat discouraged. Just before his return to Philadelphia in 1750 Dr. Cadwalader made perhaps the earliest experiment with the therapeutic use of electricity in America, and was reported thus to have saved the life of the son of Governor Belcher of New Jersey. He proved an able instructor of medical students, and Dr. John Jones, his most distinguished pupil, praised his thorough care in the teaching of "both physic and morals."

More famous than Cadwalader as a teacher and an organizer of his profession was Dr. John Redman, who after graduating from the Log College at Neshaminy came also under the tutelage of Kearsley. He practiced for a few years in Bermuda, and then, with some financial aid from his brother and a substantial loan from William Allen, crossed the Atlantic in 1746 for a year under Munro *primus* and others at Edinburgh. In 1748 he graduated from the University of Leyden, where he published a remarkable dissertation, *De Abortu,* in the same year. He completed his training with a year at Guy's Hospital, London, whence he received a certificate praising his "great application" and high qualifications for his chosen work. Returning to Philadelphia possessed of the finest medical education of any of the local faculty, Dr. Redman now, despite his early specialization in surgery and midwifery, confined himself entirely to the practice of medicine.

Under the influence of Boerhaave and Sydenham, Redman sub-

scribed to the belief that Americans required stronger doses of medicine than did the English—an idea which long prevailed in the
profession—but he proved more flexible than some of his successors
when he later accepted the milder views of Dr. Cullen of Edinburgh.
He became noted for the "anaesthetic kindness" of his bedside manner and for the promptness with which he responded to his calls,
riding about town on a little fat pony which the son of Benjamin
Rush remembered seeing him hitch "to the turnbuckle of the mansion shutter, so that she always stood on the foot-pavement." Redman's great influence on the future of medical practice in America,
however, derived from his skill and idealism as a preceptor, for
among his "professional children" he numbered Doctors John Morgan and Benjamin Rush.

The decade preceding the founding of the hospital also witnessed
medical achievements by others than the students of Dr. Kearsley.
The fact that of the seventeen physicians known to have practiced in
Philadelphia in these years only three were without some sort of
European training elevated the entire tone of the medical faculty
and made for considerable exchange of scientific views and information. From Boston late in 1743 came Dr. Adam Spencer, trained in
Edinburgh, and "justly recommended" by eminent Londoners "as a
most Judicious and experienced Physician and Man-midwife." He
it undoubtedly was who informed Cadwalader of the views of Boston physicians concerning the effects of lead-pipe stills, which had
led to the Massachusetts legislation of 1723 prohibiting their use in
the manufacture of rum.

The *Autobiography* acknowledges the indebtedness of Franklin to
Spencer in the field of electricity, a subject treated by the latter in an
epochal series of lectures on natural philosophy delivered at the
State House. On May 29, 1744, he lectured on the eye, endeavoring
"to account for the Faculties, the Nature and Diseases of that Instrument of Sight," a performance significant as the first public medical
lecture to be held in the city, as well as one of the earliest scientific
treatments of ophthalmology, a field more generally left to quacks
throughout the eighteenth century. Spencer was also the first phy-

sician to attempt, though not with marked success, to challenge the monopoly exercised by the city's midwives.

Like the Bond brothers, Samuel Preston Moore, and other Maryland doctors who were attracted to the metropolis, Dr. Adam Thompson, originally of Edinburgh, came up to Philadelphia in 1748 to "practice Physick, Chirurgery and Midwifery." His advertisement that he would keep "no publick Apothecary Shop" seems to have aroused the resentment of physicians in town whose practice it was to compound their own medicines, depending thereon for much of their income, and may have contributed to the storm of opposition that greeted his public "Oration" on preparing the body for inoculation, which he delivered at the Academy on November 21, 1750. During the newspaper controversy that followed the publication of his essay, he was forced to deny the assertion of a certain Quaker that he had "call'd most of the Practitioners in Town Quacks."

In the end Thompson won out over his critics, including even the redoubtable Dr. Kearsley. He had the satisfaction of introducing the use of mercury into Philadelphia practice, of initiating the city's first important medical controversy, of inaugurating public medical lectures at what was later to become the University of Pennsylvania, and of carrying on the work of Spencer as an accoucheur. In 1749 he joined with Dr. Graeme and other Scots in founding the St. Andrew's Society, an organization he served as an officer for many years.

Important achievements in the year 1751-52 made it a turning point in the medical history of Philadelphia and of the colonies as well. Late in 1751 Franklin and Hall published the third edition of Thomas Short's *Medicina Britannica,* with preface and notes by John Bartram, "shewing the Places where many of the described Plants are to be found in these Parts of America . . . and an Appendix, containing a Description of a Number of Plants peculiar to America, their Uses, Virtues, etc." This work was especially directed to persons in rural areas who lacked "the Helps of the Learned," but it contained as well important New World additions to the pharmacopoeia of the day. In April, 1752, Dr. Cadwalader Evans, aided by Benjamin Franklin as technician, experimented with the use of electricity to relieve a young woman who, having suffered from convulsions for ten years, consented to try the novel cure as a last resort. Publication in the first volume of the London *Medical Observations and Enquiries* (1753) of Evans's account of this case and of a paper by Dr. Thomas Bond on the appearance of a worm in the human liver aroused European interest in the work of Philadelphia physicians.

Also in 1752 Charles Moore took his degree at the University of Edinburgh, and thereby initiated the procession of Philadelphians from the Scottish institution which so significantly affected the future medical development of their city. At this time, too, Benjamin Franklin was able to report to Dr. Perkins of Boston the astounding record of only four deaths resulting from over eight hundred cases of smallpox by inoculation during the city's five epidemics since 1730. Crowning all the accomplishments of these twelve fertile months came the opening of the Pennsylvania Hospital, the particular achievement of Dr. Thomas Bond.

At the time of his proposals Thomas Bond, former Marylander and one-time student of Dr. Kearsley's, had just returned from his third trip of medical observation and study in the Old World. He had studied in Paris in 1738-39, and letters from contemporaries reveal him to have been in London in the spring of 1744. As principal organizer of the medical faculty of Philadelphia, he had been selected by Franklin to represent his profession in the newly founded American Philosophical Society of 1743. Interest in the application of medicine to problems of hygiene and epidemiology doubtless took him again to England at the close of King George's War (1748), and his experience with the newly established hospitals in London led him on his return to propose a similar institution for his own community.

The times were ripe for such a development. During the decade 1740-50 the idea of association had been taking root among medical men. As apprentices and house pupils, first of Kearsley, and later of Bond, Redman and Cadwalader, they acquired for one another a fraternal regard which, as they jointly or separately pursued their advanced studies in Europe, ripened into a sense of professional solidarity. The very generality of European training, and the interchange of views and experience it made possible, contributed to the growth of their professional spirit. Exposed by their travels to all the educational and humanitarian impulses of the age, they were able, in the prosperity of their growing urban practices—Graeme, Zachary, Bond and Cadwalader supported fine country estates—to participate, singly or in association, in movements for the social betterment of their community. Lloyd Zachary, William Shippen, Sr., and Thomas and Phineas Bond, for instance, were all trustees of the Academy in 1749.

These men demonstrated their increasing professionalism in their desire to combine practice with research and to broadcast the results of their experience and scholarship by medical publication. Between 1740 and the year of the establishment of the hospital, while the whole question of medical progress and research was enjoying widespread publicity in local newspapers, Philadelphia presses issued nine original works and two important reprints of English medical treatises. During the same period four studies by Philadelphia doctors achieved publication abroad—in London, Leyden, and Edinburgh.

The opening of the Pennsylvania Hospital provided members of the faculty with opportunity to work out together many of the ideas they had acquired in Europe. Distinguished men, who generously donated their services, composed its staff from the first. The resident group consisted of Dr. Zachary and the Bond brothers, while for "consultation in extraordinary cases" the Managers called in Thomas Graeme, Thomas Cadwalader, Samuel Moore and John Redman. Before the close of the colonial period the elder Shippen, Cadwalader Evans, John Morgan, Charles Moore and Adam Kuhn had been chosen to fill vacancies occurring on the staff.

Under such able leadership the hospital performed, as has been earlier demonstrated, remarkable services for the sick and the insane of the community. Perhaps its most signal achievement lay in breaking down the fear and suspicion with which members of middling and lower classes, from both town and country, regarded the medical profession. Experience of free and fairly effective treatment by skilled practitioners undoubtedly did much to educate the public in matters of health and hygiene, and to undermine, at least partially, the rule of quack doctors and their sovereign remedies.

From the purely professional viewpoint the hospital justified the faith and monetary support accorded it by virtually all of the faculty. Its apothecary shop adopted the most modern developments in pharmacy, and in it a number of able druggists, among them John Morgan and George Weed, underwent apprenticeship. Its wards provided physicians, surgeons, and their pupils with means of increasing their knowledge and skill. The advantages derived from clinical observation of its nearly 9,000 medical and surgical cases from 1752 to 1777 could be excelled or equaled in only a few hospitals in the largest cities of Europe. Intelligent rules, strictly observed from the beginning by Managers and staff, maintained and elevated professional standards.

America's first medical museum was begun at the hospital in 1757, when Deborah Morris presented it with a skeleton for teaching purposes. Five years later a donation valued at £350 from John Fothergill, the great Quaker physician of London, included three cases of anatomical casts, a skeleton, a fetus, and eighteen crayon drawings of parts of the body executed by the Dutch painter Van Rymsdyke. By order of the Managers these were placed in a room set aside for the purpose, and to them were later added preparations of muscles and arteries and another skeleton purchased from the estate of Dr. William Logan in 1772. Visitors might view this collection for a dollar, and any professor could give lectures and demonstrations from the exhibits at a charge of one pistole per student. In May, 1763, Dr. William Shippen, Jr., offered the first series of public lectures so illustrated, proceeds of which he donated to the hospital. A gift in 1762, also from Dr. Fothergill, formed the basis of the hospital library. Supported from the students' fees, it was greatly augmented in 1767 by its acquisition of the books of the late Dr. Zachary, one of the best medical collections in the colonies.

To such members of its staff as Doctors Redman, Cadwalader, the elder Shippen and Thomas Bond, who regularly trained apprentices, the Hospital proved a valuable adjunct to their teaching. Here students could witness operations, observe the treatment of the sick, and follow post-mortem examinations. In this fashion, Dr. Bond declared, the clinician comes "to the aid of speculation and demonstrates the Truth of Theory by facts." His own admirable procedure would do credit to any medical school of today. Meeting his students at the Hospital at stated times, he had them observe a particular patient, while questioning them "in the most exact and particular manner," in order to convince them "how many and what minute Circumstances are often necessary to form a judgment . . . on which the Safety and Life of the Patient depend." He would then himself pronounce upon the disease with regard to treatment and possible cure, giving "his reasons from Authority or Experience" for all he said.

Following Boerhaave, Bond laid great stress on the importance of autopsies in his teaching. "By exposing all the Morbid parts to View, and demonstrating by what means death was produced the doctor brings his knowledge to the Test, and fixes Honour or discredit on his Reputation," discovering whether his judgment be true or false. If the latter, "like a great and good Man," he acknowledges his mistake and suggests other methods to follow. The post-mortem examination, he concluded, "is the surest method of obtaining just ideas of Diseases." With experience thus supplementing "Language and Books," the Pennsylvania Hospital, like the great infirmaries of London, Edinburgh and Paris, became in these years, under the able leadership of Thomas Bond, one of the world's "Grand Theatres of Medical Knowledge."

While taking full advantage of the facilities of the Hospital for the education of both practitioners and students, Bond devoted much energy to the care and comfort of his patients. He was a clever anatomist and surgeon, his skillful "anatomical preparations of the

Father of the Pennsylvania Hospital and of the clinical practice of medicine in America.

Dr. Thomas Bond, artist unknown.

(Courtesy Pennsylvania Hospital)

People were proud to be able to say, "I've seen him."
Dr. John Morgan, portrait by his patient, Angelica Kaufmann.
(Courtesy University of Pennsylvania)

muscles and blood-vessels injected with wax" earning the praise of even so caustic a critic as Alexander Hamilton of Annapolis. He devised a splint which is still used today for fractures of the lower end of the radius and invented an esophageal forceps for extracting foreign bodies from the throat. His firm belief in the value of post-mortem dissection led him to perform a number of remarkable autopsies, often before large audiences of professional and apprentice doctors.

Dr. Bond was well known for his lithotomies, which elicited highest praise from students and colleagues and were admired in Europe. After witnessing his removal of a large stone from a youth-ful sufferer in 1772, one observer was moved to ecstatic comment in the *Gazette:* "instead of seeing an operation said to be perplexed with difficulty and uncertainty, and attended with violence and cruelty, it was performed with such ease, regularity and success, it scarcely gave a shock to the most sympathetic bystander." Bond's most famous operation was perhaps his removal of a cancerous growth from the nose of Caesar Rodney, though Rodney had been advised by Messrs. Allen and Chew to go to England for treatment and relief. A paper on the uses of Peruvian bark in the treatment of scrofula, published in the London *Medical Observations and Enquiries* for 1759, shows that despite his preoccupation with surgery, Dr. Bond could on occasion do research in medicine as well.

The story of the Philadelphia medical profession from 1753 to 1776 is one of growth in numbers, of wider training and experience in men of marked ability, of a developing sense of professional solidarity and obligation, of improvement in the medical facilities available to the public, and of active interest on the part of a large proportion of the faculty in the power of medical science to promote the public welfare. In the two decades prior to the War for Independence at least eighty-two physicians and surgeons, perhaps more, practiced in the city. Associated with them were some seven oculists and dentists of reputable standing, and ten apothecaries, at the least, who prescribed treatment in addition to dispensing remedies. Of this group more than half had undertaken some study in the Old World, and at least twenty are known to have possessed European medical degrees. Few cities anywhere at this time enjoyed the services of a better trained medical group.

Lest this picture seem too bright, it must be remembered that quackery easily kept pace with the growth of legitimate medicine. There was no system of medical licensing, and nothing to prevent untrained apothecaries, barbers, or those who had failed in other lines of work from peddling their miraculous cures. The marks of the quack were his flamboyant advertisements, replete with fulsome testimonials, and his glowing promises to cure anything, but especially cancer and venereal diseases. For the most part also neither eyes nor teeth were considered worthy the specialized attention of the trained doctor, and treatment of those organs was left largely to the "empirics." Existence and widespread tolerance of such charlatans explain the newspaper epigram on "The Advantage of having two Phisicians":

> One prompt Phisician like a sculler plies,
> And all his Art, and skill applies;
> But two Phisicians, like a pair of Oars,
> Convey you soonest to the Stygian Shores.

Notwithstanding the slowly widening circle of medical knowledge, much ignorance and fear of the medical profession still prevailed among the common people, and superstitious devotion to "kitchen-physic" and old wives' remedies lay deep embedded in the folkways of both town and country. To such prejudices the widely advertised patent medicines made a ready appeal, and self-medication with favorite nostrums constituted, then as now, the resort of the gullible and the ignorant.

The more highly trained physicians continued, as in the past, to be drawn from wealthy mercantile families, since training for the profession proved too costly for most others. Most of them commenced their medical education as apprentices under the more prominent local doctors already named. Historians have been inclined to write disparagingly of this sort of training, but it should be observed that the example of an able and conscientious mentor could be infinitely superior to tuition at an inferior medical school, and that the best of the training doctors inspired and encouraged their students to pursue further study abroad. In consequence, a steady procession of young Philadelphians crossed the ocean at great expense in search of the best instruction possible, under such men as Heberden, Fothergill, Pringle, the Hunters, Lettsom and McKenzie, and in the London hospitals. Increasingly, however, the University of Edinburgh became the Mecca for colonial medical students, and of the many Philadelphia practitioners who studied there eleven, at least, took degrees.

Simultaneously, a number of properly trained Europeans, such men as Dr. Lachlan Macleane of Ireland, Bodo Otto of Hamburg, Lewis Colin of Paris and Joseph Batacchi of Italy, were attracted to the capital city of the New World. Otto practiced in and about Philadelphia, and was later a prominent Revolutionary physician on the patriot side. Educated in a German university, and fresh from experience in the army and the hospitals of his native land, Dr. Ludwig arrived in 1775 to minister to his countrymen in the vicinity of the city. These men, native or foreign, discovered, as Samuel Coates informed William Logan on the latter's graduation from Edinburgh in 1770, that "a Skilful Practitioner might do well" in the Quaker city.

Philadelphia, with its multiplying population and expanding back country, offered ample opportunity for young doctors. Much the same situation prevailed in other colonies, where rural areas, especially, were rapidly filling up. This need for medical men everywhere focused the attention of the profession on the lack of educational facilities in America.

Because of the high costs of European training many "young men of genius" who lacked the necessary "Circumstances and Connections" were barred from such opportunities and the public thus deprived of their services. Moreover, the Atlantic crossing involved genuine dangers as well as expense. Cadwalader Evans's foreign studies were delayed by a brush with pirates and an enforced sojourn on the island of Hispaniola before he could make his way back to Philadelphia, and thence to Edinburgh and London. Samuel, son of Dr. John Bard, took passage for Portsmouth in 1760 on a packet which was captured off Cornwall by a French privateer, with the consequence that the young medical student endured many weeks of captivity at Bayonne before his release could be procured. Jonathan Potts, James Cummins and Benjamin Rush suffered a frightful passage to Liverpool aboard the Philadelphia packet in the autumn of 1766. All three were wretched and weak from seasickness, and the death of young Cummins shortly after their landing was the direct result of the terrible experiences of his crossing. With the growing demand for doctors at home, the facilities for practice offered by such an infirmary as the Pennsylvania Hospital, and the innumerable difficulties involved in obtaining a foreign degree, all things pointed to the logic of a good medical school in the colonial metropolis.

A tentative step in this direction was made as early as 1762. In November of that year the *Gazette* announced that at six o'clock on the evening of the sixteenth, at the State House, Dr. William Shippen, Jr., would commence, under the sponsorship of the Pennsylvania Hospital, "a course of anatomical Lectures . . . for the Advantage of the young Gentlemen now engaged in the Study of Physic, in this and the neighboring provinces . . . and also for the Entertainment of any Gentlemen who may have the Curiosity to understand the Anatomy of the Human Frame." No doctor then in Philadelphia could have been more conversant with the problems of medical education, more aware of the dangers and expense of seeking it abroad, or better qualified to introduce it in his native place.

Scion of one of the city's most wealthy and prominent families and son of one of its leading physicians, William Shippen had proceeded from the Nottingham School, where John Morgan had been a fellow student, to the College of New Jersey, of which his uncle was a trustee. Although George Whitefield, impressed by his brilliant valedictory at the commencement of 1754, had tried to persuade the eighteen-year-old Presbyterian to enter the ministry, parental pressure and example ultimately decided him in favor of the family profession. After a three-year apprenticeship with his father, he sailed for London to complete his medical education in 1757. Late in that year Pennsylvania's colonial agent in London received an urgent and eloquent letter from young Shippen at Belfast. His storm-wracked ship had put into the Irish port after a fearful voyage, the last week of which had seen both passengers and crew reduced to a meager daily ration of salt meat and one quart of water. Consequently, though equipped with letters of credit on London, he had to beg his friend Mr. Franklin to advance the funds to get him to England. Well might Shippen in later years consider the plight of the student without "Circumstances and Connections."

Letters of introduction from physicians at home, coupled with the good offices of Franklin, secured the young man a place in the household of Dr. John Hunter. In addition, he studied surgery under William Hunter and William Hewson. "I do not spend my time trifling about Playhouses or operas or reading idle romantic tales or trifling newspapers at coffee-houses, as I find many have done before me," he reported somewhat self-righteously to his uncle in Lancaster, "but rather in the rich improvement of those advantages which are not to be had in my own country." Interest in obstetrics led him to seek instruction under Dr. Colin McKenzie in the slum sections of London, and in time he added great skill in midwifery to his already acquired anatomical proficiency. In London, too, he came under the patronage of Dr. John Fothergill, whose interest was to be of considerable aid to him on his return to his homeland. In 1760, armed with an introduction from Benjamin Franklin to Dr. Cullen, Shippen went to the University of Edinburgh, where he proved an outstanding student, and where, after publication of an important thesis in the field of obstetrics, *De Placentae cum Utero Nexu,* he took his degree in 1761.

At Edinburgh Shippen conceived the idea of delivering a series of lectures on anatomy when he returned to Philadelphia, a project he discussed with his old schoolmate John Morgan, when the latter likewise appeared in Scotland for medical study. With this plan in mind, as well as from desire to round out his training as a gentleman, he determined, if possible, to make the Grand Tour. England and France were still at war, but the famous surgeon Sir John Pringle was able in those days of enlightened hostilities to arrange with French physicians and officials for Shippen to accompany a tubercular patient as medical attendant. In this capacity he toured France, visited the great hospitals of Montpelier and Paris, and became personally acquainted with prominent Continental doctors, among them the famous Senlac. Crowning his social achievements by his brilliant marriage to the beautiful Alice Lee of Virginia, he returned to his native land in the year 1762, bearing with him strong letters of recommendation and a gift of casts and drawings from Dr. Fothergill, and determined to raise the practice of obstetrics to a position of professional dignity.

The large audience of local intelligentsia which attended Shippen's introductory lecture at the State House in November, 1762, assured the success of his project. The course commenced meeting regularly the next week at his father's house in Fourth Street, its registration made up of twelve medical students, among them Benjamin Rush, and some gentlemen who desired to "learn the art of Dissecting, Injections, etc." In December Shippen procured from the local authorities the body of a Negro who had hanged himself, and thereafter was able to receive for dissecting purposes the corpses of all suicides and executed criminals.

Aware of the novelty of his undertaking and of the possibility of opposition from some quarters, Dr. Shippen shrewdly appealed not only to serious students of medicine but also to the influential and scientifically inclined among the laity. In February he announced in the *Gazette* that since he had now completed his lectures on osteology, "the most dry, though necessary Part of Anatomy," it was possible for "any Gentlemen, who don't think it necessary to attend the whole Course," but who wished to understand something of the structure of the human body, to "gratify their Curiosity, by attending any particular lecture." A list of his lecture subjects was posted at

Bradford's London Coffee House, where tickets were on sale at 5 shillings per lecture.

Successful in this effort, Shippen the next year expanded his course to sixty lectures, including in addition to anatomy, surgical operations, bandaging, midwifery, and instruction in injecting and dissection. To attract students from out of town, he arranged for extension to them of the privileges of practicing in the Pennsylvania Hospital, and further to popularize his work he gave biweekly public demonstrations of the Fothergill casts and drawings, now housed in the hospital museum.

Satisfied with the reception accorded his anatomy courses, Shippen soon turned to his second objective, the elevation of obstetrics to a professional plane. By virtue of the pioneer work in midwifery performed by Doctors Thompson, Spencer and Redman, the public at Philadelphia was perhaps better prepared for this innovation than anywhere else in the colonies. Early in 1765 Shippen informed the public through the pages of the *Pennsylvania Gazette* that he had recently assisted a number of women through difficult deliveries, "made so by the unskillful old women about them." In most cases the mothers suffered excessively and the babies died. It was because such cases abounded that he proposed his "intended" course in midwifery for "those Women who have Virtue enough to own their Ignorance, and apply for Instruction." Thus, although he also designed his course for those students of physic and surgery "who are taking Pains to qualify themselves to practice in different Parts of the Country, with Safety and Advantage to their Fellow Creatures," he did not propose any immediate attack on the vested interests of local midwives.

Perhaps the most revolutionary feature of his plan was his proposal to combine with his lectures a course in prenatal care for pregnant mothers. For "a few poor Women," who might otherwise "be unable to attend from the country, or who might lack necessaries," he provided convenient lodgings under supervision of a skilled matron. With his characteristic felicity in the handling of delicate matters, he advertised the "female Pupils to be taught privately, and assisted at any of their private labours when necessary." Thus combining instruction with finesse, Dr. Shippen laid the groundwork for the first successful practice of obstetrics in the American colonies.

All that one man working alone might accomplish to promote formal medical education in his locality, William Shippen, Jr., had performed. But he envisioned more. Announcing his fifth course, in September, 1766, he called public attention to the fact that as far back as in his initial lecture of November, 1762, he had pointed out the need for a medical school in the New World. "What place would be so fit for such a School as *Philadelphia,* that bids so fair by its rapid growth to be soon the *Metropolis* of all the continent?" Such an institution should properly begin with the study of anatomy, as did the great school at Edinburgh with the lectures of Dr. Munro. Inasmuch as the suggested seminary is now about to be founded, this extract from his Introductory Lecture is offered to the public, explained the physician, to prove to those unable to be present that he "proposed and began to execute a plan for the institution of a medical school in this place four years ago." And thereby hangs a tale.

Among Shippen's schoolmates at the Nottingham School some fifteen years before had been John Morgan, a precocious lad of Welsh Quaker stock, whose family, with the increase of their wealth and social position, had deserted the Meeting to become communicants at Christ Church. After completing his studies at school, Morgan spent six years in Philadelphia as an apprentice under Dr. John Redman, at the same time graduating from the College with its first class in 1757, and serving a year as apothecary at the hospital. He finished his apprenticeship in 1758 in time to accompany the Forbes expedition to Fort Duquesne as military surgeon with the rank of lieutenant. This adventure gained him considerable experience in both medicine and surgery, and some reputation as a physician.

In the spring of 1760 John Morgan sailed aboard the *Dragon* for England, bearing letters of introduction to British Anglicans from that patron of science and letters, the Reverend Thomas Barton. In London, where he attended the lectures of Dr. William Hunter, his genuine ability combined with his handsome appearance and genteel mien to gain him entrance to the best medical and literary society. After a year he traveled north to Edinburgh, recommended by Franklin to the patronage of Lord Kames as one who "I think will one day make a good figure in the profession, and be of some credit to the school he studies in, if great industry and application, joined with natural genius and sagacity, afford any foundation for the presage."

Thus far no American student had arrived in Edinburgh with so much medical experience behind him, and at the university Morgan amply justified the endorsement of his father's old friend and neighbor. He won the enduring friendship of Dr. Cullen, who came to regard him as more colleague than pupil. In 1763 he took his degree with an epoch-making thesis, *De Puopoiesi sive Tentamen Medicum in Augurale de Puris Confectione,* in which he set forth the novel doctrine that pus was a secretion under certain inflammatory conditions from the blood vessels, and did not arise, as the profession had hitherto supposed, from solid tissues. A century later this revolutionary discovery was confirmed by Cohnheim's demonstration that pus is secreted by the white corpuscles. "Morgan has graduated at Edinburgh with an éclat almost unknown before," reported his best friend, young Samuel Powel, in September, 1763. "The Professors give him the highest character you can imagine."

At Edinburgh Morgan again encountered William Shippen, with whom he discussed the possibilities for medical education in the colonies and the latter's plan to deliver anatomical lectures on his return. Like Shippen, he resolved to complete his medical and social education with the experience of a European tour. In Paris in 1763 he profoundly impressed members of the profession with his capacity and learning, especially by his injection of a kidney "in so curious and elegant a manner" as to surpass anything ever seen there before. Here he studied more anatomy under M. Sue, visited the Paris hospitals, about which he corresponded with Shippen, now back in Phil-

adelphia, and was made a corresponding member of the Académie
Royale de Chirurgie. In Paris also, he began to formulate plans for
a medical school in his native city, which, as he journeyed toward
Italy with Samuel Powel, were "greatly amended" by the latter's
"candid and judicious remarks."

Although, as has previously been noted, the two young aristocrats
gave themselves over to wholehearted enjoyment of travel in Holland and Switzerland and ultimately surrendered to "the softer arts
of Italy," Morgan, wherever he went, made careful investigation of
medical conditions and progress. Such indeed was his extraordinary
reputation that he was instrumental in spreading the scientific ideas
of London and Edinburgh throughout the Continent. Medical education in Italy he found "deplorable." He listened to lectures by Torre-
giani at Parma, and at Padua was greeted as an equal by the aging
Morgagni, leader of Italian medicine and father of pathological anatomy, who presented the young American with a complete set of his
works. Aided no doubt by the curious fact of his American origins
and by his intimacy with the "good Quaker" Powel, Morgan everywhere encountered leading scientists and littérateurs as well as hosts
of cultivated laymen, and his collection of medical books and specimens, assembled in the course of study and travel, now surpassed
anything of the kind in Philadelphia.

Morgan was by this time the darling of the European profession,
and there was considerable pressure upon him to remain abroad for
the rest of his life. But to Dr. Cullen he wrote in November, 1764,
of his desire, despite the pleas and advice of many prominent scientists, to return to Philadelphia and achieve something for his profession in his native land. Few honors remained for him in Europe.
He was now Licentiate of the London College of Physicians, corresponding member of the Académie Royale de Chirurgie, and
member of the Arcadian Society of Belles Lettres at Rome; and he
was about to be elected Fellow of the Royal Society and member
of the Edinburgh College of Physicians. Also, his plans for a provincial medical school were now well matured. Back in London he
received good advice and support from Fothergill, Hunter and

Watson, and, even more important, the promised backing of Richard Peters, Benjamin Franklin, Miss Elizabeth Graeme, Thomas Penn and others whose influence counted for much in the affairs of Philadelphia.

"I am now preparing for America," he wrote with determination, "to see whether, after fourteen years' devotion to medicine, I can get my living without turning apothecary or practising surgery." He mentioned his intention to give medical lectures, but neglected to enumerate among the chief reasons for his return his desire to "whisper soft things to his charmer," the lovely and accomplished Mary, sister of his college classmate Francis Hopkinson.

"Morgan comes home flushed with honors, and is treated with all due respect to his merit," George Roberts reported in May, 1765. "He appears to be the same social friendly man, not assuming the solemn badge so accustomed to a son of Esculapius. . . . I hope the Doctor may meet with success in his undertaking, tho' I fear the mode of giving fees on attendance to the sick will be too confined for this paper-monied country." So indeed it was, especially as such leaders of the profession as Doctors Redman, Cadwalader, the Bonds and the Shippens refused to accede to his new method of leaving the making of medicines to an apothecary. In this respect he accomplished little more than had Dr. Thompson many years before, though like Thompson and Dr. Redman he did succeed in limiting his practice to medical cases alone.

No one in the city doubted Morgan's ability, nor that he merited his European reputation, second only to that of Franklin among Americans. When the handsome young physician walked down Chestnut Street, bearing one of those new-fangled "umbarilloes" and an aura of slightly foreign charm, people were proud to be able to say "I've seen him." But when Morgan took to himself full credit for the establishment of the Medical School at the College and became its first professor, there were those who failed to share the opinion of his friend Roberts of his friendly and unassuming sociability.

At a special meeting of the trustees of the College on May 3, 1765,

Dr. Morgan presented his proposals for a medical school. A letter previously received from Thomas Penn had endorsed both the plan and its author, and as a result Morgan was elected "Professor of the Theory and Practice of Physick." At commencement two weeks later he delivered in two parts, on May 30 and 31, his famous *Discourse upon the Institution of Medical Schools in America,* which was shortly thereafter printed. This work, composed in Paris, dedicated to Samuel Powel, and expressed in a prose style of remarkable clearness and maturity, deservedly ranks as a classic of medical literature.

In a preface frankly setting forth his conception of his professional duties Morgan announced his intention to confine himself to medicine, eschewing surgery save only when asked to perform inoculation. He himself intended to compound no medicines, but would refer his patients for such services to Mr. Daniel Leighton, a gentleman trained in both pharmacy and surgery, whom he had brought with him from England. Because "Practitioners must be paid for their time and attendance," he would charge a fee for each visit, but on a sliding scale, so that it might no longer be claimed that medical advice was available only to the wealthy. "By this leaving the fee in a great measure, or wholly, to the free will and circumstances of the patient, a physician may be employed by the middling class of people as well as the rich." The poor he promised to attend gratis. Despite some opposition already evident, he did not believe Philadelphians as a whole to be "too narrow-minded" for such an innovation. Finally, he would endeavor to serve those at a distance from the city by giving an opinion in writing, provided the history of the case were properly drawn up and transmitted to him.

Next he took up the need for regulating the practice of physic. The position of his profession he found no longer so simple as in the days when the city was small and the costs of living moderate. With the doubled prices of his own day, the expenses of medical training, especially since it must be sought in Europe, were proving beyond the reach of any but the very rich. Moreover, everyone would admit that the practice of medicine was "the most slavish profession known in this part of the world." Its study was becoming so complex as to require some degree of specialization. Physic, surgery, and pharmacy, therefore, should be made separate studies and separately practiced, with consequent improvement to each branch of science.

Building on the logical structure thus erected, Morgan proceeded to his plan for a medical school. He praised the "number of skilled and expert physicians, qualified by genius, education, and experience to take charge of the health of their fellow creatures," who practiced in Philadelphia. These men were, he believed, good teachers, but never yet had there been gathered together "a coalition of able men, who would undertake to give compleat and regular courses of Lectures on the different branches of Medicine." The want of such facilities was the greater, since the rapid growth of the country left many communities entirely "destitute of all the aids of Medical science," while even in the larger towns many practitioners, lacking opportunities for medical education, remained "in a pitiful state of ignorance."

The need for medical schools in America thus established, Morgan had no difficulty in demonstrating the suitability of Philadelphia as the place to locate such an institution. Already it possessed the materials,—its fine medical faculty, the many students drawn thither to become apprentices to its "set of eminent practitioners," its hospital with its facilities for practice and observation, and finally, the anatomical lectures of Dr. Shippen, Jr., now in their fourth series. Also, existence of the College made it possible for students to acquire a liberal premedical training.

In erecting "medical schools" at the College, Morgan proposed to follow the natural divisions of medical science—anatomy, materia medica, botany, "chymistry," and the theory and practice of medicine. Each of these fields he defined and skillfully discussed in turn, showing its importance in a rounded medical education. Determined to reproduce in his own country the best of what he had seen and learned in Europe, he outlined, in the words of Dr. Flexner, "what in essence still is a sound medical school," and a system of training never fully attained in America until the middle of the nineteenth century. He recognized the necessity for sound preliminary discipline in the liberal arts and sciences, a standard not revived until the opening of Johns Hopkins, and the importance of thorough training in anatomy, physiology, chemistry and physics as basic to the development of clinical medicine. Finally, he understood the need to connect the medical school with the College, in order to procure the sort of preliminary training he advocated. Medicine, he maintained, "is very extensive in its researches, and presupposes the knowledge of many other sciences. The cultivation of it requires no small abilities, and demands of those who engage in the arduous pursuit an enlarged and benevolent mind."

The only reference in the *Discourse* to William Shippen's plans for local medical education was the correct though ungenerous statement that in his Introductory Lecture of 1762 the latter had "proposed some hints of a plan for giving medical lectures amongst us. But I do not learn that he recommended at all a collegiate undertaking of this kind." Morgan went on to add, rather condescendingly, that should the trustees find it desirable to found a professorship of anatomy, Shippen was well qualified for the job. The latter, justifiably resentful of the highhanded fashion in which Morgan on his own had negotiated directly with the trustees, spent three sultry months in the nursing of his wounded amour propre. Then, in a letter plainly evincing his chagrin and naming his own terms, he applied for the proposed chair of anatomy. His position, like his qualifications, was strong, and it was clearly in the interests of harmony that the appointment was made on September 23, 1765. Only three days later the *Pennsylvania Gazette* carried notices of two Proposals—Dr. Shippen's lectures on anatomy and surgery to begin on November 14, and Dr. Morgan's course in materia medica commencing on the eighteenth, both under sponsorship of the College.

So, despite politics and heartburnings, the Medical School was born, and the College of Philadelphia became truly entitled "to the name . . . of an University, in any Part of the World." Although Shippen had clearly seen the need for medical education in America and to that end had tentatively inaugurated medical lectureships in the city, it was the bolder, more original mind of Morgan that supplied the broad educational philosophy upon which the Medical School was raised. As an alumnus of the College he was able to secure its sponsorship, and as a member of the Anglican gentry he obtained the important patronage of Hamilton, Peters and Penn, which ensured the success of the new institution. In these respects Shippen was something of an outsider. Notwithstanding his impulsiveness and arrogance and the frequently irritating display of his undeniably superior training, John Morgan was the primary founder of America's first medical school. But the affair left scars, and the animosity between the two brilliant men, never fully reconciled, bore bitter fruit in later years when both were to be entrusted with the health and welfare of the Continental Army.

The next year, 1766, saw a further step in the realization of Morgan's plan for a "compleat and regular" medical curriculum. It was contributed by an older man, a trustee of the College, who combined with long experience a vision equal to that of his younger colleagues. When Dr. Thomas Bond secured from the managers of the Pennsylvania Hospital permission to offer clinical lectures there to supplement the theoretical teachings of Shippen and Morgan, that institution reached the climax of its usefulness to the medical profession. Bond's "Essay on the Utility of Clinical Lectures," delivered at his home on November 6, 1766, before an audience composed of the managers of the Hospital, professors of the College, most of the city's physicians, and "near thirty students," ranks second only to Morgan's *Discourse* in the medical history of Philadelphia. In addition to his demonstration of the value of clinical training, he revealed his firm understanding of the peculiar problems of American medicine and a glimpse of the notable social contributions of his profession in the future.

"When I consider," Bond began, "the unskillful hands the Practice of Physick and Surgery has of necessity been committed to, in many Parts of America, it gives me pleasure to behold so many Worthy Young men, training up in those professions, which from the nature of their Objects, are the most interesting to the Community, and yet a great[er] pleasure in foreseeing, that unparalleled public Spirit, of the Good People of this Province, will shortly make Philadelphia the Athens of America, and Render the Sons of Pennsylvania, reputable amongst the most celebrated Europeans, in *all the Liberal Arts and Sciences*. This I am at present certain of, that the Institutions of Literature and Charity, already founded, and the School of Physic lately open'd in this City afford Sufficient Foundation for the Students of Physic to acquire all the Knowledge necessary for their practising every Branch of their professions respectably and Judiciously." Considerable value, Bond went on, attaches to the study of medicine in the locality where it is to be practiced, since "every Climate produces Diseases peculiar to itself, which require experience to understand and Cure." Thus, in the future, even those who could afford the expense of "going from America to Europe, and thence from Country to Country, and Colledge to Colledge, in Quest of Medical Qualifications," ought to remain at home in these fine new institutions where "the precepts of *never-failing Experience* are handed down from Father to Son, from Tutor to Pupil." "Principals of Patriotism and Humanity," he believed, pointed to the same conclusion.

America, Bond asserted, was on the whole a most healthy country, yet the recurrent summer and autumn epidemics to which it was still subject constituted a challenge to the local medical profession to attack and control them. He then proceeded to review with great clarity and insight the history of the five yellow fever visitations since 1741 and, though he shared the prevailing confusion of medical theory as to whether contagion or local conditions were responsible for the spread of infectious disease, suggested possible explanations and potential remedies based upon his own experience in their treatment. Both "Experience and Reason" encouraged him in the belief that "by diligent investigation . . . the prevention of Epidemic diseases in America . . . is more within the limits of human precaution than has generally been imagin'd." Here it was that Bond, the clinician, proposed to come to the aid of the Medical School, and, by means of regular clinical lectures at the Hospital, to demonstrate "the Truth of Theory by Facts." His technique was well established by fourteen years of practice at the Hospital, and its addition to the Medical School's curriculum greatly added to the training young men were there able to receive.

The Medical School achieved continental publicity by means of articles which shortly appeared in most provincial newspapers, stressing such additional advantages as the acquisition of a valuable collection of books for the Hospital library and Provost Smith's projected lectures on pneumatics, hydrostatics and mechanics. Requirements for the degrees of Bachelor of Medicine and Doctor of Medicine, adopted in 1767 by the medical members of the board of trustees meeting with the professors, were similarly broadcast by the colonial press in October of that year. These requirements closely paralleled those of the University of Edinburgh, and demanded that all students entering the Medical School without a college degree be examined in Latin and such branches of mathematics, natural and experimental philosophy "as shall be judged requisite to a medical education."

All that now remained was completion of the faculty. This was accomplished by the appointment in January, 1768, of Dr. Adam Kuhn, recently returned from study under Linnaeus and the taking of an Edinburgh degree, as professor of materia medica, and of Dr. Benjamin Rush, also an Edinburgh graduate, as professor of chemistry in the next year. The faculty now consisted of five able men, all trained in Europe, and four of them possessing degrees from the world's leading medical school. It was a distinguished group, and like Edinburgh's first faculty when recruited from graduates of Leyden, composed with the exception of Dr. Bond of men not yet thirty-five years old.

By 1767, despite the fact that the Medical School had already acquired a rival at King's College in New York, some twenty students from Philadelphia and elsewhere were studying with Dr. Morgan and his associates. Ten of them, natives of Pennsylvania, New Jersey and the Delaware counties, received the degree of Bachelor of Physic on June 21, 1768, a date editorialized by the local press as "having given Birth to Medical Honors in America." At the same time the faculty noted with satisfaction that Philadelphia had become "the great Resort of Students for several Years past, from the distant Parts of the Continent . . . for improvement in Medicine." They confidently anticipated, since the staff had been completed by the recent appointment of Dr. Rush, the prompt conferring of the doctor's diploma.

In 1771 four such degrees were granted,[1] and the Medical School had achieved a position with respect to high standards maintained and excellence of instruction exceeded only by its parent institution, Edinburgh, in western Europe. This, it must be remembered, was more than half a century before the establishment of medical colleges in such English cities as Liverpool, Manchester and Leeds. In 1772 John Morgan undertook an extended publicity tour throughout the Southern and island colonies on behalf of his school. For ten months he spread "the knowledge of this Institution and the advantages" it offered "The Youth whose Parents may think proper" to have them educated at the College. His energetic campaign, which raised between £4,000 and £5,000 for use of "the University of Philadelphia," was a factor in the school's growing reputation which made it increasingly the objective of medical students from Rhode Island on the north to Barbados to the south.

Further clinical facilities, in addition to those offered by the Pennsylvania Hospital, became available for medical students shortly after the opening of the new Bettering House. Here was established the first lying-in hospital in the American colonies, and here, by 1770 at least, Thomas Bond was delivering obstetrical lectures to his apprentices and students at the Medical School. To preserve "Order and Decency," only those students were permitted to witness a delivery who were "of decent manners and of suitable age to attend operations of that kind." Dr. William Shippen, Jr., headed the medical staff at the Bettering House, and Dr. Cadwalader Evans, second in command to Bond at the hospital, seems to have assisted in the maternity clinic. They were joined in 1772 by a distinguished

---

[1] Although medical degrees were granted at the College in 1768, to King's College, New York, belongs the honor of conferring the first M.D. in 1770.

group of physicians, including Doctors Kuhn, Rush, Duffield and Clarkson, and to them were later added John Morgan and Thomas Parke. In the years just preceding the outbreak of the Revolution, its clinical activities, no less than its services to the poor, entitled the Bettering House to its claim of being "an Hospital, in every sense of the word, and perhaps more extensively so than any other institution on this Continent."

Stimulated by the returning enthusiasm of men trained in the finest European universities, and encouraged by the generous support accorded by wealthy laymen to the newly established medical institutions, the scientific spirit of the age found opportunity for development. A desire for association for the professional exchange of views and experience and the advancement of scientific knowledge was a natural consequence. Late in 1766 Dr. Morgan approached Chief Justice William Allen with a view to obtaining official support for a medical society he had gathered together in the previous year. Favorably impressed, Allen wrote the Proprietor, Thomas Penn, advocating the granting a charter to this organization, which "may be attended with very good Consequences," and make of Philadelphia "in some measure the Seat of the Sciences, and, in the physical way, the Edinburgh of America."

It soon appeared that Morgan had "given offense to many by being too desirous to put himself at the Head of Things," and by May, 1767, Allen felt impelled to withdraw his support and to advise Penn against incorporating the society. Characteristically, Morgan had failed to conciliate young Shippen after the affair of the Medical School, and now, with his customary intellectual arrogance, he made matters worse by highhanded procedure over the medical society. "Sundry of the most reputable Physicians," wrote Allen, "three of them Shippen, Sr., and the two Bonds, would not join Morgan's Medical Club, affronted at his forming it at first, chiefly of young men and then sending Tickets to the old Physicians to join as Members, which some did and more declined, intending or at least talking of forming another Society. . . . Such a Charter just now, I fear, would divide instead of unite." Allen hoped, by leaving matters alone, to achieve a reconciliation, which, however, was several years in being effected.

Nothing deterred by lack of a charter, nor by refusal of some of the city's leading practitioners to join his society, Morgan went ahead with his plans. On October 14, 1768, following the precedent established by Edinburgh's first medical organization when it merged with the Philosophical Society of that city, he secured the incorporation of his group into the American Society for Promoting Useful Knowledge. This move doubtless served to checkmate the Bonds and Shippens, who, still unappeased, had the previous January revived the old American Philosophical Society of 1743. Under Morgan's energetic leadership the American Society added to its roster as corresponding members most of the eminent physicians of Boston, Newport, New York and Charleston. Ultimate union of the two philosophical bodies in January, 1769, finally healed the breach among the medicos, whose work on the medical committee of the new organization proved of lasting value to their profession and to the public, not only of Philadelphia but of all the colonies as well.

Presence in the city of a large number of medical students from other colonies led to their association for discussion of their common problems in 1771. The American Medical Society, as it was called, embraced both junior and senior members, the latter including the leading practitioners of physic. Its management, however, was in the hands of the students, among the most active of whom were David Ramsay of South Carolina and William Tillinghast of Newport, Rhode Island. The group met weekly on Mondays from November to February at the College to listen to papers and take part in discussions. As students boarded about town, and many apprentices lived in the homes of their mentors, the particular value of the society lay in its fraternal features. Here young men from widely separated colonies met on a basis of common interests and ambitions. Here acquaintance ripened into understanding and friendship, a factor of importance to the Revolutionary cause when an

American medical service had to be organized at the outbreak of the war.

As Philadelphia doctors approached in practice the problems of public health and the medical battle against disease, they repeatedly sought to make scientific descriptions of local conditions and their possible treatment. In this they enjoyed the splendid co-operation of the printers, who accorded the best possible publicity to these efforts at laying the groundwork for American medical research.

Between 1753 and 1776 more than thirty publications on health and medicine issued from local presses. Of these, Franklin's account of the Hospital and three others may be considered as publicity tracts; the remainder were definitely scientific in nature. Important among them were thirteen works by members of the local faculty, including essays on inoculation by Dr. Lachlan Macleane (1756) and Thomas Ruston (1767), and a description of Dimsdale's method, probably by Dr. Morgan, in 1771. Also in 1771 Philadelphia printers published the dissertations of the four students receiving the first degrees of Doctor of Medicine from the College.

At least eight medical studies by Philadelphians achieved publication in the British Isles in these years, and Dr. Morgan's *Discourse* received most favorable comment in the *Monthly Review* and other journals. Dr. John Kearsley, Jr.'s "Observations on the Angina Maligna, or the putrid and Ulcerous Sore Throat," previously published in a Philadelphia magazine as well as separately, was reprinted in the *London Magazine* for May, 1769.

Philadelphia printers, especially Robert Bell, further assisted the medical profession by their increasing republication of important European medical books. Bradford in 1773 brought out William Cadogan's *Essay upon Nursing and the Management of Children,* a notable pioneer work in pediatrics, in which the author "sought to clear away the accumulated rubbish of folklore and to replace it with a sane, empirical hygiene." Bell made a noteworthy contribution in 1775 when he reprinted, in a pirated form to be sure, Dr. William Cullen's *Lectures on Materia Medica,* which he asserted were "in danger of being lost to the world." Of even greater significance to the profession was his 1775 subscription edition of *Lectures on the Duties and Qualifications of Physicians* (1770) by Dr. John Gregory of Edinburgh, in which was set forth a statement of the principles of medical methodology which, says Professor Shryock, "might well have served as a working program for the century that was to follow." Particularly is it to be regretted that such leaders of American medicine as Benjamin Rush gave scant heed to his analysis of the dangers and shortcomings of medical speculation. Bell's effective marketing methods of course assured a continental distribution for these works.

The publicizing of new medical and scientific developments, the breaking down of much of the average man's superstition and prejudice with regard to medical practice, and the publication of methods and directions for self-treatment in areas remote from professional medical assistance, were services of the colonial press in these years that have been largely ignored or forgotten. Its contribution to the acceptance of inoculation, especially in rural districts, was considerable. In 1760 one "Americanus" praised in the columns of the *Pennsylvania Gazette* the generosity of Benjamin Franklin which had made possible free circulation of Dr. Heberden's pamphlet containing instructions for inoculation. He added a few suggestions, such as the use of calomel before the operation and observation of a careful diet afterwards, a method prescribed by Dr. Shippen, by which not one patient in a hundred had died.

Yet acquisition of smallpox by inoculation in order to avoid contracting it in the natural way ran counter to common sense and general belief, and especially among the lower classes and in rural areas many people violently opposed the operation. In 1768 the disease raged in the little town of Reading, killing some sixty children in less than two months' time. "The German inhabitants," reported Goddard's *Chronicle,* "cannot be dissuaded from the pernicious Method of keeping the Sick in hot-Stove rooms, under a hot Regimen, to which, doubtless, so great a Mortality is principally to be attributed. 'Tis much to be lamented, that their Prejudice in this Particular, and against Inoculation, are not removed." Jonathan

Potts, just starting practice in Reading after having received his bachelor's degree with the first medical class at the College, sought to quiet German fears by publication of a paper explaining inoculation, which he had translated and printed by Henry Miller in the *Philadelphische Staatsbote*. Such newspaper publicity quietly prepared the public mind for the opening of Dr. Glentworth's private inoculation hospital in 1773, and for the good work of the Society for the Inoculating of the Poor Gratis, which began in the following year.

Prevalence in and about Philadelphia of a variety of sicknesses, grouped by eighteenth-century physicians under the general classification of "fevers," resulted, here as in Europe, in continuous interest in their causes and cure. In response to proposals of the American Society for widening its scope in 1768, Dr. Lionel Chalmers of Charleston submitted to Dr. Morgan a series of essays on the climate and diseases of South Carolina. After listening to a reading of these essays the Society ordered their publication, and Goddard ran four of them in the *Pennsylvania Chronicle* (December 19, 1768 to January 2, 1769). Dealing with apoplexy, the dry bellyache, "Catarrhal Peripneumony" and "Catarrhal Consumption," plagues very nearly as rife in Philadelphia as in lands to the south, they attracted wide interest and attention. Sparhawk & Anderton collected them as an *Essay on Fevers* in 1769, and Lewis Nicola's *American Magazine* of that year, in an appendix containing the proceedings of the American Philosophical Society, reprinted a series of extracts. In London in 1776 Dr. Chalmers included these papers in his two-volume treatise *Essays on the Weather and Diseases of South Carolina,* which earned a "rave notice" in the *Monthly Review,* and may indeed be regarded as the best and most extensive work in descriptive medicine produced in the American colonies.

Already the yellow fever was figuring prominently in Philadelphia's medical literature. The *American Magazine* for June, 1769, contained an anonymous paper on the angina maligna, which the author, although "not very fond of publishing," offered for the public benefit. The view of physic prevailing in Philadelphia, he wrote, because it accepts "reasoning from observation and facts, in preference to reasoning a priori, is the only basis on which we can rest with safety." On this basis, the essay discussed the history of the yellow fever since 1746, describing its symptoms and pointing out the failure of certain remedies prescribed by the "learned Huxham, Fothergill and others." Purging, he said, was as improper as bleeding; emetics and bathing with vinegar had proved of little value; and above all, the use of "antiphlogistic medicines" should be avoided. Experience seemed to reveal "the bark acidulated with the elixir vitrioli," with cold bathing as a prophylactic, to be the "most sovereign remedy." This essay, by Dr. John Kearsley, Jr., was reprinted in the *London Magazine* for November, 1769, and was brought out separately in Philadelphia by Cruikshank & Collins in 1770.

Dr. Thomas Young, amid multifarious revolutionary activities in 1775, found time to communicate to the *Gazette* a paper on "the bilious and putrid fevers prevalent in hot weather," wherein, for the good of the public, he opposed the traditional treatment of sweating and "the still more cruel method of blistering from crown to ancle," recommending instead a calomel purge and a diet of mild acids. Replying in a second communication to a letter from a neighboring colony he explained:

I desire to be understood as speaking in general when I speak of the virtues of medicines. I say again that no directions I am capable of giving can serve to make every man his own doctor, more than an ample description of Mr. Wood's or Mr. Birny's tools, Mr. Du Symetere [sic] or Mr. Mitchell's paints and pencils would make all the country watchmakers or limners.

The newspapers provided a most effective means of placing medical knowledge or speculation before the public. An epidemic of hives in the autumn of 1769 impelled young Benjamin Rush, fresh from the achievement of his Edinburgh degree, to publish in both *Journal* and *Gazette* the known history of that ailment and, though with some diffidence, his own objections to the theory of their cause held by local practitioners. Nerves are the trouble, he asserted, the symptoms being "entirely spasmodic." Of far more value was his *Inquiry into the Natural History of Medicine among the Indians,* delivered before the American Philosophical Society in 1774, and published in part in the *Pennsylvania Journal.* In this paper he observed the success enjoyed by the aborigines with their use of the cold bath, and took occasion to note the absence among them of nervous ailments, which he found to be on the increase in Philadelphia. By study also, he concluded that smallpox and venereal diseases, being European scourges, made correspondingly greater ravages among the red men.

In fact, venereal disease increased alarmingly in Philadelphia after about 1745, owing possibly to increasing commercial activity and the frequent presence of the British army, and here the press, rather than performing a public service, did little more than carry the advertisements of quack doctors and their useless specifics. In view of the then state of medical knowledge these sensational promises of cure probably did no real harm. With the exception of Dr. Kearsley, Jr., who published a testimonial, copied in the Boston papers, on a cure effected by Dr. Keyser's pills, most of the faculty had the good sense to hold aloof from such matters. On the other hand, the press stood squarely back of provincial quarantine regulations, and fought for better sanitary conditions and cleaner streets. The agreeable impression received by Henry Pelham in 1774 of "the regularity, the neatness and cleanness of this City," indicates the achievement of some success, at least in the latter sphere.

Of the relationship of the physician to his paying patients in eighteenth-century Philadelphia not much is known, although judging from the numbers and prosperity of the profession it was a pleasant and profitable one. Undoubtedly there was some shopping about for a medical advisor among the well-to-do, and confidence in the abilities of the doctor, once selected, may have been far from complete. The diary of Elizabeth Drinker shows her family to have been fairly faithful to Drs. Redman and Cadwalader Evans, while after the latter's death they occasionally called in John Kearsley, Jr.

Yet even they resorted to the apothecary for "worm-powder," to self-medication with such sovereign remedies as the famous "Venice Treacle," and to a variety of doubtfully qualified "tooth-drawers." For more serious ailments, however, such as "the Putrid soar Throat" or "Something very like the Yellow-Feaver," they called in a reputable physician, and children in the family were inoculated by Dr. Redman.

How less intelligent families may have fared at the hands of quacks who offered their varied treatments for cancer, venereal disease, hernia, "falling fits," all sorts of stomach disorders, skin afflictions, and the extermination of vermin, is food for the imagination. Surgeon-dentists throughout the period advertised their toothache remedies on a "no cure, no pay" basis, and promised to supply full sets of artificial dentures with dispatch and secrecy. Perhaps the most popular field for quackery lay in afflictions of the eye, and one shudders at the damage that must have been wrought by such "oculists" as James Graham, later described as "half enthusiast, half knave," who traveled the length of the colonies operating on the blind or nearly blind. People did better who went directly to Hannah Breintnall's in Second Street for her "Venetian Green Spectacles for weak or watery eyes. . . . Concave Spectacles for short-sighted Persons. Magnifying and Reading Glasses," and so on.

Despite these parasites that swarmed on the outskirts of the profession, Philadelphia on the eve of the Revolution enjoyed the services of a medical faculty perhaps unequaled outside London and Edinburgh. In the decade of the seventies there existed one reputable physician or surgeon for approximately every 600 citizens, while for every 1,100 inhabitants there was one doctor who could boast some advanced study in the hospitals or medical schools of the Old World.

To a considerable degree these men had learned to co-operate with one another in the service of their profession. With other leading humanitarians they had opened two hospitals which provided fine clinical facilities, had established a medical library, founded a great medical school, and inaugurated a medical society, institutions all made possible only by the wealth and population of an important urban center such as Philadelphia had become. It should be emphasized that the modern hospital and the professional medical society were relatively recent developments even in Europe. Philadelphia, in respect to such institutions, was more advanced than most cities of its size.

More than half of the faculty practicing in Philadelphia had undergone some graduate training in the clinics or universities of Europe, and were thus completely abreast of contemporary medical and scientific developments. The nature of this training, as well as the conditions of local practice, dictated their approach to their profession. Many of them had already practiced medicine before going abroad, and therefore built on a foundation of practical experience rather than of theoretical education. The empirical character of medical instruction in the New World, at the hands of active physicians, contributed to the same end. In Europe a majority of these young men studied medicine and surgery at the great hospitals of Paris or London, or in the critical northern atmosphere of Edinburgh, and only a very few in medical schools where the inherited fondness for theorizing predominated. Thus by temperament and training they returned home prepared to perpetuate the medical traditions of observation and experiment encouraged in the seventeenth century by Sydenham and others.

The nature of their practice at home, in a young country with its new conditions and peculiar diseases for which little European lore was available, led them in the same direction, causing them to strike out for themselves in search of effective cures. Prior to the War for Independence there was small disposition among American doctors for the "systematizing" that was so popular on the Continent. Only after the Revolution and the advent of the Romantic era did Benjamin Rush, in a burst of patriotic fervor and driven perhaps by the specter of an enemy which baffled medical science to defeat, propound his American system of medicine, with unfortunate consequences for the future. In this period American medicine confined itself to the strictly empirical, and to that end its devotees sought not so much European certificates and degrees as the best experience and most up-to-date instruction the Old World could offer them.

The expense of this sort of training meant that most doctors came from the city's wealthy mercantile families, but the costs were more than made up by the handsome livings they found it possible to achieve in the flourishing community on their return. The profession paid well and enabled its practitioners to maintain social positions of eminence and respect. Graduates of the Academy or College, and later of European universities or hospitals, broadened by extensive travel and by wide contacts with leading intellectuals in Scotland, England and France, the doctors constituted the most highly educated group in the city. Experience and training equipped them to serve as middlemen between European and native humanitarianism. Born and educated to a sense of social responsibilities, they returned from Europe with vision renewed and enlarged, and sought with considerable success to raise the ethical standards and improve the esprit du corps of their colleagues. They thus laid the permanent basis for a noble tradition in American medicine.

Their contemporary social and cultural contribution to the world in which they lived was of far greater significance than that of the legal profession, of which historians have made so much. Their work induced in them a natural interest in all science, and even apart from medicine they made important contributions to its development, as the next chapter will make clear. As logical hosts for the forces of Enlightenment, they not only applied their curiosity and experimentalism to science and things of the intellect, but they also founded the tradition of literary excellence so notable among their Philadelphia successors.

Alert to all intellectual and social currents of their contemporary world, and endowed by their profession with competent livings, the medical men of Philadelphia gave the lie to Dr. Morgan's assertion that they must be slaves to their scientific duties. They assumed social responsibilities to an extent seldom achieved today, and played important roles in the cultural life of their native city. In the promotion of higher education the names of the Bonds, Redman, Morgan,

Shippen and Zachary are pre-eminent. Dr. Cadwalader devoted his energies and his wealth to the establishment of libraries in two communities, and the services of Kearsley to architecture and Graeme to gardening were outstanding. Philadelphia's leading connoisseur of art was John Morgan, Adam Kuhn was one of its most accomplished musicians, and Benjamin Rush stood second only to Anthony Benezet in humanitarian labors for the underprivileged and the oppressed. Kearsley, Sr., Williamson, and Thomas Bond were active in politics, and Rush became a signer of the Declaration of Independence. All labored ardently for charity, and of the offices of national societies, beginning with the St. Andrew's Society of which Thomas Graeme was the first president, most were occupied by medical men.

The physicians, more than any one group save perhaps the printers, seem to have sensed the spirit of contemporary America and grasped some vision of its future. When the break came away from the mother country only two of them, Quaker Thomas Parke and eccentric John Kearsley, Jr., failed to side with their fellow countrymen. Their professional capacities and intercolonial connections were of inestimable value to the patriot cause, and at considerable sacrifice of income and convenience, sometimes even of reputation, they furnished the Continental forces with a sorely-needed medical personnel.

Chapter IX

THE LOVE OF SCIENCE: THEIR REIGNING CHARACTER

IN THE rooms of the Union Library Company on New Year's Day, 1768, Charles Thomson, a scholarly gentleman of "family, fortune, and character," one-time schoolmaster and now a successful merchant, earnestly addressed his fellow members of the American Society Held at Philadelphia for Promoting Useful Knowledge. "Knowledge is of little use," he maintained, "when confined to mere Speculation; But when speculative Truths are reduced to Practice, when Theories, grounded upon Experiments, are applied to common Purposes of Life, and when, by these, Agriculture is improved, Trade enlarged, and the Arts of Living made more easy and comfortable, and, of Course, the Increase and Happiness of Mankind promoted, Knowledge then becomes really useful." Turning from the general to the specific, Thomson continued: "As Philadelphia is the Centre of the Colonies, as her Inhabitants are remarkable for encouraging laudable and useful undertakings, why should we hesitate to enlarge the plan of our Society, call to our Assistance Men of Learning and Ingenuity from every Quarter and unite in one generous, notable attempt not only to promote the Interest of our Country, but to raise her to some eminence in the rank of polite and learned nations?"

One could search long and far before discovering a better statement of the ideals and objectives of the natural philosophers of the Enlightenment.

In a very real sense the scientific activities of its inhabitants most completely encompassed and expressed the whole of the Philadelphia mind. Sharing the faith of their European contemporaries in the ultimate triumph of reason, intellectual Philadelphians early found the study of nature and the pursuit of the New Science congenial to their tastes. To this transplanted interest their New World environment added constant nourishment. Strange and wonderful flora and fauna excited man's curiosity; the discovery and use of new herbs and minerals challenged his intelligence; and the geographic exploration of great expanses stimulated his imagination. The planting of a civilization on a virgin continent created fresh problems for the natural ingenuity of men of science to solve. It was thus no accident that Philadelphians, striving to meet new social and economic needs as they appeared, largely confined their researches to botany, cartography, astronomy and navigation, mechanics and electricity, for it must be remembered that ocean-borne commerce and inland transportation and development occupied the bulk of their gainfully invested time.

The community was rich in human materials. As the eighteenth century became increasingly a golden era for middle-class intellectuals, the British colonies, and Philadelphia in particular, where that group early rose to wealth, leadership and power, presented a most fertile soil for the nurture of their activities. The prosperous middle class of the Pennsylvania city contained many skilled craftsmen, farmers and mariners, as well as men of scholarship and leisure, persons in whom special training or a liberal education combined with no prejudice against manual labor. Stimulation to philosophic inquiry came from all quarters, and artisan and scholar, meeting in the common pursuit of scientific problems, enabled machinery to keep pace with speculation.

Science at Philadelphia never hesitated to enlist the skills of the craftsman and the gardener, the engineer and the architect, the teacher, the artist, the printer or the merchant. The democratic implications of such an approach are nearly as obvious as the practical nature of its results. In 1801, in what was probably the earliest attempt to review the achievements of the century just closed, the Reverend Samuel Miller concluded that "while the explorers of science have gratified liberal curiosity, and gained reputation for themselves, their inquiries have been rendered subservient to the abridgement of labour, the increase both of expedition and elegance of workmanship in manufactures, and the promotion of human comfort, to a degree beyond all former precedent."

The city's first burst of scientific activity well illustrates this marriage of practice with theory, of the mechanic with the sage. By the decade of the thirties there existed in Philadelphia all the elements necessary for fruitful investigation into natural and scientific phenomena. In 1727 Franklin had brought together in his famous Junto a group of young men interested in their "mutual improvement" by reading and discussion. Among them were the glazier Thomas Godfrey, the surveyor Nicholas Scull, the eager shoemaker William Parsons, and the joiner William Maugridge— all, in their respective crafts, "most exquisite" mechanics, and well able to apply their skills to the construction of instruments and apparatus without which science is powerless to advance. Also of this company was the Quaker merchant, Joseph Breintnall, whose far-flung business connections were later to supply his Junto colleagues with means of introduction to the scientists of the mother country. Finally, when one of their number should uncover unusual talents for scientific experiment and research, he could earn the aristocratic and scholarly encouragement of James Logan, universal philosopher of the eighteenth-century type and first citizen of the Middle Colonies.

Born in Ireland of Scottish parents, Logan had come to Philadelphia with William Penn in 1699, and soon achieved prominence in the political and commercial life of the colony. Highly schooled in mathematics and the classics, he was well known among prominent English scholars and leading Quakers. At Stenton, his beautiful home, he assembled the finest classical and scientific library in the colonies, including among other items the works of Archimedes,

Euclid and Ptolemy in their original tongue, many volumes of modern mathematics, three editions of Newton's *Principia,* and the works of such well-known English scientists as Wallis and Halley, the latter a personal friend. Here he pursued his studies in mathematics and the phenomena of light. Here, too, minding the injunctions of George Fox and William Penn to the Friends to interest themselves in gardening, he became an enthusiastic amateur botanist, and his researches supplied the final proof in the long-vexing question of the sexuality of plants.

His universal curiosity, which ran the gamut from the literature of the Greeks to the physics of Isaac Newton, his wide practical experience in trade and politics, and his Quaker concern with problems of public welfare brought Logan into touch with all phases of the colony's life. And though an aristocrat by birth and training, and always mindful of the distinction his wealth and position conferred, he could usually be prevailed upon, because of his deep interest in science, to recognize and encourage the work of its devotees, even though on occasion they might spring from the humbler ranks of society.

Foremost among these was Thomas Godfrey, a glazier by trade, uneducated beyond the proverbial three R's, and self-trained in mathematics from books at first accidentally acquired and later assiduously borrowed. After a painful struggle to master the Latin tongue in order to gain further access to his chosen science, he arrived at Stenton one day in 1729 with a request to borrow Logan's copy of the *Principia.* Discovering from conversation his "excellent natural genius," Logan made the artisan welcome to the use of his library. Godfrey now turned his skill in astronomy and optics to the solution of a problem that had long puzzled navigators, the discovery of a simple and accurate means for measuring longitude, supporting himself meanwhile by the calculation and publication of a single-sheet almanac "after the London manner." In October, 1730, he contrived "an easy and curious" mariner's quadrant which represented a great improvement over that of Davis then in use, and which, after a successful trial in Delaware Bay by the Quaker Joshua Fisher, was placed on a ship bound for Jamaica for further testing.

At a meeting of the Royal Society in 1731 John Hadley of London presented an account of a new quadrant, based on the same principles as that of Godfrey and invented by him in the summer of 1730, though not previously announced. When patented, this instrument became known as Hadley's quadrant. Logan, reading in the *Philosophical Transactions* of the new instrument, and anxious that his protégé should be accorded "the right of an inventor (at least), if not absolutely the first," sent accounts and drawings of Godfrey's invention to his friend Dr. Edmund Halley, and to Mr. Jones of the Royal Society. Godfrey himself defended his claims in letters to the Royal Society in 1733-34.

In 1734, when that learned body was about to bestow upon Hadley the award it had offered for the discovery of such a device, Logan again wrote Dr. Halley, enclosing a complete set of affidavits which he believed proved Godfrey's invention to have been "not only made, but used at sea six months before J. Hadley's was seen or known," while to Peter Collinson he sent a detailed description, with drawings, of Godfrey's instrument, which Collinson had published in the *Philosophical Transactions* of that year. Belatedly, as Hadley had already acquired his patent, the Society bestowed a gift of £200 upon Godfrey for his services to navigation, but, having somehow learned that the colonial was a heavy drinker, voted that the sum be expended in the purchase of a handsome clock. Logan's influence and persistence, therefore, finally won from the Old World's most illustrious scientific association the acknowledgement, however reluctant and equivocal, of the independent discovery and prior use by a plain citizen of Philadelphia of one of the century's great contributions to the science of navigation.

When under stimulus furnished by Franklin members of the Junto combined with other book-loving citizens to form the Library Company in 1731, the eager borrower, Thomas Godfrey, became one of its most enthusiastic directors. He it was who in the next year persuaded James Logan to advise the company on books to be

acquired, and who, in conjunction with the secretary, Joseph Breintnall, secured the good offices of the Quaker merchant and botanist
Peter Collinson of London for their purchase.

Breintnall, though older than most of this group, was an ardent
amateur philosopher, and utilized the opportunity afforded by business correspondence to open up channels of scientific communication. To Collinson he reported his botanizing, his experiments with
grafting, and his observations of natural phenomena. As early as
1730 he had demonstrated that the sun's rays more easily penetrate
colored materials than white, and later he wrote of experiments to
determine the differences in the sun's heat in summer and in winter.
Collinson procured the publication of two papers by Breintnall in
the *Philosophical Transactions,* one, his observation of meteors at
Philadelphia in 1740, and six years later a "curious paper" on the
treatment of snake bites. In return for this transoceanic companionship Breintnall did both Collinson and the scientific world a considerable service when he introduced to the Londoner by mail, as "a
very proper person" to procure American seeds and plants for him,
the Pennsylvania botanist John Bartram.

By the early thirties, when Collinson sought Bartram's services,
gardening and experimental botany were occupying the attention of
many men of leisure or scholarship at Philadelphia. At Germantown, "facetious and pliant" old Dr. Christopher Witt, devotee of
natural philosophy, physic, astrology and magic, divided his time
between his library and his beloved garden. He acted for some years
as agent for Collinson, sending him many American plants and
seeds, though his employer regretted that he sent only "the fine
sorts," proved "very credulous," and dealt "much in the marvelous."
In London, Collinson had encountered Dr. John Kearsley, whom
he found to be usually "of the contrary opinion" in matters botanical. However, Kearsley always defended his views "very ingeni-
ously," and in later years Collinson more than once advised Bartram
to consult with the doctor on difficult problems. During their years
in Europe both Thomas and Phineas Bond had combined the study
of botany with their medical training. Through Collinson, Thomas

Bond met and studied with the famous Antoine Jussieu of the Royal Gardens in Paris, while at Leyden his brother Phineas became an intimate of J. F. Gronovius.

It was James Logan, however, who furnished America's greatest contribution to scientific botany in these years. For forty years, since Nehemiah Grew had addressed the Royal Society concerning the sexual nature of plants in 1696, botanists had been concerned with the question of the universality of pollenization in plant reproduction. Logan experimented for some time with the problem in his gardens at Stenton, and finally in 1735 wrote to Collinson of his experiences with the planting and raising of maize in 1727, which definitely proved that this plant reproduced sexually. This admirable report, described by Collinson as "very skilful and knowing," was printed in the *Philosophical Transactions* for 1736, and greatly enhanced its author's reputation. It resulted in the publication at Leyden in 1739 of Logan's Latin treatise, which Dr. John Fothergill translated and published as *Experiments and Considerations on the Generation of Plants* (London, 1747).

Perhaps more significant than his own researches was Logan's patronage of John Bartram, who about 1728 at his farm at Kingsessing had begun his botanical garden which was eventually to contain the finest collection of native and exotic plants in North America. Perceiving here again a case of "excellent natural genius," Logan used every means in his power to encourage his friend in the systematic study of botany, making him free of his library at Stenton, and presenting him with copies of Parkinson's *Herbal* and the works of Culpepper, Salmon and Turner. From Logan, Bartram learned the use of the microscope and the Linnaean system of classification, and at the former's instigation he began in 1736 the study of Latin. Collinson informed Bartram by letter in 1737 that Logan, "fearing thee had no consideration for thy collections," had written "in thy behalf."

Actually, with characteristic Quaker shrewdness, John Bartram made botany profitable. Through the good offices of Collinson he was retained by a number of wealthy Englishmen, among them

Lord Petre, to assemble and ship regular consignments of American flora for their gardens in the mother country. Later he also furnished seeds, plants and shrubs to J. F. Gronovius at Leyden and even to Linnaeus himself.

His success in this business attracted others into the field, in particular James Alexander, the Proprietor's gardener, who, backed by William Allen and the Penns, and described by Lewis Evans as "very well skilled in every thing usefull as well as curious relating to the polite as well as the more vulgar Culture in our Plantations and Gardens," became in time a real competitor. Collinson warned Bartram in 1756 that he feared "we shall be outdone by that Alexander." Bartram, in reply, explained Alexander's ability to make extensive shipments by the fact that "he frequents the market, and discourses with all the people he can get any intelligence of . . . and offers them money for any quantity they can gather of the seeds, if they will bring them to town. So that when I go to gather seeds, where I used to find them, the people near where they grow will not let me have them." Upon the whole, however, Alexander and Bartram were friendly rivals, and the latter doubtless derived great satisfaction from Collinson's report of 1761 that his own shipments arrived in fine condition, while "there are great complaints of Alexander's seeds . . . but his will do well enough for the Scots."

With the growing interest in gardening and botany after the midcentury, Bartram could no longer lament, as he once did to Mark Catesby and Collinson, that "Our Americans have very little taste for these amusements." Among others engaged in collecting botanical specimens for English gentlemen were Thomas Lees and Humphrey Marshall, the latter a cousin of Bartram's, who furnished seeds to European gardeners "at lower prices than common." Marshall was a particular correspondent of Dr. John Fothergill, who made him presents of books and instruments, encouraged him in his astronomical observations, and took great interest in his famous botanical gardens begun at Marshallton in Chester County in 1773.

Then there was William Young, a German lad from Philadelphia, who in 1764, by some devious negotiations not altogether clear, succeeded in having himself named Botanist to the King and Queen. "My neighbour Young's sudden preferment," wrote Bartram to Collinson in an injured tone, "has astonished a great part of our inhabitants. They are daily talking to me about him, that he has got more honour by a few miles' travelling to pick up a few common plants, than I have by near thirty years' travel, with great danger and peril." He comforted himself with the thought that the Royal Gardens couldn't amount to much, since "the plants you have had, many of them known a hundred years, should be esteemed at court as new discoveries." But it pained him that £300 a year should be paid to another for such services.

At Franklin's solicitation that Bartram "might be made happy, as well as more useful," Collinson bestirred himself in his friend's behalf, and succeeded the next year in procuring his appointment as Royal Botanist, but at a stipend of only £50 per annum. To make matters worse, Young became "new modelled" in London, playing the Macaroni "with his hair curled and tied in a black bag." On his return home Bartram reported: "He cuts the greatest figure in town, struts along the streets, whistling, with his sword and gold lace, etc. He hath been three times to visit me, pretends a great respect for me." With his foreign ways and his "aimiable" London wife, William Young made doubtless far better copy than Quaker John, and always received more attention from the local press. Yet even Collinson had to admit the German youth was not lacking in scientific skill, and on several occasions John Ellis, F.R.S., and the famous Linnaeus generously acknowledged that "we are indebted to Mr. William Young, a native of Philadelphia."

Although John Bartram is best known as a collector of American plants, his botanical interests were never limited to collection and classification. He studied with great care the native habitats of the forms he gathered, analyzing their "soil requirements" and their seeds. He made important contributions to the early development of hybrid plants. Writing to William Byrd in 1739 he reported:

I have made this spring several microscopical observations upon the male and female parts in vegetables, to oblige some ingenious botanists in Leyden . . . as a mechanical demonstration of the certainty of this hypothesis, of the different sex in all plants that have come under my notice. I can't find that any vegetable hath power to produce perfect seed able to propagate without the conjunction of malle seed any more than animals and by a good microscope the malle and femalle organs is as plainly discovered.

He crossed several species of the genus *Lychnis,* "whereby I have obtained curious mixed colours in flowers, never known before," and he repeated Logan's experiments with maize. "I hope by these practical observations," he concluded significantly, "to open a gate into a very large field of experimental knowledge." In the work of Logan and Bartram Philadelphia made a notable contribution to the science of botany during this period of genetical inquiry.

In his search for specimens Bartram undertook a number of long journeys into the American wilderness, journeys which stimulated his scientific questioning and were productive of valuable results. A fieldworker and experimentalist rather than a bookish scientist, he never followed Franklin's injunction of 1769 to cease "your long and dangerous peregrinations" and devote your leisure to "a work that is much wanted and which no one besides is so capable of performing, a Natural History of our country." Yet these "peregrinations" resulted in a surprisingly large literary output. Between 1740 and 1763, thanks largely to the efforts of Franklin and Collinson, Bartram published in the *Philosophical Transactions* eight papers on a wide variety of subjects, ranging from rattlesnakes, wasps, and fresh-water mussels (which he erroneously supposed to be vegetables), to observations on the aurora borealis. Franklin and Hall incorporated his notes on American medicinal plants in their 1751 edition of Short's *Medicina Britannica,* thereby imparting to that popular herbal a definitely scientific tone.

At London in the same year Peter Collinson secured the publication of *Observations on the Inhabitants, Climate, Soil, Rivers, Productions, Animals, and Other Matters Worthy of Note, Made by John Bartram, in His Travels from Pennsilvania to Onandaga, Oswego and Lake Ontario in Canada.* This journey, one of the most appealing in the history of scientific exploration, was arranged by

James Logan in 1743 and undertaken in company with Lewis Evans, the geographer, Conrad Weiser, Indian agent, and the powerful sachem Shikellamy of the Delawares. Most popular of Bartram's writings was his *Description of Florida,* which passed through three London editions between 1766 and 1769. Many years after his death there appeared in the first volume of the *Philadelphia Medical and Physical Journal* (1804) his "Notes of the Epidemics of Pennsylvania and New Jersey in the Years 1746, 1747, 1748 and 1749."

Bartram's letters, however, constitute the most important of his literary efforts. Full of pleasing speculation and compact scientific description, they evince a steady progress in epistolary style, from the fumbling efforts of a novice with his pen to the mature productions of a master in his field. In addition to their intrinsic charm, they provide a key to the understanding of the astonishing absence of provinciality among colonial Philadelphians—a quality notoriously lacking in the nineteenth century and after. A knowledge of science was the passport to the intellectual society of the eighteenth century, and it was Peter Collinson of London who issued the visas to the initiate of many lands.

Mere enumeration of Bartram's correspondents furnishes a roster of the scientists of the Enlightenment. Philip Miller, Sir Hans Sloane, George Edwards, Mark Catesby, Dr. John Fothergill, and Dr. J. J. Dillenius of Oxford were a few of his English friends, while on the Continent he was in communication with Dr. John Gronovius and Peter van Muschenbroek of Holland, as also with Queen Ulrica, Peter Kalm, Dr. Charles Wrangel and the great Linnaeus of Sweden. These were folk who knew no nation; they were citizens of the world of science. In 1756, when a state of war existed between England and France, Collinson instructed Bartram to address his shipment for that year to M. Buffon at Paris as well as to himself, so that, in case of capture, he "should have it, one time or another."

The London Quaker also introduced his American friend by letter to interested colonials, and Bartram soon came to operate at

Philadelphia a sort of scientific clearinghouse for the colonies. Through him Franklin met Cadwalader Colden of New York, and such natural scientists as Jared Eliot of Connecticut, John Clayton, William Byrd and Dr. John Mitchell of Virginia, and Dr. Alexander Garden with his group of Charleston botanists were brought into touch with one another. Many of these men journeyed to Philadelphia to know Bartram and to see his garden, "which is a perfect portraiture of himself." All received from the genial philosopher, who happened also to be Deputy Postmaster for the Colonies, the privilege of franking letters on scientific matters. Just address me at Philadelphia, Bartram advised Collinson, "for every merchant of note in town knows me." In 1764 the canny Quaker botanist had Governor Dobbs of North Carolina and Justice Lamboll of Charleston exchanging seeds, "as they are both Irish; and they and the Scots will hang together like bees." It was no accident that this eager man of broad views and wide acquaintance should have conceived the idea for an American scientific society many years before more cautious philosophers felt the time was ripe.

Bartram's letters reveal him to have been a versatile scientist and true philosopher, a shrewd but benevolent student of humankind. Not content solely to botanize on his many travels, he observed Nature in all her aspects. He frequently made maps for Collinson, which the latter praised as "very prettily done." After 1753 he left the drawing of plants to his son William, who accompanied him on his travels, and whose fine artistic talents made him the worthy predecessor of a long line of such American naturalists. Bartram's interest was always attracted by animals and insects, especially rattlesnakes and wasps. He evolved a most practical plan for mounting the bones of a mastodon discovered by George Croghan in the West, and lamented that "the learned curiosos" of England would send no one to Ohio to take measurements before the bones were all carried away. Learning from sailors of shellfish and sand reptiles found in the bellies of large fish caught in mid-ocean, he speculated to Gronovius "whether there may not be vast chains of mountains" under the sea as well as on the land. For Dr. Fothergill he made a survey of New World mineral springs and the properties of their waters, but though like his contemporaries he believed in the efficacy of such spas, he thought their excessive use an expensive fad. "We have several springs in our province," he reported somewhat acidly, "on which many people have bestowed a large income."

On several subjects Bartram's scientific thinking foreshadowed the later developments of modern times. To his theory of the marine origin of limestones and marbles he clung tenaciously despite the withering criticisms of such correspondents as Collinson. Discovery of fossils "all over the country, even on the top of the mountains" inspired him to the "notion of the antediluvian impression of marine shells." But such "rambling observations" fell short of his practical plans for his country. In 1756 he wrote to Dr. Garden of Charleston:

I have often thought of proposing a scheme, which I am apt to believe would be of general benefit to most of our colonies. It is, to bore the ground to great depths, in all the different soils in the several provinces, with an instrument fit for the purpose, about four inches in diameter. The benefit . . . is to search for marls, or rich earths, to manure the surface of the poor ground withal. Secondly, to search for all kinds of medicinal earths, sulphurs, bitumens, coal, peat, salts, vitriols, marcasites, flints, as well as metals. Thirdly, to find the various kinds of springs, to know whether they are potable, or medicinal, or mechanical.

To carry out this design he proposed the selection for each province of an "overseer" who should superintend the borings and

write down, in a book for that purpose, the time and place, when and where, they began to bore, and the particular depth of every *stratum* they bore through, and the depth from whence it was drawn. . . . By this method, we may compose a curious subterranean map.

Here was an entirely practicable plan for a geological survey, conceived in detail long before any such useful project was attempted in either Europe or America.

In 1763 John Bartram, who, like most Philadelphians, was a careful reader of the newspapers, came upon the suggestion of a "noble and absolutely necessary scheme . . . to search all the country of

Canada and Louisiana for all natural productions, convenient situations for manufactories, and different soils, minerals and vegetables." He was willing, he wrote Collinson, to undertake the latter survey himself, but as a practical man and a realist he admitted that "before this scheme can be executed, the Indians must be subdued or driven above a thousand miles back." John Bartram belonged still to the pioneer generation: "unless we bang the Indians stoutly," he declared, "and make them fear us, they will never love us, nor keep peace long with us." It is merely one of time's characteristic ironies that his son William became a great advocate for the red man, a proponent of the concept of the noble savage, and a major influence, through his *Travels,* upon the writings of Wordsworth, Coleridge, Châteaubriand, and the whole Romantic school.

For his lifelong devotion to natural history John Bartram received ample reputation in Europe and at home. It is true the Royal Society failed to do itself the honor of electing him to membership, as likewise the London Society of Arts, though the secretary of the latter organization sought his advice on the subject of grasses in 1760 with the axiom that "the surest method of improving science, is by a generous intercourse of the learned in different countries, and a free communication of knowledge." The Scots did better, however, the Edinburgh Society of Arts and Sciences conferring upon him in 1773 a gold medal in recognition of "the many ingenious and useful discoveries he has favoured them with in the course of a long correspondence," and in 1769 the Royal Society of Science at Stockholm, where he was "well known . . . from throne to everyone that regards learning," unanimously elected him a member. This was an even greater honor than the Royal Society could confer, for the Swedish institution was famous "for the greatest delicacy in choosing members of distinction and note." Indeed, Linnaeus indulged in no burst of rhetoric when he was said to have referred to John Bartram as "the greatest natural botanist in the world."

By 1740 a small group of eager and capable inhabitants of the city on the Delaware were actively engaged in the study of natural philosophy. Such sympathetic dilettanti as Drs. Thomas and Phineas Bond, Joseph Breintnall, Dr. John Kearsley and Dr. Christopher Witt generously encouraged those in their circle who possessed real talent to pursue their studies further, and all of them benefited from the wealth and prestige, the wide connections and scholarly assistance of James Logan of Stenton. With Godfrey, whom he found "a very good master of Newtonian philosophy," Logan frequently worked on mathematical problems, and there is reason to suspect their joint authorship of an essay "On the Usefulness of Mathematicks" in the *Pennsylvania Gazette* for October 30, 1735. In addition to his defense of his friend's improvements on the quadrant, and his own investigations into the reproduction of plants, Logan wrote for the *Philosophical Transactions* two papers on astronomical subjects, and in 1739 published in Holland a Latin treatise on the refraction of light. By 1742 interest in natural history was sufficiently general among Philadelphians to enable Franklin and other friends of Bartram to solicit in the *Pennsylvania Gazette* an "annual contribution for his Encouragement" for which nearly £20 had already been subscribed.

The philosophers of Penn's city could boast two significant achievements in these years. They had made considerable contributions to the development of scientific knowledge, and by means of their contributions they had entered, on equal terms with European scholars, into the main current of Western scientific thought. James Logan, Thomas Godfrey, Joseph Breintnall, John Bartram, and such medical men as the Bonds and Kearsley had attained an international audience for their scholarly accomplishments. There was little of the provincial in this group; they exchanged views with English and Dutch scientists, who solicited their opinions and published the results of their researches, many years before Benjamin Franklin became celebrated in Europe for his electrical experiments. Interest in natural philosophy and in the association of men of learning to bring about scientific progress were in the air. The clever young printer, making his way to wealth in the thirties, no doubt learned to speculate on such things from conversations he listened to at the Library Company or about town among James Logan and his friends. Franklin was hardly *sui generis*.

Scientific advance, however, cannot be achieved by reason and inquiry alone; it is to a great degree dependent upon the instruments of precision available for its prosecution. The trade of instrument-making did not come into being until late in the seventeenth century, and attained importance only in the eighteenth, with the establishment of the craft on a broad basis by the Muschenbroeks of Leyden and by Leupold of Leipsic, who began issuing his famous catalogue, *Theatrum Machinarum,* in 1732. Before this time scientists had had either to construct their own apparatus or to resort for assistance to jewelers, watchmakers, carpenters, glass-makers, blacksmiths or locksmiths.

Lacking professional instrument-makers and finding imported instruments extremely expensive, Philadelphia scientists in the first half of the century were fortunately able to employ the services of a group of "exquisite mechanics," many of whom shared with their employers a passion for scientific knowledge. Local scientists were often themselves able craftsmen. Godfrey the glazier built his quadrant with his own hands, and the farmer Bartram constructed greenhouses and botanical equipment for himself. Scientific progress in Philadelphia was further made possible by the fact that here its votaries, even those "gentlemen of capacity and leisure," had not, like many aristocratic Europeans, a disabling aversion against joining the powers of their minds to the skill of their hands.

An interesting combination of mental and mechanical skills for scientific and social betterment is to be seen in the famous Pennsylvania Fireplace. In 1742 Printer Franklin furnished a model of this useful stove, invented and constructed by him, to his Junto crony, Robert Grace, Quaker ironmaster and skilled metallurgist, who cast the plates at his Warwick furnace. Two years later, to aid Grace in marketing them, Franklin wrote and printed *An Account of the New-Invented Pennsylvanian Fire-Places,* explain-

ing the principle of the action of heat upon which the new con-
trivances were based. The excellent drawings illustrating the
Account were prepared by Lewis Evans, engineer and cartographer, who also sold the fireplaces at his shop in Strawberry
Alley, and advertised to take care, "if required, that they are fitted
up and set to the best advantage."

By 1740 all crafts needed for the production of precision instruments were represented in the city. Schoolmaster Andrew Lamb,
erstwhile transported convict, had served an apprenticeship to a
London mathematical instrument-maker, and at Philadelphia and
New York he combined his trade with pedagogy, eventually working over almost exclusively into the former field. In 1749 he offered
for sale at his mariner's shop "the late invented and most curious
instrument, called an Octant, for taking the latitude or other
altitudes at sea, with all other mathematical instruments for sea
and land," of his own make. By 1761 James Ham was also doing
business as a "Mathematical and Optical Instrument-Maker" at the
Sign of the Quadrant, where he made all sorts of surveying, nauti-
cal and scientific instruments.

When in the 1740's several Philadelphians took up the study of
electricity, their researches were considerably accelerated by ingenious apparatus designed and constructed by local craftsmen. Foremost among these were Philip Syng, silversmith and scientifically-
minded member of Franklin's Junto, who in 1747 contrived a
simple, portable laborsaving machine for producing electricity by
friction. Ebenezer Kinnersley was also responsible for several bits
of electrical invention. As early as 1747, when electrical experimentation was in its infancy, Franklin advised Cadwalader Colden
that his New York friends who wished to conduct such investigations might procure their materials in Philadelphia; "I am satisfied
we have workmen here who can make the apparatus as well to
the full as that from London." By the decade of the fifties local
glassmakers were blowing bottles for Leyden jars. Franklin sent
eighteen of them to James Bowdoin of Boston in 1753, and in

1756 Dr. John Lining wrote from Charleston to obtain some Philadelphia-made jars.

The increase in the intellectual tempo at Philadelphia, which took place in the middle years of the century, and the effect of which in other fields of endeavor previous chapters have sought to describe, hastened the pace of scientific development, both speculative and applied. A sufficient number of men were either engaged in philosophic inquiry or well schooled in recent theory to provide a proper audience for the course of philosophical and experimental lectures delivered at the State House in 1740 by Isaac Greenwood, formerly of Harvard, and an authority on Newton's system of fluxions. These men were all loosely associated, either through membership in the Library Company, or through their common friendships with Logan and Franklin. A more formal organization to encourage correspondence with scientists in other colonies and to permit communication with European scholars was clearly desirable.

Bartram had proposed such an association in 1739, but was discouraged by Collinson on account of "the infancy of your colony." The idea did not die, however, and five years later Benjamin Franklin and Dr. Thomas Bond were ready to agree with Bartram that the time had now come for the formation of a scientific body for the colonies.

With a view to "Promoting Useful Knowledge among the British Plantations in America," Franklin issued proposals for the establishment of "one society . . . of *virtuosi* or ingenious men" from all the colonies, to be known as the American Philosophical Society. Advantages of a central situation, the colonial post office, and "a good growing library" all pointed to Philadelphia as the proper place for its location, and its promoter suggested it should always include at least seven members from that city who should meet there monthly. Inasmuch as the body was intended not only to unite American scientists by intercolonial correspondence but also to furnish a regular channel of communication with the Royal

Society of London, the Deputy Postmaster agreed to frank all letters dealing with philosophical subjects.

In the spring of 1744 the American Philosophical Society was organized according to these proposals by Franklin, Thomas Bond and John Bartram; its other Philadelphia members included Phineas Bond, Thomas Godfrey and Samuel Rhoads. Cadwalader Colden and James Alexander of New York lent considerable encouragement, and through their good offices at least five other gentlemen from that colony and from New Jersey were persuaded to send in their names. When Colden wrote Collinson of the project, the Londoner this time vouchsafed an enthusiastic reply: "I expect something New from your New World, our Old World as it were [is] Exhausted." In similar fashion Gronovius soon wrote to Bartram, inquiring about the work of the new body.

Unfortunately, things did not turn out as planned. Out-of-town members such as Colden naturally waited "for an example from those of Philadelphia" before offering any communications, and in 1745 Franklin had to confess that "the Members of our Society here are very idle gentlemen, they will take no pains." "It is certain that some have been too lazy," Colden wrote to Bartram, but he added significantly, "Others may have been too officious; which makes the prudent afraid of them." Franklin, Dr. Bond, and I "talk of carrying it on with more diligence than ever," Bartram replied, "which we may very easily do if we could but exchange the time that is spent in the Club, Chess and Coffee Houses for the Curious amusements of natural observations." Perhaps they could have succeeded, but the outbreak of King George's War put a final end to the project, which was not to be revived for many years.

Notwithstanding this failure, interest in scientific experiment and speculation increased, and these very war years witnessed the performance of the famous "Philadelphia Experiments" in the field of electricity which gave the city its greatest European repute.

Colonial interest in electricity was an overflow from that which was animating English and French scientists at the time. In the early 1730's important experimentation by Stephen Gray of England and Charles Du Fay of Paris with the many magnets, kites and other "mechanical toys" to be found among the stocks of the instrument-makers inspired much curiosity among Europeans. By 1746 Pieter van Muschenbroek and E. G. von Kleist had developed the Leyden jar, the simplest form of condenser, which for the first time enabled experimenters to obtain a high electric charge. Natural philosophers of France and England were soon agog over the problems of electricity, and a number of papers on the subject appeared in the *Philosophical Transactions,* which, being eagerly read in the colonies, induced scientific gentlemen there to take up the study with astonishing rapidity.

The first manifestation of interest in electricity in the American colonies seems to have occurred at Boston, where, in May, 1743, Dr. Adam Spencer of Edinburgh advertised a course of lectures on experimental philosophy, with demonstrations on his "compleat Apparatus." From Boston Spencer went to Newport, where he encouraged Dr. Thomas Moffatt and the ingenious clockmaker William Claggett to undertake similar experiments, and thence to New York, where he interested James Alexander and some of his friends. In the spring of 1744 Spencer arrived in Philadelphia, where he commenced a course of lectures in the rooms of the Library Company at the State House. The traveling William Black reported his lecture of May 29, wherein he "proceeded to show that [electrical] Fire is Diffus'd through all space, and may be produced from all Bodies, Sparks of Fire Emitted from the Face and Hands of a Boy Suspended Horizontally, by only rubbing a Glass Tube at his feet."

Spencer, wrote Franklin in the *Autobiography,* "showed me some electrical experiments. They were imperfectly performed, as he was not very expert; but being on a subject quite new to me, they equally surprised and pleased me." In all probability this incident occurred in 1743, during the journey which Franklin made in that year to New England (although as an old man he remembered the date as 1746), but in any event it seems quite clear that the American owed his original interest in electricity to the "imperfect" demonstrations performed by the Scottish doctor.

Franklin doubtless wrote to Collinson of his new interest, for in 1746, shortly after "the most surprising discovery that has yet been made in the whole business of electricity," the Library Company received from the Londoner a most important gift. "Your kind present of an electric tube, with directions for using it," reported Franklin in March, 1747, "has put several of us on making electrical experiments, in which we have observed some peculiar phenomena that we look upon to be new." So widespread was the interest in these demonstrations that friends of the printer came "continually in crowds to see them." Meanwhile in Newport (March, 1746) and later in Boston (August, 1747), William Claggett, assisted by Dr. Moffatt and others, had been carrying out further experiments on apparatus of his own construction. The Welsh clockmaker knew Franklin, and quite probably communicated to him some of his "great discoveries in electricity" during the latter's visit to Newport in 1746.

Virtually all scientific advance is the product of many contributions, large and small, by numbers of devoted though often obscure workers, which come eventually to be synthesized by the insight and genius of a single mind. So it was in the case of electrical research at Philadelphia. While Benjamin Franklin was without doubt the primary genius and "the real master of the new knowledge," the famous "Philadelphia Experiments" which attracted world-wide attention when published in London in 1751 were, as he himself generously admitted, the fruits of group action.

In a letter to Collinson on May 25, 1747, Franklin reported two major contributions to the field of "American Electricity." The first, based upon experiments performed by Franklin, Philip Syng, and others, was the conclusion "that the electrical fire was not created by friction, but collected, being really an element diffused among, and attracted by other matter, particularly by water and metals"; and the second, the use of the new terms "positive" and "negative" to describe the varied states of electrified bodies. At this time also the printer noted the importance of grounding in electrical experiments, and began observing "the wonderful effect of pointed bodies, both in *drawing off* and throwing off the electrical fire." The latter phenomenon had been first noted by his "ingenious friend" Thomas Hopkinson, who devised a series of experiments for its demonstration, and interest therein led ultimately to Franklin's construction of the lightning rod.

Electrical research by Franklin and his middle-class assistants proceeded with "great alacrity" in the next few years. Both Franklin and Ebenezer Kinnersley had purchased their own electrical equipment, and in 1747 the Library Company received a complete apparatus from the Proprietors. Votaries of the new science spread its popularity to other cities—New York, Boston, Newport and Charleston—whence came orders for Philadelphia-built equipment. In 1748 Franklin and his associates invented an "electrical battery," and Kinnersley contrived a "Magical picture" of the King in court dress, the crown highly charged to shock anyone contemplating the "high treason of removing it, along with other tricks which attracted public attention." But despite such activities the investigators were all "chagrined a little," as Franklin phrased it, "that we have hitherto been able to produce nothing this way of use to mankind."

A practical application of the theories of electricity, however, was not far off. The next year (1749) Lewis Evans published his *Map of Pensilvania, New Jersey, New-York, and the Three Deleware Counties,* notes to which explained the occurrence of "thunder gusts" common in those regions as caused by the "Meeting of Sea Clouds freighted with Electricity" with land clouds which were "less so"; equilibrium between the two, Evans believed, was restored by "snaps of Lightning." Franklin then proposed a demonstration to confirm the identity of lightning with electricity, which M. d'Alibard of France verified in May, 1752, and which Franklin himself independently proved by the famous "kite experiment" in June of the same year.

The printer had also sometime previously conceived the use

of lightning rods, which again were first tried out by the French in May, 1752, and which were reported to be in use on the spires of the Academy and the State House in Philadelphia in October. Kinnersley wrote to Franklin in England in 1760 of how use of this device had recently saved a house in the city from fire. To the satisfaction of the practical mind of Philadelphia, what had begun as a matter of curiosity and diversion did, indeed, redound to the benefit of mankind.

The careful accounts of all these activities which Franklin drew up he forwarded to Collinson for communication to the Royal Society, where they were eagerly discussed by the members and "Deservedly Admired not only for the Clear Intelligent Stile, but also for the Novelty of the Subjects." Two of these papers appeared in the *Gentleman's Magazine* in 1750, and the next year Collinson secured publication of the whole collection, with a preface by Dr. John Fothergill, under the title *Experiments and Observations in Electricity. Made at Philadelphia in America, by Mr. Benjamin Franklin.* In 1752 a French translation of the Fothergill volume appeared in Paris, and the Royal Society began including in its *Philosophical Transactions* papers by Franklin, Kinnersley and other colonial experimenters in this new and expanding field.

Franklin and his associates had embarked upon the study of electricity in 1746 with small knowledge of what had been accomplished in Europe, but in less than five years they had drawn fully abreast of their distant colleagues. Benjamin Franklin in fact "laid the foundations of modern electrical science" at Philadelphia in the years 1747-49. He conceived and formulated a unified theory of electrical action which explained all known phenomena in terms of a single electrical fluid, and he evolved the terminology to express that theory. More clearly and fully than any of his predecessors he elucidated familiar electrical phenomena and predicated new ones.

Franklin's vigorous and curious mind was well suited to such a task, and of all his activities this was the one he most regretted leaving for service to his country. But his accomplishment owed much to his Philadelphia environment. "Exquisite mechanics" among his acquaintance aided him in the construction of apparatus, and the eager interest and fruitful co-operation of his many associates were a continuing source of stimulation. Separated by ocean distances from European experimenters and unfamiliar with the electrical literature of the Old World, his fertile imagination was able to range freely, unfettered by long-accepted scientific conventions. In 1759 Van Muschenbroek wrote from Leyden that he was forwarding the information about all writers on the subject of electricity, as Franklin had requested. "I should wish, however," he concluded, "that you would go on making experiments entirely on your own initiative and thereby pursue a path entirely different from that of the Europeans, for then you shall certainly find many other things which have been hidden to natural philosophers throughout the space of centuries."

"While we are attending to what was done by Dr. Franklin at Philadelphia," observed Joseph Priestley in his *History of Electricity,* "we must by no means overlook what was done by Mr. Kinnersley." When his townsmen took up the study of electricity this Baptist minister without a charge, who had but recently given up shopkeeping, entered eagerly into the experiments. In 1748 he demonstrated that a Leyden jar could be electrified as well through its outer tinfoil coating as through the wire leading into it, and in Boston in 1751 he rediscovered M. du Fay's "two contrary electricities, of glass and sulphur," vitreous and resinous, with which both he and Franklin were unacquainted, and which he immediately identified with his friend's categories of positive and negative. He also suggested means for protecting buildings at Newport against lightning.

Even after his appointment as professor of English and oratory at the Academy, perhaps at the expense of the quality of the instruction he dispensed, Kinnersley continued his work on electricity. To study the effects of the new element on air he invented an "electrical air thermometer." By means of this device, which procured him his greatest reputation, he was able to demonstrate that the melting of metals by electricity or lightning was caused by heat and not, as Franklin had previously believed, by "cold fusion."

Kinnersley and Franklin were always good friends, and there is no ground for William Smith's insinuation that Franklin took credit for the achievements of his coworker. On the contrary, he encouraged Kinnersley in the extensive lecture tours by which the latter spread the knowledge of electricity and stimulated interest therein throughout the mainland colonies and the West Indies, and he faithfully communicated his friend's discoveries to the Royal Society, which published accounts of three of them.

Kinnersley enjoyed considerable contemporary fame, at home and abroad. Lord Charles Cavendish praised his air thermometer, and John Canton, F.R.S., told Franklin in conversation in 1764 that "Mr. Kinnersley's first experiment in electricity [is] truly a beautiful one . . . his second . . . an extraordinary one," which he himself had endeavored in vain to repeat in England. By 1767 Priestley could declare that if Kinnersley "continue his electrical inquiries, his name, after that of his friend, will be second to few in the history of electricity."

The desire of Philadelphians that the results of scientific knowledge be applied to social uses, voiced by Franklin in respect to electricity, bore fruit in other fields, especially in the procuring and reporting of geographic information. Lewis Evans's *Map of Pensilvania* . . . published in 1749 and revised in 1752, included roads and carrying-places, while the accompanying text contained much military and agricultural information and an account of the formation of the Endless Mountains which revealed its author's familiarity with the latest geological knowledge.

More important were his *General Map of the Middle British Colonies in America* (1755) and its attendant pamphlet, *Geographical, Historical, Political, Philosophical and Mechanical Essays,* issued in two parts in 1755 and 1756. This large-scale map, with its wealth of detail based on a wide variety of observations, surveys and reports, marked a great step forward in American cartography.

Especially for its representation of the Ohio River and surrounding country it remained a recognized authority for many years. On this map Evans made Philadelphia "the first Meridian of America," for its central position, and because "it far excels in the Progress of Letters, mechanic Arts, and the public Spirit of its Inhabitants."

Another Philadelphia geographer of note was Nicholas Scull, mathematician and surveyor, who published in 1750 his *Map of Philadelphia and Parts Adjacent,* and in 1757 his *Map of the Improved Part of the Province of Pennsylvania.* The former is important for showing the location of eastern Pennsylvania's country estates, and the latter for having a more accurate frontier line than that plotted by Evans. The Philadelphia merchant, Joshua Fisher, formerly of Lewes, Delaware, who had made the first tests of Godfrey's quadrant, devoted his leisure for many years to compiling his *Chart of the Delaware Bay and River,* based upon his own surveys. "Sundry Merchants" subscribed £1,000 in 1756 to ensure publication of this pioneer work in hydrographic charting, which recorded soundings and risks to navigation so accurately as to render pilots unnecessary to ships coming up the Delaware.

More spectacular, though less successful, were the ambitious plans of William Allen and his mercantile associates for an expedition to locate the Northwest Passage. As often, hopes of discovery and commerce went hand in hand. "We have been encouraged in our attempt," wrote Allen, "by consideration that in case our search for the passage should be fruitless, we might strike a lucrative trade in the coast of Labrador." Allen with his Philadelphia contributors, one of whom was Benjamin Franklin, and certain merchants of Maryland and Boston subscribed £900 "on a generous plan" with "no view of any monopoly" to equip the schooner *Argo,* sixty tons, under Captain Charles Swaine. After taking on a crew of ten whalemen and some tackle at Boston, Swaine set sail in April, 1753, with instructions that in event of failing to locate the passage he was to explore the Labrador coast and have a try at whaling.

Although the *Argo* became icebound and was forced to return home in November, the expedition did result in a good chart of

that northern coastline. At a meeting at the Bull's Head Tavern
the subscribers expressed "a general satisfaction," voted Swaine a
present, and laid plans for another voyage the following May. In
the second expedition John Watts, William Gordon, and several
other New Yorkers took shares. This attempt likewise failed in
its major objective, but was nonetheless productive of important
results. Swaine took the *Argo* as far north as Latitude 16° and explored a portion of Davis Strait. On his return in October, 1754,
he brought with him, not, to be sure, his intended Golden Fleece,
but a fine collection of Eskimo garments and artifacts, which, when
presented to the Library as a gift from the "North-West Company," became one of the most popular exhibits in its growing
museum.

Of more significance to the social historian than even the accomplishments of local scientists was the deepening interest in the subject displayed by the public at large. By 1750 adequate facilities for
the study of natural philosophy were available to anyone whose
tastes inclined him in that direction. The Loganian Library consisted almost exclusively of books on science and mathematics,
while the constantly growing collections of the Library Company
were as strong in science as in any other field. "Besides the books,"
Peter Kalm reported of the latter institution, "several mathematical
and physical instruments and a large collection of natural curiosities are to be seen in it."

Franklin saw to it, at the founding of the Academy in 1749, that
its mathematical school was well equipped with instruments and "a
middling apparatus for experimental philosophy." The appointment
of Theophilus Grew, mathematician and astronomer, as the school's
first master in 1750 provided real impetus to scientific study. He
was followed by Ebenezer Kinnersley, Francis Alison, and later
by Charles Thomson, all devoted students of natural philosophy.
Despite his overemphasis on the classical curriculum, Provost William Smith had a lively interest in the sciences, and from Academy
and College he and his faculty sent forth a group of able young men

who had by 1765 assumed leadership in such matters, not only for
the city but throughout the colonies.

If the study of Nature required a badge of gentility, Provost
Smith imparted it, and more and more it became fashionable for
members of the mercantile gentry to dabble in natural philosophy,
which they found to be a pleasant and useful diversion. A similar
habit of mind had long prevailed among certain Quakers. In 1749
George Mifflin bought himself a microscope, and John Smith, who
had been an absorbed listener to Adam Spencer's lectures in 1744,
became much interested in James Alexander's "Solar Microscope
and his system of the heavens in wheels," although he confided to
his diary that he couldn't understand it. Taste for science even
rendered young girls suspiciously bluestocking. "Spent this after-
noon with Molly Foulke at the widow Bringhurst's," recorded
Elizabeth Sandwith in February, 1760, "where we were entertained
with divers objects in a Microscope, and with several experiments
in Electricity."

The gentry provided patronage for science by their attendance
at public lectures, now given with increasing frequency. David
James Dove, recently arrived from England, in December, 1750,
presented at the home of Jacob Duché in Chestnut Street a course
of six lectures on physics, pneumatics, hydrostatics, optics, geography and astronomy, the last being illustrated by the use of "a
curious large Orrery." For the sum of two pistoles a gentleman
could attend these lectures, bring a lady with him, and obtain a free
syllabus to be had at the post office.

After Dove joined the faculty of the Academy, Edward Shippen
of Lancaster backed Lewis Evans in the purchase of Dove's apparatus, and arranged for the delivery by Evans in the spring of 1751
of a course of thirteen lectures on natural philosophy and electricity
before the College of New Jersey. In July Evans went to New
York, where he repeated his course at the home of the Reverend
Ebenezer Pemberton, explaining all technical terms "for the Sake
of the Ladies and Gentlemen unskill'd in Mathematics." Success in
these two ventures encouraged him to go south to Charleston,

where at Mr. Doughty's Dancing Room in March, 1752, he delivered his philosophical and electrical lectures, for which he now
provided a printed syllabus.

Greatest of colonial lecturers, however, was Ebenezer Kinnersley,
who began his career in April, 1751, with two lectures, drawn up
by Benjamin Franklin, on "the newly-discovered Electrical Fire."
So many incipient scientists were willing to pay 7s. 6d. to witness
the "entertaining and astonishing Wonders of Electricity" that
he was forced to demonstrate his experiments daily for several
months at Mr. Duché's. In September, armed with letters from
Franklin to James Bowdoin, Kinnersley took his "compleat apparatus" to Boston, where he lectured in Faneuil Hall, rediscovered
M. du Fay's two contrary electricities, and made himself "most
acceptable to the Gentlemen of Boston." In March, 1752, he repeated his lectures at Newport, and after an appearance in New
York, returned to Philadelphia for another course in September.
Eventually Kinnersley performed his electrical experiments in
"every capital town" of the mainland colonies, "and picked up
some money." A venture in the West Indies in 1753 proved less
successful, the atmosphere there being too moist for the satisfactory
performance of his demonstrations.

After his appointment to the Academy faculty Kinnersley gave
lectures almost annually in the "Apparatus Room" at the College.
In 1767 he announced his farewell appearances, but, good trouper
that he was, he returned repeatedly, giving two courses a year from
1770 to 1773. His really astonishing success lay in his constant revision of his lectures and experiments to keep them abreast of new
discoveries, and his inclusion of enough tricks and "novelties," such
as the electrified portrait of the King, to keep his audiences amused
and interested. One of Kinnersley's last public performances was a
nice piece of colonial irony, when he arranged the burning in
effigy "by Electric Fire," for their insults to its principal discoverer,
Franklin, of Alexander Wedderburn and Thomas Hutchinson, the
latter "represented with a double face."

The Philadelphia press contributed heavily to the propagation of the new science. Thomas Godfrey employed the columns of the *Pennsylvania Journal* to announce data on an eclipse of the sun which was due on July 14, 1748, and to request Bradford's "Astronomical Readers" to make observations to aid him in the calculation of longitude. "For the Sake of the Curious, and those that are provided with a good Telescope and Timepiece," the *Pennsylvania Gazette* published a timetable for the "small eclipse" of January 7, 1769. Professor Theophilus Grew regularly used the newspapers to request "Gentlemen" to communicate their observations. Benjamin Franklin, practical publicist that he was, printed accounts of his lightning rod and instructions for setting it up both in the *Gazette* and in *Poor Richard's Almanac* for 1753. Provost Smith devoted considerable space in his *American Magazine* to a "Philosophic Miscellany." Among its contributions were John Winthrop's account of the causes of earthquakes, a series of articles on the improvement of agriculture, and a reprint of Franklin's "Observations Concerning the Increase of Mankind." Outstanding, however, was Smith's own defense of Thomas Godfrey's priority over Hadley as inventor of the quadrant.

The efforts of Smith and Franklin, the activities of Evans and Kinnersley, and the good offices of the local press brought the achievements of local investigators in the natural sciences to the attention not only of hundreds of interested Philadelphians, but of European scientists and of the colonists generally. Certainly such factors played a part in stimulating the latter to pursue philosophical inquiries of their own. By 1760 the time was doubly ripe for the organization of colonial students of science.

On June 5, 1757, Benjamin Franklin sailed for England, and thereafter was to see his native land for only a brief period of two years (1762-64) before the outbreak of the War for Independence. But although colonial Philadelphia had thus lost its most versatile citizen, greatest publicist and ablest organizer, there was no hiatus in its intellectual life. Instead, the years immediately ahead witnessed a genuine flowering in many fields of endeavor, but especially in the sciences, and the successful establishment of the great intercolonial body of scholars of which John Bartram had dreamed and which he and Franklin had tried to inaugurate. This progress was consummated by a coterie of vigorous young men, many of them associated with the College of Philadelphia either as graduates or as faculty, and recruited not so much from the middle class, whence came so many of Franklin's cronies, as from the provincial gentry.

In 1750 Charles Thomson, William Franklin and other young Philadelphians, chiefly Quakers, began to meet for weekly discussions in a society which they named and modeled after Franklin's Junto. To satisfy their scientific questionings they acquired an electrical apparatus and some optical equipment, but loss of members by death and want of enthusiasm among the survivors caused the club to pursue an extremely uneven existence throughout the decade of the fifties. In the summer of 1761 Thomson and Edmund Physick reorganized the group, which was thereafter to meet weekly for "Mutual Improvement in Useful Knowledge." Samuel Powel had joined them on his graduation from the College, and more new members, including Dr. Cadwalader Evans, Lewis Nicola, Owen Biddle, and Isaac and Moses, sons of John Bartram, now brought the total to thirty. In 1766, when a period of genuine scientific activity was at hand, Dr. John Morgan was admitted to membership.

On December 13 of that year, by vote of the members, the Junto became the American Society for Promoting and Propagating Useful Knowledge, Held at Philadelphia.[1] The "extremely zealous" Charles Thomson now proposed enlarging its activities, "fabricated a plan from that of the Royal Society and the Society of Arts," and suggested inviting to membership a number of "ingenious and publick spirited Gentlemen," both at home and abroad, to aid in furthering the design. On March 7, 1768, the *Pennsylvania Chronicle* carried the complete proposals of what was now called the American Society, Held at Philadelphia, for Promoting Useful Knowledge.

---

[1] Hereinafter this organization will be referred to as the American Society, to distinguish it from its rival, the American Philosophical Society.

Patriotic as well as scientific purposes animated the reinvigorated American Society. Its reorganization must be viewed as a part of the movement for colonial cultural union that accompanied the rising tide of opposition to the mother country. Indeed, its principal sponsor was soon to become known as "the Sam Adams of Philadelphia." Among the Society's evident objectives were the desire to improve the status and increase the output of agriculture and a program to promote the growth of manufacturing in the colonies.

"The Means of conveying Knowledge," opined Thomson, "are now become easy. Printing Houses are erected in all the principal Towns on the Continent, and regular Posts established to carry Letters and Papers from one to another. There is an easy and ready Communication with our Islands [and with England and the Continent] by Vessels which are employed in carrying our Trade. Besides, Hints thrown out in our public circulating Papers are not lost, as in this Country almost every Man is fond of reading, and seems to have a Thirst for Knowledge. The Farmers employed in cultivating the Lands are intelligent and sensible, capable of Observation, and of making many useful Experiments. . . . Among our Mechanics many are expert and ingenious . . . while many of our Young Men . . . have discovered such a Degree of Judgment and Genius, as will enable them to carry their Researches far into Nature." Therefore, the American Society requests persons of all occupations in every colony to aid it in promoting and propagating useful knowledge, and stands ready to incorporate as members all "who deserve well of their Country." The only merit to which the Society lays claim is that of "encouraging and directing Inquiries and experiments, of receiving, collecting, and digesting Discoveries, Inventions, and Improvements, of communicating them to the Public, and distinguishing the Authors; and of thus uniting the Labours of many, to attain . . . the Advancement of useful Knowledge and Improvements of our Country."

The new project was an immediate success. Thomson, the corresponding secretary, Dr. Morgan, and Vice-President Powel made full use of the pages of Goddard's *Chronicle* to solicit correspondence from scientists in other colonies and in Europe. Communications deemed notable the Society ordered published in the weekly press, in the hope that others would emulate "these fine examples." The *Essay on Fevers* by Dr. Lionel Chalmers of Charleston, South Carolina, thus first saw print in the *Pennsylvania Chronicle*. To the same paper the Society sent an account of a machine for cutting and polishing crystals, built by Abel Buell of Connecticut, and "Observations on the Native Silk Worms of North America" and other papers by Moses Bartram.

The hopeful future of colonial scientific organization was beclouded at the opening of the year 1768 by old personal and social animosities and by the torrid factionalism of Pennsylvania politics. It will be recalled that the Bonds and the Shippens, resentful of Dr. Morgan's Medical Society of 1765, had not only refused to join but had threatened the formation of a rival organization. They were confirmed in this purpose by a rumor current in 1767 that Charles Thomson was contemplating a further enlargement of the American Society, in which in the meantime John Morgan had become very active.

Dr. Thomas Bond, Smith, Alison and the Shippens, therefore, according to Cadwalader Evans, "strenuously endeavoured to revive the American Philosophical Society" of 1743, by electing to membership Governor John Penn, Chief Justice William Allen, former Governor James Hamilton, Richard Peters, and "between 20 and 30 others." The claim of "revival" was somewhat specious, since of the original members of the old Philosophical Society only four besides Dr. Bond were still living in Philadelphia. The whole move had a tendency to perpetuate political animosities and personal resentments by means of scholarly bodies in which they had no place. Most of the members of this new American Philosophical Society were proponents of the Proprietary party, while a large fraction of those in the American Society belonged to the Quaker or Assembly party which under the leadership of Franklin had long been seeking the abolition of the Proprietary.

Both societies were fortunate, however, in having for leaders men whose patriotism and love of learning transcended petty partisanship, and who immediately sought an accommodation. In January, 1768, Dr. Morgan approached Dr. Bond with a suggested solution to which the latter generously agreed, promising to do everything in his power "to cultivate that harmony which should subsist among the lovers of science." Morgan's proposal had been for union "on terms equally honourable to both Societies," but the Philosophical Society, still unwilling to forget local politics, sent a committee on February 2 to inform its rival that it had elected all the members of the American Society into membership with itself. This the American Society found unacceptable, as it was the older body and would thus become not merged but completely absorbed. Firmly declining the proposition, its members were nonetheless careful to leave the door ajar for future negotiations.

The two societies now embarked upon a struggle for membership and publicity. The American Philosophical Society reprinted in the pages of David Hall's *Gazette* (the Proprietary organ) Franklin's *Proposals* of 1743, which it followed up with various scientific communications by Bond, Ewing and others throughout the year 1768. For its part, the American Society achieved in the columns of Goddard's anti-Proprietary *Chronicle* such extensive intercolonial attention that the Philosophical Society felt compelled to order the publicity of its greatest scientific contribution, Thomas Barton's description of David Rittenhouse's orrery, inserted in the *Chronicle* as well as in the *Gazette*.

In similar fashion the rival bodies engaged in a race for new members. In general, wealthy conservatives of gentility and influence, usually Anglican or Presbyterian, gravitated into the American Philosophical Society—Smith, Alison, and all the trustees of the College were members—while well-to-do Quakers, medical men, and the more active and democratic young scientists affiliated with the competing organization. The latter's program was more vigorous and successful. In February, 1768, it scored a major victory by electing the absent Franklin to membership, and in November gained immeasurable prestige at home and abroad by naming him its president. At the same time it further cut the ground from beneath its rival by electing the recently converted Anglican, Samuel Powel, to its vice-presidency, and by incorporating Morgan's Medical Society into its membership, thereby gaining the support of most of the doctors in town.

The efforts and wide connections of Morgan, Powel, Thomson and others secured as corresponding members of the American Society some sixty-seven foreign and colonial scientists, whose accomplishments far outweighed those of the thirty-six who affiliated with the other body. On the other hand, the Philosophical Society led in resident fellows, ninety-two to seventy-eight.

By the autumn of 1768 public criticism was becoming vocal at the continued existence of competing organizations with similar aims. A "Lover of Truth" penned a powerful indictment of the junior body for its attempt to secure backing from the Assembly and to "confound" the public by adopting the thoroughly confusing title "The American Philosophical Society for Promoting Useful Knowledge." The emergent unity of merchants and others in the face of British restrictions and the concurrent integration of the city's libraries and fire companies further emphasized the utter folly of thus maintaining petty differences. Fortunately, too, some fifteen gentlemen of influence, among them Drs. Evans and Cadwalader, Joseph Galloway, Francis Hopkinson and the Reverend Jacob Duché, had accepted membership in both societies and thus constituted a solid factor for conciliation. On November 18 the American Society again proposed a union on equal terms, which this time the American Philosophical Society accepted.

On January 2, 1769, at the College, officers were elected for the combined body, henceforth to be known as the American Philosophical Society, Held at Philadelphia, for Promoting Useful Knowledge. At this meeting scientists prevailed over politicians, rebels over gentlemen, and Benjamin Franklin won the presidency over James Hamilton, candidate of the Penns, while Dr. Thomas Bond, who had labored diligently to persuade his own group to bury the hatchet, became vice-president. "We are now united," Bond wrote hopefully to Franklin, "and with your Presence, may make a Figure." But Governor Penn felt otherwise. "I shall never," he declared, "be a patron of a Society that has for its President such a ————— as Franklin."

After 1769 scientific activity in Philadelphia and in the American colonies as a whole came almost entirely beneath the aegis of the American Philosophical Society. Under vigorous and tactful guidance from Vice-President Thomas Bond, and from the secretaries, Smith, Thomson and Mifflin, the members showed a remarkable capacity to ignore political and social differences. All signs of "the old party leven" had disappeared by June, 1769, when Bond reported to the absent Franklin on the progress of Society, Hospital and Medical School. Franklin replied, with pleasure at the situation, that party had no place within a body of scholars. "Here the Royal Society is of all parties, but party is entirely out of the question in all our proceedings."

At the time of the union in January, 1769, the combined Society numbered 251 members, of whom ninety were residents of other British colonies, and seventeen of various countries of Europe. From that time until the outbreak of the war only sixteen new members were added from the city, compared with forty-eight from other colonies and twenty-six foreigners, to bring the totals to 298 American and forty-three European members.

Analysis of the Society's roster reveals the shrewdness and skill with which its officers conspired to ensure its success. Hardly a colonial scientist or natural philosopher of any standing was omitted, so that in a very real sense the body comprehended intellectual America. Inclusion of prominent public figures of all parties and colonies guaranteed a measure of public sympathy, while social prestige and adequate financial support were assured by the admission of practically all the gentlemen of capacity and leisure living in and about Philadelphia. The names of such European savants as Fothergill, Nevil Maskelyne, Cullen and Hewson of Great Britain, Condorcet, Lavoisier and Abbé Raynal of France, Linnaeus, Wrangel and Bergman of Sweden, stood witness to the Society's scientific worth, while the Earl of Stanhope, Lord Mahon and the Baron de Klingstedt of St. Petersburg contributed the tone of gentility so valued in certain quarters.

Thus substantially supported by aristocratic patronage, the irresistibly unifying and democratizing forces of American culture were enabled to proceed apace. Dr. Bond and his colleagues adhered closely to Charles Thomson's original plan for making the American Philosophical Society the central colonial agency for the coordination of scientific and practical inquiry. A significant part of its function was the encouragement it bestowed on workers in other colonies. When in May, 1769, Dr. Benjamin Gale of Connecticut submitted samples of American printing types made by his friend Abel Buell, the Society referred them to Thomas Bradford, and after his favorable report recommended their use. Two years later a committee endorsed a paper by Andrew Oliver of Salem on "The Path of a Solar Shadow on a Horizontal Plane" as "more minutely discussed by him than any other," and praised "An Account of the Country of Illinois" by the King's Surveyor, Thomas Hutchins. Similar endorsement was awarded a communication from Dr. John Perkins of Boston "On Tornadoes, Hurricanes and Water Spouts," and approval bestowed on numerous plans and proposals for American manufactures.

In like fashion, residents of rural Pennsylvania who interested themselves in useful knowledge received encouragement and applause from their urban colleagues. Out on the frontier, at Lancaster, largest inland town in the colonies, the Juliana Library Company became virtually a branch chapter of the American Philosophical Society. Edward Shippen was the presiding genius of this circle, and the Reverend Thomas Barton its most learned member. But the most enthusiastic student of the New Science in this area was wealthy William Henry, maker of the famous Pennsylvania rifles and earliest patron of Benjamin West. At his gun works Henry maintained a well-equipped laboratory, and here he is said to have constructed a steam engine on principles learned from James Watt in Scotland, which he tested, unsuccessfully, in

1763 in a boat on the Conestoga Creek. The Society at Philadelphia praised his invention of a "Self-Moving or Sentinel Register," which provided automatic heat control for houses, and encouraged his other experiments with steam. Agricultural experiments at Bethlehem, undertaken by the Moravians and communicated by Dr. Bodo Otto, also received the support of the Society.

Although the American Philosophical Society had as its main object the encouraging and popularizing of "useful knowledge," it also undertook or sponsored research projects which added considerably to the world's scientific lore. Among its signal achievements in this field were its observations of the transit of Venus in 1769, and the uncovering of a great native genius in David Rittenhouse.

This scion of Welsh Quaker and Dutch yeoman stock spent his early life on a farm at Norriton, twenty miles from the city, where he divided his time between agriculture and clockmaking. Here, with the probable assistance of Thomas Barton, his brother-in-law, he made himself master of the Newtonian philosophy by reading the *Principia,* in Mott's translation, and similar works. At the age of twenty, according to his friend Dr. Rush, with only two or three books at his disposal he had become "acquainted with the science of Fluxions [the Newtonian Calculus], of which sublime invention he believed himself for a while to be the author," until he learned of the conflicting claims of Newton and Leibnitz for that honor.

From 1751, when he first met Barton, until 1770, when the latter persuaded him to move to Philadelphia, Rittenhouse made remarkable progress as an instrument-maker. Barton's influence secured him an appointment in 1763 to help survey the Pennsylvania-Maryland boundary, and it was he who fixed the famous quarter-circle line. Six years later he was employed on the boundary between New Jersey and New York. Meanwhile he studied Kinnersley's experiments on the compressibility of water, improved his clocks, designed numerous instruments, and in 1767 commenced work on his mechanical masterpiece, the orrery. By this time the fame of this self-educated countryman was such as to earn him an honorary degree of Master of Arts from the College of Philadelphia and a corresponding membership in the American Society.

In January, 1768, Rittenhouse joined the American Philosophical Society, to which in March Provost Smith communicated a description of the new orrery drawn up by Thomas Barton. This exquisite mechanism was designed to show not only the motions of the planets and their satellites, but also the eclipses of the sun and the moon. Similar, though cruder, planetaria had previously been exhibited at Philadelphia, but this one, Rittenhouse asserted, was intended not for the amusement of the ignorant, but rather to "astonish the skilful and curious examiner. . . . I would have my Orrery really useful, by making it capable of informing us, truly, of the astronomical phenomena for any particular point of time; which I do not find that any Orrery yet made can do." The Society approved the work, publishing a description in full because it did "Honour . . . to this Province." After the union the American Philosophical Society secured from the Assembly in 1771 a grant of £300 to its creator in recognition of his invention.

Rittenhouse then sold the orrery to the College of New Jersey, much to the chagrin of William Smith, who had wanted it for his own institution. "This province is willing to honour him as her *own*," he told Barton bitterly, "and, believe me, many of his friends . . . regretted that he should think so little of his noble invention as to consent to let it go to a village" such as Princeton, when in a city college like our own "so many strangers would have had an opportunity of seeing it." Rittenhouse finally mollified the irate Scot by consenting to construct another orrery for the College of Philadelphia, and by his promise not to deliver his first to Princeton until the second had been completed.

Only six days after the union of the two scientific bodies, the American Philosophical Society appointed a committee, headed by the Reverend John Ewing, to observe "the Transit of Venus across the Sun," which "rare phenomenon" was to occur on the third of June, 1769. Because of its importance to astronomy and navigation

"One of the luminaries of the eighteenth century."
Scientist and "Franklinian Democrat," David Rittenhouse, by Charles
Willson Peale.
(Courtesy University of Pennsylvania)

The Genesis of "Internal Improvements."

Survey drawing of roads and canals designed to divert western trade from Baltimore to Philadelphia. From the notebook of Thomas Gilpin. (*Courtesy Historical Society of Pennsylvania*) the event was attracting "the attention of every civilized nation in the world."

The Society designated three places as observation sites: the city, the residence of Rittenhouse at Norriton, and the lighthouse at Cape Henlopen. Dr. Ewing, an accomplished mathematician and astronomer and author of a recent improvement upon Godfrey's quadrant, assisted by the able Dr. Hugh Williamson, Colonel Joseph Shippen, Charles Thomson and two others, set up and managed in the State House yard the reflecting telescope and other equipment purchased in London by the Pennsylvania Assembly. The well-known mathematical instrument-maker Owen Biddle erected a borrowed apparatus at Cape Henlopen. At Norriton, where as early as the previous November he had begun assembling his equipment, David Rittenhouse was joined by Provost Smith, John Lukens, surveyor general for the province, and John Sellers of the Assembly. For the occasion Rittenhouse had specially constructed an equal altitude instrument, a transit telescope, and an accurate chronometer.

The Philosophical Society also encouraged the taking of similar observations at other points throughout the colonies. Prior to this time only two observations of the transit had ever been made, and these not very accurately, although, as John Ewing pointed out, the phenomenon was of great importance in determining the parallax of the sun, a fundamental desideratum in astronomy. The successful calculations of these thirteen Philadelphia scientists, together with those of John Winthrop at Cambridge, Massachusetts, Benjamin West (only important colonial scientist never elected to membership in the American Philosophical Society) at Providence, Rhode Island, and of William Alexander in New Jersey, furnished not only valuable scientific data hitherto unavailable, but also the first demonstration of American co-operative scholarship—co-operation by scientific men, generously supported by government and public.

So ably had Rittenhouse performed his task at his Norriton observatory that such learned astronomers as Smith, Williamson and Ewing readily acknowledged him a master. Urged by Smith and

Barton, he now, like many another rural genius, moved in to the city, where Smith hoped the Assembly might reward him with employment in the Loan Office and so provide the financial security to enable him to pursue his scientific work. But though Speaker Galloway favored the proposal, and William Allen declared on the floor "Our name is Legion for this vote," the Governor vetoed the bill which would have brought the appointment to pass.

Meanwhile, Rittenhouse continued his researches in Philadelphia. His observations of Lexell's comet in 1770 enabled him to detect the error of John Winthrop, F.R.S., "in supposing that it yet crosses the meridian every day" between noon and one o'clock. The next year he became a secretary of the Philosophical Society, and later its curator, as well as member of a committee for the improvement of navigation on the Schuylkill. At the College on February 24, 1775, he delivered the anniversary oration of the American Philosophical Society before a "crouded and most respectable audience." He chose astronomy for his topic, which he treated, reported the *Evening Post,* "in that accurate, sublime and masterly manner" expected of him, and which, canny Deist that he was, he "enlivened with beautiful digressions, and benevolent and moral reflexions drawn from the subject."

The success and reputation of Rittenhouse encouraged his fellow members of the Philosophical Society to petition the Assembly on March 6, under signature of Thomas Bond, to grant a lot and promote a popular subscription for the erection of a "Public Observatory," of which their distinguished colleague should be the custodian. Such an observatory should be always open to sea captains, young men desiring to learn practical astronomy, and the scientifically curious. Instruction in the calculation of longitude would be dispensed by the "Public Observer," who was also to be appointed surveyor of roads and water ways. Though we are a young colony, the petition observed, we should take pride in our reputation, which "has extended even to the remotest parts of Europe, on account of our many . . . rapid improvements in all the useful arts. . . . To give a last perfection to geography and navigation," the document continued, we have the man for this purpose, a man of genius and ability, who deserves to be rescued from "the drudgery of *manual labour.*" But the shot at Lexington had already been fired, and David Rittenhouse, "Franklinian democrat," became, instead of provincial astronomer, a member of the rebel Council of Safety.

The emphasis on the practical application of science for the improvement of life in the colonies became more pronounced as opposition to the mother country mounted and Americans began to feel a need to seek means of economic independence. The career of Thomas Gilpin combines an instance of scientific versatility tending in an increasingly practical direction with a good example of the social and economic contributions of the American Philosophical Society.

Son of a wealthy Quaker family of the Lower Counties, Gilpin inherited lands on the Susquehanna River and an estate and a flour mill on Brandywine Creek. Largely self-educated, he became a skilled mathematician and navigator, and a student of natural history and the new agriculture. A journey to England in 1753, where he observed the operation of steam pumps at the Whitehaven collieries, further stimulated his interest in applied science.

On his return from England Gilpin purchased a tract of over a thousand acres at the head of the Chester River in Maryland. Here he founded the town of Gilpinton (now Millington), which rapidly became a milling center for one of the leading wheat-growing areas of the colonies, and here he commenced his philosophical studies. Concerned over the ravages of the wheat fly in Kent County, he traced the life history of the pest in a skillful paper, and recommended as the best remedy the threshing of the grain in the fall and the immediate burning of the straw in which the eggs lay dormant through the winter. These views he communicated first to the Maryland Assembly and later to the American Society.

During this period also he wrote a fine life history of the American locust, which had appeared in 1766 for the first time since 1749, wherein he carefully differentiated the seventeen-year variety from the annual. Other subjects which Gilpin treated in scientific essays were the marine life of the Chesapeake Bay, the extensive strata of fossil shells on the Eastern Shore, and, remembering his visit to English mines, the coal deposits to be found at considerable depths in the soil of Pennsylvania.

Business and milling interests drew Gilpin to Philadelphia in 1764, where he married Lydia, daughter of Joshua Fisher the cartographer. Entering enthusiastically into the American Society, he became one of the most active of the city's merchant-philosophers. Another trip to England in 1768 preceded a new burst of scientific activity. He presented to the American Philosophical Society an account and a model of a "Horizontal Wind-mill" capable of driving three pumps for the raising of water with only one crank. Another model of this same invention had been exhibited by his friend Franklin at the Society of Arts in London, as a device which "may be of great use in draining mines, quarries, etc."

To the latter body Gilpin sent an essay on the much debated subject of the migration of North Sea herring, which he thought to be of the same species as those found along the coast of North America. He worked out the ingenious theory that the mysterious appearance and disappearance of the fish in the waters of northern Europe in the spring and autumn might be explained by their migration to America, where he knew they appeared during the fall and winter. Much as Franklin had speculated on the course of the Gulf Stream while crossing the Atlantic, Gilpin charted the migratory course of European herring in a regular circuit, beginning along the American coast and ending in Europe.

In the seventies Gilpin backed Moses Bartram in his society to encourage the growth of silkworms in Pennsylvania, and informed the Society of Arts that many "minor manufactures would succeed if parliament would but lay on a few more duties, or as I may say bounties, for such is the effect of their duties." At this time he was instrumental in founding a grammar school, preparatory for the College of Philadelphia, at Wilmington, Delaware. By 1774 he had turned engineer, designing a chain suspension bridge to span the

Schuylkill at Philadelphia, the necessary soundings for which he made himself. This project had always appealed to Philadelphians, but Gilpin's estimated costs of £8,000 currency frightened them away from it. Gilpin died at Winchester, Virginia, in 1777, whither he had been sent with other Quakers suspected of being "inimical" to the Revolutionary cause, and Philadelphia lost thereby one of its most gifted and public-spirited citizens.

Thomas Gilpin's greatest contribution to useful knowledge lay not in the solo performances enumerated above, but in the part played by him in arousing the interest of Philadelphia merchants and members of the Philosophical Society in the problems of inland transportation. Sporadic efforts to provide better means of communication between Philadelphia and its hinterland had engaged the attention of back-country residents since about 1750. Yet repeated petitions for roads and bridges and for the improvement of navigation in the Delaware and Schuylkill rivers had been largely ignored by the Quaker-dominated Assembly. Not until 1768 did city merchants awaken to the enormous inroads into their Western trade being effected by the rising port of Baltimore, which, via the highway of the Susquehanna River, was successfully attracting the produce of Pennsylvania. No one of them was in better position to appreciate the communications problem than Thomas Gilpin, who owned lands on the Susquehanna, estates and mills on the Eastern Shore and on the Brandywine, and a dry-goods business in Philadelphia.

Early in 1768 Gilpin began addressing communications to both the *Chronicle* and the *Gazette* on the necessity for constructive action. His journey to England in this year may have been primarily to investigate the Duke of Bridgewater's canal, which, completed in 1761, inaugurated the great era of artificial inland waterways. Still making use of the newspapers on his return, he shrewdly assembled mercantile support for a project he laid before the American Philosophical Society early in 1769, soliciting its support in the making of surveys to determine the most suitable route for a canal to connect the headwaters of the streams flowing into the Delaware River and Chesapeake Bay. The Society appointed a committee of investigation, consisting of John Lukens, John Sellers, Matthew Clarkson, Joseph Ellicott, Gilpin and four others, and obtained financial backing from a group of merchants inspired to action by the Gilpin propaganda.

During 1769 and 1770 Gilpin and his associates made careful surveys of five possible routes by which the Delaware and the Chesapeake might be connected, working out for each route two sets of plans, one for a barge canal, the other for a ship canal with locks. Upon a series of water-color maps Gilpin plotted out each route, the number and type of locks for each, and the estimated costs of construction, which ranged from £8,050 to £70,000. These plans reveal his considerable ability as an engineer, his skill as a draughtsman and his grasp of the basic problems of inland transportation. He further mapped out proposed courses for two highways between the Susquehanna and the Delaware, and a possible canal route to connect the two streams. All his drawings show a mastery of current transportation lore, especially his plans for the construction of locks and of auxiliary, or feeder, canals to supply them with water.

The Philosophical Society decided in favor of the route connecting Long Creek with the Delaware, where Gilpin estimated a barge canal could be constructed for the relatively low cost of £14,426, and, encouraged by reports from Dr. Hugh Williamson and David Rittenhouse concerning the navigability of the Susquehanna, it strongly urged the building of Gilpin's suggested road from Peach Bottom to Christiana Creek. In the Society's *Transactions*, published in 1771, these surveys occupied a prominent place.

All Philadelphia was now excited at the prospects of internal improvements, and many merchants, sensing the possibilities of the expanding West, agreed with "Philadelphus" that it is "indisputably certain, that what port soever on this continent can acquire the greatest share of its inland commerce, must proportionately advance in riches and importance." Now men dreamed of opening up roads, and possibly canals, to connect Philadelphia with the Potomac and the Ohio. Work was actually begun by the Assembly on the removal of obstacles to navigation from the Delaware and the Schuyl-kill, while Gilpin, promoter as well as engineer, evolved a scheme to finance his canal by private capital through the issue of shares at £10 each.

"We expect shortly to be canal-mad," Samuel Rhoads wrote to Franklin in 1771. "We can devise no other means of saving our-selves [from the competition of Baltimore] but by a canal from the Susquehanna to the Schuylkill." But though he, along with Gilpin and Rittenhouse, pored over the reports of Smeaton, Brindley, and the Scottish canal experts, forwarded by Franklin, the outbreak of war once again put an untimely end to a project about to be under-taken.

To spread popular interest in science, and to further its work of co-ordinating scientific and other useful activities throughout the col-onies, the officers of the American Philosophical Society made skill-ful use of the press. As we have seen before, the newspapers, because they reached a wide public, afforded an extremely effective means of publicity. In the *Chronicle, Gazette* and *Journal* many scientific communications first appeared that were later to be published in pamphlet form.

A volume of proceedings, similar to the *Philosophical Transac-tions* of the Royal Society, was planned by the two societies at the time of their merger, but some time was required for the maturing of so elaborate a project. In the meantime one member, Lewis Nicola, served the Society well by printing its most important papers as appendices to his *American Magazine, or General Repository,* which was issued monthly for nine months in 1769. This magazine reflected "the taste of the age" by devoting greater space to science and natural philosophy than had any previous colonial publication. Its first number, for example, contained an "Essay on the Impor-tance of Natural History," stressing its practical as well as its enter-tainment value, and pointing out the fact that great discoveries have sometimes been stumbled upon, even by the illiterate.

From Bradford's press in 1771 issued the first volume of the

Transactions of the American Philosophical Society, which, sixty-six years before Emerson's plea for intellectual independence, offered the world concrete demonstration of American scientific accomplishment. It contained, in addition to communications from European scientists, a well-chosen selection of the works of American scholars in mathematics, astronomy, medicine, agriculture and mechanics. Beautifully printed by Bradford and illustrated with excellent engravings by Henry Dawkins, the volume was widely distributed among colonial booksellers and enjoyed a ready sale. Copies were sent to sixteen learned bodies and seven universities in Europe.

The volume evoked the immediate admiration of the scientific world. The *Gentleman's Magazine* carried a long account of the union of the two societies and their distinguished European membership, and a favorable review of the *Transactions.* Dr. Wrangel wrote from Stockholm of his pride at being a corresponding member of the Society; "Your accurate Observations of the Transit of Venus have given infinite satisfaction to our astronomers; as will the rest of your Transactions to the Literary World." "They are much sought after by the Literati in London," reported an English savant, "many of whom have declared that they will do you great Honour."

Perhaps the most significant tribute came from Jean Bernoulli of the Royal Observatory at Berlin, who recorded in Volume II of his *Recueil pour les astronomes* (1772) the many well-merited compliments paid the *Transactions,* especially in regard to the writings of Smith and Rittenhouse on the transit of Venus. In particular he praised the habits of American scientists in printing "not only the conclusions from their observations, but also the data on which they are based, so that others may examine the evidence and judge for themselves; a practice well worthy of imitation by those European astronomers who are so sparing of detail and who speak only in general terms of their instruments and their observations."

There was ample reason for the *Journal's* boast to its readers that such enthusiastic notices from "so many respectable Individuals, as well as learned Bodies in different Parts of the World . . . shew that this Society is growing in *Reputation*," and for John Adams's envious comment to Abigail that as soon as the war should be over Boston must have a philosophical society. Certainly, this first volume of *Transactions* was evidence of American maturity, if not an actual declaration of intellectual independence.

One source of continuing public interest in the activities of the American Philosophical Society lay in its intimate connection with the growing body of skilled mechanics of Philadelphia. No one more loyally supported Charles Thomson in his efforts to transform the young Junto into the American Society than Owen Biddle, clock- and watchmaker and ardent devotee of science. Mathematics and astronomy were his specialties, and for his children he constructed a small orrery. Though he had received from Mr. Maskelyne of the Royal Society a letter of praise for his observations of the transit of Venus, he took perhaps even more pride in his new invention, a machine for cutting files, a description and plate of which appeared in the *Transactions* in 1771.

Biddle was only one, the best known perhaps, of many skilled craftsmen whose instruments made possible the pursuit of scientific inquiry in the city. Benjamin Condy, mathematical instrument-maker, constructed John Ewing's new quadrant in 1767, and four years later Whitehead Humphreys manufactured for sale at his steel furnace a screw-cutting machine of his own invention. At Richard Wistar's "glass works" blowers did a thriving business in "electerising globes and tubes" for Kinnersley and his fellow experimenters.

By 1771 the number of skilled mechanics and other interested persons in the city was sufficient to warrant the opening of an evening school by the Irish "engineer and architect" Christopher Colles, who taught mechanics, "hydraulics, Hydrostatics, pneumatics, optics, perspective architecture, and fortification," and the application of these sciences to the construction of waterworks, docks, bridges, "locks, sluices and aqueducts for inland navigation," and engines for "abridging the labour of men." His own newly built "Steam Engine for raising water" was given a trial by Rittenhouse and Biddle of the American Philosophical Society in 1773, and though it broke down after a few strokes, "some of the material not being sufficiently large and strong, owing to his attempting the execution at a very low expense," they perceived it could be easily improved and therefore recommended its endorsement by the Society. This backing undoubtedly assisted Colles to secure the commission to construct a steam engine, reservoir and "Water Buildings . . . ornamented in the Grecian and Roman Manner," to supply the city of New York with water in 1775.

The peer of American instrument-makers was David Rittenhouse, whose clocks were deservedly famous, and whose mathematical instruments, according to William Smith, "have been esteemed by good judges to be superior in accuracy and workmanship to any of the same kind that have been imported from Europe." In 1770, as part of the program for encouraging home manufactures, the Provost conceived a plan for putting Rittenhouse in charge of a proposed establishment for "manufacturing optical and mathematical instruments," the financial backing to be provided by his neighbors, "the Wissahickon millers." This project would save the colonies "thousands of pounds" sent annually to England for instruments "often ill-finished," would increase the importance of Philadelphia as a scientific center, and would make of Rittenhouse the van Muschenbroek or Leupold of America. Political support was enlisted in the person of Joseph Galloway, but Proprietary pique at the Assembly ultimately frustrated the design.

Rittenhouse nevertheless pursued his trade of instrument-making with great success, receiving orders from such distant sources as the Library Company of Charleston, South Carolina. His orrery was praised abroad as excelling "any Thing of the Kind that has yet appear'd in Europe." Commenting on the *Transactions* of the Philosophical Society, the eminent British astronomer Ludlam wrote to Franklin that "there is not another Society in the World that can boast of a Member, such as Mr. Rittenhouse, *Theorist* enough to encounter the Problem of determining (from a few Observations) the *Orbit of a Comet;* and also *Mechanic* enough to make, with his own Hands, an *Equal-Altitude Instrument,* a *Transit-Telescope,* and a *Time-piece."*

Two more agencies, which both reflected and encouraged the rise of popular taste for the "curious" and the scientific, flourished in the years after 1769: the "repository of learned curiosities," predecessor of the modern museum, and the public lecture. Early in the period the Library Company had begun to parallel its collections of books with a cabinet containing scientific apparatus and natural curiosities, to which the Eskimo collection, presented in 1754 by the North-West Company, constituted a considerable addition. By 1775 its most significant scientific accumulations were perhaps the "cabinet of Fossils," American and foreign, which so impressed Tom Paine that he wrote an article thereon for the *Pennsylvania Magazine* of February, 1775, stressing both the scientific value of the study of fossils and its practical application to the development of mining; and a fine collection of medals, presented to the Library by a Mr. Gray of Colchester, England, value of which as sources for the study of Roman history was pointed out by the *Pennsylvania Mercury.*

John Morgan, Owen Biddle, and other curators of the American Philosophical Society built up a museum which by 1770 contained a growing collection of natural curiosities, some fossils, the mastodon bones found by George Croghan in the Ohio country, and models of various useful inventions presented to the Society. Despite the entrance fee of one dollar, the Fothergill collection of anatomical preparations and drawings at the hospital proved extremely popular. Most of the members of the First Continental Congress were entertained with Dr. Shippen's explanation of this collection, and were then taken, to be impressed as was John Adams, with a view of the "great collection" at the "Museum" of the Society of Fort St. David's. Here were assembled Hesselius' paintings of the Delaware chieftains and some marine and Indian curiosities, but, in the opinion of Du Simitière, arranged "without choice and in very bad order." Archibald McCall, merchant, who since 1763 had instructed his supercargoes to purchase strange animals for him in foreign ports, maintained a "Zoo" in the gardens of his house. Altogether, the Philadelphia public was being prepared for the more elaborate presentations of Charles Willson Peale's American Museum.

With the exception of the exhibits of the Library Company and the Philosophical Society, these miscellaneous collections were assembled without plan, in much the same indiscriminate fashion as those of wealthy European dilettanti. The collecting fever spread also to individuals, and in 1772 a local taxidermist easily found a sale for his "Collection of Preserved North American Birds." It was characteristic of this New World society, however, that a most careful and systematically projected scheme for an "American Musaeum" was evolved by the humble miniature painter, antiquary and naturalist Pierre Du Simitière, who had devoted his entire life to the assembling of materials and specimens for a natural and civil history of America. He not only accumulated specimens of plants, animals and fishes, shells, marine life, fossils and petrifactions, but brought together enormous numbers of books, notes and papers. In a mahogany cabinet he displayed ancient and modern gold, silver and copper coins, together with some "very curious Bronzes," while his anthropological interests accounted for his possession of Indian and African weapons, utensils and "antiquities."

Without benefit of great wealth, the persistent curiosity of this Swiss craftsman brought together much the same sort of collection as that which Sir Hans Sloane made the foundation of the British Museum. It was most unfortunate that at the time of his death in 1784 the General Assembly of Pennsylvania considered it "not expedient or consistent with the state of the treasury" for the state to purchase and preserve his collections, refusal of which had been granted it by his will.

Increasing attendance at lecture courses furnished even greater evidence of public interest in the wonders of nature. At the College in 1767 Provost Smith threw open his lectures on natural philosophy, primarily for medical students, to any "gentlemen" who had formerly attended the institution. This sort of university extension proved too highbrow for many of the alumni, who found their mathematics unequal to the occasion and therefore solicited private instruction. To meet their need for adult education, the Reverend John Ewing and Dr. Hugh Williamson applied to the trustees for use of the College rooms and apparatus, but being denied it, commenced a course on natural and experimental philosophy at the Masonic Hall in Lodge Alley. So popular did this semiweekly course become that its professors had to announce that "ONLY Gentlemen who are Strangers in the City can have Tickets by the Night." In 1770 Dr. John Shippen, just returned from graduate study at Rheims, delivered a series of illustrated lectures at his brother's anatomical rooms on the general theory, description, definition and history of fossils, for those "who are daily making Collections."

Philadelphians of the eighteenth century became as inveterate lecture-goers as Bostonians of a later day. In 1772-73 Christopher Colles offered three different courses on geography, natural philosophy and pneumatics at the Philosophical Society rooms in the State House. In response to public demand Benjamin Rush delivered two series on chemistry in 1774-75, with the avowed object of demonstrating to the community the application of chemical principles to agriculture and manufacturing. Simultaneously, Arthur James O'Neile and Ebenezer Kinnersley were lecturing on electricity to large audiences, Christopher Colles was offering a course on hydraulics, and a series on the "visceral anatomy and vital oeconomy of the Human Body" was being given by Dr. Abraham Chovet at the "Anatomical Museum" in Vidal's Alley.

Dr. Chovet had come to practice in the city in 1770, soon acquiring reputation as its best anatomist, and his lectures are an interesting instance of the popularization of scientific and medical information. He demonstrated his points "on his elegant Anatomical Wax-Work Figures," to obviate the "disgust" which many otherwise interested persons might feel at "the aspect of a recent dead body." His first lecture was a Latin oration on the dignity of physic, delivered before the medical faculty and trustees of the College, the clergy, and the "most respectable inhabitants" of Phiadelphia; his later discourses, in English, were reported to be models of "fine Taste, judgment, and accuracy," revealing "extensive reading, and perfect knowledge of the subject."

To capitalize upon this popular craze, Provost Smith in 1772 arranged a great series of twenty-one public lectures at the College, to consist of two discourses on astronomy by Rittenhouse, two on electricity by Kinnersley, three on chemistry by Dr. Rush, and concluding with fourteen by himself upon natural philosophy. "Friends of Literature" were entreated to encourage this series at twenty-five shillings for the course, not only because the proceeds were to be used to purchase the Rittenhouse orrery, but also because it would be "the most compleat of any that has been exhibited in America." Smith was later able to report in triumph to Thomas Barton that the lectures were crowded and that their financial purpose had been achieved.

Interest in natural philosophy had preceded that in other fields of culture at Philadelphia, and throughout the eighteenth century kept pace with other phases of intellectual endeavor. Beginning with the amateur dilettantism of the contemporaries of James Logan, it came by the end of the period to command the professional respect of its votaries and the avid curiosity of hundreds of eager and interested laymen. While actual accomplishments in the field were considerable, perhaps the most significant achievement of these years was the very generality of popular interest in the mysteries and potentialities of nature.

That Philadelphia thought in this respect was squarely in the vortex of contemporary Western culture is demonstrated by the cordial and ready acceptance of Philadelphia scientists by the intellectual leaders of Europe, who not only showered them with praise, read their works and reprinted their books, but hastened to induct them into their scientific academies, granted them the freedom of their cities, and themselves eagerly accepted membership in the great learned body of the colonies. Old World illuminati recognized, or at least sensed, the maturing of American culture before many colonials themselves became aware of it, and in this recognition the important contributions of Philadelphia in the realm of science proved no small factor.

Scientists of the Enlightenment dwelt in an intellectual democracy which recognized no castes and no frontiers. Symbolic of its egalitarian spirit were the exchange of letters between John Bartram, the farmer-botanist of Kingsessing, and Queen Ulrica of Sweden, and the respect which European scholars accorded the self-educated David Rittenhouse. The leading citizen of this democracy was Benjamin Franklin, but he represented in his own person hundreds of his fellow countrymen who shared its franchise with lovers of learning and science in the Old World.

At home, also, science played its leveling role. It brought together the unlettered artisan and the gentleman scholar, the Scottish gardener and the physician trained in European universities. But further, it slowly knit into a common brotherhood the learned, the ingenious, and the scientifically inclined of every colony, until in 1769 the founding of the American Philosophical Society appropriately signalized the intercolonial intellectual unity which it did so much to advance.

Actually, science probably served its purpose as propaganda rather more effectively than it achieved its professed object, the bettering of human conditions. It was an irresistible force for democracy, though many a local squire or plutocrat failed to catch its full implications, for it demanded the combination not only of wealth and heads but also of hands and tools, less for the intellectual pleasures of pure speculation than for the application of learning to the problems of human advancement. Such labors, broadcast from press and lecture platform, inevitably convulsed old religious dogmas, and mightily buttressed the dynamic political theories that were emerging in these years.

Perhaps the best testimony to this accomplishment was that of an immigrant of 1775. Writing in the *Pennsylvania Magazine,* Tom Paine dwelt with enthusiastic delight on this "country whose reigning character is the love of science." He clearly perceived what was beginning to dawn in the understanding of Philadelphians themselves, that "America has now outgrown the state of infancy: Her strength and commerce make large advances to manhood; and science in all its branches, has not only blossomed but even ripened upon the soil."

Chapter X

REBELS AND GENTLEMEN

"IT SEEMS I am too much of an American," Benjamin Franklin observed to an English friend in 1774, when after triumph, insult and heartbreak he prepared to return to his native land. On the fifth day of May, 1775, after an absence of almost eleven years, he once again came ashore at Philadelphia, and was met by news of the outbreak of hostilities at Lexington and Concord. The next day the Province of Pennsylvania pressed him into service as a delegate to the Second Continental Congress. Benjamin Franklin, citizen of the world, thus became a full-fledged revolutionary in his seventieth year.

Franklin's deep faith in the future of America sprang from his profound knowledge of its people. In one of the most pregnant pieces of writing to come out of colonial Philadelphia, *Observations Concerning the Increase of Mankind, Peopling of Countries, etc.,* published in 1755, he had, while adumbrating the frontier interpretation of American development, demonstrated that without any accession from abroad the population of the American colonies doubled itself every twenty or twenty-five years. He therefore ventured the prediction that "in another century. . . the greatest number of Englishmen will be on this side of the water." At the time this fact had seemed to him only another indication of the strength and vitality of the English stock. Only slowly and reluctantly did he come to the conclusion that the future of the great American branch of that family lay no longer within the framework of the old British Empire. By 1775 the experiences of twenty years had made him ready to abandon the thought of accommodation with Britain, "this old rotten state," and to stake his hopes on an independent America, whose character and interests, no less than its wealth of natural and human resources, should enable it to pursue a separate destiny.

On his return Franklin might well have considered a revision of the *Observations* to include his new faith in the quality as well as the numbers of the American breed. As colonial agent he had seen his fellow townsmen hold their own in intercourse with the best minds of Edinburgh and London, and back at home he discovered in the city on the Delaware men as able as any he had encountered abroad. Here were Bond, Morgan, Peale, Rittenhouse, the Bartram family, Thomas Gilpin, Charles Thomson and the rest, all avid participants in the cultural life of the community. He could see the evidences of their energy and vitality, and acknowledge the collective force of the growing democratic society they comprised. Certainly it was no longer necessary to speak, as once he had, of Philadelphians "lisping" in the arts; they now filled their own needs to satisfaction and furnished examples to the mother country. Their educational institutions and their civic and charitable foundations were well abreast of the age if not actually models for it, and he knew from personal experience that in scientific achievement they need bow to no one in the Western world. In short, his fellow townsmen had proved themselves a mature people.

Franklin had lived in Philadelphia for only fifteen of the thirty-five years chronicled in these pages. Had not the renewed pressure of public affairs so wholly absorbed his aging energies, he might, in well-merited retirement, have reflected with considerable pleasure upon the social and cultural achievements of Philadelphians during that time. And as he was both an honest and a generous man, it is highly probable he would have been greatly struck by the large number of "projects" for civic and human betterment accomplished by his fellow townsmen without his aid and during the years of his absence.

In that period the city on the Delaware had become a great commercial center, the metropolis of the colonies. It is probably fair to say that nowhere else in the Western world did the rising middle class enjoy such prosperity or such opportunity as within its precincts. Founded upon what English observers denominated a "surprisingly extensive" sea-borne trade and an expanding hinterland traffic, and nourished at all social levels by abundant immigration, Philadelphia had developed swiftly from a quiet little provincial seaport into a bustling commercial community, comparable in extent, population, social complexion and volume of trade with all but a few of the greatest cities of Europe.

Rapid growth, general prosperity, and continuous immigration characterized these years at Philadelphia, and their natural consequence was to produce a considerable cultural ferment. The new importance of the individual and the richness of opportunity in the new land led members of all classes to seek some kind of schooling, and educational facilities for all levels were provided with varying degrees of success. For its time the educational standard at Philadelphia was high, and its crowning achievement was the establishment of a university capable of producing leaders for community and province. Despite prevailing confusion concerning the objectives of education, virtually all inhabitants save the most recently arrived immigrants had achieved literacy by the end of the period. "In this Country," Charles Thomson declared, "almost every Man is fond of reading, and seems to have a Thirst for Knowledge." This important fact brought about a rapid expansion of the press, as it sought to provide newspapers, pamphlets, magazines and books for the growing reading public of Philadelphia and the surrounding country. It also encouraged the unprecedented development of subscription and circulating libraries.

A natural concomitant of widespread literacy and knowledge and the general taste for reading was the impulse to self-expression. The greatest development of this sort was of course literary, and its results ran the gamut from unimaginative imitation of pseudoclassical examples imported from Augustan London through the vernacular vigor of local pamphleteering to the sober elucidation of scientific observations and discoveries that delighted the scholarly world. But the colonial urge to self-expression was not limited to letters, and the arts of the drama, music and painting not only took root in these years, but began the production of a native crop.

Mounting wealth concentrated in the hands of a few who were likewise possessed of political power resulted in the emergence of a privileged and leisured aristocracy. Often its members were generous patrons, devoting their wealth and leisure to the social and cultural welfare of the community. In particular did they encourage and support the development of such minor arts as architecture, wood-carving and silversmithing, while the patronage they accorded to the fine arts was a fundamental condition of their existence. Extensive foreign travel broadened these men, even while it simultaneously impelled many of them to reject much that was useful and beautiful in their own land in favor of things prized because they were English or European.

For the notable humanitarian advances of these years, the alleviation of human suffering and the care of the sick and the insane, the gentry generously opened their purses. But the importance of eighteenth-century humanitarianism in the life of this New World community is attested by the widespread support of charities from the hard-won treasure of the middle and even of the lower classes.

The prosperity of upper and middle classes enabled them to provide increasing numbers of recruits for the learned professions, especially medicine and the law, so that by the decade of the seventies the trained immigrant played a far less important role in this phase of Philadelphia life. The medical profession consisted almost wholly of the sons of gentlemen, since they alone possessed the time and the funds for European training. This situation was remedied in the middle sixties by the opening of a local medical college, which in quality both of faculty and of graduates came shortly to rival most European institutions, and by the development of hospital facilities that compared favorably with those of London and Paris. The physicians as a body stood in the vanguard of movements for humanitarian betterment and scientific advance. They were the most liberal of the gentry, and the least bound by Old World fetters.

Both in performance and in extent of popular interest the outstanding achievements of Philadelphia in this period were scientific. Its scientific activities gave Philadelphia its greatest repute in Europe, where its votaries were everywhere accepted as equals by the leading natural philosophers of the day. But interest in science also proved a strong force for Americanization, bringing together persons of all ranks in close and increasingly democratic association for the accomplishment of a common purpose.

It was through Philadelphia that the Enlightenment, our second major strain of European culture, largely entered America. Far more eclectic and cosmopolitain than the tightly knit Puritan strain brought to New England in the previous century, it proved in the long run to be of even greater influence and importance, for by it the mind of America was drawn from its provincial eddies into the main current of Western thought. As a result in the years after 1740 a surprisingly large number of Philadelphians, the men who have peopled the preceding pages, revealed themselves to be not only alert, curious, energetic and economically successful persons, but in addition as urbane and civilized, as widely cultured and as deeply scholarly as the citizens of such Old World centers of thought as Edinburgh, London and Paris. On the basis of its citizenry and their intellectual accomplishments no apology need be made for Philadelphia, nor for its sister communities on the Atlantic seaboard.

In one important respect, one fraught with momentous future implications, Franklin's city surpassed its European contemporaries. Much of what we call the Enlightenment was merely the intellectual and philosophical expression of the practical, secular, humane genius of the rising middle class. Hence the accomplishment of many of its objectives was the greater in what was probably the leading, certainly the most unfettered, middle-class community of the Western world, the city on the Delaware, where admission to the middle class was freest, its opportunities and privileges greatest, and the literate base of society most broad.

In Philadelphia dwelt a people with ability not only to select with some discrimination what Europe had to offer, but to transform and remodel what it borrowed to suit native needs and further native aspirations. There was here no accumulated rubbish of ideas and institutions which, gathering for centuries, had to be swept aside before progress and enlightenment could begin. Government, though oligarchical, was largely in the hands of those sympathetic with the spirit of the age, and no clerical opposition existed as in France and Scotland to absorb the energies of local illuminati. Instead the clergy of Philadelphia, such men as Smith, Alison, Peters, Barton and Ewing, served as leaders in the establishment of new instruments of knowledge and in inquiry into the new science of nature. At Philadelphia also free rein existed for the exercise of the middle-class genius for co-operation, association and organization. In social and cultural realms this genius proved sufficiently effective to triumph over the disruptive forces of political partisanship and factionalism, and reaching beyond the bounds of the province to meet kindred spirits in other colonies, it succeeded in partially mitigating the centrifugal effects of colonial particularism.

The charge of subservience to middle-class practicality has often been leveled at Philadelphians, and their foremost citizen has been dismissed as "the first bourgeois," exponent of a cautious, materialistic, honesty-is-the-best-policy philosophy which left small room for noble thought or daring aspiration. Actually, these men of the eighteenth century believed first and foremost in the social function of all knowledge; in them practicality and idealism were finely blended. They sought, in the later words of De Tocqueville, not "the arrogant and sterile researches of abstract truths," but "the immediate and useful results of the sciences." "What signifies Philosophy," demanded Franklin, "that does not apply to some Use?" Knowledge to such men had value chiefly as it could be employed to better the lot of mankind; that it was capable of so doing, they never doubted.

Out of such stuff Philadelphians in these years produced a better integrated culture than their city has since enjoyed. Here were no oversophisticated cynics, no wayward intellectuals, no devotees of art solely for art's sake. In the leisurely atmosphere of eighteenth-century Philadelphia the leaders who surrounded Franklin, while not as "specialized to versatility" as he, were nevertheless men with great minds, expansive views, capacious imaginations, and the willingness to think deeply on human problems, immediate or remote. Their experience with the practical application of their speculations made them a self-confident group, unafraid to deal with the mysteries of the universe, or for that matter with King George himself.

In its transference to Philadelphia the Enlightenment underwent two divergent interpretations, and the conflicting forces thus generated appear at work in every field of artistic and intellectual endeavor. First of these was the tendency of the great middle class, aided by some of the gentry, to re-form European culture in an American mold. Its proponents held that the society evolving in America out of new combinations of people, conditions and ideals required for its expression other intellectual standards and institutions than those which adequately answered Old World needs and purposes. Their emphasis was on the native rather than the European; their attitudes were American rather than colonial.

For the most part this leaven worked beneath the surface, until in the late sixties the blunders of Imperial authorities thrust it into the open and men began consciously to speak of themselves as Americans. In general, it was a force more felt than talked about. Change proceeded at so rapid a pace in the colonial metropolis that the minds of most men inevitably harbored a confusion of ideals. Franklin himself seems hardly to have grasped the real nature of the problem, the actuality of the chasm separating two cultures and two ways of life, until the early seventies.

Opposed to this slow drift toward revolution were the powerful forces of convention and tradition. Their strength lay mainly in the gentry, whose wealth, conservatism, and considerable stake in the society of the British Empire bred in them a great reluctance to experiment and a timid devotion to the status quo. Conscious of the social disadvantages inherent in their status as colonials, they sought to make American life as much as possible a copy of what their class enjoyed in England. Frequent visits to the mother country led them to worship all things English and pronounce them good, and obsessed with "the evil itch of overvaluing foreign parts," they hoped to impose upon the magnificent distances and complex social and racial patterns of colonial America the tight little stylized culture of Georgian England. With regard to manners, morals, society and its embellishments, many local aristocrats echoed the plaint of Edward Shippen, "How much we are excelled by those in Europe!"

Actually, these Anglophile gentlemen were more American than they knew. Recently risen from the middle class, they could not escape responsibilities to their society that its very generosity to them imposed, and more than they realized the comparative fluidity of society and freedom of opportunity in the New World city affected their attitudes. Though members of a privileged oligarchy, none of them could have said, with Catherine of Russia, *"Je suis aristocrate; c'est mon métier."* The American virus had infected even those who remained loyal to the Crown. In 1777 Lord Howe's secretary found the conversation of Andrew Allen, Tory son of the Chief Justice and last attorney general under the Proprietary, though intelligent, "rather seasoned with Notions highly in favour of America."

While historians have customarily regarded these upholders of an imitative culture as the most significant intellectual force in colonial America, such appears not to have been the case. Especially after 1760 Philadelphians—and Americans as a whole—were outgrowing their colonial point of view and, gentlemen as well as rebels, were becoming to varying degrees Americanized. But the two opposing forces, at first with unconscious dichotomy and later with growing awareness of the struggle between them, conditioned Philadelphia's acceptance and absorption of the culture of the Enlightenment.

The process was accomplished with amazing speed. The importation of the Enlightenment from Europe and its acclimatization in Pennsylvania, which made Philadelphia one of the outstanding urban communities of the century and a center of civilization and culture for the continent, took place within a period of thirty-five years, from 1740 to 1775. The pace was so rapid that it escaped the understanding of intelligent foreign observers and frequently bewildered those at home. In the early days the immigration of able men was an important factor, but by the decade of the sixties it was abundantly evident that in such personalities as the Bartrams, Benezet, Cadwalader, Claypoole, Hopkinson, Morgan, Rittenhouse, Rush and the Shippens Philadelphia could breed its own geniuses. This is the acid test of any people, and a tribute to the society that produced Benjamin Franklin. Another striking fact is the youth of these men; they were a people who, much sooner than Edmund Burke anticipated, had hardened into the bone of manhood.

Just as Philadelphia became the leading commercial entrepôt of the colonies, pushing out lines of trade in all directions, so also did it serve as the principal center whence the ideas of the Enlightenment were broadcast to rural and frontier areas, especially in the Middle and Southern Colonies. Its geographical location gave it a commanding position from which to exert a sort of cultural imperialism. As the main port of entry for Scotch-Irish and Palatine immigrants, and as an urban community in constant communication with the rest of colonial America by land on three sides and by water on the fourth, Philadelphia was probably known to more Americans, by influence or experience, than any other city. Its culture ran out over the roads via stage wagons and post riders, with the great intercolonial migrations, and especially through the output of the press. As the capital city of both Quakers and Presbyterians, two religious bodies noted for their intercolonial solidarity, and as an important stronghold of Anglicanism, the city was a Mecca for adherents in distant communities and rural areas. From its College, Medical School, and private institutions of learning it sent forth to the South and the West cultural influences of increasing importance. In like fashion the American Philosophical Society brought widely scattered intellectuals into fruitful contact with one another through its membership, and unified colonial scientific activity.

While dispersing the ideas of the Enlightenment, Philadelphia also served as a magnet to attract from rural districts men of talent and capacity to whom the advantages and interchange of ideas in an urban center presented a wide appeal. Joseph Galloway, Charles Willson Peale, David Rittenhouse and Thomas Gilpin are but a few who abandoned country living for the opportunities of a city career. At the same time rural and frontier areas constantly looked to the city for leadership. Philadelphia's march to American pre-eminence occasionally inspired the jealousy of other urban centers, though at the same time they reluctantly admitted its superiority. "What fruit is the good seed sown likely to produce in the minds of our great," wrote Nathaniel Ames of New England in his *Almanac* for 1771, "who can supinely behold the Philadelphians not only outstrip us in the liberal arts but also in the mechanical arts?"

The citizens of Philadelphia enjoyed fame and influence in Europe as well as at home. No colonial community has ever been so well or so widely publicized. From the days of William Penn downtrodden peasants of the Palatinate and rack-rented Scotch-Irishmen had been flooded with come-to-Pennsylvania "literature." When the city began to produce artists and men of science, it was the European intellectuals who first became aware of its rapid cultural development. They welcomed such men as John Bartram, Benjamin West, John Morgan and Henry Bembridge into the international fellowship of arts and sciences. Upon traveling Philadelphians they conferred the freedom of their cities, membership in their learned bodies, and honorary academic degrees. In Benjamin West rulers of taste in the mother country thought they perceived a British painter who for the first time rose above the lushness of Correggio and the nobility of Raphael; in John Morgan the English medical profession found a scientist it would have been happy to claim for its own. Conversely, European illuminati eagerly sought correspondence with American scholars and gladly accepted membership in the American Philosophical Society.

After 1760 the spectacular rise of Penn's city attracted more and more European attention. Even a cursory survey of the *Gentleman's, London,* and *Scot's* magazines reveals a mounting interest in the thought and life of Philadelphia and an increasing audience for its writings. Moreover, those Philadelphians who crossed the ocean exhibited a mature capacity and a confident poise that elicited respect and admiration. Dr. Morgan held his own in conversation with Voltaire, John Ewing talked back to Dr. Johnson, and West wore his hat before the King, while back at home John Bartram took the illuminati of several countries in his stride from eminent scientists to crowned royalty. Franklin's neighbors performed on the stages of London, Edinburgh and Paris with almost as much distinction as did he.

Gradually the intellectuals of Europe sensed that the evident ability of the city's representatives, their absence of provinciality and their quiet self-assurance presaged the emergence of a new kind of society. They began to realize that Philadelphia and its sister cities were in the process of demonstrating what had hitherto been categorically denied, that culture could thrive and flower in a democratic society where the voluntary and ample support of the few was buttressed by the broadening interest of the many. So Turgot wrote to Dr. Price in 1778 that the Americans were "the *hope* of the world. They may become a *model* to it. They *may* prove by fact that men can be free and yet tranquil." Philadelphia, the first urban community of the Western world to develop a mature and broadly based culture, furnished one step in Turgot's desired proof.

The consequence of all this cultural ferment was the maturing of the Philadelphia mind. Membership in the old British Empire had proved of incalculable benefit in hastening this process. The mother country contributed not only military defense and economic support but also people and ideas. Until about 1760 Philadelphians were in the position of favored sons growing up in a prosperous and cultivated home with all the advantages parental care and protection could provide. Between 1760 and 1775, however, Philadelphia came of age and was now spiritually prepared to go its way alone. Silently and for the most part unconsciously, it had undergone an intellectual revolution; it had shaken off its early allegiance to Old World standards and conventions and had chosen for itself the democratic direction.

While many of the British intelligentsia recognized that the indigenous culture of Philadelphia constituted a powerful solvent for independence, the King's Ministers remained wofully blind and ignorant of the vast changes developing overseas. The blundering policy of Imperial authorities coupled with the internal mistakes of Pennsylvania's ruling classes from 1763 to 1775 finally exasperated the city's great middle class, forcing from the backgrounds of their consciousness to the forefront of their minds the conviction that aristocratic control must be abolished, socially and culturally as well as politically.

Culturally and intellectually Philadelphia had by 1776 achieved a democratic society. In the Pennsylvania constitution of that year, therefore, the "Franklinian Democrats"—Judge Bryan, Schoolmaster Cannon, Dr. Thomas Young and Printer Franklin—deliberately sought to embody in fundamental law safeguards for the people's political and social liberties, to ensure that "the danger of establishing an inconvenient aristocracy will be effectually prevented." This most democratic instrument of the Revolutionary era contained provisions for rural education by well-paid masters, for the regulation of entails, and for the preventing of long-time imprisonment for debt. It also provided for exercise of the franchise by every freeman paying taxes, and that every son of a freeholder when he reached his twenty-first birthday might likewise vote.

Such men as David Rittenhouse, holding full and free franchise in the great republic of letters, saw no reason why they should be denied a share in determining the public affairs of Philadelphia and

Pennsylvania, nor why possession of fifty acres or a £50 freehold made any man legally or politically more competent than they. They therefore broadened political control to parallel the cultural achievement of their own middle class, and sought to rebuild political institutions to conform with the economic and cultural conditions their own brains and energy had brought about.

The forces of democracy met with a stubborn and increasingly effective resistance from property and conservatism, and the gentry engaged in deliberate sabotage of government under the new instrument. Yet, despite the mild counter-revolution they effected in the Federal Constitution and the reactionary state constitution of 1790 which perceptibly slowed the democratic trend, the broadened franchise remained to form the basis for a revival under the aegis first of Jeffersonian and later of Jacksonian democrats. The concept of a native cultural tradition persisted and, despite vicissitudes and periods of outright denial, passed on into the main stream of American life.

The purpose of this book has been to examine the transfer of the Enlightenment to Philadelphia and its fusion there with native elements to provide the beginnings of an American culture. There was a brief struggle between rebels and gentlemen as to who should have the dispensing of the new culture, but in the end the native strain prevailed. This process, effected in the short span of thirty-five years by hundreds of eager, able, intelligent Philadelphians, produced upon the banks of the Delaware a city owning the first broadly democratic society of modern times. As Franklin was its finest product, so his city was in many respects the best fruit of the culture of the Enlightenment.

But Philadelphia was not alone in its response to the forces of the future. In varying degrees, according to their talents and their convictions, the citizens of other New World communities were similarly thinking for themselves and preparing for the management of their own cultural and political destinies. Their self-recognition as a mature and independent society supplies the true explanation of John Adams's wise and well-known statement—"The Revolution was effected before the war commenced. The Revolution was in the minds and hearts of the people. . . . This radical change in the principles, opinions, sentiments, and affections of the people, was the real American Revolution."

BIBLIOGRAPHICAL NOTE

This volume is based upon a study of the sources. The materials used will appear obvious to anyone familiar with the history of Philadelphia or any other colonial city. For that reason we are not including an exhaustive bibliography. Earlier writers have not been primarily concerned with social and intellectual history and it has thus been necessary to piece our account together with scraps of information taken from literally hundreds of different places. Below, we have sought to indicate the principal sources of information and to single out those monographs or studies which seemed to be particularly valuable for the study of a given topic.

GENERAL

SOURCES. Philadelphia newspapers have proved the most fruitful single source for this study, especially the *Pennsylvania Gazette* (1728-76); the *Pennsylvania Journal* (1742-76); the *Wöchentliche Philadelphische Staatsbote* (1762-76); and the *Pennsylvania Chronicle* (1767-74). Generous use has also been made of the files of the other eleven newspapers, the necessary guide to which is Clarence S. Brigham, "Bibliography of American Newspapers, 1690-1820," in the *Proceedings* of the American Antiquarian Society (N.S., Vol. XXXII, 1922). Similarly, the *American Magazine and Monthly Chronicle* (1757-58), the *American Magazine, or General Repository* (1769), and the *Pennsylvania Magazine, or American Monthly Museum* (1775-76) provide an abundance of material for the cultural history of the city. Lyon N. Richardson's *Early American Magazines* (New York, 1931) contains an excellent finding list of these early periodicals.

From the several Philadelphia presses came an annual flood of broadsides, sermons, pamphlets, and books, which is of inestimable value in gauging the literary and reading habits of the citizens. The indispensable guide to this is the bibliography of Charles R. Hildeburn, *A Century of Printing: Issues of the Pennsylvania Press, 1685-1784* (2 vols., Philadelphia, 1885). The well-known works of Evans and Sabin are also useful. Items listed in these bibliographies, as well as books, newspapers, prints, maps, and manuscripts, were consulted at the John Carter Brown (JCB) and John Hay (JH) Libraries, Providence; the Historical Society of Pennsylvania (HSP) and the Library Company (LCP) at Philadelphia; the Massachusetts Historical Society (MHS), Boston; and the Harvard University Library (HU), Cambridge.

The sixty-five volumes of the invaluable quarterly *Pennsylvania Magazine of History and Biography* contain a vast historical treasure of letters, diaries, journals, and other remains of colonial Philadelphia. Next to the newspapers this work yielded the most material. No student should overlook the "Notes and Documents" section at the end of each number.

In addition to the familiar city and province records, extensive tribute has been exacted from the colonial travelers. The accounts of Dr. Alexander Hamilton, Peter Kalm, Andrew Burnaby, Alexander Macraby, Dr. Robert Honyman, Patrick M'Robert, and Ambrose Serle, and the letters, diaries, or journals of William Black, Hannah Callender, Elizabeth Drinker, John Adams, Silas Deane, and Peter Pelham, have been particularly useful. Alexander Graydon's delightful *Memoirs of a Life Chiefly Passed in Pennsylvania within the Last Sixty Years* (Edinburgh, 1822, and other editions) is a classic. No author can write about colonial Philadelphia without consulting the voluminous writings of Benjamin Franklin in the editions of Sparks, Bigelow, and Smyth, and without examining the vast collection of Franklin manuscripts at the American Philosophical Society. In general, no very extensive use has been made of manuscripts; most of those consulted are in the Historical Society of Pennsylvania and are described in the *Guide to the Manuscript Collections* (1940).

SECONDARY WORKS. Weekly, from 1867 to 1875, Thompson Westcott published a chapter on the history of the city in the *Philadelphia Sunday Dispatch*. All who have worked in the primary materials must pay tribute to Westcott's thoroughness and accuracy. The Historical Society of Pennsylvania has two sets of this history; one is bound in 32 vols. illustrated with drawings and contemporary documents by D. M. Stauffer. In 1884 an abridgment, with added chapters, was published as J. T. Scharf and T. Westcott, *History of Philadelphia,* 3 vols. Many odd facts may be found in Joseph Jackson's not altogether accurate *Cyclopedia of Philadelphia* (4 vols., Harrisburg, 1932). Two other works of immense value are Charles H. Lincoln, *The Revolutionary Movement in Pennsylvania* (Philadelphia, 1901), and Carl Van Doren's admirable *Franklin* (New York, 1938). Sketches, varying in value and usually political in emphasis, of many of the persons mentioned herein may be found in the *Dictionary of American Biography.*

The materials listed above constitute the principal sources of this book. Below are listed selected primary works and such special studies and monographs as proved useful in the writing of a given chapter. All books were published at Philadelphia unless otherwise noted, and all articles listed are in the *Pennsylvania Magazine of History and Biography,* unless otherwise indicated.

Chapter I. THE PHILADELPHIA OF BENJAMIN FRANKLIN. Population figures are based on a wide variety of sources, an analysis of which we hope shortly to publish. Colonial statistics are far more reliable than contemporary English estimates. It is clear, however, that before 1776 English cities were much smaller than is generally supposed. Religious conditions in Philadelphia warrant extended study. There is nothing of value on the Quakers. See G. S. Klett, *Presbyterians in Colonial Pennsylvania* (1937); and the useful sources in W. S. Perry, *Historical Collections Relating to the American Colonial Church,* Vol. II (Hartford, 1871). Westcott wrote a *History of the Philadelphia Fire Department* for the *Sunday Dispatch* which is now in HSP, where are also the minutes of the Fellowship, Star, and Cordwainer's Fire Companies. The minutes of the Union Fire Company are in the LCP. The only full account of a club is the *History of the Schuylkill Fishing Company* (1889), which also includes the records of the Gloucester Hunt. Some idea of the economic status of the persons mentioned in this volume may be had from "Proprietary, Supply and State Tax Lists of the City and County of Philadelphia," 6 *Pennsylvania Archives,* Vol. XIV.

Chapter II. EDUCATION FOR A LITERARY REPUBLIC. James Mulhern, *History of Secondary Education in Pennsylvania* (1933) is excellent. For religious education, Thomas Woody, *Early Quaker Education in Pennsylvania* (New York, 1920), and two articles in Pa. German Society, *Proceedings,* Vols. XXXVIII, XL, on Reformed and Lutheran schools. On its subject, S. E. Weber, *Charity School Movement in Pennsylvania* (1905), though brief, is adequate. For the Academy and the College, all works earlier than E. P. Cheyney, *History of the University of Pennsylvania* (1940), which appeared after this chapter was written, are partisan. Thomas Woody collected the opinions of the founder in *The Educational Views of Benjamin Franklin* (New York, 1931); the Anglican side is in Perry, *Historical Collections,* noted above. Something of

Alison's ideas may be gleaned from the *Itineraries and Correspondence of Ezra Stiles* (New Haven, 1916). A biography of Francis Alison is badly needed. T. H. Montgomery, *History of the University of Pennsylvania* (1900), is almost a source collection, but its conclusions are untrustworthy.

Chapter III. PRINTERS AND BOOKS: THE MAKING OF FULL MEN. This chapter, with a complete set of references, appeared as "The Press and the Book in Eighteenth Century Philadelphia," in the *Pennsylvania Magazine of History and Biography,* Vol. LXV (January, 1941, pp. 1-30).

Chapter IV. GENTEEL VERSE AND REBEL PROSE. The writings of Philadelphians naturally formed the basis of this chapter. Hildeburn's *Issues of the Pennsylvania Press* proved invaluable. Richardson's *Early American Magazines* gives an exhaustive account of each periodical. George E. Hastings, *Life and Work of Francis Hopkinson* (Chicago, 1926) is a capital biography; the same can hardly be said for Horace W. Smith's adulatory, biased, and inaccurate *Life and Correspondence of the Rev. William Smith, D.D.* (2 vols., 1879). The LCP and the Boston Public Library have first editions of Thomas Forrest's *The Disappointment;* and the JCB copy of Charles Thomson's *An Enquiry into the Causes of the Alienation of the Delaware and Shawanese Indians* (London, 1759) has important marginal notes made by Thomas Penn. Every student of the literature of this period will find Lawrence C. Wroth, *An American Bookshelf* (1934) required reading.

Chapter V. THE ARTS MOVE WESTWARD. On the theater, T. C. Pollock, *The Philadelphia Theatre in the Eighteenth Century* (1933) gives all the details and playbills in conventional manner. The effect of the stage on the people must be studied in newspapers and letters. See Graydon's *Memoirs;* "Letters to Sir Philip Francis," Vol. XI; the *Burd Papers* (Pottsville, 1899); and *Extracts from the Diary of Jacob Hiltzheimer* (1893). On music, O. G. Sonneck in his *Francis Hopkinson; Early Opera in America* (New York, 1915), and *Early Concert-Life in America* (Leipsic, 1907), brought together a wealth of data. R. R. Drummond, *Early German Music in Philadelphia* (1910), treats a neglected subject. Scattered references may be found in letters and diaries which show the musical life of the people. On painting, C. Brinton, *Gustavus Hesselius* (1938), and Theodore Bolton in *Art Quarterly,* Vol. II, on Hesselius and Peale. C. C. Sellers, *Artist of the Revolution* (Hebron, Conn., 1939) is based on family manuscripts. J. T. Flexner, *America's Old Masters* (New York, 1939) is notable for its fresh point of view. Scattered through the volumes of *International Studio, Antiques,* and the *Antiquarian* are useful articles by Theodore Bolton and William Sawitzky. The latter's "American Work of Benjamin West," LXII, is admirable. Most books on colonial painting borrow from one another, leaving the student greatly confused. Special attention is called to the bibliography, *Early American Artists, 1665-1860* (Newark, 1940), published by the N. J. Historical Records Survey; and William T. Whitely, *Artists and Their Friends in England, 1700-1799* (2 vols., London, 1928). The HSP, LCP, Independence Hall and the Pennsylvania Academy of Fine Arts possess works by most of the painters mentioned in this book. There is no study of John Meng of Germantown.

Chapter VI. GENTLEMEN OF CAPACITY AND LEISURE. This chapter has been composed almost wholly from the sources. William Allen is one of the major eighteenth-century figures without a biography. Some information can be found in L. B. Walker, *Extracts from Chief Justice William Allen's Letter Books* (1897); and Ruth M. Kistler, "William Allen, Provincial Man of Affairs," *Pennsylvania History,* I. For architecture, one must view the houses themselves. P. H. B. Wallace and M. L. Miller, *Colonial Houses, Philadelphia. Pre-Revolutionary* (New York, 1931) is an admirable collection of photographs taken by an artist and student. Joseph Jackson, *Early Philadelphia Architects and Engineers* (1923), and F. Cousins and P. M. Riley, *The Colonial Architecture of Philadelphia* (Boston, 1920), though inaccurate are frequently useful. Scull and Heap's *Map of Philadelphia and Parts Adjacent* (1750) indicates most of the country estates. For gardens, see Hannah Callender's "Diary," XII. Most travelers comment on gentlemen's estates, especially Josiah Quincy in 49 Mass. Hist. Society *Proceedings.* B. Sprague Allen, *Tides of English Taste* (2 vols., Cambridge, 1937), and John Steegman, *The Rule of Taste* (London, 1936) are vital for English background. No account of Samuel Powel exists. An enlightening study of the colonial craftsman could be made from something more than the collector's or antiquarian's viewpoint. It would tell the story of colonial manufactures. For Philadelphians, the files of *Antiques* contain some useful articles on furniture-makers and silversmiths; a convenient collection of newspaper advertisements is found in A. C. Prime, *The Arts and Crafts in Philadelphia, Maryland* etc. (Walpole Society, 1929). The privately-printed *Journal of Dr. John Morgan* (1907) is the best account of a Grand Tour. Copies are in HU and HSP.

Chapter VII. SOCIAL USE OF THE FAVOURS OF PROVIDENCE. August Jorns, *The Quakers as Pioneers in Social Work* (New York, 1931) provides a good introduction. The work of the city authorities in caring for the poor may be traced in *Minutes of the Common Council of the City of*

Philadelphia (1847), in the Ms Alms-house Accounts, and the Ms Catalogue of the Contributors to the Poor in the HSP. Most travelers visited and described the Bettering House. On hospitals consult T. G. Morton and F. Woodbury, *History of the Pennsylvania Hospital* (1897) whose excellent appendices have been seldom read, and the informing article by Robert J. Hunter, "The Origin of the Philadelphia General Hospital," *Medical Life,* XL, or in *Pa. Mag.,* LXVII. On national friendly societies, see F. V. A. Cabeen, "Society of the Sons of St. Tammany," XVII, T. C. Knauff, *History of the Society of the Sons of St. George* (1923), and O. Seidensticker, *Kurtze Geschichte der Deutschen Gesellschaft von Pennsylvanien* (1910). Mary S. Locke, *Anti-Slavery in America* (Boston, 1901) is a fine introduction to the subject. George S. Brookes's, *Friend Anthony Benezet* (1937) is superb. Consult also H. S. Cadbury, *Colonial Quaker Antecedents to British Abolition of Slavery* (London, 1933).

Chapter VIII. THE MEDICAL PROFESSION: A COALITION OF ABLE MEN. No study deals with the social aspects of medicine. There are two good works on Philadelphia medicine: F. P. Henry, *Standard History of the Medical Profession of Philadelphia* (Chicago, 1897), and George W. Norris, *Early History of Medicine in Philadelphia* (1886). Woodbury and Morton's *History of the Pennsylvania Hospital,* previously mentioned, includes a wealth of information miscellaneously arranged. It is very useful and contains Dr. Thomas Bond's hitherto unnoticed "Essay on the Utility of Clinical Lectures." The latter should be edited and reprinted. N. G. Goodman's *Benjamin Rush* (1934) is useful and has a fine bibliography. Dr. Phineas Bond's account book is in the HSP. The Library of the Philadelphia College of Physicians has the daybooks of the Bonds (5 vols.), a collection of letters relating to the University of Edinburgh, biographical sketches of the members (6 vols.), and the printed works of many of the early physicians, including theses from European medical schools. The JCB has Dr. John Jones, *Plain Concise Practical Remarks on the Treatment of Wounds and Fractures* (1775). John Morgan's *Discourse* has been reprinted in *Bibliotheca Medica Americana,* II (Baltimore, 1937). A series of fine studies of Philadelphia Physicians by W. S. Middleton and others appeared in *Annals of Medical History,* II, IV, VIII and IX. See also, David Riesman, "The Oldest Medical School in America," *General Magazine and Historical Chronicle* (April, 1936), and J. Carson, *History of the Medical Department of the University of Pennsylvania* (1869). The quarrel over the medical society has never been worked out. Richard H. Shryock's *De-*

velopment of Modern Medicine (1936) is one of the major achievements of recent American historical scholarship.

Chapter IX. THE LOVE OF SCIENCE. THEIR REIGNING CHARACTER. The social implications of scientific development at Philadelphia have never been explored. The delightful letters in William Darlington's *Memorials of John Bartram and Humphrey Marshall* (1849) are essential, and Ernest Earnest's *John and William Bartram* (1940) is useful. Professor Joseph E. Johnson of Williams is preparing the definitive life of James Logan. I. Bernard Cohen has made a fundamental contribution to the history of electricity in his critical edition of *Benjamin Franklin's Experiments* (Cambridge, 1940). Joseph Priestley had the benefit of Franklin's corrections in his *History and Present State of Electricity* (London, 1767). On the Northwest Company, see E. S. Balch, "Arctic Expeditions sent from the American Colonies," XXXI, and the HSP copy of Thomas Jeffrys, *The Great Probability of a North West Passage* (London, 1768) which has some additional material bound with it. L. H. Gipson's *Lewis Evans* (1939) is most useful. On the origin of the American Philosophical Society, the political and social aspects of which have never been studied, see Junto Minutes (Ms) in the HSP, *Historical Account of the Origin and Formation of the American Philosophical Society* (1914), which contains good sources but little interpretation, and H. T. Wood, *History of the Royal Society of Arts* (London, 1913). Rittenhouse should have a biography; W. Barton's *Memoir of the Life of David Rittenhouse* (1813) is antiquated. An introduction to Pierre Du Simitière's manuscripts is available in the Pa. Historical Records Survey's *Descriptive Catalogue of the Du Simitière Papers in the Library Company of Philadelphia* (1940). Many papers by Philadelphians appear in the *Transactions* of the Royal Society of London. Especially interesting are the *Early Proceedings of the American Philosophical Society* (1884), and *The Transactions of the American Philosophical Society* (1771; 2nd ed., 1789). Two excellent works on the English background are N. G. Brett-James, *Life of Peter Collinson* (London, 1925), and R. H. Fox, *Dr. John Fothergill and His Friends* (1919).

INDEX

The East Prospect of the City of PHILAD[ELPHIA]

THE CENTER OF THE BRITISH

1. Christ Church   2. State House

         3. Academy

4. Presbyterian Church   5. German Church

         6. Town Hall and Market